Interventions is produced on the land of the Wurundjeri people of the Kulin Nation. We acknowledge the Traditional Owners of country throughout Australia and recognise their continuing connection to land, waters and culture. We pay our respects to their Elders past, present and emerging. Their land was stolen, never ceded. It always was and always will be Aboriginal land.

"This work combines a remarkable number of features. It is vast in scope but judiciously focusses on key moments of workers' struggle between 1917 and 1956. Full of fascinating information and detail, it is never a detached academic history but is a guide to activists today, both in terms of theory and practice. By focussing on workers' self-activity, in combination with Marxist theory, the authors steer clear of the traps of Stalinism and reformism, remaining true to the essence of revolutionary socialism. In the midst of all that, they still manage to present debates around important political questions. This book should be of interest to readers worldwide, though the three chapters on Australia will give it special value there."

—Donny Gluckstein
Lecturer in history in Edinburgh, member Socialist Workers' Party (UK); author of *A People's History of the Second World War* (Pluto Press 2012) and *The Nazis, Capitalism and the Working Class* (Haymarket 2012).

"We are seeing a global revival of interest in socialism. Like their predecessors, this generation of socialists will try to draw lessons from the history of the struggle against capitalism. *The Fight for Workers' Power* is an invaluable resource for the education of socialists today."

—Charlie Post
Member of the editorial board of *Spectre: A Marxist Journal* and *Tempest*, a US-based revolutionary socialist collective.

"These stories of past revolutions are not only exciting and inspiring. They also point the way to successful socialist revolution in our time."

—Rick Kuhn
Australian Marxist scholar, activist and Deutscher Prize winner.

Tom Bramble has written extensively on the politics of the workers' movement in Australia and internationally. His books include *Introducing Marxism: A Theory of Social Change (2015)* and *Trade Unionism in Australia: A History from Flood to Ebb Tide* (2008). He is a founder member of Socialist Alternative and a life member of the Australian university staff union. Tom has been active in a wide range of social and political movements in Britain and Australia since the 1970s.

Mick Armstrong has been a socialist, political activist and organiser in Australia since the early 1970s. He writes regularly for the *Marxist Left Review* and *Red Flag* newspaper and has authored a range of books and pamphlets, including *From Little Things Big Things Grow: Strategies for Building Revolutionary Socialist Organisations* (2007). Mick is a founder member of Socialist Alternative.

The Fight for Workers' Power

Revolution and Counter-Revolution in the 20th Century

Tom Bramble and Mick Armstrong

INTERVENTIONS
MELBOURNE

First published 2021 by Interventions Inc

Interventions is a not-for-profit, independent, radical book publisher. For further information:
    www.interventions.org.au
    info@interventions.org.au
    PO Box 24132
    Melbourne VIC 3001

Cover design after a photo of Republican women fighters, Spanish Civil War. Photographer unknown (Gerda Taro?).
Cover design by Lachlan Stewart.
Interior design and layout by Viktoria Ivanova.

Authors: Tom Bramble and Mick Armstrong

Title: The Fight for Workers' Power: Revolution and Counter-Revolution in the 20th Century
ISBN: 978-0-6487603-5-1: Paperback

© Tom Bramble and Mick Armstrong 2021

The moral rights of the authors have been asserted.
All rights reserved. Except as permitted under the Australian Copyright Act 1968 (for example, a fair dealing for the purposes of study, research, criticism or review), no part of this book may be reproduced, stored in a retrieval system, communicated or transmitted in any form or by any means without prior written permission.

All inquiries should be made to the author.

 A catalogue record for this work is available from the National Library of Australia

CONTENTS

Acknowledgements   1

Introduction   3

BIRTH OF A NEW INTERNATIONAL, 1914 to 1923

1. Reformist Betrayal, Revolutionary Hope   9
2. The Creation of Mass Revolutionary Parties   41
3. The Fight Against Ultra Leftism   75
4. Germany: An Opportunity Lost   101

THE DEGENERATION OF THE INTERNATIONAL, 1923 to 1928

5. Counter-Revolution in Russia   125
6. The British General Strike   151
7. The Chinese Revolution   173

THE COMINTERN'S ULTRA LEFTIST TURN, 1928 TO 1933

8. 'Social Fascism': the Path to Nazi Victory in Germany   203
9. Communism in Australia During the Great Depression   219

POPULAR FRONT: GRAVEYARD OF STRUGGLES, 1935 to 1945

10. The Popular Front in France   239
11. The Spanish Revolution: Anarchism Put to the Test   261
12. Sit-Down Fever! US Workers' Struggle and the Roosevelt Administration   287
13. Saluting the Flag: Australian Communists During WWII   309
14. Anti-Fascist Resistance in Italy and Greece   329

STALINISM AND ANTI-STALINISM AFTER WORLD WAR II

15. Post-War Upsurge in Australia and the Communist Challenge   357
16. The Communists Come to Power in China   383
17. Anti-Stalinist Revolts in Eastern Europe   405

Acronyms and Abbreviations   429

Endnotes   433

ACKNOWLEDGEMENTS

Particular thanks to Eleanor Morley and Jordan Humphreys, who read drafts of the whole book and gave invaluable advice. Thanks also to the following, who made helpful suggestions on chapters: Gregor Benton, Andrew Bonnell, Llanon Davis, Phil Deery, Charlie Fox, Sarah Garnham, Joel Geier, Duncan Hart, Charlie Hore, Lian Jenvey, Phoebe Kelloway, Rick Kuhn, Dimitra Kyrillou, Sean Larson, Panos Petrou, Charlie Post, Darren Roso, Luca Tavan and Alexis Vassiley. While most of our readers would support the general line of argument in this book, none bears responsibility for interpretations with which they may not agree or for any errors that may remain.

We would also like to express our appreciation to the team at Interventions: Janey Stone (editor) and Viktoria Ivanova and Lachlan Harris (designers).

INTRODUCTION

The 20th century saw the exploited and oppressed repeatedly rise up against the brutality of the capitalist system. This book recounts some of the key moments in this history of class struggle. It starts with the 1917 Russian Revolution, which inspired millions of working class militants and anti-imperialists to rise up and fight for power. It ends with the magnificent 1956 uprising against Stalinism by the workers of Hungary.

As the masses revolted against their rulers, they turned conventional politics upside down. Leon Trotsky explained in the preface to his classic account of the Russian Revolution:

> The most indubitable feature of a revolution is the direct interference of the masses in historical events. In ordinary times the state, be it monarchical or democratic, elevates itself above the nation, and history is made by specialists in that line of business – kings, ministers, bureaucrats, parliamentarians, journalists. But at those crucial moments when the old order becomes no longer endurable to the masses, they break over the barriers excluding them from the political arena, sweep aside their traditional representatives, and create by their own interference the initial groundwork for a new regime... The history of revolution is for us first of all a history of the forcible entrance of the masses into the realm of rulership over their own destiny.[1]

Revolutions do not consist of a conspiratorial elite seizing power behind the backs of the masses or a palace coup where one ruler replaces another. They are occasions when workers and the oppressed who have been denied any control over their lives, and who live in fear of unemployment and all its attendant miseries, stand up to assert their basic humanity. As they do so, they subvert everything that is 'normal' and 'proper,' all those conventions that constitute and reinforce ruling class power. Workers begin to establish *their* authority and *their* power, acting in ways that prioritise the needs of humanity, not the interests of the rich.

This is why, time and again, workers form workers' councils, or *soviets*, to use the Russian term. They do so not because they have read Marxist texts or been instructed by revolutionary agitators but because the demands of the class struggle impel them to. Workers need to organise their struggles. They need to provide for the essentials of life once the bosses start to sabotage production, and they need to defend themselves from ruling class violence. This book illustrates the phenomenon of workers' councils, appearing everywhere from St Petersburg and Berlin to Turin, Shanghai, Barcelona and Budapest.

Karl Marx described the working class as the 'universal class' because its struggles, at their height, point to a solution to every aspect of capitalist oppression: when the working class emancipates itself, it emancipates humanity. The Russian Revolution demonstrated this very practically, introducing reforms to women's conditions far in advance of those made by any capitalist democracy. We also see women coming to the fore repeatedly in the revolts discussed in this volume. Their very oppression often made them the most determined fighters.

Workers' councils throw up the fundamental question of politics: who is to rule? They pose an alternative to the capitalist state. That is why the capitalist class, the landlords and government authorities invariably try to crush them, often by force of arms. This applies not only in high points, where fully fledged workers' councils appear, but also every time workers rise up *en masse*.

Not only capitalists oppose workers' power. Reformist parties that emerge out of the workers' movement also play a role in preventing workers from taking power. Trotsky's quote above suggests that workers will 'sweep aside their traditional representatives' at crucial moments. The episodes described in this book, however, tell us that these representatives, wedded to the capitalist state, will do their utmost to obstruct the struggle and channel it back into the capitalist order. Very often, they succeed.

Openly reformist parties have frequently been responsible for extinguishing working class struggles. However, for much of the history covered in this book, it was those who called themselves 'Communists' who took on this role or who, as 'Communist' governments, openly opposed the working class. How was it that Communist parties came to play such a role?

The betrayal of the social democratic parties in 1914, when they lined up to support their own ruling classes at the outbreak of war, and the victory of the Russian Revolution in 1917 demonstrated the bankruptcy of social democracy and the crying need for new workers' parties, like Lenin's Bolsheviks, dedicated to the revolutionary conquest of power. In 1919 the Communist International (Comintern) was born; its mission, to assist in the creation of revolutionary parties and to help them win the majority of class conscious workers away from the social democrats and other forces hostile to revolution. Very soon, the parties affiliated to the Comintern had within their ranks hundreds of thousands of worker militants.

Tragically, the working class upsurge in the period following the Russian Revolution was beaten back. Repression by Western governments and capitalists was partly responsible. But the capitalists could only put down the postwar revolt with the help of the social democrats who strained every nerve to bring it to an end.

The Comintern's failure to establish new revolutionary beachheads outside Russia gave the capitalist system a new lease of life. In Russia, it condemned the revolution to isolation. Lenin and his comrades had staked everything on revolutionary victories elsewhere in Europe. In their absence, Russia was in no position to advance towards socialism. It had suffered enormous damage in the three years of civil war and foreign intervention that had followed the Revolution. The economy was virtually destroyed and the working class reduced almost to a political nullity.

In the absence of workers' power in Russia, a new bureaucracy, headed by Stalin, could rise. By 1928, Stalin's victory had become secure. Those gains from the 1917 Revolution that had not been wound back by this stage were now completely eliminated. No hint of the Revolution now remained, and those in the Russian party who embodied it were pushed to the margins and eventually, in thousands of cases, executed.

The counter-revolution in Russia had a devastating impact on the Comintern. The revolutionary International that had been founded to lead workers to power now became an instrument of counter-revolution cynically wielded by the Stalinist bureaucracy to secure its own power. Resting on the reflected glory of 1917, the Comintern attracted millions of workers to its ranks in the first half of the 20th century but in every case frustrated their desire to settle accounts with capitalism.

The history of workers' struggles in the 20th century confirms the importance of political leadership. The Russian Revolution succeeded only because Lenin and his comrades had spent two decades building a revolutionary party which brought together the most advanced layers of the working class movement to fight for workers' power. Building a revolutionary party that can pick up the tradition established by the Bolsheviks is the motivation of the authors of this book.

The world today is very different to the period covered in this book. But capitalism rules now, as it did then. The working class continues to be exploited. Oppression of minorities and of women continues unchecked. Poverty continues to exist alongside obscene luxury. The working class remains the social force that can bring these evils to an end. Socialist Alternative, of which the authors are members, is committed to leading struggles by workers and the oppressed to tear this rotten system down. Understanding the history of the workers' movement – what worked and what failed in the fight for workers' power – is essential if we are to succeed in this task.

BIRTH OF A NEW INTERNATIONAL

1914 to 1923

1.
REFORMIST BETRAYAL, REVOLUTIONARY HOPE

At Easter 1916, a band of Irish rebels took up arms against British rule, sparking off a revolt that inflicted a historic defeat on the world's mightiest empire. In 1917, the workers of Russia rose up, disposed of the centuries-old Tsarist regime and then overthrew capitalist rule. In November 1918, the German empire, the most powerful state in Europe, collapsed under the impact of a mass revolution. Workers' and soldiers' councils sprang up throughout Germany and wielded effective power. In Bavaria, a Soviet Republic was proclaimed. The other great central European power, the Austro-Hungarian empire, ceased to exist, pulled apart by the revolutionary risings of late 1918. In German-speaking Austria, for example, the only effective armed force was the People's Army, controlled by the Social Democrats. In Hungary, a Soviet Republic was formed in March 1919. All the new or reconstituted European states – Czechoslovakia, Yugoslavia, even Poland – were unstable. Italy saw a wave of factory occupations. In France, massive strikes broke out late in the war. In Britain, the government sent a gunboat to quell a general strike in Glasgow. In Spain, workers rose up in industrial Catalonia.[1]

The wave of revolt spread well beyond Europe: to Australia, Latin America and the colonial world. In Iraq, there were uprisings against British rule. In India, an explosion of popular anger following a massacre at Amritsar transformed the independence movement. In China, students rose up, demanding democracy and an end to the imperial carve-up of their country.

The ruling classes were well aware that their system was in danger. In 1919, British Prime Minister David Lloyd George warned his fellow rulers that:

> The whole of Europe is filled with the spirit of revolution. There is a deep sense not only of discontent but of anger and revolt amongst

the workmen against the pre-war conditions. The whole existing order in its political, social and economic aspects, is questioned by the masses from one end of Europe to the other.[2]

He was correct. The world stood on the edge of revolutions that could smash capitalism and create a world free from exploitation, poverty and war.

Tragically, the established leaderships of the working class movement in most of Europe, grouped together prior to World War I in the Second International, had no interest in taking this struggle forward to victory. In the name of 'democracy,' they supported counter-revolution. Some of them had been and still claimed to be Marxists and internationalists. But they were now a major prop of capitalism. They mouthed socialist phrases and used the credit established by their years of agitation to prevent the establishment of workers' power; where it was temporarily established, they blocked its consolidation.

One of the few exceptions to this pattern was the Bolsheviks. Lenin's Bolsheviks had argued from the outset that a revolution in Russia, one of the weak links in the imperialist world, could be the detonator for revolution elsewhere. Such revolutions were also important because the future of the Russian Revolution was in the balance – it could only be sustained if the revolution spread beyond its borders. But these revolutions required new revolutionary parties, with influence in the working class, to realise their enormous potential. This could not be delayed; the future of humanity was at stake.

Driven by the urgency of the situation, the Bolshevik Party, renamed Communists after the Revolution, issued a call in early 1919 for revolutionaries to come to Moscow to form a new Communist International (Comintern). It was named the Third International in recognition of the fact that the Second International had betrayed socialism and collapsed. The numbers who came together at Moscow's invitation in March 1919 were limited. Just 51 delegates represented 35 organisations in 22 countries; most were small organisations in countries which had been part of the Russian empire. But for such a small organisation, the new Comintern had big ambitions, declaring in its *Manifesto*:

> Our task is to generalise the revolutionary experience of the working class, to cleanse the movement of the disintegrating admixture of opportunism and social patriotism, to mobilise the forces of all genuine revolutionary parties of the world working class and thereby facilitate and hasten the victory of the communist revolution throughout the world.[3]

Reformist betrayal

The Comintern was born and soon became a pole of attraction for revolutionaries in every corner of the world. But its creation had been a long time coming. The Second International's counter-revolutionary role in 1919 came as no surprise to Russian Communists. The International's pretensions to be revolutionary had been exposed at the outbreak of war in 1914, when it carried out the worst betrayal in the history of the socialist movement.

War magnifies to the most extreme degree all the contradictions and barbarities of capitalist society; it also tests the politics of those who stand for a different society. The Second International failed that test. In Germany, France, Austria-Hungary, Britain, Australia and many other places, social democratic parties voted for the war budgets that let loose the greatest slaughter the world had ever seen. They renounced the numerous motions denouncing war and calling for the world's workers to join hands in resistance to patriotic calls to arms. Virtually every member of the international league of socialist parties, most notably the International's leading party, the German Social Democrats (SPD), abandoned its internationalist principles and rallied behind its own ruling class.

Rosa Luxemburg of the revolutionary left of the prewar SPD was so stunned by the betrayal of her colleagues that she briefly considered suicide. She invited SPD parliamentarians identified as radicals to attend a meeting to oppose the decision of the party leadership to back the war. Only two responded: Karl Liebknecht and Franz Mehring. An incredulous Lenin assumed that newspaper reports of the SPD's vote for the military budget were a lie. Finally convinced of the betrayal, he declared: 'The Second International is dead, overcome by opportunism.'[4]

Leading figures in the Second International soon became champions of the war. They joined war cabinets and urged workers and peasants to enlist in the armed forces. They encouraged workers in the factories to sacrifice all the conditions they had won over decades of struggle in order to increase production of munitions and war supplies. The socialist leaders joined the monarchists and empire loyalists to glorify the nation and used racist rhetoric to denounce its enemies. They were not alone. Syndicalist and anarchist currents not part of the Second International also came out for the war. In France, there had been massive anti-war demonstrations on the streets of Paris just days before the war. Then, the syndicalist daily newspaper *La Bataille Syndicaliste* (Syndicalist Battle) made an about turn and supported the war. Léon Jouhaux, leader of the French General Confederation of Labour (Confédération Générale du Travail, CGT), which had a longstanding anti-militarist tradition, declared his support for the war. The CGT paper declared: 'Against German militarism, we must save France's democratic and revolutionary tradition.' The Russian anarchist movement split over the question; as late as 1916, its most famous international figure, Peter Kropotkin, signed an Open Letter by anarchists supporting the war on the grounds of opposition to 'German militarism.'

Why were the mass workers' parties of the Second International able to betray their members and support a nightmare bloodier than even the most trenchant critics of capitalism had imagined? How were they able so readily to abandon the letter of their own politics and the numerous anti-war statements that they had produced?

The trajectory of the SPD helps us to explain the betrayal of the International at the time of its greatest test. The SPD was a major force in Germany. By 1914, it had a million members and, with one-third of the vote, had become the country's largest political party in the Reichstag, the federal parliament. It had deep roots in every aspect of working class life, with dozens of daily papers, weekly periodicals and theoretical journals. It ran youth clubs, cultural groups and theatres and organised credit unions, sporting clubs and consumer and producer cooperatives. The SPD was intimately tied to the trade union movement, whose membership rose from 237,000 in 1892 to 1.8 million in 1907 and to 2.6 million in 1912.

The SPD had a leading role in the International not only because of its impressive size, but also because it was the party most identified with Marx (and Engels, who had been active in it after its foundation in 1875). It boasted the leading theoreticians in the International, including 'The Pope of Marxism,' Karl Kautsky. Its Erfurt program, proclaimed in 1891, was regarded as the last word in Marxism by many other socialist parties, and Germany was the country most Marxists believed would be the first socialist state.

The Second International proudly boasted its commitment to conquering political power. But how was this to be accomplished? This question formed the basis of big debates in the International: did workers need to wage a revolutionary struggle, or could socialism come about in the gradual evolution of the capitalist system through a series of parliamentary reforms? In Germany, following the lifting of illegality in 1890, a reformist or 'revisionist' current emerged in the SPD. Its leading theoretician, Eduard Bernstein, argued that capitalism could gradually and peacefully grow into socialism by parliamentary means. Bernstein was heavily defeated in party congresses at the turn of the century, but it was a sign of things to come.

The debate opened up by Bernstein exposed a contradiction that had lain at the heart of the SPD since its formation. This was embodied in its 1891

Erfurt Program. Alongside its 'maximum' program – the complete abolition of capitalist society – it contained a 'minimum' program of immediate reforms, demands it thought attainable under capitalism, like the eight-hour day. As the SPD grew, the 'minimum program' became the real focus of activity, while the 'maximum program' was reserved for rousing speeches at May Day rallies. Reforms and the growth of the SPD became ends in themselves. Humdrum routine, working within the system without any attempt to struggle against it, became the bread and butter of the union leaders and the parliamentarians. One of Bernstein's right wing colleagues, Ignaz Auer, wrote to him to draw attention to the fact that the party's practice now diverged substantially from its 'maximum' program. He pointed out Bernstein's 'mistake' in advancing his revisionist program: 'What you call for, my dear Ede, is something which one neither admits openly nor puts to a formal vote; one simply gets on with it.'[5]

Kautsky, who led the SPD's 'centre,' opposed the revisionist argument that capitalism would gradually give way to socialism. Against those in the Second International who advocated pacts with bourgeois parties, he argued that social democracy must maintain its independence from all the other parliamentary forces. But Kautsky still believed that parliament must be the vehicle by which workers would take power:

> The objective of our political struggle remains…the conquest of state power through the conquest of a majority in parliament and the elevation of parliament to a commanding position within the state. Certainly not the destruction of state power.[6]

Socialism would come about through inexorable historical processes arising out of capitalist contradictions and the gradual accumulation of parliamentary seats. Any notion that the SPD might *force* the pace, might use mass struggle to advance the revolution, was ruled out:

> The Socialist Party is a revolutionary party but not a revolution-making party. We know that our goal can be attained only through revolution. We also know that it is just as little in our power to create the revolution as it is in the power of our opponents to prevent it. It is not part of our work to instigate a revolution or to prepare a way for it.[7]

But capitalism would not simply collapse. Only the conscious intervention of revolutionaries could turn the possibilities offered by historical developments into actuality.

Roots of reformism

The SPD's reformist trajectory had its roots in two phenomena. One was the gradual emergence of a distinct labour bureaucracy comprising politicians and trade union officials who rose above the working class movement to form a buffer between workers and the bourgeoisie. The other was the belief by participants in the big debates, from left to right, that the party was a catch-all party, containing both reformist and revolutionary currents. This view inhibited the emergence of a revolutionary pole of attraction within the SPD's ranks.

The growth of a labour bureaucracy provided the material basis of the Second International's reformism. Parliamentarians, at the summit of the bureaucracy, became a substantial force by 1914 and the outbreak of war: the SPD had 110 deputies in the national parliament, the French party 102, the Italian 78 and the Austro-Hungarian 82. In addition to these national parliamentarians, there were hundreds, if not thousands, of party representatives in state and provincial assemblies, along with municipal councillors and parliamentary staff. The unions accounted for thousands more full-time functionaries in the International's bigger affiliates.

There was also the army of party officials, journalists, benefit agents and office staff managing the steadily accumulating financial assets and property in the hands of the party and unions. Such people became a real force within the SPD as their numbers rapidly increased after Friedrich Ebert's appointment as general secretary in 1906. For many labour bureaucrats, the party and union apparatuses were gradually transformed from a means to an end.

In the quarter century of social peace that prevailed in many European countries prior to World War I, most of these Second International labour bureaucrats had in common a belief in the peaceful reconciliation of workers' interests with the capitalist order – although some still mouthed phrases about social revolution in their May Day speeches.[8] This trend was particularly obvious among the trade union leaders, whose social role inclined them to form a conservative bloc. Their essential function was to negotiate the terms under which their members were to be exploited, gradually improving the wages and conditions of employment, a franc here, a mark there, an hour off the working week. These gains also had to be set alongside the need for the capitalists to turn a profit. The union leaders were not about replacing the capitalist system, but making it work better for their members. Once recognition of the capitalists' needs to make a return on their money became a central consideration, with negotiations regularised every year or every three years, the trade union leaders increasingly began to see their role not as workers, which they may have been once, but as *intermediaries* between labour and capital, balancing the interests of each. Trade-offs and compromises were the natural outcome. This tendency was further exaggerated by what the German party called the 'two pillars' principle: a division of labour whereby the union leaders attended to the economic interests of the working class, the parliamentarians the political. Separating workers' economic and political demands in this way only dulled the revolutionary potential of workers' struggles, a potential that Luxemburg vividly described in her 1906 pamphlet *The Mass Strike*.

Once trade unions had become an accepted fact of life in Europe, union leaders hailing from working class backgrounds underwent a transformation in their personal circumstances. Removed from the factory bench, construction site or railway yard, the trade union leaders were no longer exploited. Their lives began to deviate from those of their members. They enjoyed definite perks – higher salaries, better working conditions, isolation from the dangers and monotony of the capitalist workplace. In Britain, at least, they also began to enjoy a certain social status. By the turn of the century, British union leaders had become notable figures, invited to important conferences or to appear before royal commissions and appointed as justices of the peace. This 1890s account puts it clearly:

> Nowadays the salaried officer of a great union is courted and flattered by the middle class [the capitalists]. He is asked to dine with them, and will admire their well-appointed houses, their fine carpets, the ease and luxury of their lives… He goes to live in little villa in a lower middle-class suburb. The move leads to dropping his workmen friends; and his wife changes her acquaintances. With the habits of his new neighbours he insensibly adopts more and more their ideas.[9]

Keen observers of the British labour movement Sidney and Beatrice Webb, members of the Fabian Society, noted of the union leaders that they had become 'a separate governing class…marked off by capacity, training and habit of life from the rank and file.'[10]

The situation varied from country to country. Union officials in Germany were more shut out from political influence than in Britain, but this did not significantly change their political character. They were consistently a pro-reformist bloc in the leadership of the SPD and vigorously fought the party's radicals.

The Webbs noted how the elevation of worker militants to trade union leaders and well-paid professional negotiators had important ideological effects:

> Whilst the points at issue no longer affect his own earnings or conditions of employment, any disputes between his members and their employers increase his work and add to his worry. The former vivid sense of the privations and subjection of the artisan's life gradually fades from his mind; and he begins more and more to regard all complaints as perverse and unreasonable.[11]

It was not just that strikes involved more work for the union officials. Strikes, particularly if they were substantial and militant, endangered the unions' accumulated assets, whether through depletion or through seizure by government authorities. Big strikes also created opportunities for militant workers to challenge the union leaders' control over the union. None of the union leaders wanted to lose their positions and be forced to go back on the tools. So they were cautious, at times leading strikes under pressure from below or when forced into action by employer intransigence, but doing their best to avoid major confrontations with the bosses and governments.

The same social pressures to conform bore down on both left officials and right officials; their differences were of secondary importance at times of crisis.

Reformist tendencies also became obvious among the SPD parliamentarians as the atmosphere of wheeling and dealing took their toll on what might once have been radical aspirations. It is unsurprising that reformist tendencies were particularly strong in the southern states, where relatively liberal constitutions and electoral laws created more opportunities for parliamentary collaboration with middle class parties and more potential for involvement in government. In Prussia and Saxony, by contrast, repressive, property-based franchises at the state and local government levels ensured the exclusion of the party from power on these levels and the party was notably more radical in those states. In the national parliament, the Reichstag, there was no prospect of the Kaiser and aristocracy allowing SPD members to become ministers, and so Reichstag deputies were able to maintain a certain amount of radical speechifying, but their practice was usually far removed from their lofty rhetoric.

There were some tensions between the parliamentarians and trade union leaders, but they generally coalesced behind reformist policies and practice, reinforcing each other.

This bureaucracy of union officials, parliamentarians and party officials formed the material basis for the ideology of reformism in the Second International. They identified with their ruling classes: some because they aspired to join them, some because they negotiated with them over the terms of workers' exploitation, and some because they provided intellectual cover to those in the party who carried out these tasks.

Importantly, the drift to reformism within the SPD was not a plot imposed on the party's members. It occurred in a period of economic expansion, steadily rising wages and advances in social legislation in Germany. In these circumstances, the reformist bureaucracy could be seen to deliver higher living standards, and, in the absence of stormy industrial struggles, they were never seriously tested in the eyes of the working class.

Reformist trends in the SPD were also assisted by an inbuilt bias in their favour in the party's constitution. Delegates to party congresses were elected on the basis of Reichstag electorates which were heavily skewed in favour of rural areas and small towns at the expense of the big cities dominated by industrial workers. The reformist wing of the party used the conservative bloc of delegates from the provinces to drive the party platform to the right in the years leading up to the outbreak of war.

The reformist nature of the SPD labour bureaucracy was clearly revealed in its hostility to general strikes. In the 1890s and 1900s, the SPD had repeatedly opposed resolutions moved at Second International congresses for a Europe-wide general strike in the event of a declaration of war. SPD representatives sought refuge in Marxist orthodoxy to justify their opposition: Marx and Engels had repudiated the anarchist demand for general strikes as an artificial schema put forward without regard to the actual state of the class struggle. They also argued that it would be impossible to organise a general strike in conditions of martial law. The SPD's real objection, however, was that a general strike immediately raised the question of a frontal challenge to the state, endangering the legality and the assets of the SPD.

The question of the general strike became particularly pointed in the SPD in 1905-06, in the context of a strike wave of insurrectionary proportions in Tsarist Russia and a big coal strike at home in the Ruhr. The emergence of the 'political mass strike' became the talk of the SPD, exciting radicals in the party and stirring up the enthusiasm of union militants. This coincided with moves by the national and various state governments to restrict the franchise, to try to limit the steady rise in the SPD's electoral support. Even this threat to the electoral success of the SPD did not convince the union bureaucracy to support the tactic. With support growing in the party for a general strike to defend political freedoms, the union leaders fought back. At a quickly convened conference in Cologne in March 1905, union leaders declared that a general strike was out of the question.

Many SPD members were not prepared to let the issue simply die. At the subsequent SPD congress in Jena in September 1905, delegates endorsed a resolution moved by leader and founder August Bebel which obliged party members to carry on a broad, mass agitation for the mass strike. Who would carry the day? The resolution of this dispute would reveal the real balance of forces in the party and its overall trajectory.

Had Bebel and the party executive taken the Jena resolution seriously, they would have been obliged to break the resistance of the union bureaucracy in the SPD and to make plans for revolutionary agitation. Bebel had no such intentions. He understood that a serious general strike, on Russian lines, would inevitably raise the possibility of insurrection – which he completely opposed. This was apparent even at the Jena Congress; he told delegates that it was incorrect:

> to say that the Social Democrats are working towards a revolution. This idea does not even occur to us. What interest can we have in bringing about a catastrophe in which the workers will suffer first and foremost?[12]

The party executive and the SPD union leaders held a secret conference in February 1906. The executive bowed down to the union leaders, disavowing any idea that it might agitate for a general strike; on the contrary, the executive pledged to 'try to prevent one as much as possible.'[13] In September 1906, the Mannheim Party Congress accepted a resolution in these terms, with Bebel explaining away his support for a general strike at the previous Congress:

> If at Jena I enthusiastically recommended the general strike as an ultimate means of struggle, no word of mine can be taken to mean that I am prepared to recommend one for the coming year.[14]

Nor the year after that, nor the year after that... The general strike had been buried, much to the pleasure of the union leaders. They now understood themselves to be the masters of the SPD, because the resolution gave them veto power over any decision that might intrude on their affairs. The Mannheim decision also suited the open reformists who were no keener on a confrontation with the state, while also indicating that Bebel, who had historically backed the radicals in the party against the open reformists, had now definitely shifted to the right wing. Mannheim confirmed that the revisionist trend in the party was now winning in practice.

The SPD's orientation to the state – rather than class struggle – as the way to lift workers' conditions inevitably meant that it accommodated to nationalism. The capitalist state it sought to work through was by definition a national state. While party leaders declared their support for working class internationalism, they were more and more adapting to the project of 'national defence', by which they meant defending Germany's supposedly superior civilisation against Russian absolutism. The party fiercely opposed the Prussian officer class and the existence of a standing army paid for by taxes on the working class. It advocated instead the creation of a volunteer militia. But it still believed in defending 'the fatherland,' even under capitalist rule. In 1900, Bebel told the Reichstag that 'if it came to a war with Russia... I would be ready, old boy that I am, to shoulder a gun against her.'[15] He returned to the theme in 1907 at the Party Congress in Essen:

> If ever we should really be called upon to defend the fatherland, we will defend it because it is our fatherland, the soil on which we live, whose language we speak, whose customs we possess, because we want to make our fatherland a country that is inferior to none in the world in perfection and beauty.[16]

The door was thereby opened for the betrayal in August 1914, which was, inevitably, pitched by the German High Command as 'national defence' against Russian barbarism. When the decision came, many in the SPD felt immense relief. They no longer had to bear criticism from the right that they were 'anti-national.' One of the SPD's newspaper editors, future Prussian minister Konrad Haenisch, illustrated this mood best:

> The conflict of two souls in one breast was probably easy for none of us. [It lasted] until suddenly – I shall never forget the day and hour – the terrible tension was resolved; until one dared to be what one was; until – despite all principles and wooden theories – one could, for the first time in almost a quarter century, join with a full heart, a clean conscience and without a sense of treason in the sweeping, stormy song: 'Deutschland, Deutschland über alles.'[17]

Lenin quickly drew lessons from the SPD's betrayal and summarised the outlook of the labour bureaucracy that explained its capitulation:

> Advocacy of class collaboration; abandonment of the idea of socialist revolution and revolutionary methods of struggle; adaptation to bourgeois nationalism; losing sight of the fact that the borderlines of nationality and country are historically transient; making a fetish of bourgeois legality; renunciation of the class viewpoint and the class struggle, for fear of repelling the 'broad masses of the population' (meaning the petty bourgeoisie) – such, doubtlessly, are the ideological foundations of opportunism. And it is from such soil that the present chauvinist and patriotic frame of mind of most Second International leaders has developed.[18]

The capitulation of the Second International in August 1914 confirmed the counter-revolutionary nature of the labour bureaucracy. It demonstrated that social democrats could combine verbal radicalism with political passivity in practice, so long as they were not confronted by life and death questions. The outbreak of war presented them with a simple choice: maintain their formal political position of internationalism and hostility to imperialist war, and return to illegality, persecution, prison and the seizure of their assets; or abandon the principles to which they formally subscribed, support their 'own' imperialist state and gain an honoured role in capitalist society. They capitulated and became recruiting sergeants for World War I. There was no turning back. The reformists had now made their stand as agents of the bourgeoisie in the labour movement. They dragged in their wake Kautsky and his centrist followers.

The SPD's betrayal was not a simple matter of a few individuals having the wrong idea about how to fight for socialism. But why did the party not split, between those who were rapidly accommodating to the Imperial state and those who held firm to the party's 'maximum program,' in which was inscribed the fight for socialism? The revisionist debate gives us some answers. Bernstein and his supporters were trounced at three successive congresses, each time more soundly than the last, but they were not expelled. They should have been; they were arguing that the SPD abandon its basic principles. Allowing them to remain members meant that the party's formal adherence to Marxism became increasingly meaningless. But one principle held in common across the Second International was that the working class in each country must have just one party, which must embody *all* currents within the working class movement. So splitting the party would be tantamount to splitting the working class. This commitment to party unity meant that the majority took no steps to force the revisionists out, and the latter gradually gained ground in the party whose practices were much more in line with their theories. And so, while Kautsky supported Luxemburg's fight against Bernstein, the leader of the centre would not argue for an open break with the reformists.[19] Fudging the differences with the reformists in the name of party unity was his priority.

Even Luxemburg, more sharply critical of Bernstein and deeply hostile to the results of the Mannheim Congress, allowed the struggle to be largely confined to an ideological battle and failed to argue for a sharp organisational demarcation between revolutionaries and reformists. Luxemburg spelled out her approach to the battle with the reformists in her *Organisational Questions of Social Democracy*, written in 1904 as a polemic against Lenin's *What is to Be Done?* She argues that the SPD must represent the whole working class and must reflect the diversity of its experiences. Yes, the reformist current within the party was a problem, but organisational measures, such as expulsions and tighter definitions of membership, imposed through rule books and constitutions, could not insulate the SPD from conservative currents of opinion within the working class. Nor was it advisable for the party to try to do so, argued Luxemburg; this would only cut the party off from the vital energy of the class.

The problem with the SPD was not so much the presence in the party of reformist rank and file worker members with mixed and contradictory ideas reflecting their experiences under capitalism. These layers could be radicalised in the course of struggle, as the 1918 November Revolution showed (Chapter 2). The real problem was the presence in the party of professional labour bureaucrats whose reformist ideas were entirely in accord with their underlying class interests. The labour bureaucrats would respond to the November Revolution by shifting hard to the right, not the left; they became the main bulwark of German capitalism in its time of need.

Luxemburg had no illusions. She understood that the labour bureaucracy would try to hold back any revolutionary rising in Germany. But – and here is the second problem – she believed that the spontaneous energy of the masses would push the labour bureaucracy to one side. She wrote:

> If at any time and under any circumstances, Germany were to experience big political struggles, an era of tremendous economic struggles would...open up. Events would not stop for a second in order to ask union leaders whether they had given their blessing to the movement or not. If they stood aside from the movement or opposed it, the result of such behaviour would only be this: the union or Party leaders would be swept away by the wave of events and the economic as well as the political struggles would be fought to a conclusion without them.[20]

This was a serious misassessment. It overlooked the tremendous unevenness within the working class which, at one pole, comprised more advanced layers ready to break the grip of the labour bureaucracy to take struggles to the next step, and, at the other, less class conscious workers more easily swayed by the labour leaders. What was needed was organisation by the more advanced layers, who could challenge the bureaucracy's grip on the less advanced. Luxemburg's approach also overlooked the fact that mass struggle only raises the question of power; it cannot resolve it. Only the destruction of the old state power through insurrection can do that. And, as the Bolsheviks were to demonstrate in 1917, insurrection calls for revolutionary organisation, politically and organisationally distinct from reformist parties. The absence of such an organisation could only lead to disaster, as Luxemburg was to discover during the November Revolution.

The Bolsheviks: a very different kind of party

The Russian Bolsheviks reacted very differently to the outbreak of war. After Lenin overcame his initial shock about the collapse of the International, the Bolsheviks came out stridently against the war, arguing that 'the conversion of the present imperialist war into a civil war is the only correct proletarian slogan.'[21] They faced immediate repression by the Tsarist authorities; Lenin was forced into exile in Switzerland. Despite persecution, however, the Bolsheviks were still able to issue dozens of illegal leaflets denouncing the war and Russia's imperialist war aims.

Why were the Bolsheviks able to resist the Second International's collapse into what Lenin called 'social patriotism' in August 1914? It was not that the Bolsheviks thought of themselves as a fundamentally different party to the SPD. Lenin regarded their project as trying to build a party on the same lines as the SPD, involving the fusion of the socialist intelligentsia with the most active and purposeful worker activists, albeit in Russian police-state conditions. But while Lenin may not have been consciously trying to build a different party to the SPD, in practice, by the time war broke out, the Bolsheviks and the SPD had become quite different parties. August 1914 demonstrated this with stunning clarity.

There was an important contextual difference between Russia and Western Europe: the Tsarist state apparatus was not capitalist but absolutist. The result was that neither of the foundations of working class reformism – parliamentarians and the union bureaucracy – could flourish in Russia. Reformism was much weaker in Russia, no more than an ideological current; in the West, it had a material base, the labour bureaucracy. Social democracy in Western Europe was characterised by a division of labour between the parliamentarians campaigning for political reforms for the working class and trade union leaders fighting for economic gains. No such distinction was possible in Russia because of Tsarist repression. Historian of the revolution Steve Smith writes:

> Attempts at home-grown reformism never got very far, however, for the simple reason that even the most 'bread and butter' trade union struggles foundered on the rock of the tsarist state; all efforts to separate trade unionism from politics were rendered nugatory by the action of police and troops. In this political climate trade unions grew up fully conscious of the fact that the overthrow of the autocracy was a basic precondition for the improvement of the workers' lot.[22]

The major difference between the Bolsheviks and the SPD, however, was that the Bolsheviks had split with the reformist current in the Russian socialist movement, the Mensheviks. The two wings of Russian social democracy had moved closer and further apart from each other since the formation of the two factions of the Russian Social Democratic and Labour Party (RSDLP) in 1903 – at times virtually uniting, but at other times engaged in heated polemics. In 1912, however, on the eve of a resurgence in workers' struggle, the issue of relations between the two forces came to a head. At a conference in Prague early in the New Year, the Bolshevik majority used its strength to impose its political line, in effect forcing a split with the Mensheviks on the grounds of the latter's 'liquidationism,' their tendency to restrict their work to legal work and to abandon the underground work which was necessary to sustain a revolutionary organisation in an absolutist regime.

The Bolsheviks may have believed that they were building a party along the lines of the SPD. In practice, they were building a party of revolutionary worker leaders, a militant minority, independent of, and capable of politically contesting, the forces of capitalist liberalism and working class reformism. While the SPD sought to represent *the class* in all its diversity, the Bolsheviks aimed to represent *the interests of the class*, bringing together those who understood the need to smash capitalism and excluding those who did not, precisely using the 'rules' and 'constitution' abhorred by Luxemburg to effect this separation. Outside the climax of a revolution, this meant restricting membership to the most advanced layers. While the SPD was a 'catch-all' party, the Bolsheviks built a combat organisation bringing together the most advanced layers of workers. The point was not to cut the party off from the rest of the class, the outcome Luxemburg believed would result. 'On the contrary,' Lenin wrote:

> the stronger our Party organisations, consisting of *real* Social-Democrats, the less wavering and instability there is *within* the Party, the broader, more varied, richer, and more fruitful will be the Party's influence on the elements of the working-class *masses* surrounding it and guided by it. The Party, as the vanguard of the working class, must not be confused, after all, with the entire class.[23]

Unlike the majority of the Second International, the Bolsheviks did not see their task as merely 'educating' workers in socialism and waiting passively for the contradictions of capitalism to play out. Sandra Bloodworth argues: 'The aim was to build a party capable of organising the most advanced workers so they would be capable of shaping events, maximising the possibility of working class victories.'[24] That involved building a cadre who learned by building a party in the course of struggle by workers and other oppressed groups. It involved not simply tailing popular moods but taking an intransigent stance when necessary – and also learning how and when to compromise with their rivals and survive with principles intact. After the experience of the 1905 Revolution in Russia, it also meant preparing for a second revolution, no matter how hard the experience of working class retreat and demoralisation was in the years of reaction that followed. Bloodworth explains:

> to chart a course through these complex situations, an organisation needed a cadre with roots among workers and with sufficient experience to enable them to make the assessments each concrete situation demanded; and crucially, they had to have the authority to inspire workers to carry it through.[25]

Because the Bolsheviks sought to build on this basis, they attracted the more advanced workers in the big workplaces of St Petersburg[26] and Moscow. This tendency, which Paul Le Blanc calls 'the "proletarianization" of the Bolsheviks and the Bolshevization of the "conscious workers",'[27] accelerated after the 1912 split in the RSDLP. By 1914, Lenin could claim that the Bolsheviks overwhelmingly dominated all 13 trade unions in Moscow and, in St Petersburg, were predominant in the Metal Workers, Textile Workers, Tailors, Wood Workers, Shop Assistants and others. The Bolshevik paper *Pravda*, which appeared for the first time in 1912, very quickly established a strong influence among politically conscious factory workers who supported it financially through workplace collections. By the time of the February 1917 Revolution, the Bolsheviks had trained many thousands of worker militants who played a vital role in organising the workers. During 1917, these workers looked instinctively to the Bolsheviks for a lead, and Lenin relied on them for support in his arguments against right wing tendencies within the party.

The Mensheviks, by contrast, attracted workers in smaller workplaces, such as printing, where working class attitudes were accordingly more sectional and reformist. Compared to *Pravda*, the Menshevik papers were far more dependent on financial support from non-workers. They were a looser organisation, less demanding on members. Like the SPD, they attracted a coterie of public figures who became a bridge to bourgeois democratic trends. In 1914, many Mensheviks backed the Russian war effort and, following the February Revolution, they demanded the continuation of the war and backed the bourgeois Provisional Government.

In summary: whatever Lenin may have believed about the Bolshevik project and its place in the Second International before the war, he built a party profoundly different to the SPD by shearing off the reformist wing and building on an explicitly revolutionary basis.

Resistance and the rebirth of the socialist left

The Bolsheviks were not the only party in the Second International to stand against the patriotic tide in 1914. The Serbian and Bulgarian parties also intransigently opposed the war, as did small numbers of leftists in the German SPD. In December, Liebknecht reclaimed the honour of the German socialist movement when he voted against the military budget in the Reichstag. The Italian socialists were not forced to decide on the question immediately, because Italy did not enter the war for another year, but the majority opposed the war. The Socialist Party of America opposed the war but suffered significant splits over the question. In Australia, the syndicalist Industrial Workers of the World (IWW) and the small socialist groups to the left of the ALP also opposed the war. Elsewhere, only scattered individuals or sections of parties took a principled stand.

Although they constituted only a tiny minority and recognised their isolation, revolutionaries who opposed the war believed that popular support for the war would eventually fade and that opponents of the war would begin to get a hearing. The immediate task was to lay the basis for a new International that could prepare for that political break. Lenin argued that a new International had to be built on the basis of a revolutionary rejection of imperialist war:

> To the present-day bourgeoisie's attempts to divide and disunite them by means of hypocritical appeals for the 'defence of the fatherland' the class-conscious workers will reply with ever new and persevering efforts to unite the workers of various nations in the struggle to overthrow the rule of the bourgeoisie of all nations.[28]

Lenin was not a pacifist. Civil war, not 'peace,' was the urgent necessity:

> It is the duty of every socialist to conduct propaganda of the class struggle, in the army as well; work directed towards turning a war of the nations into civil war is the only socialist activity in the era of an imperialist armed conflict of the bourgeoisie of all nations.[29]

Intransigent revolutionaries were a smaller minority within the anti-war minority. The Italian and Swiss socialist parties, for example, opposed the war but held a 'centrist' line. They lay between the outright reformists and the revolutionaries, often talking revolution but practising reformism. They were dubious about – or were unwilling to recognise – the potential for class struggle that the war had created. They were keen to reconstitute international links between the socialist parties that had been broken by the war. They saw the war as a disastrous interruption of 'normal' political life, not as an opportunity for socialist revolution.

In September 1915, the Italian and Swiss parties convened a conference of anti-war socialists in the Swiss village of Zimmerwald. Lenin's Bolsheviks and representatives from the German, French, Swedish, Norwegian, Dutch, Polish and other parties attended. Numbers were low, just a few dozen, reflecting both the isolation of the anti-war camp and the difficulty of attending such an event in wartime when contact with 'enemy' nationals was regarded as treason. Debates at Zimmerwald revealed a clear demarcation between revolutionaries and centrists, with centrists in a majority. Lenin's resolution, which contained the call: 'Turn the imperialist war into a civil war!' was rejected by 19 votes to 12. Nonetheless, Lenin declared, the congress was a first step; the majority manifesto stated: 'The capitalists of all countries claim that the war serves to defend the fatherland... They are lying.'

In April 1916, anti-war socialists convened a second conference in Switzerland, this time in Kienthal. The Bolsheviks pressed their revolutionary line harder this time, stating that the Zimmerwald manifesto was inconsistent and muddled. They argued that the centrists were too eager to maintain good relations with the Second International to be able to offer a way forward to those who wished to fight imperialism. The task of socialists was not to rebuild the Second International, but:

> to explain to the masses the inevitability and necessity of breaking with opportunism, to educate them for revolution by waging a relentless struggle against opportunism, to utilise the experience of the war to expose, not conceal, the utter vileness of national-liberal labour politics.[30]

This entailed a sharp break with the centrists.

The Bolshevik attempt to stiffen the resolve of the anti-war socialists matched a turn in the public mood. As initial hopes that the war would be over in a few months faded, sentiment began to weary. The death toll climbed, food and essential items fell into short supply, prices rose dramatically, and awareness grew of the fortunes accumulated by well-connected generals, politicians and capitalists. Significant minorities in the combatant nations started to turn against the war.

The 1916 Easter Rising in Ireland, which broke out just as the Kienthal Conference began, was the first open signal of rebellion against war and imperialism. In Germany, Liebknecht and Otto Rühle had broken with the SPD and were agitating in the Reichstag against the war. Liebknecht's arrest for treason in May provoked a strike by 50,000 workers in Berlin in June and a wave of clashes with the police. Strikes and desertions on the Western Front began to rise.

Into this context of growing dissatisfaction with the ruling classes, the February 1917 Revolution in Russia burst like a thunderclap. The revolution brought down within days the Romanov dynasty that had ruled the Russian empire for 300 years. Tsar Nicholas II was forced to flee. The February Revolution inspired hundreds of thousands of German workers to strike in April for an immediate peace without annexations, an end to censorship, the release of all political prisoners, improved food supplies and a democratic franchise throughout Germany. In May, French soldiers mutinied *en masse*. In the summer of 1917, German sailors in the North Sea Fleet rebelled against harsh discipline and the privileges enjoyed by the officers.

The February Revolution and dual power

The February Revolution in Russia starkly posed all the questions that divided the socialist movement during World War I. In particular, it raised the question of which class was to take power. Were reformist and centrist forces going to patch up the old system and put the capitalists back on their feet? Or could revolutionaries convince workers of the need to smash capitalism and take power? Every party in the workers' movement was put to the test.

The fundamental fact about 1917 in Russia was the phenomenon known as 'dual power,' characterised by the existence of two powers side by side, one of which ultimately imposed its will on the other. Organs of workers' power were one element. The February Revolution saw a massive outburst of popular struggle and popular democracy in Petrograd. Workers flocked to institutions both old and new. Unions were formed from scratch, others were revived, and trade union membership exploded. Factory committees sprang up in all the big workplaces and made decisions about what would be produced and how. The factory committees were immediately accountable institutions and, over the course of 1917, most readily drew revolutionary conclusions. In the barracks and in the naval bases, solders' and sailors' committees started to agitate against brutal treatment by their officers. And then there were the workers' councils, or soviets, composed of delegates elected from the big workplaces, but also including representatives of soldiers and sailors, peasants and other layers. The Petrograd Soviet could pose the basis of an entirely new way of organising society, without capitalists, landlords or generals. Very quickly, workers in other cities and regions followed Petrograd's example and set up soviets and factory committees of their own.

The Russian soviets and even the most democratic parliamentary systems in Western Europe embodied two entirely different forms of rule. Soviet democracy is not merely an alternative to parliament, it is its antithesis, combining as it does power at the point of production with the battle for class dominance. The soviets in Russia unified political and economic power, whereas parliament leaves the most important power of the bourgeoisie, its economic strength, untouched. The soviets brought under democratic control the administrative and legislative functions of government – unlike parliament, which leaves the public service, army and police in unelected hands. The soviets were an organ of struggle responsive to the will of the workers and capable of organising strikes and protests, whereas parliament is an organ dominated by the bourgeoisie and far removed from democratic accountability. Delegates to the soviet were immediately accountable to their workmates and enjoyed no special privileges, while parliamentarians enjoy far superior conditions of life to their constituents and only have to answer to them once every three or four years. Obviously, not every soviet in Russia met these standards, but their formation created the potential to bring workers' power into being, whereas parliament only entrenches the power of the capitalists.

The other power in Russia in 1917 was the unelected Provisional Government. Having filled the vacuum as the Tsarist regime collapsed, and comprising only appointees from the old Tsarist toy parliament, the Duma, the Provisional Government had no revolutionary ambitions. It was dominated by the bourgeois liberal Cadet party, and its leader for the first four months of its existence was the Cadet representative Prince Lvov, a nephew of the Tsar. It did not formally declare a republic until September. The new government sought no more than modest democratic reforms, a constituent assembly, civil rights, land reform and some improvement to workers' living standards. But all this was to await victory in the war. The Provisional Government, whether led by Prince Lvov or, later, by the moderate socialist lawyer Alexander Kerensky, was committed to pursuing the same imperialist war as the old order, anxious to defend and extend Russia's ambitions in Europe and Asia.

Prioritising winning the war meant that none of the ambitions for democratic change or increased living standards could be realised. 'Win the war' meant that the generals had to command the soldiers. 'Win the war' meant that the peasants could not be granted land. 'Win the war' meant that workers had to work long hours to make munitions. 'Win the war' meant that the old social hierarchies, with their Russian nationalism and religious, sexual and racial oppression, remained intact. The millions of poor peasants who had seen the overthrow of the Tsar as an opportunity to finally have land for themselves faced constant delaying tactics. The workers in the factories demanding food to feed their families and an end to the dictatorship of the supervisors and managers were snubbed. The faces at the top of the state apparatus may have changed, and the Tsarist double-headed eagle had vanished from the halls of power, but nothing much had changed for most people following the February Revolution.

The Provisional Government lacked firm foundations. As the War Minister, Alexander Guchkov, advised the army chief of staff in March:

> The government, alas, has no real power: the troops, the railroads, the post and telegraph are in the hands of the Soviet. The simple fact is that the Provisional Government exists only so long as the Soviet permits it.[31]

That was the essence of 'dual power.' Such a situation could only survive while neither the soviets, representing the working class, nor the Provisional Government, representing the interests of capitalists, landlords and generals, was able to prevail. Ultimately, either the soviets would sweep aside the Provisional Government and establish a governing authority of their own, or the Provisional Government would gather its forces and smash the soviets.

The crucial question in 1917 was the attitude that the workers' and peasants' parties would adopt towards dual power. The misleadingly named Socialist Revolutionaries (SRs) Party, led by the urban intelligentsia, oriented to the interests of the wealthier farmers. They opposed the land seizures by the peasants after the Tsar was overthrown. War still came first. The Mensheviks were a working class party and regarded themselves as Marxists; but, like the Western social democrats, they were opposed to workers seizing power. At best, they believed, the soviets might have an auxiliary or a consultative role in politics and must not usurp the power of the Provisional Government. Once the promised elections had been held and a constituent assembly established, they argued, the role of the soviets would become marginal. The fact that neither the SRs nor the Mensheviks saw the February Revolution as opening the door to workers' power explains why the Petrograd Soviet, dominated by these two parties, backed the Provisional Government. Only their support allowed the Provisional Government to survive eight months.

The Mensheviks snubbed the prospect of workers seizing power because they believed that the infant Russian proletariat, confined for the most part to a few large cities in European Russia, was incapable of carrying through a revolution and taking power into its own hands. Therefore, the Mensheviks argued, workers should tag along behind the liberal bourgeoisie in its demands for political reform. Proletarian demands and actions should be moderated so as not to scare the capitalists. The bourgeoisie would lead, the workers would follow, giving the capitalists a little shove when needed. Once the bourgeoisie had gathered political power into its own hands, the working class would have to allow a prolonged period of capitalist development before it became strong enough to challenge the capitalists for state power. It was this schema that explained the counter-revolutionary role played by the Mensheviks in 1917 – they did not want workers to take power. They feared that the revolutionary impulse of Russian workers would scare the bourgeoisie and drive them into the arms of reaction.

The official program of the Bolsheviks at the time of the February Revolution started from the same premise as the Mensheviks: that socialist revolution was not on the immediate agenda in Russia because of the country's economic backwardness. From this point of initial agreement, they diverged. The Bolsheviks argued that the late-developing Russian bourgeoisie, unlike its forebears in Britain and France in centuries past, was too cowardly to lead a revolution against autocracy; it had too much to gain from the status quo and too much to lose from a working class uprising. On the other hand, while the Mensheviks saw the peasantry, who comprised 100 million of a population of 170 million, as a fundamentally conservative, property-owning class incapable of transcending capitalism, Lenin understood the powerful revolutionary impulse that peasant land seizures could play. Lenin argued that the proletariat, just three million of whom worked in factories and mines, must forge an alliance with the peasantry in revolutionary battles to bring down autocracy.[32] This was the basis of the 'democratic dictatorship of the proletariat and peasantry.'

The 'democratic dictatorship' schema involved the formation of a revolutionary government in which the worker and peasant organisations would hold a majority and carry out the basic tasks of bourgeois democracy: abolition of Tsarism, implementation of land reform and the eight-hour day, and the establishment of a democratic capitalist republic. Once the 'democratic dictatorship' had completed these tasks, particularly after the peasants had received land, the alliance would break up; the peasants would abandon the working class and shift their support to the parties of private property. Given the voting power of the peasantry in a democratic franchise, this shift would allow the capitalist parties to form governments, throwing the working class parties onto the opposition benches until such time as industrial development made the working class sufficiently strong to overthrow capitalism and establish proletarian rule.

The Bolsheviks scorned the passive tailism of the Mensheviks. But the program of 'democratic dictatorship' did not prepare them to respond adequately to developments when dual power began to emerge in the weeks after the February Revolution. The formation of soviets had begun to point to a very different trajectory for the Revolution, one in which the working class, leading the peasants in struggle, could fight for power in its own right.

The Bolshevik leaders in Russia in the first weeks of the Revolution, Joseph Stalin and Lev Kamenev, editors of *Pravda*, stuck to the old formula: bourgeois democracy was all that was possible. This position dragged them rapidly to the right. They began to adopt a position of support for the Provisional Government as the best defence of the gains of the February Revolution. In particular, they argued that the February Revolution had changed the character of Russia's participation in the war. It was no longer a war waged by an absolutist monarchy, but a war to defend the gains of the Revolution against German imperialism. Had the Bolsheviks held to the line of Stalin and Kamenev, the party would soon have become indistinguishable from the Mensheviks.

Lenin's return from exile in Switzerland in early April turned the Bolsheviks around. He had received letters from Russian workers expressing their anger at the *Pravda* line, demanding that Stalin be expelled from the party. They wanted the Bolsheviks to end their support for the Provisional Government. Lenin instinctively understood that they were right. While not formally rejecting the 'democratic dictatorship' line, Lenin now argued that the revolution could not stop at a mere constituent assembly. The workers themselves must take power. In a letter to the *Pravda* editors, Lenin described the Soviet of Workers' Deputies as:

> the embryo of a workers' government, the representatives of the entire mass of the poor…i.e. of nine-tenths of the population, which is striving for peace, bread and freedom.[33]

Arriving in Petrograd, Lenin told the crowd that greeted him: 'We don't need any government except the Soviet of workers', soldiers' and farmhands' deputies.' He attacked the Petrograd Soviet majority backing the Provisional Government as 'the same old opportunists, speaking pretty words but in reality betraying the cause of socialism and the worker masses.' Lenin's argument was conveyed powerfully in his *April Theses*. He called for the party to withdraw its support for the Provisional Government and instead to demand 'All Power to the Soviets,' with three main demands: an end to the war, land to the peasants, and bread to the workers.

Lenin's changed line astounded and horrified many of the Bolshevik Central Committee. Stalin and Kamenev had refused to publish his letters to *Pravda*. Only Alexandra Kollontai, who had been passing on Lenin's letters to the *Pravda* editors, supported him at the Central Committee meeting convened to debate the *April Theses*. Nonetheless, Lenin knew that he was supported by the thousands of Bolshevik worker militants who were voting in district after district in favour of the *April Theses*. So, when a party conference was held three weeks after his arrival, Lenin's perspective swept the board.

Lenin recognised that having the formally correct position did not give the Bolsheviks the capacity to lead the soviets to take power in April. Nor, despite the claims of right wing historians, were they plotting to take power in a coup. The Bolsheviks were only a minority of delegates to the soviets in Petrograd and Moscow. At that stage, the majority of workers still backed the Mensheviks and SRs, hoping that the Provisional Government would deliver on its promises. The demand 'All Power to the Soviets' appealed only to the most politically advanced worker militants. Consequently, Lenin argued that the main task of the Bolsheviks in the spring of 1917 was to 'patiently explain' their case to workers in order to win a majority in the soviets.

Lenin renounced, in practice if not explicitly, the slogan of the 'democratic dictatorship.' This demonstrated his reluctance to be held back by old party shibboleths. It also shows his understanding of the needs of the revolution, based on his ongoing connections over many years with working class militants engaged in the project of building a revolutionary party. It also coincided with the arguments of the Marxist Leon Trotsky. Having opposed Lenin's Bolsheviks for many years, Trotsky would shortly join the party.

Trotsky had been elected president of the St Petersburg Soviet following the 1905 Revolution, when workers' soviets made their first appearance. He set out a revolutionary path very different to either the Mensheviks or the Bolsheviks. In his theory of permanent revolution, which he outlined in his 1906 work *Results and Prospects* in the aftermath of the 1905 Revolution, Trotsky advanced two fundamental points of difference.

The first concerned the relationship between the working class and the peasantry. Trotsky acknowledged that no one could doubt the Russian peasants' bravery and capacity for self-sacrifice, which they had demonstrated during numerous uprisings, but he argued that they could not lead a revolution. Their individualistic character, each peasant family toiling on their own plot of land, meant that they were incapable of ruling in their own right; the peasantry must always fall under the sway of one urban class or another. The fundamental question of the Russian Revolution, on which its whole future would rest, was: which urban class would the peasantry follow – the capitalists or the workers? Trotsky argued that the working class, a collective class, concentrated together in the strategic centres of capitalist power, must lead the peasants. The working class was a minority class in Russia; but, if it seized state power, it could confirm and consolidate the spontaneous seizure of land by the peasants, thereby winning the peasants to their side.

The second point of difference concerned what would happen once the basic tasks of the bourgeois revolution were completed. Lenin had argued that, having carried out a basic program of legislative reform, the working class would be forced into the role of the opposition. Trotsky said that workers would see no reason to stop halfway. In a situation where workers were on their feet, why would they simply accept capitalist rule with all its injustices? Instead, the struggle against feudalism and Tsarist autocracy would inevitably develop into a socialist revolution, whose final victory could be realised only on a world scale. The prerequisite for success – here Trotsky agreed with Lenin – was that workers had to be organised independently, not subordinated to the bourgeoisie who would only look for ways to cut short any struggle.

Trotsky's use of the term 'permanent revolution' and his argument were not new. Following the 1848–49 revolutions in France and Germany, Marx and Engels argued that liberal bourgeois forces could not be trusted in the fight for democracy. Their experience with these bourgeois friends of 'liberty' and 'democracy,' who wrote fine speeches denouncing autocracy, was that they decamped to reaction when the plebeian and rising proletarian forces began to insist on their rights. The working class, Marx and Engels argued, was the only reliably revolutionary class. With no stake in the status quo, the working class had no reason to pull back from a thoroughgoing settling of scores with the autocracy.

Where Trotsky differed was in his greatest insight: his insistence that the Russian Revolution had to be situated in its world context, specifically a world characterised by uneven and combined development. Yes, those Marxists who said that the small proletariat in backward Russia could not possibly build socialism were right. The material wherewithal would simply not be available to them, and they would soon be crushed by imperialist invasion and internal counter-revolution. Trotsky argued, along with Lenin, that a revolution in Russia could be the spark to ignite revolutions in more advanced countries. If such countries followed Russia's revolutionary lead, the new workers' states could band together to repel imperialist intervention and could share foodstuffs, agricultural equipment, machine tools and the basic necessities sufficient to sustain themselves.

Although there is no indication that Lenin read *Results and Prospects* before the October Revolution, his thinking and Trotsky's were clearly running along the same path in 1917. In July and August, Lenin resumed work on a book begun before the February Revolution, one of his most important works, *State and Revolution*. With its call to smash the capitalist state and to establish a workers' state based on soviets, *State and Revolution* clearly echoed Trotsky's argument that there was no Chinese Wall between the democratic revolution and the socialist revolution, and that the former, as Trotsky put it later, must 'grow over' into the latter.[34]

From April to October

Properly oriented now by Lenin, the Bolsheviks hammered away at the treachery of the Provisional Government, emphasising that it would not deliver for the workers, soldiers and peasants. They warned that the generals, landlords and industrialists were preparing to crush even the limited democratic reforms the people had won. The Provisional Government persecuted the Bolsheviks relentlessly.

In July, the Bolsheviks faced their sternest test yet. Masses of Petrograd workers rose in revolt when the Provisional Government ordered the machine gun regiment, a revolutionary stronghold, to the front. The Bolsheviks refused to turn their backs on the impatient workers who wanted to move into revolution ahead of the majority of workers in other cities. They joined them on the streets, the better to steer them away from a premature attempt to seize power that would only have led to their isolation and destruction. Following the July Days, the repression became even more severe, with leading Bolsheviks thrown into jail or forced into exile or hiding.

The Bolshevik warnings that reaction was preparing to strike to wipe out the limited gains of the February Revolution were proven correct. In August, General Lavr Kornilov, commander in chief of the Russian army, attempted a coup to bring down the Provisional Government. Prime Minister Kerensky had for some weeks been encouraging plotting by the military to smash the soviets. He only turned against Kornilov once he realised that the military would not be satisfied with destroying the soviets but would go on to crush the Provisional Government itself. The compromised Kerensky was in no position to rally workers to defeat the coup. It was the Bolsheviks who took up the challenge. They offered the Provisional Government no political support but understood the threat that the coup represented to the entire working class. As Kornilov's armies began to approach Petrograd, the Bolsheviks organised the defence of the capital by mobilising the Military Revolutionary Committee of the Petrograd Soviet, which they dominated. Armed workers defeated Kornilov in just four days. His armies crumbled in the face of the working class mobilisation.

The Bolsheviks' role during the Kornilov coup convinced many workers that the Bolsheviks were the only party serious about defending democracy and delivering the reforms that the Provisional Government refused to enact. The party had constituted only a minority in the working class in February, but its militants now began to draw tens of thousands of new followers behind them. It was the experience of struggle that drove workers towards the Bolsheviks, as Lenin had anticipated on the eve of the February Revolution:

> The real education of the masses can never be separated from their independent political, and especially revolutionary, struggle. Only

struggle educates the exploited class. Only struggle discloses to it the magnitude of its own power, widens its horizon, enhances its abilities, clarifies its mind, forges its will.[35]

The party's popularity in the barracks and in the factories surged over the summer and early autumn of 1917. Membership rose from 20,000 in January to 250,000 by October. The Kornilov coup demonstrated that the Bolsheviks were the most significant force in the workplace militias set up to maintain order and to smash counter-revolution. Army units in the rear and sailors of the Baltic fleet turned towards the Bolsheviks in large numbers. Discontent became increasingly obvious on the front lines. By October, such was the demand for the party's material that the Bolsheviks were printing four daily newspapers. In the villages, peasants were seizing the land and ignoring the objections of the SRs, the party that traditionally claimed their allegiance. They were increasingly prepared to lend a sympathetic ear to the Bolsheviks who, although based in the cities, were the only party prepared to support their actions.

Soviets continued to flourish as the revolution deepened. In May, there were at most 400 soviets; in August, 600; and by October, 900. The most important was in Petrograd, where attendance could be as high as 3,000 in full session. It was in this city, the cradle of the revolution, that the Bolsheviks first won a majority in September. Moscow and many other regional cities soon followed. Support for the Mensheviks and SRs in the soviets collapsed. The same result was evident in municipal elections in Petrograd and Moscow. Workers and soldiers (mostly peasants in uniform) were clearly swinging behind Lenin and the Bolsheviks. This was reflected in the left wing of the SRs, who effectively split from the right under the impact of the upsurge in the towns and villages. The left SRs, with a majority of the party's followers behind them, backed the Bolshevik demands for peace, bread and land.

The question of who was to rule became critical. The generals, capitalists and landlords understood that the Provisional Government could no longer control the workers or peasantry. From their perspective, the only solution was savagery, military rule, dictatorship. With Kornilov defeated, they yearned for German invasion. The capitalists hoped that the German army on Russia's borders could crush Petrograd workers. Trotsky's prognoses concerning the reactionary attitude of the bourgeoisie were proven correct. Only the working class, leading the peasantry, was capable of delivering the basic demands of the people: peace, bread and land.

As autumn wore on, a curious process unfolded in Petrograd. Even as peasants were rousing themselves by the millions to seize land, workers in the capital began to retreat from the strikes and demonstrations that they had been using for months to organise themselves. What use were demonstrations and strikes when the question of state power was in the balance? Either the workers had to seize power themselves, through their soviets, or they would have to succumb. The Bolsheviks had to move. If they faltered, workers would cast them aside as a party that talked big but did nothing. Lenin persuaded the Bolsheviks to mount an insurrection; the time for talking was over. In the days leading up to the convening of the Second All-Russian Congress of Soviets, scheduled for 25 October, the Military Revolutionary Committee under Bolshevik command steadily seized control of key sites in the capital.

When the Congress of Soviets convened in the early hours of 26 October, it was Bolshevik and left SR delegates who filled two-thirds of the seats – a stark turnaround from the previous Congress, when the Bolsheviks were a minority. The Congress now learned that the Winter Palace, home to Kerensky's beleaguered Cabinet and the last building still under his control, had fallen to the Military Revolutionary Committee. By a large majority, the Congress endorsed the overthrow of the Provisional Government and the transfer of power to the soviets. The declaration read out decreed a democratic peace, the elimination of landlord estates and redistribution of land to the peasants, workers' control over industry, democratisation of the army, provision of bread for workers and the right of self-determination for all nationalities in the Russian empire. The right to practise any, or no, religion was established. Despite all the lies that have been told about the October Revolution in the century since it took place, this was no 'Bolshevik coup.' Even one of the party's opponents, the Menshevik Julius Martov, was forced to admit:

> Understand please, what we have before us after all is a victorious uprising of the proletariat – almost the entire proletariat supports Lenin and expects its social liberation from the uprising.[36]

The revolution sparked off an explosion of ingenuity, creativity and innovation. Poets, artists, architects and engineers were inspired to rethink how both the physical world and the imaginary could be transformed – not for profits, or the comforts and enjoyment of a privileged minority, or the glorification of a repressive state, but for all. Experimentation in every field burst the limits set by class society, searching for a new truth for a world worth living in. Some 125,000 literacy schools were set up, and factories established Education Commissions that put on theatre productions, poetry readings and orchestral concerts that were patronised by huge numbers of working women and men. The schools could not start on time in 1918 because the teachers were debating the latest and best methods of instruction.

The legal changes made by the soviets went far beyond economic reorganisation. They opened the possibility of individual freedom and personal liberation. In the first year, the decrees of the soviet government established universal suffrage, ended the authority of heads of families, abolished the right of inheritance and established divorce and civil laws that made marriage a voluntary relationship free of state and church control. Free abortion on demand, introduced in 1920, was the first such reform in the world. All of these gains, backed up by the eight-hour day, equal pay, literacy programs, child care and communal kitchens provided the basis for economic and sexual freedom for women – to take control over their own bodies and to take their place in public life.

Revolutionary hope

The October Revolution announced to the world the battle for the loyalty of the working class movement internationally – between the reformists, who had thrown their lot in with the generals, capitalists and landlords, and the Communists, who represented a revolutionary alternative: working class rule through soviet power. Soviet power provided workers with the concrete answer to the parliamentary reformism of the Second International, which had led workers into the barbarism of world war. If social democracy meant the continuation of capitalist rule, with all its miseries, soviet power meant ending the imperialist war, land for the peasants, bread for the workers, national liberation for oppressed countries, women's liberation and religious freedoms for minority faiths. Social democracy involved working through the capitalist state; soviet power was about smashing it and replacing it with organs of working class rule, the soviets.

But soviet power was not going to triumph unless revolutionary parties could win workers away from their traditional loyalty to the parties of the Second International. That was obvious from the experience in Russia, where the reformist parties, the SRs and Mensheviks, had done their best to destroy soviet power. Winning militant workers was the mission of the Communist International, founded just 18 months after the October Revolution.

The collapse of the Second International and the victory of the Russian Revolution amid a rising tide of workers' struggle meant that the issue of political leadership dominated debates among leading working class militants of every country with an organised workers' movement. As with the anti-war congresses in Zimmerwald and Kienthal, many in the socialist movement sought to resuscitate the Second International under a new leadership or to build a halfway house. They were not convinced that a new International needed to be organised and demarcated on the basis of revolutionary politics. Others argued that the betrayal of the Second International showed that the party was itself the problem and that trade unions could substitute for it. A minority, however, argued that parties of a whole new type were needed; workers in Europe and elsewhere should learn the lessons of the Bolsheviks. They need not replicate the Bolsheviks in every detail, but workers needed a revolutionary party in place of the social democratic parties which, while purporting to represent the whole working class or even the nation, actually represented the interests of the capitalists. Revolutionary parties had to be forged on the basis of sharp anti-capitalist politics and draw together the vanguard of the working class, the most advanced, clear-sighted and class conscious workers. Their central task was to break the hold of social democracy on the majority of the working class. Extensive debates in the early Comintern Congresses addressed the best way of achieving this.

Tens of thousands, hundreds of thousands of working class activists and militants who were breaking from reformism were invested in this fight about the future for working class politics. At stake were both the survival of the Russian Revolution and any chance for international revolution. Socialism, Lenin was well aware, could not be built in Russia alone. Russia was only the spark; the Bolsheviks hoped for a Europe-wide revolution. Only if this took place could the counter-revolution in Russia, backed by the imperialist powers, be crushed. Only if revolution jumped across national borders could workers' states be consolidated on the basis of an economy in which all the resources of the continent were marshalled to provide for the sustenance of the people. Socialism could not be created in a single country. Lenin and his comrades hoped that the formation of the Comintern in 1919 marked the first step towards world revolution. The Comintern's fate was to decide the future of the world for decades to come.

FURTHER READING

S. Bloodworth, 'Lenin vs "Leninism"', *Marxist Left Review*, no. 5, 2013.

V.I. Lenin, *State and Revolution*, Melbourne, Red Flag Books, 2020 [1917].

V.I. Lenin, *April Theses*, Moscow, Progress Publishers, 1980 [1917].

R. Luxemburg, *Reform or Revolution?* Melbourne, Red Flag Books, 2020 [1900].

R. Luxemburg, *The Mass Strike*, Melbourne, Red Flag Books, 2020 [1906].

A. Rabinowitch, *The Bolsheviks Come to Power: The Revolution of 1917 in Petrograd*, Chicago, Haymarket Books, 2004 [1976].

J. Reed, *Ten Days that Shook the World*, Chicago, Haymarket Books, 2019 [1920].

C. Schorske, *German Social Democracy, 1905-1917: The Development of the Great Schism*, Cambridge, MA, Harvard University Press, 1983 [1955].

N.N. Sukhanov, *The Russian Revolution 1917 - A Personal Record*, Princeton NJ, Princeton University Press, 1984 [1922].

L. Trotsky, *The History of the Russian Revolution*, London, Pluto Press, 1977 [1933].

2.

THE CREATION OF MASS REVOLUTIONARY PARTIES

The most pressing issue facing the Comintern after its formation in March 1919 was the need to draw mass forces to its ranks. There was some urgency to this project, because the discredited parties of the Second International were busily trying to stitch together a new, reformist International. Communists had to raise their banner to provide a rallying point for all those disgusted by the social democratic parties that had betrayed workers in 1914. The situation in Russia, where the revolution was beleaguered on all sides by counter-revolution within and invasion from without, made this even more urgent. The Russian Revolution could only survive with the help of revolutions internationally.[1]

The formation of the Comintern was controversial. The German Communist Party (KPD), formed only three months earlier, argued that creation of a new International was premature without the prior establishment of mass parties in a number of countries.

Those advocating the formation of a new International, most importantly the Russian Communists, argued that it was crucial to act now to consolidate the split with the Second International. The Russian party would obviously be dominant, both in size and because of its credentials as the only party to have successfully led a revolution, but could use its experience to help train the leaderships of the new parties. The Russians certainly hoped that their dominance would be temporary. Their entire project was founded on the premise that mass communist parties would come to power elsewhere in Europe within two or three years.

The Russians' optimism about the impact of the founding conference of the new International was confirmed in practice. In the three months following the conference in Moscow, two big workers' parties joined, the Italian Socialist Party (PSI) and the Norwegian Labour party, along with smaller but still significant parties in Bulgaria, Yugoslavia, Sweden and Romania. Two other mass parties opened negotiations with a view to joining the Third: the French Socialist Party (SFIO) and the German Independent Social Democratic Party (USPD). Indeed, the very act of establishing the Third International created the conditions for the left wing to split from the USPD and merge with the small KPD, as this chapter explains. Syndicalist union federations in Italy and Spain also expressed interest in collaborating with the new International. Other parties broke with the politics of the Second International without joining the Third. By 1920, the ranks of the former Second International had been severely depleted.[2]

The Comintern sought to rally communists on the basis of support for three basic principles: overthrow of the capitalist state and the creation of workers' states; the dictatorship of the proletariat, based on soviets, not parliament, as the basis for a higher form of democracy; and no faith in any parliamentary road to socialism.

The problem of centrism

Having raised the banner for communism, the Comintern confronted the problem that most of the newly formed Communist parties had, at best, a few tens of thousands of workers in their ranks, as against the hundreds of thousands in the more established working class parties.

The main task of the Comintern for the 12 months after its foundation was abundantly clear: to use the prestige of the Russian Revolution to draw in the mass ranks from the rival parties. The political issue was not particularly problematic for the outright reformist parties, those who had backed their own rulers in 1914: their reformist rivals had to be beaten in open combat. There would be no place for them in the new International.

But how to respond to the centrist currents that had developed in the later stages of the war, combining revolutionary and reformist politics in shifting proportions? Centrism existed both as a mass working class current and as a tendency among leaders of the workers' movement. As workers in Europe shifted sharply to the left, many of them looked beyond the established reformist parties that had betrayed them. Some of them moved straight to revolutionary socialism. Most were not yet ready to abandon working within the capitalist system. The Russian Revolution exercised a powerful pull on their imaginations, but they were still not yet convinced of soviet power as an alternative to parliament. Centrist moods within the working class were unstable. The class struggle and political debates pulled adherents of centrism one way or the other – back towards reformism or forwards to revolution. The situation could not prevail indefinitely. Centrism as a mass current is usually a short-term phenomenon, because it straddles a contradiction that has to be resolved one way or the other, usually within months or a few years. Winning centrist workers to communism before they lapsed back into reformist despair was the task for the Comintern in its bid to build mass parties.

The centrist leaders were another matter. At the time of the Comintern's formation, there was tremendous flux in the labour movement. Some established reformist leaders shifted left – in some cases sincerely, but mostly opportunistically – in an attempt to hold on to their following. They began to mouth left wing phrases and declared their support for the Russian Revolution. However, as parliamentarians and leaders of well-established trade unions, most were never going to throw in their lot with revolutionary socialism. They were willing to steer their parties to the left. In some cases, they were thrown out of their own parties, forcing them to form new organisations, but they did not break with reformism. At best, they occupied a space between reformism and revolution, but their every instinct was to lapse back into reformism. They tolerated open reformist leaders in their own ranks and generally saw the betrayal of the Second International in 1914 and the resulting split in the socialist movement as an unfortunate incident that could be overcome with goodwill on both sides. Their problem was that their life's political project had been undermined by reality. They clung to the gradualist formulations of how socialism would be built, but these had been trampled on by the reformist parties during the war. On the other hand, the centrist parties they led only existed because a revolutionary situation was opening up, which meant that every peaceful, gradualist tactic was being rendered redundant. Torn by this contradiction, the centrist leaders were unstable. They vacillated, sowing only confusion among the workers who looked to them.

The problem for the Comintern was that the centrist leaders' left wing phrases could deceive radicalising workers who took it as good coin. Unlike the leaders of the openly reformist parties, centrists were not regarded by militant workers as traitors; many had broken with the social democrats during the course of the war. In the last year of the war and in its immediate aftermath, organisations led by centrist leaders grew rapidly. They commanded a much greater following than the outright communists, who didn't even have separate organisations in most places. The Comintern, therefore, had to find ways of dealing with the centrist parties. It had to pull the revolutionary elements towards the new International without dragging the reformist leaders in with them. The three main parties where centrists predominated were to be found in France, Italy and Germany.

France

The French SFIO, which had supported the war in 1914, swung to the left as workers' enthusiasm for the war gave way to opposition. At the party congress in October 1918, an alliance of right centrists, grouped around Jean Longuet, and left centrists, led by Ludovic-Oscar Frossard and his colleague Marcel Cachin, defeated the pro-war bloc led by Pierre Renaudel, a parliamentarian and editor of the party's daily newspaper, *Humanité*. While Frossard and Cachin could turn on revolutionary phrases, neither of them had any conception of building a revolutionary party, of taking the best of what the Bolsheviks had built in Russia but adapting it to the conditions of French parliamentary democracy. They were reluctant to drive Renaudel and the right out of the party. The hard left of the party centred on Fernand Loriot, who worked closely with the revolutionary syndicalists Alfred Rosmer and Pierre Monatte.

As workers radicalised at the end of the war, the SFIO drew in tens of thousands of new recruits. By December 1920, the party had 180,000 members, up from just 38,000 in 1918. The party began to secure big votes in elections; by 1920, it had captured between 1,500 and 1,800 local councils. Any new communist party in France would have to work with this raw material to grow beyond a small propaganda group.

Italy

The PSI was another mass party shifting to the left. It won over one-third of the votes at the 1920 general election and had 156 deputies. It ran many local councils, including the key industrial cities Milan, Turin and Bologna. By 1920, the party had 180,000 members, compared to 50,000 in 1914, and its daily paper sold 300,000 copies.

Although the PSI expressed support for the Russian Revolution and the dictatorship of the proletariat, and its executive voted to join the Comintern in March 1919, it was far from a revolutionary party. A hard reformist minority led by Filipo Turati, who had supported the war, occupied an important place in the party. They controlled the main trade union federation, the General Confederation of Labour (CGL) and could count on the allegiance of a small army of union officials and most parliamentarians and city councillors. This reformist minority therefore exercised influence out of proportion to their size.

The majority of the Italian party were centrists (labelled Maximalists), led by Giaconti Serrati. Serrati's group criticised the reformists from an apparently radical Marxist position but failed to distinguish themselves from the reformists in practice, focusing on agitation for democratic reforms and pouring endless energy into election campaigns. Most of the leadership opposed the war but had a fundamentally passive approach to it, stating that they would 'neither support nor sabotage' the war effort. Serrati was a sincere supporter of the Russian Revolution but absolutely not a revolutionary leader. Although the war had radicalised Italian workers, and the Russian Revolution enthused Italian radicals more than any others, this did not shift the centrist leaders' passivity. As Kautsky had in Germany, Serrati and his comrades believed that steady electoral gains would bring Italy closer to socialism: 'We, Marxists, interpret History, we do not make it, we move in time according to the logic of facts and things.'[3] The evolution of capitalism would simply bring socialism closer. Thus could revolutionary rhetoric be combined with passivity in practice.

This same passivity was also evident in the PSI's revolutionary faction, led by Amadeo Bordiga. Bordiga had been an intransigent opponent of the war and imperialism. A chronic ultra leftist, with a purist, sectarian approach to building the party, he regarded any collaboration with reformists as unprincipled; the party would take power, not the working class. Only once the party was in power could soviets be established, and only by the party and under its control. Bordiga's politics became a major problem for Italian Communists in the following years.

The limitations of the Italian party were starkly shown up in the *biennio rosso*, the two red years of 1919-20. In the summer and autumn of 1919, the class struggle in the northern industrial citadel Turin advanced in leaps and bounds. The shop steward committees in the big factories began to develop into workers' councils, urged on by Antonio Gramsci, a revolutionary in the PSI and editor of the newspaper *L'Ordine Nuovo* (New Order). Gramsci envisaged these councils going beyond the traditional bread and butter concerns of the steward committees to assert workers' control over production. The councils drew up a program enshrining workers' control, which Gramsci considered a new form of proletarian power. By the end of 1919, more than 150,000 workers were organised in such councils in Turin. Their limitation was the widespread belief that they could challenge the capitalist class for power simply by controlling production. In reality, it was impossible for workers to liberate themselves completely while private property prevailed and political power remained in the hands of the capitalist state. The councils had to be extended, like the soviets in Russia, to encompass political as well as industrial organisation. By March 1920, Gramsci was beginning to develop a program to overcome these limits. In the party's newspaper, *Avanti*, he outlined the tasks of the councils. They included arming the proletariat and creating a powerful movement of peasants and smallholders in solidarity with the industrial workers' movement.

In early 1920, Gramsci and the PSI's Turin branch demanded that party leaders help spread the council movement. They were met by rejection or stonewalling. Turati's reformist wing feared the potential for the councils to pose a direct challenge to the trade union bureaucracy and the parliamentarians. Serrati's supposedly left wing Maximalists were horrified at the idea of workers' councils, condemning them as anarchistic. Bordiga also rejected the councils, on the basis that workers' control of production was a reformist illusion so long as the capitalist state prevailed. He made no argument for providing revolutionary leadership to the powerful movement in order to develop it into a revolutionary challenge to the state. Instead of workers' power emerging organically through working class struggle, Bordiga believed that the institutions of a workers' government would be decreed from above following the communist party's victory. If workers wanted to fight, they should join the party – a position no different to that of outright reformists such as Turati. The PSI was left to stand passively by when the class struggle in Italy surged forward again in the spring.

By the summer of 1920, the situation in Italy was extremely polarised. The engineering bosses' organisation, Confindustria, declared war on the factory councils and urged the government to smash them up. The first fascist organisations, bankrolled by the bosses, attacked the PSI headquarters. In rural areas, widespread peasant land occupations burst out. The workers were shifting sharply to the left. One non-socialist writer could barely hide his disgust when he described the revolutionary mood sweeping the country:

> Until September 1920, Italy really gave the impression of having fallen prey to the most excessive disorder and the most exaggerated revolutionary madness – mainly in verbal form. The strike-mania among all categories of workers, even in the public services, verged on tragi-comedy. The slightest cause was pretext for stopping production. Everything that had a 'bourgeois' appearance was subject to attack; cars could not travel through the countryside or the suburbs of certain 'red' towns without running the risk of being the target for stones thrown by workers and peasants… The Russian myth was more widespread than ever. Communist Russia became the ideal of the great majority of the working class.[4]

The workers and peasants looked to the PSI for leadership. Serrati told the French revolutionary syndicalist Alfred Rosmer:

> The towns and countryside are with us; the workers follow our calls. The peasants are no less keen: in many rural communes, the mayors have replaced the portraits of the king in the town halls with pictures of Lenin. We have the strength; we have it so absolutely that no one, friend or foe, would think of disputing it. The only problem for us is how to use that strength.[5]

The PSI failed to use its strength, betraying the workers' hopes.

In April 1920, Confindustria locked out the engineering workers in Turin. That provocation sparked a general strike which brought out 500,000 workers and drew in millions behind it. Tramways, public services, many private businesses and all of industry stopped work for 11 days. The action spread beyond Turin. Labourers in the city's rural hinterland struck and forged links with industrial workers. The authorities tried to intimidate the strikers, surrounding Turin with machine guns, cannons and 50,000 troops, but they did not have to resort to a bloodbath. The PSI let the workers down badly. Its newspaper refused to print their appeals for assistance, and the leadership even moved the party congress from Turin to Milan because, as Gramsci remarked sarcastically, 'a city in a general strike was not adapted to socialist discussions.' The city's anarcho-syndicalists, who were heavily involved in the council movement, rallied behind the workers. They led strikes that shut down the railways and port, preventing the movement of troops, and issued clear national appeals for solidarity. However, militant action by such a minority was not enough to dislodge the reformist leadership of the PSI and the unions. Isolated and demoralised, the strikers returned to work after a month. The experience clearly demonstrated that the PSI was not the party that workers needed if they were to have a revolution.

Not only the reformist and centrist leaders of the PSI failed. The party's left was incapable of meeting the challenge. It was incumbent on Bordiga to offer a fighting leadership for the workers in Turin. Instead, he offered doctrinal criticism, stating that its defeat only confirmed his scepticism about the movement. Throughout September, Bordiga's paper, *Il Soviet*, made not one reference to factory occupations in its editorials. Gramsci's *L'Ordine Nuovo* group, by contrast, threw itself into the struggle; but it failed to offer a political lead and suspended publication of the paper for the duration of the strike, leaving it without a political platform. Gramsci's reluctance to split with the PSI prevented him from organising with the anarcho-syndicalists.

Germany

The third and most significant centrist organisation facing the new Comintern was the German USPD. It grew out of anti-war sentiment among the working class, the soldiers and the sailors in the latter half of the war. Many thousands of SPD members were growing sick of the war but were not yet ready for revolution. Many SPD politicians had harboured private doubts about the war in 1914 but had not wanted to jeopardise their careers by coming out against it. Now that anti-war sentiment was more widespread, these politicians voiced some opposition to it more confidently. But this layer had not changed their hostility to revolution. They wanted an end to the war, but they did not want a great social upheaval; they saw peace as coming through diplomacy. Even such half-hearted opposition to the war was, however, too much for the SPD leadership. In May 1916, the SPD suspended 34 parliamentarians who had voted against the renewal of repressive government powers. In January 1917, the SPD carried out a more thorough purge, forcing the dissidents to form a party of their own. The USPD was born in April 1917.

The USPD provided a mass focus for the aspirations of those who were, however hesitantly, beginning to oppose the war. It boasted some of the well-known figures from the SPD, along with much of the old SPD apparatus – daily newspapers, union offices and meeting halls – and it was legal and able to hold open meetings, even if still constrained by censorship. Six months after the split, the USPD had 120,000 in its ranks – among them many militants from the factories and the naval bases – compared with the SPD's much reduced figure of 170,000.

The USPD was politically fuzzy from the outset. It had not formed on the basis of a left wing program in opposition to the reformist SPD. It had not seriously assessed any of the questions raised by the political battle over the war and the rising class struggle: the role of the unions, the role of the state and the prospect of gradually reforming capitalism into socialism. Its creation was the result of the SPD right clarifying *their* ideas and program and forcing out those who disagreed. Many of the USPD's functionaries, parliamentarians and trade union officials still saw themselves as tied to the SPD and assumed that they would one day merge back into it. Some were outright reformists, including Eduard Bernstein and Rudolf Hilferding. Karl Kautsky was also moving into the openly reformist camp by this time. The right of the new party was the most hostile to revolution, the most equivocal about the war and the most determined to reunify with the SPD and return to the relative social peace of pre-1914.

The main leadership of the USPD, headed by former SPD chair Hugo Haase and Wilhelm Dittmann, were to the left of this bloc but were nonetheless right centrists. They used revolutionary language but acted in a reformist manner. There was also a left centrist current, led by Ernst Däumig and Emil Barth, which was veering further left under the impact of the Russian Revolution but was still committed to the idea of unity with the SPD. The left centrist leaders were generally closest to the vanguard elements of the working class, and they operated in cities or areas where the revolutionaries were a strong force, However, they were quite hostile to Rosa Luxemburg's Spartacus League.

The left edge of the left centrist current in the USPD was the Revolutionary Shop Stewards (RSS), a militant minority established in Berlin in May 1916 within the strategically central metal workers' union. They were led by Richard Müller and oriented to the veteran leftist Reichstag deputy, Georg Ledebour. Although only 1,000 strong, the RSS was able to mobilise workers against the war; they proved this in June 1916, when they called a strike in response to the imprisonment of Liebknecht for anti-war agitation; in April 1917; and again in January 1918, when hundreds of thousands of metal workers struck against the war.

The Spartacus League, a revolutionary current founded in January 1916 which included Luxemburg, Karl Liebknecht, Clara Zetkin, Franz Mehring, Leo Jogiches and Paul Levi, formed the far left of the USPD. Luxemburg was repeatedly imprisoned for her agitation against the war. Liebknecht had been a longstanding Reichstag deputy and a leading anti-war agitator who had been sent to the front by the authorities for his opposition to the war and jailed on his return. The Spartacists were expelled from the SPD in September 1916 and, following intense internal debate, a majority voted to join the USPD soon after it was formed. They were only a few hundred strong and very isolated, holding few positions of any authority in the USPD and lacking a single organising centre. They were paying the price for not having formed a coherent revolutionary organisation earlier.

These conflicting layers within the USPD made the party incapable of acting decisively at key moments of the class struggle. While sections of the membership were straining to the left, its leaders pulled in different directions. At key points, they acted as a restraint on radical workers and provided a left cover for the SPD. This became clear during the November Revolution which ended the war.

Centrism in the German Revolution

In late September 1918, the German High Command realised that the Imperial regime was at risk on two fronts: military defeat on the battlefield and growing rebellions at home. They told the Kaiser that concessions had to be made to the Allies and that, to provide a stable government while armistice negotiations proceeded, the SPD must be brought into the government. The Kaiser's Secretary of State said: 'We must forestall an upheaval from below by a revolution from above.'[6] To that end, they foisted a change of government on the Kaiser, with Prince Max von Baden, regarded as a 'progressive,' appointed Chancellor. Military rule was withdrawn, and the Reichstag was given powers of oversight over the government for the first time. But the new government's only goal was to defend the imperial status quo. For that, the supposedly republican SPD, led by Friedrich Ebert following Bebel's death in 1913, was eager to offer its services. Ebert's view was that the involvement of the SPD in the Cabinet and parliamentary rule constituted the only revolution that Germany needed. In the coming weeks, the capitalists and military command would look to the SPD for support in their attempt to hold up their system when the authority of the established powers fell to pieces.

The sense of crisis in the regime created openings for working class agitation in the factories. October 1918 brought an explosion of demonstrations and mass meetings. The attempt to negotiate an armistice came to nothing, because the Allies were determined to impose savage terms on Germany. Rather than subject the Reich to such humiliation, the High Command ordered the fleet to embark on what was effectively a suicide mission against the British navy in the North Sea. Unwilling to sail to certain death, sailors at Wilhelmshaven mutinied on 29 October, locking up their officers and raising red flags. The authorities then arrested some of the alleged 'ringleaders.' On 3 November, thousands of sailors marched through the streets of Kiel, protesting against the arrests. They were joined by local workers. Clashes with government patrols left nine dead and dozens wounded. But the sailors fought back, driving the patrols from the city. That evening, a 20,000-strong mass meeting elected a sailors' council, and the army garrison organised a network of soldiers' councils. The red flag was hoisted over the ships.

The Kiel rising was the spark that fired the German Revolution. Delegations of sailors carried word of the revolt to every major city. Hamburg was the first big city to fall to the rebels. On 5 November, 40,000 joined a demonstration in the city and voted for a republic of workers' councils. That evening, a workers' and soldiers' council was formed in the city, headed by a revolutionary. Its newspaper declared:

This is the beginning of the German revolution, of the world revolution. Hail the most powerful action of the world revolution! Long live socialism! Long live the German workers' republic! Long live world Bolshevism![7]

On 7 November, workers from Munich's giant Krupp factory marched for peace. The march escalated into a general strike and an attack on the army barracks. By the end of the day, the Bavarian king had fled, and the local USPD leader became the president of the workers' and soldiers' council of the new Bavarian Republic. Everywhere, fraternisation between workers and members of the armed forces led to the soldiers and sailors coming over to the side of the revolution.

It was not all plain sailing for the revolution. The SPD did its best to hold back the growing revolutionary tide. It understood that the monarchy needed a new lick of paint; propping up Kaiser Wilhelm was no longer an option. On 3 November, with Kiel aflame, a joint delegation of SPD leaders and union officials insisted that the Kaiser had to go to preserve capitalism. One SPD leader explained their thinking:

> The problem is to resist the Bolshevik Revolution, which is rising, ever more threatening... We must sacrifice the Kaiser to save the country. This has absolutely nothing to do with dogmatic republicanism.[8]

The openly counter-revolutionary SPD was not the only obstacle. Despite Liebknecht's consistent urging, the USPD refused to determine a date for an insurrection in Berlin. Even with the established authorities losing their grip on town after town, the USPD leaders, including the RSS's Müller, argued that the situation was not ripe. On 6 November, when every passing day increased the prospect of the authorities stamping out the revolution, the USPD leaders would not commit to a date earlier than 11 November. The right centrist Haase was even more reluctant to move; he had promised the SPD's Gustav Noske not to do anything which could compromise the 'unity' between the two social democratic parties. The USPD leadership passively waited on events.

Developments soon threatened to overtake the two parties. On the one hand, the Berlin police were watching every move of the USPD and RSS and arresting their leaders. On the other, the USPD and SPD leaders were finding it increasingly difficult to hold back the Berlin workers. Workers' and soldiers' councils were being elected. The prisons were attacked and prisoners freed, and the red flag was raised over government buildings. On

8 November, the SPD, USPD and RSS called on their forces to march on 9 November, the day that had been chosen by the Spartacus League. On that morning, huge crowds of workers advanced towards the centre of Berlin, led by armed troops from the front. The High Command and government had reinforced the capital to prepare for the revolutionary challenge. But, as workers marched past the barracks, soldiers flooded out to join their ranks. The police and the reactionary forces were overwhelmed and capitulated. One account described the scenes:

> The Kaiser Alexander Regiment had gone over to the revolution; the soldiers had rushed out of the barracks gates, fraternised with the shouting crowd outside; men shook their hands with emotion, women and girls stuck flowers in their uniforms and embraced them. The officers were being stripped of their cockades and gold lace.
>
> Endless processions of workers and soldiers were passing without break along the road... Army lorries passed by with red flags; they bore soldiers and red-ribboned workers, crouching, kneeling or standing alongside the machine guns, all in some fighting attitude, all ready to fire... All the men around the machine guns on the lorries or resting their rifles on their knees in commandeered private cars were manifestly filled with iron revolutionary determination.[9]

The RSS, supported by the Spartacists, took the initiative in directing this vast marching horde. A column of workers and soldiers led by Müller seized the Reichstag. Liebknecht led a contingent to seize the Imperial Palace. Another column, led by the USPD's Emil Eichhorn, took the police headquarters and freed 600 political prisoners. Another took over the city hall. By midday, Berlin was in the hands of the revolutionary workers and soldiers.

While these momentous events were under way, Ebert, his deputy Philipp Scheidemann and the SPD union leader Heller were holding discussions with Prince Max in an attempt to cobble together a new government that would forestall a full-blooded revolution. They all understood that only the SPD could now hold the situation in check and that the Kaiser had to go. Without the Kaiser's knowledge or approval, Prince Max announced the emperor's resignation and handed the Chancellery over to Ebert. Ebert immediately issued a call for calm and discipline and demanded that order be maintained.

But Ebert knew that his position would be unstable without the USPD's backing, given its support among militant workers. He immediately offered the USPD Cabinet positions.

Even at this late stage, Ebert still favoured a constitutional monarchy. This was unacceptable to workers. When huge crowds assembled at the Reichstag, SPD deputies dragged Scheidemann from his lunch and demanded that he speak to the crowd to calm them down. He started by urging them to remain orderly, but such was the passion of the crowds demanding an end to the monarchy that he was forced to finish his speech with the words 'Long Live the Great German Republic!' Scheidemann had no choice. He knew that Liebknecht was about to issue a call for a socialist republic, and the SPD would have been bypassed if all it could offer the people was continuation of the monarchy. Later that afternoon, Liebknecht addressed a large crowd from the balcony of the Imperial Palace:

> The rule of capitalism, which turned Europe into a cemetery is henceforward broken... We must not imagine that our task is ended because the past is dead. We now have to strain our strength to construct the workers' and soldiers' government and new proletarian state, a state of peace, joy and freedom for our German brothers and our brothers throughout the whole world. We stretch out our hands to them and call on them to carry to completion the world revolution. Those of you who want to see the free German Socialist Republic and the German Revolution, raise your hands![10]

A forest of arms greeted his call.

The revolution had triumphed. It had brought down the Hohenzollern dynasty after centuries of power in Prussia. Two days later, the new government signed an armistice with the Allies, bringing to an end the bloody war that had destroyed millions of lives.

The November Revolution in Germany demonstrated that the Russian Revolution was not an exceptional event, the result of Russia's particular political backwardness, unconnected to democratic Europe. The question of reform versus revolution had now moved to the heart of Europe, laying the basis for the worldwide political separation of reformists and revolutionaries. In Russia, with the revolution besieged by civil war and famine, workers greeted the news with euphoria. The Bolsheviks knew that the only chance for their revolution to survive was for it to spread – and Germany was the most developed economy in Europe.

Centrists and dual power in Germany

Toppling the old order was not the same as beginning the new. To destroy the German empire, spontaneous strikes and street fights were enough. To build a new socialist order, the majority of workers had to be conscious of what they were building, and they were not yet at that stage. The two speeches by Scheidemann and Liebknecht on 9 December clearly revealed what was at stake. Could the social democrats put back together the collapsed capitalist state, or were revolutionaries going to lead workers, soldiers and sailors forward towards socialism?

The SPD, with the USPD tailing along behind it, wasted no time in frustrating workers' desire for a fundamental overhaul. Luxemburg's comrade and biographer Paul Frölich explained:

> The General Staff of old Social Democracy – Ebert, Noske, Legien, Scheidemann, Landsberg, etc. – were conscious opponents of the revolution from the very beginning. Determined to take up the power that the November storm had blown into their lap, they opposed every socialist policy, every initiative of the masses to transform society.[11]

Just hours after the Kaiser was deposed, the SPD and USPD stitched together a provisional government, the Council of People's Deputies. The six posts were split equally between the parties, but the SPD and its counter-revolutionary politics dominated. Ebert, with two SPD colleagues and two representatives of the USPD right, Dittmann and Haase, created a bloc of five on the Council. The sixth post was offered to Emil Barth of the USPD left; he was used to give the Council an unwarranted left colouring. At the insistence of Liebknecht, backed by Müller and Barth, it was decided that the new Council would be subject to formal election at a meeting of workers' and soldiers' councils, hastily scheduled by the USPD and RSS for the following day.

When Müller and Barth opened the meeting of Berlin Workers' and Soldiers' Councils on the afternoon of the 10th, the SPD dominated the ranks of the 1,500 assembled delegates – not the USPD, still less the RSS or Spartacists. While the revolutionaries had been out on the streets on the previous day, the SPD had mobilised its party machine to set up 'soldiers' and workers' councils,' in some cases little more than paper bodies, which duly elected SPD supporters as delegates. The SPD flooded the barracks with leaflets demanding 'no fratricidal strife,' to give the soldiers the impression that anyone who criticised 'socialist unity' between the SPD and USPD was a splitter or saboteur. By contrast, the USPD made no attempt to influence the creation of the councils, while the Spartacus League was much too weak to have a significant impact.

More than bureaucratic manipulation ensured the SPD majority. The spontaneous nature of the upsurge meant that many workers were taking action for the first time. Many workers still looked to the SPD and did not yet differentiate one 'socialist' party from another. Only the hard lessons of experience would enable them to do that.

Müller and the USPD left's Barth moved at the meeting that a new Action Committee, formed exclusively from members of the RSS and Spartacus League, be elected as the highest organ of the revolution, taking precedence over the Council of People's Deputies. The SPD majority on the floor meant that they were overruled by the delegates. A new body formed instead, an Executive Council of Greater Berlin Workers' and Soldiers' Councils (hereafter Executive). It consisted of seven nominees from each of the SPD and USPD and 14 representatives from the soldiers' councils. It would be headed by Müller. Given that the more conservative soldiers backed the SPD, the result was a built-in majority for the SPD. And, although this carve-up gave the SPD an overwhelming majority, the USPD went along with it in the name of socialist unity.

For the SPD and the USPD right, the main business of the meeting was to endorse the Council of People's Deputies. To that end, Ebert announced the formation of what he called the new 'revolutionary government.' USPD leader Haase repeated the message, and the meeting formally elected the Council of People's Deputies as the new provisional government. Barth, who had earlier told delegates that he would rather commit suicide than work with the SPD, agreed to take his allotted place on the Council as the third USPD representative. A motion declaring Germany a 'socialist republic' was passed overwhelmingly, with the support of both the SPD and USPD. When Liebknecht warned the delegates that the SPD was carrying out a counter-revolution, he was shouted down by angry soldiers who wanted no dissension.

The radicals were outvoted on the day, but the situation remained extremely fluid. There were now two powers in the land, both claiming authority – the Council of People's Deputies, chaired by Ebert, and the workers' councils and the Executive, chaired by Müller. There existed, just as there had in Petrograd in February 1917, a situation of dual power. Ebert was certainly aware of this fact; he was still, formally, responsible to the Executive and to the councils, and so to the revolution. Ebert and Haase wanted to end that situation as soon as possible.

Over the course of November, the masses became more radical. The overthrow of the Kaiser spurred on workers, and the radicalism of the workers increasingly infected the soldiers in the rear. In one industrial centre after another, soldiers' councils joined with workers' councils in putting their elected leaders in charge of state and city governments. According to historian Pierre Broué, 10,000 councils were in existence in November.[12] One right wing newspaper described the situation:

> The workers arrive on time, then take off their coats, read their newspapers and slowly begin work. This is interrupted by debates and meetings. The employers are as powerless as the managerial staff. All power is in the hands of the workers' committees. On all questions ranging from the reconversion of the factory to peacetime production, the supply of labour, the employment of demobbed soldiers, the implementation of agreements, work methods and sharing out of work, on all these the workers' committees have the last word.[13]

Dual power is an unstable phenomenon. As with Russia in 1917, the key question became which parties would win the majority in the councils: the SPD and USPD right, which wanted to wind back the councils in favour of the Council of People's Deputies, the first step towards establishing a new constituent assembly; or the revolutionaries, who wanted to advance towards a council republic?

The USPD left, supported by revolutionaries of various stripes, led some of the most important workers' councils – in Berlin, Munich, Stuttgart, Chemnitz, Leipzig, Brunswick and Hamburg. However, the SPD, backed by the USPD right, attempted to win control of the movement in order to destroy it. They were very well aware of the fate of the Provisional Government in Russia. They used the more conservative councils of soldiers returning from the front as a weapon against the workers' councils. Just as important were the various steps the SPD took to block fresh elections to the councils; they would have resulted in much stronger votes for the radical left, because the working class and soldiers were shifting to the left.

The Council of People's Deputies pulled in the opposite direction to the working class in November. It was a thoroughly moderate body, committed to the old political order. The radicalisation that was growing in the army was a threat to the SPD leaders. They needed to shore up support from within the state apparatus to buttress their authority. That meant keeping in place, as far as possible, all the conservative loyalists who had staffed the Kaiser's bureaucracy and military command. The SPD leaders kept in their posts all the higher civil servants who had administered the country prior to the revolution, as well as the judges, police officers and secondary school teachers, loyalists of the old order. Likewise, the officer class, the real power in Imperial Germany, was left untouched, allowing it to repeatedly sabotage democratic reform in Germany over the following years – culminating in 1933 with its installation of Hitler. The SPD was helped by the willingness of the USPD, including many of the USPD left, to accept these arrangements.

The SPD also used its apparatus in the trade unions to push back against the workers' councils. Union leaders feared the workers' councils, sensing that they might supplant them in the big factories. The employers were ready to make concessions to the unions to bolster them against the councils. On 15 November, the trade union leaders and big employers signed an agreement in which the employers promised to introduce the eight-hour day and to recognise the unions, in return for which the unions agreed to end wildcat strikes, restore normal production, oppose nationalisation of industry and sideline the councils.

From late November, the military began to plot openly to crush the revolution, with Ebert's full support. The head of the army, General Wilhelm Groener, ordered 10 army divisions from the Front to march on Berlin, to arrive in the capital prior to the opening of the first all-German Congress of Workers' and Soldiers' Councils, called for 16 December. On 10 December, Groener's troops reached Berlin. Ebert greeted them on their arrival: 'Now Germany's unity lies in your hands!' But Groener's plans to smash the workers' councils fell to pieces when the soldiers, now aware of how they were being used, deserted.

With so much of the army 'unreliable,' Ebert redoubled his efforts to build a reactionary paramilitary, the Freikorps, under the command of General Kurt von Schleicher. General von Schleicher blamed left wing political groups and Jews for Germany's problems and called for the 'elimination of traitors.' The new military corps was assembled out of NCOs and officers who had been loyal to the Kaiser, supplemented by various military adventurers, fanatical nationalists and elements of the unemployed who could be trusted to do the government's dirty work. The Freikorps was only 5,000 strong but was disciplined, well armed and committed to the task of suppressing workers and smashing the revolutionary left.

It was a political initiative by the Council of People's Deputies, rather than military force, that decided events in December. From the outset, the Council wanted to push the Executive and the workers' and soldiers' councils to the sidelines. Real authority had to rest with a new parliament, the National Assembly, to be elected at the earliest opportunity. The Executive had a very different conception of the revolution. At its opening meeting on 10 November, it drew up a proclamation to 'the working people':

> The old Germany is no more... Germany has become a socialist republic. The holders of political power are the workers' and soldiers' councils.[14]

At stake were two different conceptions of power – one bourgeois, one socialist. Luxemburg highlighted this point, attacking not only the SPD, but those like the USPD's Haase who were promoting the National Assembly. Luxemburg argued:

> What is gained, then, with this cowardly detour called the National Assembly? The bourgeoisie's position is strengthened; the proletariat is weakened and confused by empty illusions; time and energy are dissipated and lost in 'discussions' between the wolf and the lamb; in a word, one plays into the hands of all those elements whose intent is to defraud the proletarian revolution of its socialist goals and to emasculate it into a bourgeois democratic revolution.[15]

The struggle, Luxemburg stated, had to be for socialist democracy, or council power:

> Without the conscious will and action of the majority of the proletariat, there can be no socialism. In order to intensify this consciousness, to steel this will, to organise this action, a class organ is necessary: a national council of the urban and rural proletarians.
>
> The convocation of such a representative body of labour in place of the traditional National Assembly of the bourgeois revolutions is in itself an act of the class struggle, a break with the historical past of bourgeois society, a powerful method of arousing the proletarian masses, a first open and abrupt declaration of war against capitalism.[16]

It soon became clear early that the Executive was not ideologically prepared to withstand the pressure from Ebert's provisional government. It made concession after concession. On 12 November, the Executive voted on a motion from the USPD left's Däumig, with SPD representatives in support, to set up a Red Guard to defend the revolution. This would initially consist of 2,000 revolutionary workers with military training. Such a body was essential, because the armed forces were otherwise under the command of the Kaiser's generals. But as soon as the soldiers' councils objected, on the grounds that it demonstrated a lack of faith in their loyalty to the revolution, the Executive backed down. Less than a week later, SPD chairperson Otto Wels struck back against the Executive, announcing the formation of a 'Republican Soldiers Corps' of between 13,000 and 15,000 to maintain 'order' in Berlin. Volunteers quickly flooded in. So did money from the capitalists who recognised the potential value of this body during future uprisings. The Executive had been completely outmanoeuvred by the provisional government; unlike the Executive, it was resolute in seizing control of the political situation.

Further concessions by the Executive followed in the third week of November, when a string of meetings only succeeded in piling confusion upon confusion. Müller was a political novice, quite out of his depth in the fight with the SPD's experienced operators. He had no greater ambition for the Executive than to merely 'oversee' the Council of People's Deputies, when that Council was hellbent on consigning the Executive to history. He was also overly concerned with papering over cracks on the Executive, in the name of a false 'unity.' So, one moment the Executive rejected the call for a National Assembly, stating that it would be the death of the councils; the next, they voted in favour of it. On 23 November, the Executive took the big step of conceding executive powers to the Council of People's Deputies. Müller also agreed to hand the Executive's authority for economic questions to the trade unions, a gift to the union bureaucracy. With each step, the Executive allowed itself to be pushed further to the margins.

The Council of People's Deputies exploited the USPD left's indecisiveness. The SPD press hailed progress towards the calling of elections and attacked the Executive for its supposed 'dictatorial tendencies' and unwillingness to submit to a National Assembly. Incapable of holding the line, the Executive retreated step by step. On 25 November, with the Executive in disarray, the Council of People's Deputies announced that elections to the Assembly would be held on 16 February 1919, a date soon brought forward to 26 January.

The Executive had called for the convening of an all-German meeting of delegates' councils on 16 December to finally settle the question of the power of the councils. But the outcome was already obvious days before its opening. Luxemburg wrote on 11 December:

> It is clear that it was in the Executive Council and in the workers' and soldiers' councils that the masses should have discovered their role. But their organ, the organ of the proletarian revolution, is reduced to a state of total impotence. Power has slipped out of its hands, to pass into those of the bourgeoisie. No organ of political power lets power escape of its own free will, without having made some mistake. It is the passivity and the indolence of the Executive Committee which has made possible the game of Ebert and Scheidemann.[17]

The first national Congress of Workers' and Soldiers' Councils duly took place from 16 to 21 December. Proceedings opened in the context of a fresh wave of strikes. In the days leading up to the Congress, the Spartacists, knowing that they would have little ability to influence the Congress from the inside, organised demonstrations to pressure the Congress. On the day of the opening, they led masses of workers in a march outside the hall demanding 'All power to the workers' and soldiers' councils!'

This new militancy found no expression at the Congress. The SPD's manipulation of the councils, only allowing fresh elections where they were sure to win, and demanding parity with the USPD where they were not, gave the party 288 of the 489 delegates, compared with 80 for the USPD and just 10 to the Spartacus League. Liebknecht and Luxemburg were barred from the hall. Full-time political functionaries dominated: 164 of the 499 delegates were journalists, parliamentarians, trade union and Social Democratic officials or professionals, and a further 71 were intellectuals, together far outnumbering the 179 manual or white collar workers.

The chief debate at the Congress was over the role of the workers' and soldiers' councils. The SPD was adamant that the National Assembly should rule; anything else would be 'dictatorship.' The USPD was split down the middle. Müller and Däumig made the case for a council republic, but Dittmann and Haase voted to give the National Assembly pride of place in the new constitution and spent a considerable part of their time attacking the Spartacists.

With the SPD dominant, there was never any doubt about the outcome. By 344 votes to 98, the Congress rejected a proposal calling for the creation of a republic based on workers' and soldiers' councils. By 400 votes to 50, the congress then voted in favour of elections for a National Assembly on 26 January. They further agreed to 'transfer legislative and executive power to the Council of People's Deputies until such time as the National Assembly may make other arrangements.' Outside Berlin, the Executive had now effectively ceased to function. Richard Müller made no secret of his disappointment:

This central congress was Germany's first revolutionary tribunal, but there was no revolutionary atmosphere at all. My expectations were none too high going in, but I had no idea that this congress was going to turn into a political suicide club.[18]

Luxemburg attacked the Executive leadership for its failure to resist the pressure from the provisional government, but she lacked the forces to make a difference. The tragedy of the November Revolution and the months that followed was the absence of a revolutionary party on the lines of the Bolsheviks. Luxemburg and her revolutionary comrades had to break the hold of the USPD leaders over their members and draw them towards their side. To do so, they had to move beyond simple rhetorical attacks on the USPD leaders. They had to demonstrate to the radicalising workers flocking to the USPD that the leaders were more loyal to the reformist minority – figures such as Hilferding and Kautsky, and through them to the capitalist state – than they were to revolutionary politics. Had a sizeable revolutionary organisation with deep roots in the working class and with trusted cadres existed by November 1918, it could have made big inroads in these weeks by arguing that the workers' own actions demonstrated the alternative to parliamentary politics. Such an organisation could have appealed to those in the ranks of the USPD looking for a forthright revolutionary lead and seeing only vacillation and confusion from their own leaders. In the absence of such an organisation, the potential was lost.

The interim Chancellor, Ebert, now took a step too far. While the Congress of Workers and Soldiers' Councils was in session, Ebert announced that the People's Naval Division, the several thousand strong military force loyal to the revolution, would be reduced to 600 men and transferred away from the centre of Berlin. This manoeuvre blew up in the Chancellor's face. On 23 December, the sailors retaliated, occupying government buildings and arresting members of the Council of People's Deputies. After a promise by Ebert that the Cabinet would discuss their grievances the following day, the sailors released the arrestees and spent the night in the Imperial Palace. On the following morning, however, Ebert ordered artillery troops loyal to General Groener to fire on the Imperial Palace. The attackers seemed likely to overwhelm the sailors, but word of the fighting spread. Tens of thousands of workers and their families marched on the palace to demonstrate their support for the sailors. By midday, they had beaten back the attack. The troops who had attempted to drive out the revolutionary sailors were themselves forced to leave Berlin. They were disbanded and integrated into the Freikorps.

For many, Liebknecht's warnings about the counter-revolutionary nature of the SPD began to resonate.

Several days later, the USPD representatives Haase, Dittmann and Barth were compelled to resign from the Council of People's Deputies because of the attack on the People's Naval Division. But the damage was already done. The party had propped up the SPD for seven weeks while it shored up the old state apparatus. Without the left cover the USPD provided, the SPD would have found this task immensely more difficult. The USPD left allowed itself to be dragged along with the right in this project. Barth had begged the workers not to 'debase the Revolution to a movement for wages.'[19] By mid-December, militants had lost all faith in Barth. Desperate to avoid a reckoning at the hands of their rank and file, the USPD leaders refused to call a party congress. The Spartacus League now walked out of the USPD, taking only a few hundred with them. They invited other revolutionaries who had stayed out of the USPD, as well as the RSS, to join them in forming a communist party.

The USPD had demonstrated its inability or unwillingness to lead a revolutionary struggle during the November Revolution. But this did not stop it growing rapidly – from 100,000 in November 1918 to 300,000 in March 1919, and then to 750,000 by the end of the year. It was also shifting to the left under the impact of the Russian Revolution. Many of the new recruits were working class militants in big workplaces formerly loyal to the SPD but now repelled by their former party. The Comintern could not, therefore, simply ignore the USPD if it was to construct mass communist parties.

The move to the left did not apply to the USPD leaders. Centrism – revolutionary talk but reformist actions – remained their defining characteristic. In November 1919, the party conference adopted workers' councils as the organisational form for socialism, but most of its leaders tried to graft this onto an outlook that remained embedded in the traditions of the Second International. Their objective was not backing workers in struggle but overcoming the 1917 split in German social democracy and forming a coalition government with the SPD.

In the spring of 1920, the Kapp Putsch, an attempt by right wing generals to overthrow parliamentary democracy (see Chapter 3), proved to many USPD members that there was no prospect of a return to prewar social arrangements. The Putsch would be crushed by a massive mobilisation of workers, coming out at the call of the USPD and SPD union leaders, but the USPD leaders would join forces with the SPD to call off the strike. Further, USPD leaders would do nothing to stop the SPD government from dispatching detachments of the same right wing troops to crush a revolt in the Ruhr by thousands of armed mine workers who had occupied the mines.

By the time of the Comintern's Second Congress in July 1920, hundreds of thousands of rank and file USPD members were beginning to evolve away from centrism towards revolutionary politics. How to pull those radicalising German workers away from their centrist leaders was a crucial question for the Comintern. The Russian leadership knew that it could not rely on the new KPD that had formed early in 1919 with just 3,000 members. Not only was it much smaller than the USPD; its membership was drawn predominantly from younger militants and the unemployed, people with little experience in the trade unions. Indeed, in its first two years (see Chapter 3), the KPD repeatedly fumbled its intervention in working class struggle. For example, soon after its formation, it was carried away by impulsive elements in Berlin who were incapable of responding to an SPD provocation. In the reactionary bloodbath that followed, Luxemburg and Liebknecht were both murdered on the orders of the SPD, decapitating the party. During the Kapp Putsch, the KPD again demonstrated the weaknesses created by its lack of a stable cadre of experienced leaders: it lagged behind the mass strike called to defeat the generals. The KPD's problems in 1919-20 make it understandable that militants would look first to the USPD. The task for the Comintern, therefore, was to orient the KPD towards attracting radicalising USPD members away from their loyalty to their centrist leaders.

The Second Congress of the Comintern

Dealing with the centrist parties such as the SFIO, PSI and USPD was central to the Comintern's Second Congress, held in July 1920 in the context of an upswing in revolutionary struggle. The Red Army was at the gates of Warsaw. German workers had crushed the Kapp Putsch. In Italy, the defeat of the April strikes did not halt the rising tide of militancy across the country. There was still much to play for.

The Second Congress was the first real congress of the International. It was much bigger and more representative than the First Congress. It comprised 217 delegates from 67 organisations from 36 countries, including Asia and Latin America. At its First Congress, the Comintern's chair, Grigorii Zinoviev, called it 'a propaganda society organised on a large scale that tried to take the ideas of communism to the working class.'[20] Now, however, the Comintern had the opportunity to be much more, 'to become a fighting organisation of the international proletariat…that not only propagates communism but also wants to turn it into deeds.'[21]

Circumstances were propelling centrist leaders towards the Comintern. The leaders of the SFIO, the USPD and a range of others had wanted to create a centrist International, but the Russian Revolution had radicalised their members, who pressured them to apply to join the Comintern. Fearing a loss of credibility if they refused, they complied. The Comintern Second Congress now had to decide the terms under which the centrist parties could join or, in the case of the PSI, remain members.

The approach of the Russian Communist leaders was to put the radical credentials of the centrist leaders to the test by requiring them to act against the reformist leaders in their ranks. They devised conditions of membership for the Comintern, the '21 Conditions.' If the centrist leaders agreed to, and carried out, those measures, good. If they baulked at agreement or implementation, then they stood exposed to their followers as revolutionaries in word but not in deed.

What were these 21 Conditions? The most important was that all members of the Comintern were required to purge their parties of reformist elements, to carry out 'a complete and absolute break with reformism and with the policy of the centre.' To ensure that there was no misunderstanding, the Comintern listed some of those who must be driven out; these included Kautsky, Hilferding, Longuet and Turati.

The Third International was to be centralised and internationalist. The Second International, for all its internationalist rhetoric, had operated as a collection of national parties. When the crunch came in 1914, the majority of them pursued the interests of their 'own' ruling class and sacrificed those of the working class. The Comintern hoped to become a party of the international proletariat and world revolution. It had to develop an international line of march, and the policies of national sections must accord with this. The 21 Conditions required all sections to submit their national programs to the Comintern for ratification and to abide by all decisions of the Comintern. The Executive Committee of the Comintern was to be the general staff of the new International.

As part of the drive to purge the revolutionary movement of reformists, who had long used the labour movement as a vehicle for their own careers, all parties were required to organise on the basis of democratic centralism. They were to bring parliamentarians, union officials and other privileged layers within the party under party control. To ensure that new sections were thoroughly committed to the project of building a revolutionary International, only those parties where two-thirds of party leadership bodies had been supporters of admission to the Comintern *before* the Second Congress could apply to join. To combat the tendency evident in the Second International for the editorial boards of party publications to become strongholds of the right, the Comintern demanded that party publications be under the control of the national leaderships and run by 'reliable Communists.'

As part of the Comintern's desire to weed out parties and groupings within parties that focused exclusively on parliamentarianism and legal work, the 21 Conditions required that parties establish parallel underground networks, to be activated if government repression made legal work impossible. As a further token of their commitment to revolutionary and internationalist work, parties were required to conduct propaganda against social patriotism and pacifist illusions in the League of Nations, the new international forum in which the victorious imperialist powers sought to impose their postwar division of spoils on the world.

The 21 Conditions also spelled out areas of work and goals for parties. To undercut 'ultra left' parties and leaders who, on principle, abstained from parliamentary activity or working in trade unions, the Comintern argued that parties had to work in the unions and workers' cooperatives in order to secure leadership of these bodies for the Communists. Communist parties were also charged with fighting for revolutionary leadership among women and in the anti-colonial struggle and to agitate within the armed forces. Communists were also to break with the reformist trade union international and to campaign for affiliation with the Profintern, the union federation set up by the Comintern.

The 21 Conditions were an extremely extensive set of demands, and the Comintern leadership knew that no party in, or applying for, membership met all these conditions. However, it was important for the program to spell out the Comintern's goals clearly to all who had joined and to clarify the expectations for those who wished to join.

Implementing the 21 Conditions

The Russian Communists did not believe that the 21 Conditions were a magical talisman for winning radicalising workers from their centrist leaders. They regarded the 21 Conditions as one weapon in their battle to win these workers to the communist cause – a battle that went on for at least two more years. But by making demands on the centrist leaders that they commit firmly to the revolutionary camp and disown their reformist wings, Lenin and his comrades did draw clear lines at a time when the reformists in the centrist camp wanted to muddy the waters and centrist leaders wanted to make excuses for them.

Of the big three centrist parties, the best outcome, in terms of winning over radicalising workers trapped in centrist formations, was in the German USPD. The USPD right, which included the party's big cohort of functionaries, newspaper editors and parliamentarians and the majority of the Central Committee, hated the 21 Conditions, either because they were reformists themselves or because their project was to have revolutionaries and reformists coexist in the one organisation. The USPD told the Comintern Executive that they had already expelled the Right, that Kautsky had moved into semi-retirement and had no influence, and that no more splits were needed. They could not, therefore, accept the 21 Conditions.

But the USPD apparatus did not get away with it; the party was no longer theirs. Under pressure from radicalising members who saw in the Comintern the embodiment of the Russian Revolution, the USPD leaders were forced to call a conference in October 1920 to consider affiliation. Furious debates erupted in every party branch in the weeks leading up to the conference. The leadership mobilised the entire apparatus to campaign against affiliation to the Comintern and refused to publish its articles in the party paper *Freiheit* (Freedom). But they were losing the argument. In Berlin, where all eight *Freiheit* editors, including Hilferding, opposed affiliation, 16 out of 18 organisations voted in favour. The referendum to select delegates to the conference resulted in a solid 58 percent majority for those in favour of the Comintern. By the time delegates took their seats on 14 October, the party had essentially split.

The October conference became the focus of international attention. The future of German communism, and thus the German and European revolution, was at stake. The keynote speakers at the conference in Halle were Hilferding, followed by the Russian Menshevik Julius Martov (for the Second International) and Zinoviev (for the Third). Many delegates to the conference were predisposed to joining the Comintern, and Zinoviev's four-hour speech in favour of affiliation helped to win over some of the waverers. The result was a striking victory for the revolutionaries, with 237 USPD delegates voting in favour of affiliation, 156 against. The left of the USPD fused with the KPD, creating the United KPD (VKPD) with 350,000 members, growing soon to half a million.

A new mass Communist party was thus established – the largest outside Russia, in the most important country for the future of the Russian Revolution. It had a mass membership, a solidly organised vanguard with strong fractions in the big unions, control over local unions in several industrial towns, 40 daily papers, an underground military organisation and considerable financial resources. The USPD rump kept going in name for two years, then rejoined the SPD.

Matters were less clear cut with the French Socialists. The centrist representatives of the SFIO at the Congress, Cachin and Frossard, were anxious to be identified with the Comintern to protect their left flank at home. They stated that they were in full agreement with the 21 Conditions. At the Tours Congress of the SFIO in December 1920, the party voted by three to one to accept the 21 Conditions and join the Comintern. The motion was moved, from prison, by the left's Loriot and Boris Souvarine but was backed by Cachin and Frossard. The result was the creation of a 110,000-strong French Communist Party (PCF), which took out the youth wing of the Socialist Party and the party's newspaper, *Humanité*. Opposing the majority were Longuet, who argued for affiliation but rejected the 21 Conditions, and Léon Blum, who opposed both. Longuet and Blum walked out with the rump of 30,000 to re-establish the SFIO, taking with them most of the MPs and municipal councillors.

The formation of a mass Communist party in France was a step forward. The problem was that its new leaders, Frossard and Cachin, were opportunists who had only dressed themselves up in communist clothes. They had more in common with those in the SFIO, from whom they had separated, than with communism. Cachin had actually backed World War I in 1914 but was now editor of the party's main outlet *Humanité*, an intolerable situation for a revolutionary party. The genuine revolutionaries, led by Loriot and Souvarine, were a minority in the new party.

The lack of a clear Marxist leadership meant that the PCF was a confused mishmash. There was a strong ultra left element in Paris and among the youth. Syndicalism still strongly influenced many of the party's union activists. The Russian Communists intervened, trying to straighten things out while recognising that creating a revolutionary party almost from scratch is not easy. Trotsky explained that, if the Russians had pushed too hard, almost everything could have been lost:

> [The] Frossard group gave good reasons for us to break with them. But at the time the rupture would not have been understood by the great majority of the membership… It was necessary, therefore, to give the left elements the time to see their tasks clearly, to acquire ideological cohesion and to bring around themselves a large number of party members.[22]

In December 1922, under pressure from the Comintern, Frossard resigned from the PCF. The left took over the leadership. Although Frossard took with him the majority of the parliamentarians, journalists and councillors, the bulk of the worker membership remained loyal. Here was a real chance to transform the PCF into a genuine Bolshevik-style party. But the problems were far from solved; the left was not a cohesive group capable of providing astute leadership, and there were no figures among French Marxists with the authority of someone like Luxemburg.

The outcome for the Italian party was also mixed. At the Comintern's Second Congress, PSI centrist leader Serrati voted for the 21 Conditions but refused to immediately expel the reformist Turati. Congress delegates were told that the party would expel Turati at some point – 'now isn't the right time' – and, anyway, Turati was quickly being marginalised in the party. In another indication of his lack of commitment to the Comintern project, Serrati demanded 'relative autonomy' for national parties, code for avoiding the Comintern's censures for reformist backsliding. The matter of breaking with the reformists would be decided at the party's forthcoming congress in Livorno.

Before the Livorno Congress, the PSI again demonstrated its unfitness for revolution. The end of the April 1920 strikes in Turin had done nothing to lower the profound class tensions in Italy. The bosses were still intent on crushing the workers' councils; the workers were still determined to make good their loss of living standards through wartime inflation. At the end of August, bosses at the Romeo car plant in Milan shut the gates on their 2,000 workers. In response, workers occupied 300 factories in the city. Metal industry bosses then ordered a lockout across the country, and a rash of factory occupations took place. Half a million workers took over their factories, armed themselves and prepared for a decisive struggle for control of production.

Fearing that an armed confrontation with the occupying workers would only cause tremendous damage to the factories, Prime Minister Giovanni Giolitti decided to wait them out. He put his hopes in the Socialist leaders to compromise. He had their measure. From 9 September, representatives of the PSI and the PSI-aligned union federation, the CGL, met in Milan to attempt to find a way out of the conflict. The CGL leaders had no intention of leading a revolution but said that they would support one if the PSI were willing to lead it. Faced with the prospect of workers under arms challenging for state power, the PSI leaders retreated, saying that they would put the question of a revolution to the vote of CGL members. Two motions were put. One, moved by the union bureaucrats, called for recognition of union participation in management, the most right wing possible variant of 'worker control.' The other motion, moved by the PSI leadership, called for the immediate socialisation of the means of production. The union bureaucrats' motion was carried by 600,000 to 400,000. The PSI leaders breathed a sigh of relief when their motion failed, since it removed pressure on them to actually lead an insurrection. They had done nothing to win support for the occupations outside of the northern industrial centres and made no preparations to see the struggle through.

Most bosses were hostile even to the prospect of union participation in management, but Giolitti convinced them that it was the best way to regain control. The more astute bosses understood this, recognising that the union leaders had saved their skins. The return to work was uneven. Some workers held out for a month against all odds, isolated and abandoned by their leaders. By November, a wave of fascist terror began to sweep the country, and it became clear that the revolutionary period had come to an end.

The *biennio rosso* had demonstrated the profoundly counter-revolutionary role of the PSI reformist leaders and union bureaucrats at a time when the working class was striving for power. But the Comintern Executive could not simply wash their hands of the party. They had to win over the tens of thousands of workers who had flooded into the PSI to revolutionary politics and break them from the reformist Turati. Bordiga, the figure most identified with the project of building a new communist party and the one to whom the revolutionary youth in the party looked, would have to take on this task. That meant a split in the PSI, and many questions arose. On what terms? Who would take the mass of members with them? How would the split be understood by the masses? Would the new party be capable of leading workers to power – or, at the very least, organising serious defensive action to repel attacks by the ruling class and the rising threat of fascism?

The best course of action for the revolutionary wing in the PSI would have been to try to pressure the centrists to split from the reformists. Driving the right wing minority out of the PSI would shift the centrists left, some possibly towards revolutionary politics. Unfortunately, Bordiga and his faction were not interested in pursuing that course of action. In line with his ultra left politics, Bordiga favoured a split at all costs – with the centrist leaders as well as the reformists. He believed that the very act of trying to convince centrists, workers and leaders alike, was a betrayal of the revolutionary program. This approach was disastrous, only confirming the political isolation of the revolutionary wing from the mass of centrist members.

By the time of the Livorno Congress of January 1921, the stage was set for the communists to split on a very narrow basis. Serrati's centrists, the majority, refused to break with the reformist minority. Bordiga's communist faction, with only minority support on the floor, walked out of the Congress and formed the Italian Communist Party (PCI) the next day.[23] Bordiga's ham-fisted approach achieved nothing. The communists under his leadership did not win over one group of members throughout the Congress. They came out of it with the same numbers they had going into it – 60,000 out of a party of 175,000, leaving 100,000 in Serrati's camp and 15,000 in Turati's. It was probably true that, by the time the Congress began, it was already too late to put in place a sensible strategy to win over workers influenced by the centrist leaders. Bordiga and his followers had made no effort to do this in the months leading up to it. The Comintern Executive itself, however, did not help matters; shortly before the Livorno Congress, it decided that the main fire should be aimed at the centrist Serrati, not the reformist Turati. The Comintern emissaries sent to carry out this line, the Hungarian Mátyás Rákosi (whom we will encounter again in Chapter 17) and the Bulgarian Khristo Kabakchiev, went about it so belligerently as to all but guarantee that most of the centrist delegates would side with the reformists.

The result was that in Italy, unlike Germany, the new Communist Party failed to win over many of the centrist members and was stuck with an ultra left leadership incapable of working with centrists *or* reformists. Such was Bordiga's intransigence that the membership of the new PCI had sunk to 25,000 by the end of 1921. The Italian Communists missed a vital opportunity to take advantage of a situation in which hundreds of thousands of workers were shifting to the left.

The revolutionary mood in Italy had evaporated by the end of the year, and the bosses and fascists went on the attack. The combined membership of the PSI and PCI by the middle of 1921 was just 100,000 – half the figure for the PSI alone a year earlier. Union membership also collapsed. None of the workers' parties gave any lead to workers attempting to resist Mussolini's bid for power in 1922. The PCI under Bordiga stuck to its sectarian guns, turning its back on the anti-fascist militias that sprang up spontaneously. Gramsci adapted to Bordiga's positions. By the autumn of 1922, PCI membership had slumped to just 9,000 in a country of 40 million. The reformists and the CGL, for their part, told workers to turn the other cheek, while trying to arrange a truce with Mussolini in the hope that the unions would be able to survive under fascism. Serrati's Maximalists, which by now had split away from the PSI, intensified their rhetoric about revolution as if it were still an imminent prospect. All three simply denied that fascism was on the agenda in Italy or that it was any different to any other conservative government that would soon fail. Thanks to the failures of the left, Mussolini was able to impose himself as Italian prime minister just two years after the country had stood on the brink of revolution.

Assessment of the 21 Conditions

As is evident from our account of the USPD, SFIO and PSI, the application of the 21 Conditions and their success varied from party to party. They are best understood as indicative of a general approach of the Comintern to build mass revolutionary workers' parties, an approach that met with considerable success. By early 1921, the Communist parties had the support of millions of politically conscious workers in Germany, Czechoslovakia, France, Bulgaria, Yugoslavia, Poland, Norway and Sweden.

The 21 Conditions have been the topic of controversy in the Marxist movement ever since they were formulated. The dominant line of attack is that they were too harsh and alienated the centrists unnecessarily, driving them back into the arms of the reformists. Generally, this criticism comes from those who are hostile to revolutionary Marxism, doubt the entire Comintern project and regard the whole split in the socialist movement as regrettable; Julius Braunthal, a leading figure in the Socialist (Second) International and historian of the Internationals, is one such example.[24] But it was not the Comintern which created that split in the Second International. The split had its origins in the chasm between workers fighting and dying in the trenches in the Great War and the reformist leaders who had tied themselves so closely to the state machine of their respective nations.

Another historian of the Comintern, Fernando Claudin, was a leading Spanish Communist who broke with Stalinism in the 1960s and gravitated towards social democracy. Claudin argued that the 21 Conditions excluded many fine revolutionaries and were responsible for:

> a sectarian and dogmatic spirit [that] began from the very beginning to clear a way for itself in the Communist parties, disguised under revolutionary verbalism that concealed its remoteness from its reality.[25]

This line of attack ignores the fact that the hold of centrism had to be defeated if radicalising workers were to be drawn towards revolutionary politics and not abandoned in a centrist cul-de-sac. The centrist leaders demonstrated in Germany in 1918–19 and in Italy in 1920 that they were incapable of leading a revolutionary struggle to victory. The entire experience confirmed the argument of Lenin, Gramsci and others that the mass parties needed to break with the vacillating leaders in their ranks, as the Bolsheviks had finally done in 1912. Had the Comintern not succeeded in winning workers in centrist parties to its ranks, the only outcome would have been their demoralisation and drift back to the reformist parties or out of politics altogether. French historian Pierre Broué noted perceptively:

> For the Communists the split was not simply a state of affairs destined to last for some time, but an immediate necessity in order to eliminate definitively from the workers' movement the reformist leaders who acted as 'agents of the bourgeoisie.' It was the preface to the reconstitution of unity on the basis of a revolutionary programme, a condition for victory in the struggle for power.[26]

Responding to the charge that the 21 Conditions were too prescriptive, Zinoviev explained to the USPD Congress in Halle that the Conditions were negotiable once all the communist elements from the USPD and KPD had been united in the one party – but only once the reformists were excluded.

The problem with the 21 Conditions was not that they were too draconian, but that they were, in the end, only words. They could be implemented effectively if the people charged with carrying them out did so with conviction; but Serrati in the PSI and Frossard and Cachin in the SFIO lacked this conviction. They agreed to the 21 Conditions without any intention of following through by purging the reformists. As Zinoviev told the Second Congress: 'It is possible to accept 18,000 conditions and still remain a Kautskyite.'[27]

Another line of criticism is that the 21 Conditions were simply a means by which Moscow could dominate the Comintern. The 21 Conditions are regarded as the beginning of the slippery slope that led to Stalinism, which substituted bureaucratic decree for political argument. This question is discussed in Chapter 4; for now, it is worth noting that the Executive Committee was far from being a monolithic bloc at this stage.

The final criticism of the 21 Conditions, and one that was made at the time, came from the left. This was that the Conditions allowed the centrists to disguise themselves as communists in the eyes of radicalising workers at home, without any real pressure on them to follow through. Several French delegates to the Second Congress complained that leaders such as Frossard and Cachin could not be trusted: they would agree to anything in Moscow but, once back in the cosy surroundings of bourgeois Paris, would resume their opportunist practices and give cover to the reformists. The delegates argued that such figures should be absolutely barred from the Comintern. The KPD had a similar perspective, arguing that the USPD should never have been allowed to attend the Second Congress because of the party's counter-revolutionary role in the November Revolution. Only Lenin's insistence ensured that the USPD was able to attend. Bordiga warned that the right wing of the PSI would readily agree to the 21 Conditions but not practise them: 'We would therefore be in great danger if we made the mistake of accepting these people into our ranks.'[28]

The problem with the left's criticism of the 21 Conditions was that it avoided the central issue: how to expose the centrist leaders in the eyes of their mass working class following? The point of the 21 Conditions was to test these leaders, to insist that they take the action that many of their followers wanted – to purge the reformists. Their failure to do so would teach their followers what these figures were made of. Simply denouncing the centrist leaders, without forcing them to undertake this test – essentially the method adopted by Bordiga – was to cut the revolutionary forces off from the mass of leftward moving workers whom they needed to pull over to their side. That was Lenin's response to the KPD: they had to find ways of winning over the USPD rank and file, not spit in their faces by cutting off communication with the USPD leadership. For Lenin, the 21 Conditions were never intended to be the end of the struggle against centrism. They were a beginning of the task of weeding out the worst elements and clarifying the central issues. Unfortunately, this struggle had barely begun before the beginnings of the degeneration of the revolution in Russia cut the process short.

FURTHER READING

P. Broué, *The German Revolution 1917–1923*, Chicago, Haymarket Books, 2006 [1971].

D. Gluckstein, *The Western Soviets: Workers' Councils versus Parliament, 1915–1920*, London, Bookmarks, 1985.

D. Hallas, *The Comintern*, Chicago, Haymarket Books, 2008 [1985].

C. Harman, *The Lost Revolution: Germany 1918 to 1923*, London, Bookmarks, 1982.

B. Lewis and L.T. Lih (eds.), *Zinoviev and Martov: Head to Head in Halle*, London, November Publications, 2011.

J. Riddell (ed.), *Workers of the World and Oppressed Peoples, Unite! Proceedings and Documents of the Second Congress of the Communist International, 1920*, New York, Pathfinder, 1991.

P. Spriano, *The Occupation of the Factories: Italy 1920*, London, Pluto Press, 1975 [1964].

3.
THE FIGHT AGAINST ULTRA LEFTISM

Many of the new Communist parties that came together in the Comintern were born in the immediate aftermath of a sharp turn to the left among militant workers.[1] These parties bore the imprint of the time, drawing towards them many workers sickened by reformist betrayals and impatient for revolution. They demonstrated a natural and understandable tendency towards ultra leftism, seeking to jump over stages needed to win the majority of workers over to revolutionary consciousness. The specifics of the ultra leftist current varied from country to country, but common tendencies included: abstention from workers' struggles; a refusal to work in established unions and instead to pull members out of them and into their own unions; and in-principle opposition to engaging in election campaigns and parliament, on the grounds that parliamentary democracy was obsolete or irrelevant. Their general approach was one of 'no compromise or retreats.' They spurned alliances with forces to their right, even short-term tactical alliances to fight a common enemy. While espousing very radical-sounding rhetoric, they were mostly defined by political passivity when facing the key political questions of the moment and the need to appraise the concrete truth of an actual situation.

Examples included the Dutch Communist Party, whose leaders, Herman Gorter and Anton Pannekoek, believed that they needed a pure party of only intellectuals and a few workers. In the Italian party, Bordiga had already established his ultra left credentials in 1920 by refusing to back the Turin workers' councils on the basis that they were not set up by Communists. In 1921, he would oppose anti-fascist militias formed to fight Mussolini for the same reason. Bordiga also opposed any cooperation with reformists, declaring: 'Fascists and social democrats are but two aspects of tomorrow's single enemy.'[2] Bordiga's ultra leftism masked a political passivity that opened the door for Mussolini's march to power. In Britain, Willie Gallacher and Sylvia Pankhurst, who were soon to help form the Communist Party of Great Britain, refused to orient in any way to parliament or the Labour Party, arguing that this only gave credibility to Labour's right wing leadership. In the USA, the Communist Party only wanted to carry out underground work, spurning any opportunity to conduct open propaganda – such as holding public meetings – on the grounds that this was the start of opportunist degeneration.

Ultra leftism in the KPD

Ultra leftism was most disastrous in the German party, the KPD, causing a string of disasters as the party steered erratically between adventurism and abstentionism.

The KPD was founded in the New Year of 1919, just a few weeks after the November Revolution. One of its first decisions at its founding congress was to boycott the forthcoming elections for the National Assembly, the new parliament being established as a counter to the workers' and soldiers' councils (Chapter 2). The leading ultra leftists in the KPD could have argued their case on the basis that the conditions still prevailed for power to be transferred to workers' and soldiers' councils, something that could be debated soberly and empirically. Instead, they opposed participating in parliamentary elections as a *matter of principle*. They asserted that parliament was politically obsolete and that any involvement in elections would lead to the KPD's degeneration along SPD lines. A group of the boycottists, as they were called, wrote that the KPD must have nothing to do with any parliament, because that could only confuse workers:

> All compromise with other parties, all reversion to parliamentary forms of struggle, which have become historically and politically obsolete, and any policy of manoeuvring and compromise must be emphatically rejected.[3]

The KPD ultra lefts' in-principle opposition to participation in parliament reflected a mechanical and undialectical understanding of how Communists could win workers away from their reformist illusions: all that Communists had to do was plant their flag and wait for the workers to flock to it. It was also quite wrong, given that the initial wave of revolt had subsided. A workers' seizure of power was no longer on the immediate agenda in Germany. By January, workers were looking to the National Assembly elections which, for the first time in

German history, allowed all adults, male and female, to vote. Most workers did not conceive of the Assembly as a counter-revolutionary instrument to crush the councils, but as a victory. Communists had to be where the masses were, and Rosa Luxemburg, Karl Liebknecht and Clara Zetkin recognised this – as did Karl Radek, an emissary from Russia. These leaders argued at the founding congress that the KPD should not isolate itself but should participate in the elections, so that it could expose the hypocrisy of the new capitalist 'democracy' in practice. They were outvoted by the majority of delegates, for the most part very new to the communist movement, who expected an imminent revolution. On the next resolution, the ultra lefts were joined by Luxemburg herself in arguing that the established unions, at this time recruiting hundreds of thousands of workers, had become outdated, and revolutionaries should seek to convince workers to quit them in favour of workers' councils. Fortunately, this resolution was delayed to a future congress.

The KPD decision to boycott the National Assembly elections and its ultra left dismissal of the unions only signalled to the most militant and serious sections of the working class that the KPD could not be treated as politically serious. Richard Müller, leader of the Berlin revolutionary shop stewards, used these decisions as an excuse for the RSS not to join the new party. The shop stewards would have given the KPD a significant base in the most advanced sections of the Berlin working class at this critical moment in its history. Without them, the KPD started life as little more than a propaganda sect.

The January uprising

Just three days after the KPD's founding congress, the new party was tested and found seriously wanting. The SPD, having used the USPD as its left flank during the November Revolution (Chapter 2), turned on its former ally, sacking the USPD Berlin police chief, Emil Eichhorn. This was a clear provocation: the SPD hoped to lure the USPD and the revolutionary shop stewards into a premature rising, so they could crush the vanguard of the Berlin working class – while claiming to protect the newly won democracy. The USPD, the RSS and the KPD called a peaceful demonstration for the following day, Sunday 5 January. Its demands were for the cancellation of Eichhorn's dismissal, the disarming of counter-revolutionary troops and the arming of the workers. None of these implied overthrowing the Council of People's Deputies, now calling itself the Imperial Government, only opposition to its provocative actions and its ever-closer alliance with the High Command. The turnout at the demonstration far exceeded expectations. Hundreds of thousands of angry workers, many of them armed, showed up bearing red flags and demanding action. Those who called them out, however, deliberated for hours fruitlessly, not knowing what to do with this immense force, leaving frustrated workers to drift back to their homes at the end of the day.

The demonstration's size and its militant mood caused the organisers to reassess the situation and to escalate their demands. No longer simply registering opposition to Eichhorn's dismissal, the leaders decided that the way was now clear to overthrow the Ebert government. They set up an unwieldy revolutionary committee of 52 members, jointly chaired by representatives of the USPD, KPD and RSS, as a step towards the creation of a provisional revolutionary government. As they were putting the finishing touches to this committee, a group of armed workers stormed the offices of the SPD newspaper *Vorwärts* and dumped the following day's edition in the canal.

The decision to shift from a limited defensive action on the Sunday to an all-out attempt to bring down the Ebert government on the Monday was a mistake. Berlin workers, with their massive turnout, were well ahead of the mood in other cities. The SPD leaders still enjoyed the goodwill of the majority of workers nationally at this point, so an insurrection would have been isolated and easily crushed. The KPD Central Committee, which, on the day before the demonstration, had supported the plan for a limited defensive action, understood this.[4] Liebknecht, however, lost his head. Although he had been a voice of moderation at the founding congress and had agreed with the Central Committee's defensive position, as one of the chief organisers of the Sunday demonstration, he now joined the revolutionary committee as one of its three chairs – without even consulting his comrades. With them, in defiance of his KPD comrades, he urged the overthrow of the Ebert government.

Liebknecht's actions were extremely foolish. Everything about the behaviour of the USPD leaders since the outbreak of the November Revolution should have told Liebknecht that they were incapable of leading a revolution. Just a fortnight earlier, the USPD conference had voted nearly three to one against a revolutionary perspective. But now the USPD's Georg Ledebour, without even slightly moderating his hostility to workers taking power into their own hands, was planning to use the situation to leverage himself and his comrades into government. Nor was the RSS leadership committed to insurrection; in fact, Müller and Däumig were opposed to the new plan. By joining the revolutionary committee, Liebknecht only lent his immense authority to a body that would completely mishandle the situation.

As soon as the call went out for insurrection, it became obvious how out of step it was. The revolutionary committee had calculated that the city's garrisons were all on its side. But it became clear very quickly that the troops in Berlin, while not inclined to fight for the Ebert government, were also not ready to throw their weight behind an insurrection against it. The same was true of the workers. They had risen up to defend their revolutionary gains, embodied in Eichhorn's position at the head of the police, but what they wanted was 'socialist unity' and the formation of a government made up of the SPD, USPD and KPD. The revolutionary committee closed its eyes to the reality that only 10,000 workers and soldiers, at best, were willing to back its call for insurrection. The vast majority were unwilling to take sides in what they saw as a squabble between the socialist parties.

Ebert's Imperial Government took advantage of the disarray and indecision of the leaders. In Berlin, it could call on the loyalty of only a few thousand soldiers. But Ebert and his defence minister, Gustav Noske, had at their disposal the Berlin troops of the Republican Soldiers Corps and other forces formed during the November Revolution from workers and soldiers loyal to the SPD. They arranged for these regiments to take up positions inside the Reichstag, which they occupied without resistance from the revolutionary committee. From this stronghold, they seized building after building from the revolutionaries, driving them from their positions.

Victory against the uprising was not enough. Ebert and Noske wanted a bloodbath. They brought in thousands of Freikorps who had assembled outside the capital. Together with the Berlin police, the Freikorps began to butcher the remaining resistance forces. Those surrendering were shot on the spot. While the press whipped up the middle classes into a counter-revolutionary frenzy, the police and Freikorps shot anyone even suspected of having taken part in what the government now called the 'Spartacist Rising.' The SPD's *Vorwärts* was no less bloodthirsty than the worst bourgeois papers, calling for the murder of the leading Communists. On 15 January 1919, Luxemburg and Liebknecht, still in hiding in the city, were captured and killed, felling in one blow Germany's pre-eminent revolutionary leaders. Counter-revolutionary 'order' was restored in the capital. The middle classes and capitalists rejoiced. After the blows the state machine had suffered since early November, this was an important victory from which to rebuild.

Could the outcome have been different? Liebknecht's decision to throw in his lot with the revolutionary committee, falsely signalling the KPD's support for its actions, shocked Luxemburg when she heard of it. In discussions with her comrades, she advocated a level-headed approach, arguing that the party's orientation should primarily be defensive. But she was also acutely aware that the KPD could not simply go to the workers and tell them to call off their demonstrations, as Radek advised the Central Committee. The party had only just been formed on the basis of providing a clear revolutionary lead for workers, distinct from the vacillating USPD. Sounding the retreat would only have destroyed the party's credibility among the militants. They would have been just like the wretched centrists and reformists, talking big but acting cowardly. If the USPD abandoned the battle, the KPD could draw the militants to it by standing firm. Luxemburg therefore castigated the revolutionary committee for failing to provide a serious lead to workers thirsting for direction, while the SPD government was preparing to counterattack:

> Act! Act! Courageously, consistently – that is the 'accursed' duty and obligation of the revolutionary shop stewards and the sincere leaders of the USPD. Disarm the counter-revolution. Arm the masses. Occupy all positions of power. Act quickly![5]

This clearly paralleled the situation facing the Bolsheviks during the premature rising in Petrograd in July 1917. They determined not to turn their backs on, or denounce, the impatient workers who wanted to move to an insurrection ahead of the rest of the country; instead, they joined them on the streets, the better to steer them away from a premature attempt to seize power that would have led to their isolation and destruction. Once the Bolsheviks had demonstrated their willingness to fight alongside other militants, they successfully organised a tactical retreat after three days, limiting the losses while defending their honour.

The KPD were not the Bolsheviks. The German party did not have the same authority to carry out such a retreat. They were too small and lacked the loyalty that the Bolsheviks enjoyed among leading militants in Petrograd. Further, they had not developed collective ways of operating, of allocating their tasks according to their strengths. They correctly assessed that an insurrection was premature but were incapable of providing a coherent leadership for the masses in the streets. The result was predictable. Chris Harman argues: 'Rosa's own ideas were reduced to the level of commentary on the revolutionary events, instead of providing them with direction.'[6]

On 26 January, with the uprising in Berlin crushed, the National Assembly elections were held. The SPD emerged as the biggest party, with 11.5 million votes against the USPD's two million. Ebert was elected president. A new coalition government, headed by the SPD's Philipp Scheidemann, took office.

There followed a period of virtual civil war. Workers spontaneously rose up against attempts by the bosses and SPD leaders to smash the councils and destroy the basis of working class power. Noske declared himself the 'bloodhound' and ordered the Freikorps to move from city to city, breaking strikes, opening fire on protests, assassinating radical workers and jailing thousands. Because the resistance was not coordinated, the Freikorps could successfully pick off the workers' uprisings one by one. By the time the fighting was over, thousands of workers lay dead at the hands of the Freikorps – including veteran communist, Leo Jogiches. In the wake of the massacres, the bosses blacklisted tens of thousands of revolutionary workers. By the end of May, any flickering embers that remained of the November Revolution had been extinguished.

The first wave of the revolution was now over, but events in the following years were to demonstrate that the working class was by no means decisively beaten.

Battles with the ultra lefts in the KPD

The dramatic events in the first half of 1919 drew an influx of new members to the KPD, now forced to operate underground. By the middle of the year, membership topped 80,000. Compared to the USPD, however, it was still an insignificant force. To get anywhere, the KPD had to break out of its isolation by winning over militants from the USPD. This could not be done just by denouncing their leaders. Patience was needed, to win over broader layers to revolutionary politics – even more important in the context of a retreat.

The ultra lefts who dominated the KPD were not won to such a perspective. Their reaction to the events of January and the betrayals of the SPD and union leaders was to assert even more fiercely their in-principle opposition to work in trade unions and parliament. The unions were an obstacle to revolutionary struggle and must be destroyed. Boycotting elections would help to free workers from their bourgeois democratic illusions. They fetishised 'the masses' and 'spontaneity,' which they counterposed to 'the leaders' and 'bureaucracy.' They made it a principle of 'local autonomy' to thumb their noses at the Central Committee. In practice, this meant an amateurish approach to building the party, associated with the belief that the revolution was around the corner. In July, the Central Committee reported to the Comintern Executive that most KPD branches were not functioning, and dues were not being paid. Why bother with building the party and establishing it on a sound footing if the SPD government was about to collapse and the dictatorship of the proletariat would be established in a matter of a few weeks or months?

In Hamburg, a stronghold for the ultra lefts, the leadership veered in a syndicalist direction. They developed the idea of putting an end to the division of labour between party and trade unions. They argued that Communists should attempt to split the unions to form 'factory councils' to which only those agreeing with the dictatorship of the proletariat should be admitted – in essence, 'red unions.' Once the factory councils were of sufficient size, the party should then liquidate into them in order to 'eliminate the division between economics and politics.' Accordingly, the Hamburg branch decided that KPD membership was incompatible with membership of the trade unions. Other ultra lefts still upheld the need to build the Communist Party but agreed with their Hamburg comrades that the traditional unions should be dispensed with and replaced by red unions. This only prevented the KPD from relating to serious union militants.

Paul Levi, leader of the KPD since Luxemburg's murder in January, pushed hard against the ultra leftists, with support from the majority of the Central Committee. Levi knew that, for the KPD to become a home for USPD militants shifting towards revolutionary politics, it had to break the hold of the ultra lefts on the party. The Central Committee majority had on its side the only substantial KPD branch dominated by worker militants, in the industrial city of Chemnitz in Central Germany. Here, experienced worker militant Heinrich Brandler, leader of the building workers' union, had pulled virtually the entire USPD branch into the KPD. Levi and the Central Committee were also backed by the jailed Radek. Levi and Radek were not in complete agreement on every tactical question, but they did agree on the fundamental issues: the need to reverse the party's decision at its founding conference to boycott parliament in principle; and the need to commit the party to work in the unions.

There was a vigorous debate in the KPD, with the ultra leftist majority condemning Levi and the Central Committee for supposedly preparing to liquidate the party to rejoin the USPD. They denounced the leaders as reformist, as dictators. Levi and his supporters fought back and, after extensive debate in the party, Levi's theses on the necessity of participating in parliament and the unions were carried at the party's Heidelberg Congress in October. A motion to expel those who opposed these theses was carried by just 21 votes to 20.

Meetings in most of the large branches in the aftermath of the Congress voted overwhelmingly to reject its decisions; on 4 January 1920, the Central Committee followed through with its threat and expelled all the branches which had voted to reject the theses. The result was that the KPD lost tens of thousands of members and was reduced to little more than a shell in big cities such as Berlin and Essen and to nothing at all in Hamburg, Bremen, Hanover and Dresden. Everywhere except Stuttgart and Chemnitz, where the party grew following the Heidelberg congress, the KPD now only existed in small groups. The ultra lefts formed a new organisation, the Communist Workers' Party of Germany (KAPD), with 30,000 members. However, the KAPD was made up of disparate elements bound together only by their hostility to Levi and the Central Committee, and it very quickly began to break apart. By early 1921, the KAPD had only 8,000 members. By 1923, it had ceased to exist.

The purge did not eliminate ultra leftism from the KPD. Just two months after the expulsions, ultra leftism raised its head again, instrumental in the KPD's missing out on a big opportunity to make inroads amongst organised workers. In March 1920, right wing army officers launched a coup against the SPD-led Imperial government to install their puppet, a minor politician by the name of Wolfgang Kapp, as president. Without a shot fired against them by the army or police, the officers seized government ministries and declared the government overthrown. Ebert and his ministers fled to Stuttgart in the face of the revolt by the very officers on whom the SPD had depended to crush the revolutionaries a year previously.

If the government would not fight in its own defence, many in the broader working class rallied for democracy. The call for resistance came initially from Carl Legien, leader of the SPD union federation. Although notorious as an enemy of the left, Legien understood that, if the generals forced the SPD out of office, the unions would be their next target. Legien conferred with USPD and SPD leaders who remained in the capital, and together they proclaimed a general strike. Within hours, hundreds of thousands of workers rose against the coup. Next day, the strike had spread throughout the country, with 12 million stopping work – the biggest general strike in German history. When Kapp issued a decree threatening to shoot strikers, the workers took further steps to defend themselves. In the industrial heartland of the Ruhr, the mining and industrial areas of Central Germany and the northern region between Lubeck and Wismar, armed workers formed councils, effectively taking power into their own hands. Hearing rumours of a Communist rising in Berlin, the bourgeois parties began to have second thoughts. The officers also began to question their decision to back the coup as stories of troop mutinies became widespread and the security police began to switch sides. Kapp lost his nerve and fled.

The coup collapsed after just three days. But the KPD failed to make much of the situation. This was a great opportunity for the KPD to throw itself into the defence of the Weimar Republic and so demonstrate the bankruptcy of the SPD, much as the Bolsheviks had mobilised their forces to defend the Provisional Government against General Kornilov. But the party leadership failed dismally in the first hours of the coup. It issued a statement defining the struggle as a fight between two counter-revolutionary wings:

> The revolutionary proletariat...will not lift a finger for the government of the murderers of Liebknecht and Luxemburg, a government which has collapsed in ignominy and infamy. It will not lift a finger for the democratic republic which was only a paltry mask for the dictatorship of the bourgeoisie.[7]

Indeed, at a time when workers across the country were enthusiastically joining the strike, the Central Committee explained that the workers were 'at present not capable of action.'

Not until later in the day did the Central Committee catch up with reality and swing over to supporting the strike. Even then, it did not call for the arming of workers, although Communist militants in the Ruhr were putting this into practice. Nor did the Central Committee formulate concrete demands to take the struggle forward, relying only on abstract demands for a council republic.

Part of the problem was that the KAPD split in the previous autumn had stripped the party of a base in some major centres. In Berlin, for example, the KPD had had to be rebuilt from scratch. Where it did have some influence, in Central Germany in particular, the local leadership responded to the coup with appropriate speed. In Chemnitz, Brandler organised united action in opposition to the coup and forged links with the USPD that were to stand the party in good stead when the two parties later merged. Arrests of party leaders, including that of Levi, had also taken their toll on the party's ability to navigate the situation. With Brandler occupied in Chemnitz and Levi in jail, the Central Committee lacked two of its best leaders.

The Central Committee was motivated partly by fear of another January uprising – when what began as a mass movement ended in the isolation and slaughter of the Communists and USPD left. But that does not explain its statement equating parliamentary democracy with an all-out right wing dictatorship, a travesty that equates two forms of bourgeois rule with dramatically different consequences for workers' ability to organise. The problem was the continued influence of ultra leftism, which combined maximal slogans with abstention from mass struggle.

By the time that the Central Committee finally endorsed the struggle, the leadership of the movement rested firmly in the hands of the union leaders, the SPD and the USPD right, who were intent on a shoddy compromise to end the strike. Levi noted a month later that, by this stage: 'The masses were not going to be won to another leadership.'⁸ During the Kornilov Coup, the Bolsheviks' determination to lead the resistance established in the minds of tens of thousands of workers that they were the only party serious about defending the revolution. During the Kapp Putsch, the passivity of the KPD leadership meant that the party lost an opportunity to prove its leadership qualities to workers or to position itself to shape developments after the coup's defeat. Instead, it was the USPD that picked up thousands of new members. The KPD continued to pay the price for its late formation. It lacked the battle-hardened leadership and the roots in the working class necessary to implement the correct strategy and tactics at crucial moments. Levi rued this later in the year:

> There is not a single Communist in Germany today who does not regret that the foundation of a Communist Party did not take place long ago, before the war, and that the Communists did not come together in 1903, even in the form of a small sect, and that they did not form a group, even a small one, which could at least have expressed clarity.⁹

Lenin joins the fight against ultra leftism

This was the context for the publication in July 1920 of one of Lenin's most significant works: *'Left-Wing' Communism: An Infantile Disorder*. It was a polemic aimed at the ultra lefts, in particular within the KPD and KAPD in Germany, but also elements in the British and US parties and Bordiga's faction in the PSI.

The first thing to note was that Lenin had much more patience with the ultra lefts than with the centrists (Chapter 2). Lenin's attitude was that the ultra lefts had good revolutionary instincts but pursued wrong tactics because of their inexperience. The ultra lefts should be argued with, in order to win them, Lenin believed; the centrist leaders who would not act against their reformist right wing had to be driven out. This was the basis on which Lenin had urged Levi and the KPD not to expel the ultra lefts. It also explains why, despite heated opposition from Levi and his comrades, the KAPD was invited to attend the Comintern's Second Congress as a sympathising organisation.

Lenin had some sympathy with the ultra lefts' disgust with the opportunism of the reformist leaders, but he understood that their strategies only consolidated these leaders' grip on workers. The ultra lefts had to be steered towards relating to the working class as it actually was, to find ways of breaking them from their illusions in parliament and the democratic system. This could not be achieved by disowning all who would not automatically agree to revolutionary politics.

Lenin starts *'Left-Wing' Communism* by recounting the Bolsheviks' own history: the extraordinary challenges they faced between 1903 and 1917. The party's experiences conveyed important lessons to the infant Communist parties outside Russia.

In order to build the Bolsheviks, Lenin recalls, the party had to struggle against both social democratic opportunism and petit bourgeois revolutionism. The early Russian Marxists had to combat the influence of the Narodniks,[10] who advocated terrorism. The Bolsheviks also had to fight ultra leftism in their own ranks, from those who advocated boycotting the Tsar's parliament, the Duma, in 1907–09 or from Left Communists who opposed signing the 1918 Brest-Litovsk Treaty establishing peace terms with Germany. Waging these internal battles was not easy:

> The Bolsheviks achieved this only because they ruthlessly exposed and expelled the revolutionary phrase-mongers, those who did not wish to understand that one had to retreat, that one had to know how to retreat, and that one had absolutely to learn how to work legally in the most reactionary of parliaments, in the most reactionary of trade unions, co-operative and insurance societies and similar organisations.[11]

'No compromises' is no guide to effective political practice, Lenin argued. Every situation must be judged concretely, and revolutionary leadership involves being able to judge each case on its own terms:

> It would be absurd to formulate a recipe or general rule ('No compromises!') to suit all cases. One must use one's own brains and be able to find one's bearings in each particular instance.[12]

Revolutionaries need to avoid battle when it is advantageous to the enemy and to make the most of temporary alliances even with the most unreliable of allies. The key to any such compromises or retreats is not to lose contact with the masses and to clearly perceive and pursue the final aim, that of revolution. There is a profound difference between workers who compromise at the end of a strike by returning to work without winning all their demands and the reformist leader who, in the name of compromise, sells out workers' interests to the bourgeoisie.

Lenin cited several cases where the Bolshevik caucus in the Duma made compromises even with bourgeois parties, for example, with the SRs. The Bolsheviks sought to exploit rifts in SR ranks and to seize opportunities to make temporary alliances, while maintaining the right to criticise the party. The same was true during the Kornilov coup; the Bolsheviks formed a defensive bloc with the SRs and Mensheviks to drive back the coup. So the ultra lefts could not point to the experience of the Bolsheviks as support for their slogan 'No compromises!'

As for parliaments, Lenin argued, so long as Communists do not have the mass following to replace parliaments with workers' councils, they must intervene in them. On this question, he met stiff opposition from the ultra lefts in Germany, the Bordigists in Italy, the Austrians, the Hungarians and Gallacher from the British shop stewards movement. Bordiga led the opposition, arguing that 'the tactical experience of the Russian Revolution cannot be transported to other countries where bourgeois democracy has functioned for many years.'[13] Any participation in parliament, according to Bordiga, contained the 'twofold danger' of assigning too much importance to elections and wasting valuable time that could be spent on mass work. In effect, Bordiga was arguing that the parliamentary cretinism of the prewar socialist parties was the only possible experience that socialists could have in the electoral arena.

Lenin responded that Bordiga and his supporters were correct to see parliament as a bankrupt institution; the whole history of the Second International had proved this. But the rest of the working class did not. They continued to look to reformist and centrist parties. Parliament was obsolete, said the ultra lefts. 'Obsolete to whom?' Lenin asked:

> Parliamentarianism is of course 'politically obsolete' to the Communists in Germany; but – and that is the whole point – we must not regard what is obsolete to us as something obsolete to a class, to the masses.[14]

Boycotting parliament was only permissible when the conditions for insurrection were ripe:

> As long as you are unable to disperse the bourgeois parliament and every other type of reactionary institution, you must work inside them...otherwise you risk becoming mere babblers.[15]

By boycotting elections, revolutionaries only cut themselves off from reformist workers who still had illusions in their leaders, leaving the way open for the social democrats to dominate.

Lenin pointed to the experience of the Bolsheviks in the Duma. The Bolsheviks advocated an 'active' boycott of the first Duma at the end of 1905, a time when the revolution was still driving ahead. Once the revolution began to ebb in 1906, Lenin changed his position and argued that socialists should participate:

> We were obliged to do – and did – everything in our power to prevent the convocation of a sham representative body. That is so. But since it has been convened in spite of all our efforts, we cannot shirk the task of utilising it.[16]

Lenin had had to wage a determined fight against those who argued that Marxists should boycott the Duma on principle. He argued that the boycott was meaningless under changed, non-revolutionary conditions:

> The boycott is a means of struggle aimed directly at overthrowing the old regime, or, at the worst, i.e., when the assault is not strong enough for overthrow, at weakening it to such an extent that it would be unable to set up that institution, unable to make it operate. Consequently, to be successful the boycott requires a direct struggle against the old regime, an uprising against it and mass disobedience to it.[17]

Lenin therefore attacked the idea of a 'passive' boycott – simply abstaining from elections, refusing to 'recognise' existing institutions even if the movement cannot destroy them. He did not glorify parliamentary work, but: 'since the accursed counter-revolution has driven us into this accursed pig-sty, we shall work there too for the benefit of the revolution, without whining, but also without boasting.'

Even so, Lenin was clear that revolutionaries considered participation in elections as only a small part of their activity. The struggle in the workplaces and streets was far more important:

> We shall not refuse to go into the Second Duma… We shall not refuse to utilise this arena, but we shall not exaggerate its modest importance; on the contrary, guided by the experience already

provided by history, we shall entirely subordinate the struggle we wage in the Duma to another form of struggle, namely strikes, uprisings, etc.[18]

To Bordiga, who argued against participation in parliament on the grounds that it was merely an instrument by which the bourgeoisie deceived the masses, Lenin said:

> this argument should be turned against you, and it does turn against your thesis. How will you reveal the true character of parliament to the really backward masses, who are deceived by the bourgeoisie? How will you expose the various parliamentary manoeuvres or the positions of the various political parties if you are not in parliament?[19]

In *'Left-Wing' Communism*, Lenin also attacked red unionism – breaking away from the existing unions to set up new ones comprising just those convinced of revolution. Rather than setting up red unions, Lenin argued, Communists had to throw themselves into the existing unions. The unions had grown extensively in the immediate postwar years, with membership in Germany rising from 2.8 million in 1918 to 7.3 million in 1919. This was a healthy development, indicating rising class consciousness. Boycotting the established unions, on the grounds of their treacherous leadership, only meant leaving the mass of workers in their hands. That would fence the Communist Party off from the more backward workers. Nothing would please the right wing union bureaucrats more. Lenin wrote:

> If you want to help the 'masses' and win the sympathy and support of the 'masses,' you should not fear difficulties, or pinpricks, chicanery, insults and persecution from the 'leaders'…but must absolutely work wherever the masses are to be found.[20]

The job of Communists, Lenin wrote, was not to leave the workers in the hands of the union bureaucracy but to penetrate the unions and drive out the right wing bureaucrats.

Lenin's approach in *'Left-Wing' Communism* was underpinned by his understanding that proclaiming revolutionary propaganda from the sidelines did not address the relative lack of influence of the Communists, compared with the social democrats and centrists, in so many countries. Communists must relate to the mass of the class to win it over. The point was to reach workers in struggle. Communists must work out how to bridge the gap between the smaller struggles of today and the revolutions of the future. In these battles, revolutionaries must learn to use all weapons at hand, both legal and illegal, and to make all manner of compromises in order to loosen the grip of the reformist leaders over workers.

The positions of the ultra leftists on parliament and trade unions were the expression of an erroneous political world view. Bordiga, for example, finally dropped his opposition to running for parliament but remained irredeemably ultra left. He counterposed 'rank and file action' against 'the bureaucracy' and was extremely wary of genuine, elemental mass mobilisations, explaining his suspicion of the peasant uprisings and the factory occupations in Italy. He still believed that soviets would have to be formed by the Communists, and only after the party had taken power. The ultra lefts in the KAPD condemned the KPD as a 'party of leaders' mired in compromises and parliamentarianism and determined to form a coalition government with the SPD. They contrasted this with themselves, a 'mass party' rejecting all parliamentary and opportunist methods. The KAPD would establish not a dictatorship of the leaders but a 'dictatorship of the masses.' Lenin made short work of such anarchist-influenced, classless thinking, pointing out that the KAPD brought forth new leaders from within their own ranks while shouting 'Down with the leaders!'[21]

Dealing with the revolutionary syndicalists

The Comintern also had to deal with the revolutionary syndicalists, who were convinced of the need for a revolution but opposed the very idea of building a revolutionary party – or downplayed its importance. Like the ultra lefts, they were disgusted by the reformist betrayals of 1914 and were a real force in the workers' movement in several countries. They, too, were inspired by the Russian Revolution. Some were gravitating towards the Comintern: veterans of the IWW (the Wobblies) in the US, Canada and Australia; the National Confederation of Labour (CNT) in Spain; Irish syndicalist and founder of the Irish Transport and General Workers Union, Jim Larkin; the CGT in France; the Italian Syndicalist Union (USI); and leading British militants J. T. Murphy and Jack Tanner. Syndicalism also had some prominence in Chile and Argentina. In Australia, the IWW had been a force during the Great War, as an important militant and radical wing of the anti-conscription movement. Membership peaked at 2,000 in 1917. After World War I, the demand for One

Big Union in Australia became the focus of radical syndicalist attention (and of some union leaders with less radical purposes).

Lenin and Trotsky were keen to establish friendly relations with the revolutionary syndicalists. The Congress was not all of one mind on this. Levi challenged the Russian leaders by asking why the Comintern was talking to people who had not been convinced of the need for a party when this principle had been long established in the European workers' movement. Trotsky responded that this was indeed the case, but some of the most ardent advocates of a party were reformist scoundrels who propped up capitalism, whereas the revolutionary syndicalists 'really want to tear its head off.'[22] Lenin also championed the presence of the syndicalists at the Comintern's Second Congress as a useful counterweight to the right wing influence of the centrist delegates.

It is difficult to summarise revolutionary syndicalism adequately. It is a highly variegated phenomenon, with similarities and commonalities. The basic beliefs of the revolutionary syndicalists were that reorganised industrial unions could be transformed into revolutionary organisations and could serve as the organs of worker self-government after the revolution. Revolutionary parties were at best of secondary importance, suitable for modest propaganda work, and at worst downright harmful. Most syndicalists believed that a general strike was the vehicle to bring down capitalism.

It is often said, not altogether correctly, that the revolutionary syndicalists ignored politics or socialist organisation. Some, such as Jim Larkin and James Connolly, saw the need for socialist organisation to propagandise for socialism. On that basis, they established separate political parties. The Australian IWW was politically eclectic, running weekly *Capital* reading groups and publishing lengthy excerpts by the anarchist Bakunin in its newspaper *Direct Action*. Its eclecticism and refusal to take theory seriously meant that, when it collapsed in 1917, it left behind no solid theoretical tradition to help train future generations of revolutionaries. Other syndicalists tended to lump together parliamentary politics and politics more generally and sheeted home responsibility for the betrayal of the Second International simply to 'politics.' Avoiding politics, they argued, could avoid opportunism, bureaucratism and the other problems that plagued the workers' movement. The French syndicalists in the CGT, for example, were generally 'anti-politics' – by which they meant anti-parliamentary politics, although at times they formed alliances with the SFIO. All that mattered to the CGT was that the worker was a good unionist; politics was a private affair.[23]

Syndicalist approaches to the existing union movement also varied. In France, syndicalists dominated the union movement; the French CGT was a hybrid federation bringing together small craft unions and a few large industrial unions. Elsewhere, syndicalists were divided between those who favoured 'boring from within' (working inside the established unions) and dual unionism (positioning the syndicalist organisation as an alternative to existing unions). William Z. Foster in the US was a champion of the former tactic and oriented to unions affiliated to the American Federation of Labor. By contrast, the US IWW, along with the Italian syndicalists, practised dual unionism.

Given that the syndicalists were a mixed bag, criticisms that applied to one school would not necessarily apply to another. Nonetheless, some general comments can be made. Firstly, the mere separation of economic and political struggle was no guarantee that opportunism would not dominate the movement. The CGT abstained from the Dreyfus Affair, which split the country between pro-republican, anticlerical supporters of Dreyfus – a Jewish army officer falsely accused in 1894 of spying – and pro-Army, mostly Catholic 'anti-Dreyfusards.' The Affair contributed significantly to the radicalisation of sections of the population. Many French syndicalists, however, simply stood aside, asking why they should concern themselves with a wealthy officer, a convenient cover for an opportunist refusal to fight anti-Semitism. The CGT's attitude to war was more problematic. It took a strong anti-militarist stance against the use of the army to break strikes; but it collapsed into a pro-war position in August 1914, leaving the radical syndicalist Alfred Rosmer to rally French opponents of the war at the Zimmerwald conference.

Secondly, those syndicalists who sought to put 'politics' to one side in an attempt not to divide workers simply surrendered the realm of politics to the capitalists and the reformists, both of whom enthusiastically advocated that organised labour should not busy itself with affairs of state. Neither capitalists nor reformist union officials wanted to see revolutionaries fight for their politics inside the unions. In reality, 'no politics' in the unions meant that bourgeois politics prevailed. So, for example, the CGT refused a woman a job in the print industry and expelled her husband for failing to persuade her to quit her job. Even Connolly's conception of syndicalism, involving industrial unionism working alongside a socialist party, was problematic. Connolly still saw the industrial union as being the key force in the class struggle; there was no need for a revolutionary party to lead the working class. Instead, the party should operate largely passively, as a propaganda and electoral arm.

Dual unionism left the majority of workers who do not join such unions in the hands of the existing bureaucrats. This was why the IWW in Australia, formally committed to dual unionism, operated mainly within the existing union structures. Anything else would have been suicidal, given that Australia had the highest rate of union membership in the world at this time.

Finally, the syndicalists tended to underestimate the state. Some believed that the state would crumble under a general strike; industry would halt, profits would stop flowing, and the army would starve. In reality, a general strike can halt production and paralyse the capitalists, but revolution requires an insurrection against the state. Unless the state is smashed, the capitalists can always regroup and deploy the army and police to break strikes and factory occupations. Insurrection requires a revolutionary party to prepare workers for this task.

The underestimation of the state had devastating consequences for the Australian IWW. Any revolutionary organisation, especially during wartime, must be prepared to go underground in the face of repression, to keep its basic structures and leadership intact as much as possible. But the IWW leaders in NSW reacted to their banning by the Hughes government in 1917 by openly defying the ban, challenging the authorities to arrest them. The police obliged, resulting in the jailing of much of the IWW leadership and the collapse of the organisation.

In Spain, the CNT was certainly committed to armed insurrection against the state, but it did not prepare politically, leading to a string of doomed risings at the cost of hundreds of lives. Fetishising the state as the source of evil, the CNT equally denounced the idea of a workers' state and the capitalist state, something that was to have a disastrous effect two decades later (see Chapter 11).

Comintern intervention on trade unions

The Russian Communists had demonstrated by their leadership of the first successful workers' revolution that they had something to offer revolutionary syndicalists searching for a way forward. On this basis, representatives of several syndicalist organisations found their way to Moscow for the Second Congress of the Comintern. The Congress drew up a program for union work designed both to fight treacherous union leaders loyal to the Second International and to draw revolutionary syndicalists closer.

The Second Congress resolved that Comintern sections should adopt the following principles: to promote union unity within nations and to oppose splits; to work within established unions, rather than establish dual unions; and to work to win over the established unions to Communist leadership. The Comintern advocated unity of unionism within nations but sought to smash the newly formed, reformist International Federation of Trade Unions, known as the Amsterdam International; this the Comintern called 'the agent of the bourgeoisie in the workers' camp' and 'the last stronghold of international capitalism.'[24] Workers must drive out the reformist union leaders and then affiliate their unions to the Red International of Labour Unions (the Profintern). This would bring together Communist-led unions and Communist elements in reformist unions and syndicalist unions (since unions could not be members of the Comintern). The Red International's program would be the program of the Communist International.

Negotiations with the syndicalists led to some useful expansion of Comintern understanding of trade unionism in the West. The Russian leadership had barely had to deal with the question when building the Bolsheviks, because Tsarist repression stunted the growth of unions. These discussions won some of the syndicalists to communism, including 'Big Bill' Haywood and James P. Cannon, former members of the US Wobblies, Monatte and Rosmer of the CGT, Larkin in Ireland and leaders of the Czech syndicalist federation. The majority, most importantly the US IWW and CNT, kept their distance.

There were several sticking points: dual unionism, contesting parliamentary elections, united front work with reformist parties, the relationship between the Profintern and the Comintern and the question of the revolutionary party. The syndicalists who remained aloof from the Comintern were opposed to working within established unions, objected in practice to standing for parliament or joint work with reformist parties, did not agree with the need for a centralised workers' state, and disagreed with revolutionary parties. They also attacked the Profintern as an appendage of the Comintern and could not be convinced otherwise, even when the Comintern granted the Profintern significant autonomy. The US IWW was perhaps most forthright in saying that it had nothing to learn from the Comintern:

> We have no reason to be excited by this invitation. The programme of the IWW was valid before the war, survived the war without the necessity to alter even a single point, it is valid now and will with absolute necessity be the programme of every revolutionary party.[25]

The IWW inevitably became a spent force. Its determination not to learn anything from the Russian Revolution meant that it was bypassed by radicalising workers.

The Comintern faced another issue. By the time the Profintern was established, in the summer of 1921, the industrial upsurge had ended. The general trend in the workers' movement was now to the right. The Comintern adapted its tactics accordingly. At the Third Congress, Lenin and Trotsky abandoned the Comintern's goal of 'destroying' the Amsterdam International and instead advocated the united front approach towards the reformist union leaders.

But there were other problems with the Comintern's orientation to union work. For several reasons, the very project of the Red International of Labour Unions was misconceived. There was a basic contradiction between the Comintern's stated goals of working within established unions within nations and its determination to split the unions on an international basis by getting them to break from the Amsterdam International and affiliate with the Profintern. This allowed the union bureaucrats to appeal to workers' hostility to division, saying 'Look, the Communists want to divide the workers' movement.' The fact that the Comintern referred to the Amsterdam International as a 'scab' outfit was also a problem. Although the Russian leaders tried to distinguish between leaders and members, writing off the unions that brought together 21 million workers in 1921 as scab operations naturally annoyed members of those unions. The whole operation appeared to be in bad faith, and the right wing bureaucrats were happy to play this up. The existence of multiple international federations also made the prospects for unity more difficult within countries that had multiple federations, for example, Spain and France. The Comintern believed that the leaders of the Amsterdam International unions would quickly be swept aside; in April 1921, on the eve of the Third Congress, Zinoviev confidently predicted their 'imminent and complete collapse.'[26] This was far from true; the reformist union leaders could not just be wished away.

While they differed on the need for a revolutionary party, both the Comintern and revolutionary syndicalists believed that it was possible to create 'revolutionary unions.' But this conception confuses the revolutionary party – the vanguard of the working class, the most politically advanced layers – with the trade unions, which by their very nature must seek to include the mass of workers. Unions gather all workers of extremely diverse forms of political consciousness, but such organisations cannot cohere the more advanced workers convinced of the need for revolution. They dilute them into a mass of more backward workers. The vanguard needs to be organised in its own party, not to separate those workers from the rest of the class, but to organise the revolutionary minority to win over their fellow workers.

'Revolutionary unionism' conflates the task of organising the insurrection (of which only a small minority of the class is convinced in anything but revolutionary situations) with collective bargaining over wages and conditions (what most workers see as the purpose of unions). To the extent that some self-styled revolutionary unions, like the prewar French CGT, did good mass union work, they dropped or diluted their 'revolutionary' politics. And to the extent that they sought to cohere the revolutionary minority around 'no agreements,' and 'permanent war with the bosses,' they repelled the mass of workers who looked to unions to win higher wages and better conditions in collective agreements.

The Russian Comintern leaders believed that unions in Western Europe with an established bureaucracy could be won over to revolutionary politics before the revolution. But the union bureaucracy in advanced Western countries has always proved to be a big obstacle to the creation of mass 'revolutionary unions,' attacking radicals in the union ranks. The Russian Communists consistently underestimated the strength of the union bureaucracy in the Western unions, never having had to confront mass reformist union bureaucracies themselves. This oversight related to another point: their misunderstanding of the roots of reformism in Europe.

During World War I, the Bolsheviks attributed the Second International's betrayal in 1914 to the influence of what they called the 'labour aristocracy.' Lenin and Zinoviev saw the labour aristocracy as combining the labour bureaucracy – social democratic politicians, the social democratic party apparatus and union leaders – *and* the well-paid, usually skilled workers.[27] They differed on how big the last component was; Zinoviev focused on the highly paid metal tradespeople working in the munitions factories as exemplary 'labour aristocrats,' while Lenin once considered the labour aristocracy to be 'an insignificant minority of the proletariat and the toiling masses'[28] and, at another time, the entire, millions-strong membership of the British and German trade unions.[29]

Lenin and Zinoviev viewed the labour aristocracy, whatever its size, as the bedrock of reformism in the West. This 'aristocracy' had been 'bribed' by the capitalists of the imperialist countries from the proceeds of imperialist plunder and had 'become completely petty-bourgeois in their mode of life.'[30] The result was loyalty to capitalism.

The labour aristocracy thesis does not explain reformist tendencies in the working class and only leads to a misunderstanding of the tactics needed to build revolutionary minorities within the unions.[31] It very obviously fails on empirical grounds: the skilled metal workers who were meant to constitute a conservative bloc were actually in the vanguard of working class struggle in country after country during World War I and afterwards. The reason why this supposedly conservative layer could form the vanguard is because it remained exploited. No matter that its wages were double or even triple those of labourers; it produced value for the capitalists at a still higher rate. Opposition to this exploitation and knowledge of their central role in production, particularly in wartime, meant that skilled and well-paid engineering workers were frequently at the leading edge of struggles. These included the revolutionary shop stewards in Berlin who had a policy of only including skilled workers in their ranks. Any revolutionaries who allowed themselves to be guided by the 'labour aristocracy' thesis would have been completely left behind by developments in Berlin but also in Petrograd, Turin and Glasgow. Lenin himself did not: he relied upon the revolutionary metal workers of the giant Putilov works in Petrograd for support for his arguments within the Bolshevik party. The problem was that Lenin never reflected on the incompatibility between the Bolsheviks' theory and their practice in this regard, which meant that the theory of the labour aristocracy became a shibboleth in the Comintern.

The 'labour aristocracy' theory glides over the real differences between union leaders and parliamentarians, on the one hand, and skilled workers on the other. The former do not labour for a boss and so are not exploited. Social democratic parliamentarians form a bulwark of the bourgeoisie in the workers' movement, most obviously when they are in government. Union leaders are a buffer layer between bosses and workers; they tend towards conservatism because of the privileged existence that they enjoy as wholesalers of labour power (see Chapter 1). Skilled workers, by contrast, have no objective interest in the maintenance and promotion of capitalism. This means that they can be won to revolution, while the labour bureaucracy will always be a barrier to it.

The labour aristocracy theory also fails to understand that reformism constantly reproduces itself within the working class because of the conditions of its existence. Even without unions or labour parties, reformism within the working class arises out of the fact of its exploitation, which, while contributing to a sense of collective grievance, can also generate a feeling of powerlessness and fatalism. Where there are reformist parties and unions, hopes for redress against the injustices of capitalism are often directed towards parliamentarians and union leaders. No matter how many times these parliamentarians and union leaders betray the workers, conditions of life for workers continually generate reformist illusions. These are the conditions that allow the labour bureaucracy to thrive. Collective struggle, by contrast, gives workers a sense of hope that their *own activity* can address their exploitation. Political intervention by revolutionaries challenges the authority of reformist politicians and union leaders. Together, they may convert reformist illusions into revolutionary action.

The labour aristocracy theory encouraged Russian Communists to believe that revolutionary unions could be built in the West if the 'treacherous scab leaders' were driven out of the unions. Leadership must be in the hands of Communists inoculated against the pull of the labour aristocracy. Capturing leadership positions would be the means to revolutionise the unions. In practice, this usually proved beyond the capabilities of small Communist parties in countries such as Britain and the US. Where it did happen, as in some instances in Australia, the Communists lost capable worker leaders who abandoned their party loyalties once in union office. They rationalised their situation: how much more realistic to influence the working class as the head of a great union than when confined to the margins in small communist parties? They were soon drawn into the types of compromises needed to maintain their positions as full-time officials and were quickly converted into hardened reformists. Marx had explained many years earlier: 'It is not the consciousness of men that determines their being, but, on the contrary, their social being that determines their consciousness.'[32]

Some delegates to the Second Congress, chiefly from the US and British Communist parties, such as Louis Fraina and Gallacher, were well aware of the entrenched nature of the union bureaucracies and the impossibility of revolutionaries overturning these bureaucracies this side of the socialist revolution. They emphasised instead the need for independent rank and file movements to organise within the unions. In 1915, the Clyde Workers' Committee, in which Gallacher had played a leading role, explained its attitude to the union officials:

> We will support the officials just so long as they rightly represent the workers, but we will act independently immediately they misrepresent them. Being composed of delegates from every shop and untrammelled by obsolete rule of law, we claim to represent the true feeling of the workers. We can act immediately according to the merits of the case and the desire of the rank and file.[33]

The following Comintern Congress, the Third, took place in 1921. It did actually advise sections to establish Communist workplace cells, although such cells were not to work towards independent rank and file action so much as: 'revolutionising the trade unions, ridding them of reformist influence and the treacherous reformist leaders, and transforming them into a genuine stronghold of the revolutionary proletariat.'[34] Capturing the unions replaced the earlier tactic of splitting them. This potentially opened the door to opportunism, in the form of making alliances with left officials.

While fighting the ultra left tendency to boycott work in the trade unions, Comintern policy on the trade unions contained several confusions. In the short term, these misoriented the Communist parties. By the mid-1920s, however, these confusions were replaced by policies that were distorted not by misunderstandings but by the needs of the party bureaucracy inside Russia which looked not to spreading revolution but to entrenching its own privileged position. This was to have devastating consequences for workers' struggles.

FURTHER READING

M. Armstrong, 'Socialist trade union strategy in the Bolshevik era', *Marxist Left Review*, no. 6, 2013.

P. Broué, *The German Revolution 1917–1923*, Chicago, Haymarket Books, 2006 [1971].

T. Cliff and D. Gluckstein, *Marxism and Trade Union Struggle: The General Strike of 1926*, London, Bookmarks, 1986.

R. Darlington, *Syndicalism and the Transition to Communism*, Aldershot, Ashgate, 2008.

D. Hallas, *The Comintern*, Haymarket Books, 2008 [1985].

C. Harman, *The Lost Revolution: Germany 1918 to 1923*, London, Bookmarks, 1982.

V.I. Lenin, *'Left-Wing' Communism – An Infantile Disorder*, Melbourne, Red Flag Books, 2020 [1920].

4.
GERMANY: AN OPPORTUNITY LOST

Between May and October 1923, Germany was in ferment. Inflation had reached extreme proportions; money depreciated by the hour.[1] Hunger stalked the streets. The angry and desperate masses became restless and rioted across the country. A Social Democrat politician reported:

> One cannot deny that the mass of the working class is moving away from the old union tactics and looking for a new way. With the best will in the world, we can no longer hold the working class in check.[2]

The Communist Party stood 220,000 strong at the beginning of the year and new recruits continued to flood into the party.

Everything seemed ripe for revolution. Even sections of the middle classes who had been driven to the wall by hyperinflation were looking to the KPD for a solution. But the opportunity was missed, and October ended in tragedy. The Communist Party did not even attempt to seize power, suffering the most demoralising of defeats. KPD member Rosa Levine Meyer points out:

> The workers were never able to find out by their own experience whether the revolution was betrayed or whether they lost the battle in a square fight. They felt humiliated and cheated.[3]

For a revolutionary party to fight and be beaten is no disgrace. Marxists can learn important lessons for the future from defeats. The defeated 1905 Revolution in Russia was a vital dress rehearsal for the successful Bolshevik Revolution of October 1917. But for a Marxist party in a revolutionary situation not to give battle, to hesitate, to waver, can only discredit the party and the very ideas of Marxism in the eyes of the masses and deliver them into the arms of the reformists. Trotsky explains in his 1924 pamphlet *The Lessons of October*:

> A party which carries on a protracted revolutionary agitation and then, after the confidence of the masses has raised it to the top, begins to vacillate, such a party paralyses the activity of the masses, sows disillusion and disintegration among them and brings ruin to the revolution; but in turn it provides itself with a ready excuse – after the debacle – that the masses were insufficiently active.[4]

The failure to seize the revolutionary opportunities in 1923 was a vital historical turning point for the international workers' movement. It marked the shift from a period of revolutionary struggle to one of capitalist stabilisation. It left the Russian Revolution isolated and paved the way for Stalin's victory. The failure of the German October of 1923 also opened the road for the triumph of Hitler just 10 years later. Why did it fail?

From 'Open Letter' to March Action

Some background to the German October will help to explain why the revolutionary potential of 1923 was wasted. The United KPD (VKPD) was born as a mass party in December 1920, when the KPD merged with the left wing of the centrist USPD (Chapter 2). Levi from the KPD and Däumig from the USPD were elected joint VKPD leaders. The new party of 350,000 members was filled with revolutionary enthusiasm. Levi and Radek felt confident enough to issue an Open Letter in January 1921 to the leaderships of the SPD, the USPD and the unions, calling for joint action against the rising fascist threat and a fight to defend living standards against an employer offensive.[5] Radek explained their rationale in the KPD's theoretical journal, *Die Internationale*:

> The mobilisation of the proletariat must entail consistently attempting to lead the working masses with all our energy in struggle for their immediate vital interests, the interests that unite them and not what separates them. [For it is] not a particular demand, but the *unity* of the working class, its *collective action*, that is the pivot of the current situation: *that* is the Archimedean point from which the working class can take the step forward, the step towards the overcoming of capitalism.[6]

Levi and Radek drafted the Open Letter, but the initiative came from the VKPD's local organisation in Stuttgart, responding to widespread sentiment for working class unity. VKPD members active in the metal workers' union had proposed a list of five demands to the union leadership for joint action to defend living standards. The union accepted the demands; an effective joint campaign followed, involving the VKPD and SPD. Levi and Radek now proposed to make this a national program for action. The party agreed. Members successfully pursued the united front tactic among wood workers in Berlin and metal workers in Essen, significantly enhancing the reputation of the VKPD and drawing into its ranks SPD unionists disillusioned by their party's attempt to avoid joint action.

The Open Letter approach ran into ferocious opposition from the ultra left current within the VKPD, led by Ruth Fischer and Arkady Maslow in Berlin. Having seen the SPD's Gustav Noske use the Freikorps to slaughter thousands of worker militants in the first months of 1919, many KPD members, in Berlin in particular, believed that any cooperation with the SPD was out of the question. Another source of rejection of the Open Letter came from former USPD members who had broken with centrism to join the VKPD and were now demanding that the party take immediate revolutionary action. Impatience among such members was healthy, but their thirst for action was simply used by committed ultra leftists in the party to build support for their foolhardy adventurism. They wanted to build a party untainted by any form of joint action necessary to initiate serious class struggle – in short, they wanted to build a sect. They had failed to transition from the priority of the first stage of party building – winning workers over from their centrist leaders to form the united party – to what was now required, learning to prepare for revolution and to win a majority of workers to their side. All they could see was the danger of accommodation to reformism.

The ultra left leaders slammed the Open Letter tactic and accused Levi of right wing opportunism. They also seized on criticisms Levi had made of the way in which Comintern emissaries Mátyás Rákosi and Khristo Kabakchiev intervened in the Livorno Congress of the PSI – which Levi attended as a representative of the KPD (Chapter 2). A meeting of the VKPD Central Committee attended by Rákosi, at which he aggressively defended his intervention at Livorno, saw a motion of support for the Comintern Executive's handling of the Livorno Congress passed by 28 votes to 23. Refusing to take responsibility for such a position, five members of the Central Committee – including Levi, Däumig and Zetkin – quit, a foolish decision that gave the ultra lefts more room to move.

Heinrich Brandler now assumed the leadership of the party and worked closely with one of the party's leading theoreticians, August Thalheimer. Brandler had a cautious disposition and had been a supporter of Levi. Other national leaders, however, most notably Paul Frölich, lined up with Fischer and Maslow, who had picked up Nikolai Bukharin's 'theory of the offensive.' This was not so much a theory as a justification for impatient adventurism. The Central Committee approved a statement reading:

> The party's slogan must therefore be: Offensive, offensive, whatever the cost, by every means, in every situation that offers serious chances of success.[7]

The ultra lefts ignored the important proviso that offensive was appropriate in situations that 'offer serious chances of success.' The idea that Communists should launch an all-out assault on capitalist power, even with only minority support among workers, now guided the VKPD. The results would be disastrous.

Unfortunately, the ultra lefts received backing from Russian leaders, including Bukharin and Zinoviev. Bukharin had first advanced his 'offencist' approach during the debate within the Russian party over Brest–Litovsk, arguing that, instead of signing the treaty, the Communists should wage 'a holy war in the name of the interests of the proletariat.' Although Bukharin was defeated on this question, he retained a generally ultra left method in the years following the Russian Revolution. He and Comintern leader Zinoviev had no time for the Open Letter tactic and wanted to force the pace in Germany. To this end, Zinoviev sent the Hungarian exile Béla Kun and two others to Germany as Comintern emissaries. Already responsible for contributing to the defeat of the short-lived Hungarian council republic in 1919, and now swinging to violent ultra leftism, Kun was a loose cannon. Regardless of the exact authority and general line of march that Zinoviev provided to Kun (and it is not clear exactly what he was told), the emissaries proceeded to throw their weight around in the VKPD as if their instructions for a 'revolutionary offensive' had the full authority of the Comintern Executive. Thus was born the 'theory of the offensive' and the disaster of the March Action.

On 16 March 1921, the SPD government in Saxony sent police into the coalfields of Mansfeld, a VKPD stronghold, to crush the state's militant miners. The VKPD leadership took the bait and sought to turn the local fight into a revolutionary struggle for power. The party issued a call to arms; Frölich declared: 'Previously we waited, but now we will seize the initiative and force the revolution.'⁸ On 24 March, the VKPD declared a national general strike. 'Whoever is not with us is against us,' thundered *Rote Fahne*.

The VKPD strategy was madness. Workers were in a passive and demoralised mood at this time. The VKPD membership, despite an influx of more seasoned USPD members, still consisted mainly of unemployed and inexperienced young men without roots in the major industries. The SPD retained the loyalty of most core groups of workers, who were not moved by the VKPD's strike call. Rather than retreat, however, the VKPD doubled down and sent its unemployed members to the factories to try to prevent workers loyal to the SPD from going to work. They abused them as scabs, fought them and, in some cases, shot at them. The workers responded, blow for blow. The ultra lefts also drew up plans to dynamite the Halle railway station and a munitions depot and to carry out kidnappings to intensify the armed conflict; thankfully, these did not eventuate.

The 'national' general strike was a disaster, with at best 200,000 taking part from a working class of tens of millions. Demonstrations called in support were dismal. Only 4,000 rallied in Berlin, a tiny fraction of the 200,000 who had voted for the VKPD in elections in the capital just weeks earlier. Heavy fighting took place in Central Germany between Communists and the authorities, but the government got the upper hand within a few days.

The March Action never had a chance of succeeding, because it was dreamt up without any regard to the balance of forces. The SPD government had hoped to provoke the VKPD into action that would demonstrate its isolation from the big battalions of the working class – and it succeeded. The government and courts now took full advantage of the situation, arresting 6,000 workers and jailing 4,000. Eight were sentenced to life imprisonment. Thousands of workers were sacked. The VKPD suffered heavy losses; 150 members were killed, and hundreds, including Brandler, jailed. The party had to go underground. The VKPD's name was now mud. Many members simply walked away from the party. Membership collapsed from 400,000 to 180,000. Regardless, the party continued to declare the adventure a 'temporary defeat, a prerequisite for victory in the future' and 'the only possible way a revolutionary party can win the masses for itself.'⁹

Levi was horrified by the March Action. He went public with his blunt criticisms, calling it 'the greatest Bakuninite putsch in history to date, a declaration of war against the working class.'¹⁰ The many thousands of desperate workers and unemployed involved in the fighting made it more than a putsch, but Levi's description was not far off the mark: the idea that the miners' fight could be the basis for an insurrection was completely wrongheaded. Accurate though the thrust of Levi's criticisms were, his bitter invective against the Central Committee and its publication in a public forum gave the ultra left an opportunity to rally members against him. They accused him of denigrating the entire party and exposing it to even more state repression. The Central Committee faced little opposition when it first suspended, then expelled, Levi. Zetkin appealed to Lenin to intercede on Levi's behalf, but he refused. Lenin acknowledged that Levi had brought the situation upon himself but expressed hope that the passage of time would see Levi back in the party. Having lost Luxemburg, Liebknecht and Jogiches to the Freikorps in 1919, the German Communists now lost another of their most capable leaders.

The united front

Four months after the disaster of the March Action, Lenin and Trotsky used the opportunity of the Comintern's Third Congress in July 1921 to push for a sharp turn in the international Communist movement. The Congress banner, 'To the masses!' conveyed the need for the Comintern to turn its attention to the most vital question of the day: now that big Communist parties had been formed, how could they win the loyalty of the majority of workers away from the reformist parties in order to contend for power?

The overall political situation was less favourable than during the First and Second Congresses. Trotsky's opening speech recognised that the revolutionary wave had subsided, and a limited capitalist stabilisation was in progress. Revolution was not off the agenda, but it might be a matter of years, not the months anticipated by the First Congress.[11] At home, the Russian Communists had defeated the counter-revolutionary armies but now faced intense pressure from a population resentful of wartime regimentation, where they were not in open revolt. In the absence of any international breakthrough, the Soviet government was forced to make concessions to the rich peasants and merchants in the form of the New Economic Policy.

Lenin and Trotsky had already attacked ultra left tendencies at the Second Congress but had soft-pedalled their criticisms in order to focus on fighting centrism. At the Third Congress, they pushed much more strongly against ultra left currents that threatened to wreck the Comintern. They believed that they had to push the Comintern to the 'right,' as Lenin put it. They were helped by some rethinking by VKPD leaders Brandler and Thalheimer, both of whom had gone along with the theory of the offensive.

In a letter to Zinoviev immediately before the opening of the Third Congress, Lenin pointedly praised Levi's Open Letter tactic and the 'right' turn in the VKPD in the period before the March Action, admitting his own mistake in supporting the KAPD's admission to the Comintern. It was now necessary, Lenin argued, for the Comintern to adopt a united front policy to build mass parties in this period of relative capitalist stabilisation. Workers could go on the offensive when the situation turned back in their favour. Any party that refused to adopt the Open Letter, Lenin argued, must be expelled from the Comintern within a month after the Congress.[12] Lenin openly attacked Kun and described the 'theory of the offensive' as 'an illusion, romanticism, sheer romanticism.'[13] Trotsky described the 'method' of the offensive:

> This celebrated philosophy of the offensive, which is completely non-Marxist, has arisen from the following curious outlook: 'A wall of passivity is gradually rising, which is ruining the movement. So let us advance, and break through this wall!'... We are obliged to say frankly to the German working class that we regard this philosophy of the offensive as the greatest of dangers and that to apply it in practice is the greatest of political crimes.[14]

Lenin faced stiff resistance at the Congress. Many delegates, having only just emerged from their fights against reformist and centrist currents, still believed that the right were the greatest threat. The German ultra lefts, backed by Zinoviev, Bukharin and Kun, fought to prevent a full accounting for the March Action fiasco. They tried to bluster their way through, claiming that the VKPD suffered no loss of influence as a result of the March Action - quite the opposite.

Facing the prospect of a further split in the VKPD (now known as the KPD)[15] and in the Russian party itself, Lenin accepted a compromise, supporting resolutions that fudged responsibility for the March Action (not putting Zinoviev and Bukharin on the spot, for example) and included no outright condemnation of the March Action. Indeed, the Comintern Commission on Tactics and Strategy described the March Action as 'a step forward.' Lenin was also required to abandon Levi, whom he regarded as the most capable KPD leader. Lenin made these compromises to persuade Congress to condemn the theory of the offensive and to approve the united front strategy. Even that was only partial; not until December did the Executive Committee pass a resolution spelling out in detail what was required to implement the united front tactic, and only at the Fourth Congress in December 1922 was it ratified by a full Congress - once all but the most committed ultra lefts had been won over.

The united front strategy was spelled out fully in Trotsky's 'On the United Front' in February 1922.[16] It was based on the method that lay behind the

KPD's Open Letter: to activate the mass of workers to resist the capitalist offensive by appealing to the social democratic leaders for common action around certain defensive, partial demands, for example, to fight wage cuts or a fascist mobilisation. If the social democratic leaders agreed to support the action, fine. With the majority of the working class moving into action at the call of social democratic and Communist leaders, workers would be in the best position to fight the capitalists and, if successful, to go on the offensive. Defensive in nature, the tactic also had an offensive purpose. Unleashing mass action offered the Communists the best opportunity to demonstrate to social democratic workers that they were the better fighters – presuming that they pursued the correct strategy and tactics. If, on the other hand, the social democratic leaders refused proposals for joint action, the Communists could argue that the reformists were not serious about combating the threat to the working class.

A united front could not be any pact between rival parties, Trotsky argued. For it to be successful, it must include only working class parties; bourgeois parties were excluded in principle. This proviso was important. Its violation in the following decades, in the form of 'Popular Fronts,' would contribute to a string of disasters.

Further, Trotsky believed that the united front must be a method of struggle for influence, not a paper agreement for cooperation (e.g. an electoral bloc) or an agreement for joint propaganda. In the majority of cases, no written agreement between the parties would be signed. The united front was an agreement with the social democratic leadership, precisely in order to attack their vacillations: a way of 'working with and against' reformist leaders. Its underlying premise was 'March separately, strike together.' Revolutionaries must retain their freedom to criticise the social democratic leaders (or it would be pointless).

In order for the united front to be a meaningful strategy, the Communist party had to be an organised force within the working class, claiming the loyalty, Trotsky suggested, of about one-quarter to one-third of workers. No smaller body could exert sufficient force on the social democratic leadership in response to its overtures. Any larger body would not need a united front; the Communists could call workers to action directly, challenging the reformists in an open contest for influence. Finally, it was not to be a 'united front from below,' a direct appeal to the membership of the reformist parties dependent on their ditching their leaders before commencing joint action. Lenin and Trotsky's conception of the united front involved winning reformist workers through the course of struggle, not through ultimatums.

The KPD's application of the united front

The united front policy was applied with considerable vigour and success in Germany in 1922. In June, fascists assassinated Walter Rathenau, a moderate Jewish liberal politician. The KPD called for joint action with the SPD and the unions around demands for disarming the right wing paramilitaries, the formation of armed workers' militias, joint action against inflation and seizure of industrial property by the state, under the control of the factory councils. Under pressure from their rank and file, SPD leaders were forced to agree to joint demonstrations. Where the SPD did not agree, the KPD went ahead.

The KPD made successful inroads by using the united front approach in the factory councils, which mushroomed during the economic distress. Late in 1922, the KPD called for a national congress of factory councils. When the SPD refused to cooperate, the KPD proceeded without them. The executive elected from the congress played an important role in national political life over the following 12 months. The factory councils were not merely economic bodies; they took on social and political functions. Many councils linked up with others and with working class housewives' groups to form control committees to fight price rises.

Although the ultra lefts in the KPD attacked the united front policy, calling any talk of collaboration with the SPD leaders 'class collaborationist,' the results were clear. During 1922, the KPD demonstrated that they stood for united working class action and were the best fighters. A steady inflow of worker recruits to the KPD resulted, partially reversing the mass exodus that had followed the March Action. By autumn 1922, the KPD claimed 250,000 members, an increase of 100,000 over its nadir in mid-1921. Some of the new recruits came from the SPD, which lost 50,000 members in 1922. The KPD also registered increasing support in local elections and built support and won leadership positions within the unions.

Hyperinflation and the occupation of the Ruhr

The economic situation deteriorated badly in the second half of 1922. Inflation spiralled, largely because of financial speculation by big industrialists such as Hugo Stinnes; he saw inflation as a means of both wiping out debts and paralysing the Imperial government. A political crisis also emerged in the government over the payment of war reparations to France.

At the end of the year, a new right wing coalition, headed by Wilhelm Cuno, formed government without the SPD. Cuno announced that he would not pay war reparations. In response, French troops occupied the Ruhr, the industrial heartland of Germany. An atmosphere of overwhelming nationalist sentiment against the occupation prevailed, encouraged by the ruling class, who saw hostility to France as a way of softening worker hostility to themselves. The big industrialists announced that they would refuse to cooperate with the French forces. However, it soon became clear that the capitalists' passive resistance to the occupation was a farce; the industrialists who controlled the coal and steel industries were doing deals with the occupiers. At the same time, the bosses refused to distribute coal to the families of laid-off workers. The hypocrisy of the capitalists stoked worker resentment.

On the right flank, the nationalists and the Nazis prospered from nationalist propaganda. They proclaimed that Germany had been betrayed by the Weimar Republic. The middle classes were increasingly disillusioned with Weimar. Hyperinflation had destroyed their savings. In desperation, they sought a 'strong man' who would fix up the country and restore them to what they believed to be their proper place in society; they began to look with increasing favour at the far right, which was cohering in Bavaria. The military top brass was firmly aligned with the mainstream nationalists, but middle and lower ranking officers gravitated to the Nazis.

The intertwined crises of hyperinflation, the occupation of the Ruhr and the growth of fascism all increased political polarisation. Germany was now clearly divided between the south (including Bavaria), largely dominated by the nationalist right and the fascists; the centre (Saxony and Thuringia), where the KPD was a force alongside the SPD; and the north (including the country's biggest state, Prussia and its capital, also the national capital, Berlin), which was in the hands of the SPD and centre parties.

The revolutionary moment approaches: April to August 1923

Although the patriotic atmosphere generated by the French occupation of the Ruhr dampened working class struggle for some months, the desperate economic situation forced workers back into combat in the first half of 1923. Communist influence began to mount, and nationalism to recede. The KPD formed workers' militias, the Proletarian Hundreds, to defend strikes and to push back against the increasingly confident far right. On May Day in 1923, 25,000 of these militants marched through central Berlin. Many of the Proletarian Hundreds were purely KPD operations; but, by the spring and summer of 1923, workers in the big factories were beginning to build them themselves. The Imperial government tried to ban them but could not stop workers establishing them on a firm footing in the Ruhr and Central Germany, where they were tolerated by left SPD governments. In May and June, a strike wave rocked the Ruhr as workers fought back against rapidly rising inflation.

The KPD, however, was slow to switch gear in response to the mounting workers' offensive. It did not change from its relatively defensive united front policy – well suited to the preceding years, but not when workers were on the advance. The number of strikes exploded, workers' militias were formed, workers were fighting police on the streets, and KPD membership shot up by tens of thousands, with many party militants leading struggles in the factories. Still, the KPD leaders remained adamant that immediate revolutionary prospects were dim. Brandler, who had been released from prison and returned to the leadership in January 1923, stated that the tide of revolution was 'receding not rising.'[17] When strikes did break out, the KPD did its best to encourage them, but the leadership was nervous, over-correcting for the disastrous March Action and failing to recognise that a qualitative change had taken place in the mood of the masses.

Even reformist politicians recognised the rapidly developing situation. In June, prominent SPD spokesperson Rudolf Wissell wrote:

> A mixture of bitterness and despair rules among the great masses and among all those who are forced to go without food...the atmosphere is such that in the last few weeks, it has frightened me and filled me with great worries for the future...a revolutionary and activist spirit is rising in the most quiet and most stable of the masses... It only needs a little incitement to explode everything.[18]

A mass revolutionary party had been built up in the few previous years just for this moment. Yet the 'little incitement' was not forthcoming.[19]

The SPD's hold over workers collapsed dramatically over the course of 1923. In local elections, the KPD vote jumped extraordinarily at the SPD's expense. The hyperinflation ravaging living standards hit the SPD in two ways. It provoked workers to go on strike repeatedly, bringing them into conflict with union leaders and SPD-controlled police in Prussia, and it destroyed the finances of the SPD and unions. Chris Harman writes: 'There was a visible falling apart of the apparatus that had constrained the German working class since the war.'[20]

The scale of the crises racking Germany demonstrated that only a resolute and determined radical approach could offer any solution for workers. Clearly, the KPD was capable of offering a lead of this type. Local union sections and, above all, the factory councils took on a new directing role in the struggle. KPD militants led the way. A *pessimistic* Communist account at the time spoke of 5,000 factory councils the KPD could mobilise. Even the far from overoptimistic Brandler claimed that the KPD held the leadership of the working class in key areas of Germany in June. Still, the majority of the leadership was not prepared to act. Part of the problem was that the Berlin ultra lefts were engaged in unscrupulous manoeuvring, tying up the time of the Central Committee. Faced with a developing revolutionary situation, the ultra lefts were obsessed with bringing down Brandler while posing no alternative course of action themselves. Far from urging the KPD to respond more forcefully, one of the Berlin ultra left's leaders, Werner Scholem, began to warn against revolution and factory occupations, saying that the government was too powerful.

The one attempt to reverse the KPD's defensive stance came not from the ultra lefts, who had long been posturing about the imminence of revolution while actually abstaining from big struggles, but from Brandler. On 12 July, *Rote Fahne* carried a front page article by Brandler calling for the KPD to prepare for decisive action: 'We are on the verge of bitter struggles, we must be entirely ready to act.'[21] The same issue of the paper announced a national anti-fascist day of demonstrations a fortnight later. The offensive against the right would be unleashed, and this show of force could attract other workers, horrified by the fascist threat, to the Communists. However, the party proved reluctant to act. Brandler later wrote:

> This call had a peculiar effect on the party. In the working masses, it caused hope, but in the ranks of the party functionaries, they thought 'Brandler is deranged and will make a putsch again.' This was even the view of the left.[22]

The ruling class certainly understood the importance of the planned day of anti-fascist action. The Berlin city government, backed by the SPD, banned the proposed demonstrations, as did other local governments. But strikes escalated further, and workers flocked to the Proletarian Hundreds.

The KPD leadership, with the memory of the March Action still hanging over them, began to prevaricate. The Comintern was no help. With a revolutionary opportunity crystallising over the summer of 1923 – which, had it been taken in hand, would have transformed not just Germany but the future of the Russian Revolution – the Comintern Executive appeared not to take any notice. Not only did it call no emergency Congress, but the extended Executive meeting it did call in June did not advance any strategy to take the struggle forward. When the KPD leadership consulted the Comintern Executive about how to respond to the banning of the anti-fascist day of action planned for 29 July, things were not much better. Lenin was very sick, having suffered a stroke, and Trotsky, Zinoviev and Bukharin were all on holiday. Radek received the telegram and warned against a repeat of the March Action. Zinoviev and Bukharin urged the KPD to ignore the ban and proceed. Stalin disagreed. Trotsky admitted that he did not have enough knowledge of conditions in Germany to advise them. In the end, Radek telegraphed Brandler: 'We fear a trap.' Lacking the confidence to draw their own conclusions from the rapid shift to the left among workers, the KPD leaders called the action off three days ahead of the date, sacrificing an opportunity to test the party's strength and to build confidence in the party among layers of militants.

An August general strike brought social tensions to the boil. Economic conditions were going from bad to worse. Inflation was running at over 3,000 percent per month; workers needed wheelbarrows of cash just to buy a loaf of bread. The bosses were sacking hundreds of thousands of workers, which, far from demoralising them, only deepened their bitterness. Workers were taking to the streets, chanting slogans such as 'The exploiters to the gallows.' Simple strikes for a mark or two were now insufficient. A wage rise won one day would be wiped out by inflation the next. Increasingly, the options for workers were to abandon the wages struggle, or to go forward to revolution. Factory council delegates called a three-day general strike for 9 August, demanding the overthrow of the Cuno government and the formation of a workers' and peasants' government. Even SPD delegates supported the strike call. Workers marched from pit to pit and from factory to factory to rally fellow workers. Demonstrations took place across the country. If the KPD had moved onto the offensive a few weeks earlier rather than retreating from the anti-fascist day of action, it is possible that the general strike could have turned into a revolution. In the absence of such preparation, the bourgeoisie, supported by the SPD, was able to manoeuvre. The Cuno government fell; a new coalition government was patched up, this time with four SPD ministers. Its immediate effect was to take the sting out of the general strike, because workers hoped that the new government might address their plight. Attempts by the KPD to extend the strike were defeated.

The lost revolution: September–October 1923

Although the general strike ended after three days, and workers returned to work, the revolutionary crisis was far from over. The Weimar Republic tottered under the impact of French occupation of the Ruhr, hyperinflation, the rise of fascist forces and working class unrest. It had lost all credibility in the eyes of millions. In many respects, Germany in the late summer and autumn of 1923 was as ripe for revolution as Russia in October 1917, with the ruling class in a crisis and the working class alternating between despair at their condition and anger at the ruling class. The middle classes were joining the fascists but could have been pulled behind the workers' movement if the working class took decisive action.

The August general strike did not turn into a revolution, but it did awaken the Comintern Executive. The news of a developing revolutionary situation in Germany sparked hope among Russian workers that their isolation would finally end. Workers accepted pay cuts to provide funds for German workers, despite privations in Russia at the time, and volunteers were organised to go to Germany and fight in the International Brigades. The Russian leadership started to put pressure on the German leaders to act. But, underconfident as ever, the KPD sent its leaders to Moscow to confer with the Russian leaders – not for a few days, but for a full month – precisely when momentum was picking up at home. Sensing that time was critical and recalling the prevarication on the Bolshevik Central Committee in October 1917, Trotsky urged the KPD not to delay; they should set a date and prepare for an insurrection. Its duty was:

> to fix a definite time in the immediate future, a time in the course of which the favourable revolutionary situation cannot abruptly react against us, and then to concentrate every effort on the preparation of the blow, to subordinate the entire policy and organisation to the military object in view, so that this blow is dealt with maximum power.[23]

Zinoviev and Stalin disagreed with Trotsky about setting a date. Zinoviev prevaricated, not wanting to take decisive action unless the SPD could be convinced to join. Stalin agreed; it was better to wait for the fascists to attack first, because that would 'solidify the entire working class around the Communists.' Brandler backed them up but also invited Trotsky to Berlin to help the KPD prepare for an insurrection. Fearing that any success Trotsky might be responsible for would advantage him in the party leadership fight then unfolding in Russia, Zinoviev overrode Brandler's invitation. There was, however, agreement that the KPD should step up preparations for a revolution.

Technical and military preparations were made for an uprising, and the 60,000–100,000 workers in the Proletarian Hundreds prepared for battle. However, the necessary *political* changes were not made. The KPD leaders did not switch to campaigning politically for a rising. Rather, Communist work among the masses tended to be neglected in favour of conspiratorial technical preparations. Still, all that was needed was a spark.

On 26 September, the Imperial government announced harsh measures to control inflation. This hurt workers. Unemployment was beginning to bite, eating into workers' confidence to fight, and the ruling circles were regaining their confidence because the KPD had not taken the initiative over the summer.

Even now, it was not too late. The ruling class still had not reimposed its authority over workers. The KPD strongholds in Central Germany, the states of Saxony and Thuringia, were crucial to the coming battle. These states were run by left SPD governments, but the Proletarian Hundreds and control committees were the real power. The Imperial government resolved to smash workers' power in these states. The head of the army, General Müller, prepared his soldiers to enter Saxony. The KPD planned to use the army intervention as the basis for calling a general struggle and armed uprising. Revolutionaries around the country awaited the call.

With the situation on a knife edge, with the SPD doing its best to push back against working class militancy and to stabilise bourgeois rule, the Comintern instructed the KPD to enter the SPD governments in Saxony and Thuringia. Brandler opposed this but allowed himself to be overruled by the Russian leaders, accepting the post as head of the State Chancellery in Saxony at the invitation of SPD Premier Erich Zeigner. This was a profound mistake. Now was not the time for a defensive manoeuvre – entering a supposed 'workers' and peasants' government' – but an offensive. Joining these governments gave workers the impression that they could rely on *them* to mount a successful defence against Müller's troops, rather than relying on their own strength. The working class had not been given the opportunity to test its own power on the cancelled anti-fascist day of action, and the KPD entering the Central German governments only reinforced that passivity.

Zinoviev argued in defence of the tactic: by being in these governments, the KPD would have access to weapons held in police armouries. But the question of access to weapons was not a technical one – which party held the keys to the armoury – but a political one. Which party had won the loyalty of those who held the arms? Focusing on the police armouries only indicated the problem with the defensive orientation the KPD had maintained for far too long. What was required was many months of agitating in the armed forces to win over the soldiers, much as the Bolsheviks had done in 1917. On the eve of the October Revolution, the Provisional Government could hardly find one loyal regiment in Petrograd, allowing the Military Revolutionary Committee to overthrow the government with barely a shot fired. But in Germany six years later, the Imperial government could be much more confident that the soldiers would fire when ordered, because the KPD had undertaken no such preparatory work.

On Friday 21 October, General Müller ordered troops into Saxony to crush the Zeigner government. This was the final showdown, the ultimate test. Most workers were no longer prepared to engage in struggles for limited demands. The level of unemployment was such that employers found victimisation easy. Had the working class anger that had brought down the Cuno government grown into revolutionary determination? It could only be tested by action.

As Müller's troops were marching into Saxony, Brandler explained the party's plan to KPD representatives assembled in Chemnitz: to win support at a meeting of local workers' organisations the following day for an immediate general strike. The strike would form the backdrop for armed revolutionary units to execute an operation the KPD had been planning for weeks, seizing control of police stations, barracks, communication centres and railway stations. The insurrection would then begin.

On the following day, Saturday 22 October, with workers' militias patrolling the streets of Chemnitz, nearly 500 delegates from factory councils, union branches, control committees, the KPD and SPD met to decide on the general strike. After speeches by Saxon government ministers outlining the dire economic conditions, Brandler took the rostrum, declaring that the workers of Saxony must now call for assistance from the rest of Germany or face certain destruction at the hands of Müller's army. The only salvation lay in the immediate call for a national general strike of solidarity. Brandler expected the figure who followed him to the rostrum, Saxon Minister of Labour Georg Graupe, to confirm SPD support for the plan. Graupe, however, despite being on the SPD left, was very much a reformist. He was well aware that a general strike must be the precursor to civil war, which would pitch the workers' movement against the army. Graupe told the delegates that the SPD rejected the call for a general strike. The conference must not abrogate the government's powers. Defence of Saxony must rest in the hands of the SPD–KPD government. If a motion was moved for a general strike, Graupe declared, the SPD delegates would walk out.

Brandler and the other KPD leaders were shocked by Graupe's refusal. Their strategy had been premised on the SPD's willingness to join an uprising. Now, they believed that the whole project lay in ruins. They rapidly backtracked. Determined to maintain unity with the SPD, the KPD leaders refused to appeal over Graupe's head to SPD delegates and demand that they back the general strike. Instead, Brandler replaced his proposed motion for a general strike with one simply calling for the formation of an Action Committee to sound out the 'official movement.'

With no general strike in prospect, the KPD also called off the uprising. Müller's forces occupied the streets of Chemnitz unopposed. More disastrously, news of the cancellation of the insurrection did not reach the KPD in Hamburg until too late. They went ahead with the plan and were crushed: 21 were killed and hundreds wounded or taken prisoner. Several days later, the army arrested Zeigner and installed a right wing SPD premier. Only now did the left SPD agree to a general strike; but, with the earlier momentum gone, the strike was only modestly observed and far from the kind of resistance needed.

The collapse in Saxony spelled an end to hopes for a revolutionary outcome to the year of hunger. Not only was the state, the most powerful base of the revolutionary left, now occupied by the army; more importantly, there had been no coordinated resistance. The KPD, more than a quarter of a million strong and by far the largest Communist party in Europe, had abandoned the field of battle. Throughout Germany, millions of starving, desperate people had hoped that the Communists would provide an alternative to the misery they faced. Instead, the KPD declared itself impotent. Those who would have acquiesced with relief in a revolutionary seizure of power now acquiesced to military reaction.

The lessons of October

Numerous excuses were invented to cover up the failure in Germany. The KPD leadership justified its inaction in the late summer and autumn partly by fear of a repeat of the March Action. But the two episodes were as night and day: it was absurd to equate Germany in the crisis year of 1923 with that of the relative stability of 1921. In 1921, the ultra leftist current assumed that the SPD leadership could simply be brushed aside; in 1923, the KPD overestimated the strength of the SPD leaders and their influence among workers. There are never guarantees that a revolution will succeed, but the situation had become so fluid that only an offensive by the revolutionaries could reveal the real balance of forces. Without an attempt, defeat was certain.

Trotsky thought that the KPD leaders had made a terrible mistake in not pressing ahead in October. But, he argued, this was only a final expression of the fact that they had been lagging behind events throughout the summer. In *Lessons of October,* published in 1924, he wrote:

> Why didn't the German revolution lead to victory? The reasons for it are to be sought in tactics, not in the existing conditions. After all the German proletariat had gone through, it could be led to a decisive struggle only if it were convinced that this time the questions would be decisively resolved and that the Communist Party was ready for the struggle.[24]

The party executed the turn very irresolutely and after a long delay. The KPD leadership, both the Berlin ultra lefts and Brandler, viewed fatalistically the process of revolutionary development. It was a situation in which decisive leadership at the top of the party could tip the situation either way.

Those defending the KPD's hesitancy in October argued that the masses were not yet ripe for revolution and that Trotsky's proposals to set a date for the revolution were adventurism. However, blaming the masses for the failures of the leadership is a poor excuse, a means by which the role of revolutionary leadership is minimised and downplayed. Of course, there are whole historical periods where even the most far-seeing revolutionary leadership could have done absolutely nothing to drive forward the pace of events. But there are other periods when revolutionary leadership can make the decisive difference.

Trotsky drew a parallel with the situation in October 1917, when the Bolshevik Central Committee was faced with the question of going ahead with an insurrection. Zinoviev and Kamenev vacillated and argued against launching an insurrection, using arguments very similar to those used by the KPD six years later. Lenin, however, resting on the revolutionary sentiment of the masses and the worker rank and file of the party, had been able to turn around the Bolshevik Party with his *April Theses* and, in October, he compelled the leadership to decide on an insurrection.

The conservatism displayed by the KPD leaders in 1923 is inherent in any party. A right opposition had emerged in the Bolsheviks at every decisive turning point during the course of 1917. The inevitability of a conservative tendency does not, however, make it invincible. The Bolshevik Party had taken years of struggle, the 1905 Revolution, the period of reaction following that and the test of World War I to steel itself. Building the leadership and building the revolutionary party went hand in hand. A selected and tested leadership led workers to victory.

In Germany, the bitter five-year struggle which began with the November Revolution created several opportunities for a revolutionary breakthrough. But the KPD was not up to the task, and German workers were not able to settle accounts with the capitalists. Previous chapters have discussed the disastrous impact that the late formation of the KPD had in the November Revolution. Five years had now passed, but this factor still weighed on the party. Events repeatedly overtook the KPD leaders before they were able to develop their party into one capable of leading a revolution. They made a string of errors as a result of their inexperience, resulting in constant turnover in their ranks and exacerbating the effect of Luxemburg and Liebknecht's murders. KPD leaders repeatedly misjudged the situation confronting them, and they failed to strike decisively in 1923. Nor did the Berlin ultra lefts offer any alternative, shouting about revolution and warning constantly of betrayal while passively observing developments and spending more time sniping than intervening in the class struggle. Radek later described their role:

> Although they had criticised the leadership for 'dodging the armed struggle,' they had also failed to mobilise any class forces whatsoever…the opposition demanded revolution but was unsure of itself when the decisive moment arrived.[25]

These errors could have been overcome by a leadership which combined scientific stringency in assessing events with the ability to respond to sharp and sudden changes in the mood of the masses – the sort of response Lenin made in 1917. The clear lesson from Germany is that those who wish to lead workers at the height of struggle need to lay the foundations for such leadership long beforehand, on the basis of revolutionary clarity and organisation.

Russian domination?

Assessments of the failure of the German October raise the broader question of relations between the Comintern Executive and its various sections, a topic first broached in Chapter 2.[26] A common criticism of the Comintern, both in its early years and since, is that 'Russian dominance' was the source of many problems faced by the new revolutionary parties. Critics suggest that ham-fisted interference by the Comintern Executive in the local sections, offering instructions that had little to do with the class struggle in the country concerned, did much to destroy the revolutionary moment in Europe after World War I. For example, following the disaster of the March Action, Levi attacked not only the German leaders, but also the Comintern Executive for the fiasco. While it was clear to Levi that Comintern emissary Béla Kun had probably acted well outside his mandate from the Executive, Levi wrote that the Comintern was not blameless in the matter:

> The method of dispatching irresponsible people, who can later be approved or disavowed as need be, is certainly very convenient, but even if it was blessed by long party-tradition, it is fatal for the Third International.[27]

And, whatever the failing of the emissaries, Comintern leaders Zinoviev, Radek and Bukharin had all played a part in encouraging the madness of the March Action and bore some responsibility for the mishandled Italian split at the PSI's Livorno Congress as well.

Comintern errors cannot be the end of the story, however. Several additional points can be made. One is that an international leadership, distant from events, is incapable of understanding the dynamic in each individual country and is bound to make errors. The extremely limited means of communication available inevitably led to delays and misunderstandings. For this reason, an effective central leadership needs a strong and reliable local leadership on the ground that can both argue back, when directives from the centre are obviously wrong or misinformed, and provide an accurate picture of the actual situation. This applies even within a country, and it is still more the case with an international organisation.

It is also vital to see that the problems in the individual parties were not primarily the result of the intervention of the Comintern. The ultra lefts in the German party played a destructive role from the very first KPD Congress – before the Comintern even existed. Their errors in the Kapp Putsch were also nothing to do with the Comintern, which backed Levi, but were the result of their own political failings. The same is true in Italy. The errors of the PSI in 1920 during the strike wave happened *in spite of* the views of the Comintern. The leaders of the PSI – Serrati, who wanted to accommodate to the reformists, Bordiga, who opposed the councils from an ultra left standpoint and Gramsci, who was correct on many of the political arguments but would not fight for leadership of the party – reflected weaknesses in *Italian* socialism, not the International. The Comintern's errors came about in the course of trying to rectify these problems, but it did not cause them.

On many points, the Comintern played a crucial part in establishing, both practically and on the theoretical level, a strategic approach to building revolutionary organisations around the world. It established the need to fight for clearly revolutionary organisations, to build organisations that were not self-absorbed sects, but parties that would fight to win over the mass of workers in the course of common struggle. On a whole range of issues, from the national question and the question of state power to the approach to parliamentary elections, the Comintern in its early years played an enormously positive role.

Similarly, the fact that the emissaries of the Comintern Executive were often inadequate reflected the weaknesses not just of Russia, but of the international movement. The Comintern was politically starved of resources, lacking in authoritative leaders, and its policies and particularly their implementation suffered accordingly. The very fact that Zinoviev and Bukharin, two figures who had consistently misjudged the situation in Russia, were in charge of the Comintern is one indication of the problem. Had the situation at home been more favourable, the far more capable Lenin and Trotsky could have played more of a role in the affairs of the Comintern.

The authority of the Russians rested on their status as the only party that had carried out a successful revolution. Only revolution in a second country, led by a new mass organisation with its own independent leadership, could turn this situation around. Lenin and Trotsky themselves regarded Moscow's leadership of the Comintern as a temporary phenomenon and eagerly anticipated the Executive's relocation to Paris or Berlin following a French or German workers' revolution. In the meantime, what was the alternative to 'Russian domination'? To refuse to try to generalise the lessons from the Russian Revolution internationally – a revolution that had succeeded when all others had so far failed?

While Luxemburg believed that the lack of mass organisations at the time of its declaration made the formation of the Comintern premature, the KPD could never have turned itself into a genuinely mass party without the Comintern. It is true that Levi – along with the Comintern leaders – had the correct view that a fusion with the left wing of the USPD was essential if the party was to go forward. But if it had been left to the KPD, this would not have happened. The fusion that did take place after the Comintern's Second Congress in 1920 was driven by the USPD left's respect for the Russian Revolution and desire to be part of the Third International, not by the tiny and often ultra left KPD. Zetkin observed that people made up their minds at the USPD's Halle Congress 'for or against Moscow.'

The flow of ideas was not just one way. Some of the tactics necessary for Communists in the West – like the united front – were assisted by direct experience in the Western countries. For example, Radek said that the Open Letter tactic conceived by him and Levi in Germany in 1920, one of the first instances of the united front tactic, would not have occurred to him if he had been in Moscow at the time. On the other hand, the experience of the Russian Revolution, in particular the Kornilov coup, prefigured the method of the united front that was to be developed in the following years. On all of the key problems of the revolution in the West – the role of workers' councils, parliamentarianism, the hold of reformism – the policies developed by the Russian leaders of the Comintern played a crucial role in correctly orienting the Communist parties across Europe.

It is undeniable that the Comintern in its early years made many mistakes. But the problems of the International were basically problems with the weakness of the revolutionary movement in Germany, Italy, France and elsewhere. The key problem, and the reason that capitalism survived the turmoil of the postwar years, was that there were not mass communist parties whose leaderships were up to the task of leading revolutions in Western Europe.

The Comintern attempted to overcome this problem. In the final analysis, it failed. But it certainly did not make the situation worse; it helped to build mass parties that posed the greatest threat to capitalist rule in its history. Its general orientation exerted a clearly revolutionary influence on socialists around the world.

FURTHER READING

P. Broué, *The German Revolution 1917–1923*, Chicago, Haymarket Books, 2006.

C. Harman, *The Lost Revolution: Germany 1918 to 1923*, London, Bookmarks, 1982.

J. Riddell, 'The origins of the united front policy', *International Socialism*, no. 130, 2011.

J. Riddell (ed.), *To the Masses: Proceedings of the Third Congress of the Communist International, 1921*, Chicago, Haymarket Books, 2015.

L. Trotsky, 'On the United Front', 1922.

THE DEGENERATION OF THE INTERNATIONAL

1923 to 1928

5.

COUNTER-REVOLUTION IN RUSSIA

The Russian Revolution affirms workers' ability to rise up, create their own organs of power and overthrow the capitalist state. Its very existence gives heart to workers and reproaches those who argue that capitalism is the best system and that there is no alternative.

But the Russian Revolution did not survive. The attacks on it started on the day of its birth and intensified. Within a few short years. its democratic, revolutionary content had been severely curtailed. By the end of the 1920s, it had been definitively destroyed. Joseph Stalin emerged as a new dictator, more fearsome even than the monarchy that the workers had toppled in 1917.[1]

The enemies of the Russian Revolution invariably seize upon its defeat and the rise of Stalin as proof that revolutions give way to dictatorships; better to accept the status quo than embark on a project that will only end up in the repression of the population under a totalitarian dictatorship. Commonly, explanations for the defeat of the revolution blame some feature of human nature: that people are incapable of running things democratically and collectively or that they naturally yearn for strong leaders. In this view, there is no break in the 1920s between revolution and counter-revolution, only a seamless process, with Lenin just the same as Stalin. More sophisticated hostile accounts recognise that a break of some kind occurred after Lenin's death but argue that Stalinism was simply the natural outcome of Leninism. This amalgamation of revolution and counter-revolution mystifies and distorts the real history of struggle that took place.

Often, those who promote these narratives do their best to hide the responsibility of their own political traditions for the rise of Stalinism. It was the social democratic parties – whose ideologues make much of the failure of the Russian Revolution in order to promote their own gradualist approach

– which suppressed the revolutionary uprisings in Europe. They were, therefore, responsible for the isolation of the Russian Revolution, which formed the context for the triumph of Stalinism.

This chapter traces the complex interplay of class struggle, changing economic conditions and imperialist pressures that brought about Stalin's rise to power. The triumph of the dictatorship had nothing to do with human nature, or with Stalin driving Lenin's politics to their natural conclusion. It was the absolute antithesis of the project that Lenin and his comrades had carried through in 1917.

Revolution under siege

Within months of the revolution's victory, the infant workers' state was under attack from all sides. The German High Command saw the collapse of the old Russian army as an opportunity to seize more territory. When the German army advanced on Petrograd, the Communists were forced to sign the humiliating Brest-Litovsk Treaty in March 1918 – sacrificing enormous amounts of money, supplies and territory. The collapse of the German Imperial state during the November Revolution rendered the treaty null and void, ending one threat. But Russian landlords, capitalists and generals – the counter-revolutionary force known as the Whites – were raising armies to overthrow the new government in Moscow, helped by foreign intervention. At its peak, the armies of 14 foreign powers, including Australian troops, invaded Russia to assist the Whites. Hostile governments provided substantial amounts of weapons to the counter-revolutionary forces, while the Red Army was forced to rely on weapons inherited from the Tsar's armies and those it captured. By the latter half of 1919, only one-fifth of European Russia was in the hands of the Communists. The foreign blockade cut off many of Russia's trade links, exacerbating the economic collapse.

Over the course of several campaigns, the Red Army beat back the Whites. The generals and the landlords and capitalists who backed them may have had superior weapons at their disposal and the help of foreign armies, but they promised only a return to Tsarist era repression and servitude. In most cases, they received little support from the local populations. However, no sooner were the Whites defeated than Poland, with the encouragement of the Allies, invaded the Ukraine in the spring of 1920. Six more months of bloody fighting took place.

By the end of 1920, Communists had defeated the counter-revolutionary forces, but victory came at a tremendous cost. Industry was in a ramshackle state. Factory production had declined to 13 percent of its 1913 level. Conditions of life in the cities were diabolical, the population was close to starving, and diseases ran unchecked. Desperate workers were forced to steal from their factories to buy food. It was impossible to build socialism in conditions of such poverty, as Marx had explained in *The German Ideology*:

> This development of the productive forces is an absolutely necessary practical premise [of communism], because without it want is generalised, and with want the struggle for necessities begins again, and that means that all the old crap must revive.[2]

By 1921, the Russian working class was unrecognisable, compared to the time of the October Revolution. The most militant and politically conscious workers had left the factories to fight against the Whites or to work for the new government. Hundreds of thousands of other workers fled the towns for the country in search of food. The citadels of the revolution were hardest hit. By 1921, only 50,000 of the 400,000 who had been employed in Petrograd's factories in 1917 were still at work, and the city's population fell from 2.3 million to 740,000.[3] In Moscow, the population fell by more than half. People forced to scavenge for a living were in no position to participate in political life. Lenin told the Tenth Party Congress in 1921:

> The industrial proletariat...owing to the war and to the desperate poverty and ruin, has become declassed...dislodged from its class groove and has ceased to exist as a proletariat... It has sometimes figured in statistics, but it has not held together economically.[4]

This was a dire threat to the survival of a revolution that had depended on mass worker participation in running society.

Within 12 months of the revolution, the Communist Party had established a virtual monopoly of political power. This was not because of any totalitarian instinct but because, one by one, the parties who opposed them passed over to the camp of armed counter-revolution. There could be no question of the Whites and their open supporters, the Cadets, having the freedom to organise in the areas still held by the Reds. The right SRs joined the counter-revolutionary forces within days of October and were indistinguishable from the Cadets during the Civil War, while many Mensheviks also came out in opposition to the Communist government. In response, the Communist-dominated central executive of the soviets excluded Mensheviks and right wing SRs from the soviets and instructed local bodies to do the same. The left SRs broke with the Government in March 1918 in response to the signing of the Brest-Litovsk Treaty and then attempted to launch a coup against it, mounting a wave of attacks on Communist leaders, killing several and seriously wounding Lenin. In August, the left SRs shot the German ambassador in Moscow in the hope of provoking a fresh war with Germany, something that could only have brought new disasters to the infant workers' state. They too were excluded from the soviets, although it is worth noting that, during the next 18 months, opposition parties, including the Mensheviks and right SRs, were occasionally reinstated and allowed to have their representatives elected to soviet bodies.

With the party holding a monopoly of power, the separation of party and state became unrealisable. Political life in the soviets dried up. Quite soon, the party branch secretary in each region had replaced the leader of the soviet as the leading official. At the Sixth All-Russian Congress of the Soviets in November 1918, 933 of the 950 delegates were members of the Communist Party. The fact that the country was now a one-party state raised the potential, Lenin believed, for representatives of hostile class forces to enter the party. This view led to the banning of factions at the Tenth Party Congress in March 1921.

In the factories, the government instituted 'one man management' and placed restrictions on strikes in an attempt to revive production. In rural areas, it was forced to rely on compulsory grain requisitioning, because the abolition of money that went with the introduction of emergency measures known as War Communism and the absence of any agricultural or consumer goods meant that the peasants were not prepared to trade their grain voluntarily. With many of the best party cadres diverted to the Civil War or other duties, the Communist government had to rely on officials, industrial managers and technical experts from the Tsarist era – with few sympathies for communism – to run the administrative machinery and the factories.

There is no dispute that the situation by 1921 was far removed from the Bolsheviks' initial plans and far from a model for socialism. Nor did Lenin and his comrades deceive themselves otherwise: they believed that they were conducting a desperate holding operation until relief came from a revolution abroad.

The Bolsheviks had taken the gamble of leading a revolution in the expectation that it would trigger successful revolutions across Europe. In particular, they saw Germany as the key to the situation: a successful revolution in Germany, with its wealth and industry, could alleviate the crushing poverty that gripped Soviet Russia. Russia had grain supplies, oil and other foodstuffs;

the Russian workers' state could trade these for the agricultural equipment, fertilisers and railway locomotives that the German workers' state, with its heavy industry, could produce in abundance. A German revolution would add materially, but it would also shift the whole centre of the European revolution from its eastern fringes into the heartland. If German workers had seized power, which country would be next? Unfortunately, as Chapter 4 explained, the German workers did not win power. The result was that the Russian Communist Party was forced to act as the revolutionary agency, something that could only succeed for a short period before degeneration set in. In the absence of working class democracy, the revolution could not survive.

A further problem was that the party itself was changing as a result of its new status as the supreme authority in the land. Two trends were obvious. Firstly, many Communists who had been revolutionary agitators in the factories in 1917 were drafted into the state apparatus and managerial positions in the factories as party officials and as Red Army officers. Following a decision in 1922 to abolish the old Communist provision that such appointees be paid no more than skilled workers, they enjoyed superior pay and conditions; this inevitably made their outlook more conservative over time.

Secondly, the party was flooded with new recruits of sometimes dubious quality. Membership rose from 250,000 in October 1917 to 730,000 by March 1921. Many arrived enthused by the revolution and a desire to build a new social order, but many thousands joined for careerist reasons: party membership offered the prospect of privileged jobs in the emerging bureaucracy. The core of members who had withstood Tsarist repression and been tested by the fires of 1917 became a shrinking minority. By 1922, only 15 percent of Petrograd party members had joined before the October Revolution. Less than one-quarter of the Bolshevik delegates to the Petrograd Soviet in 1920 had joined before October. Only on the Petrograd Soviet executive was there any continuity of the revolutionary cadres: 90 percent had been members prior to October.[5] There was, therefore, a gap not only between party and class, but between leaders and members within the party. This had serious consequences for the health of the party. Lenin told the Eleventh Party Congress in March 1922:

> If we do not close our eyes to reality, we must admit that at the present time the proletarian policy of the Party is not determined by the character of its membership, but by the enormous undivided prestige enjoyed by the small group which might be called the Old Guard of the Party.[6]

The defeat of the Whites and the foreign invaders brought relief to the Communist government but also new problems. The very success of the Communist program of land redistribution had dramatically reduced the number of landless peasants and rural labourers and also the number of very wealthy peasants, creating the conditions for a united front of the peasantry against compulsory grain requisitions. Once the threat of the landlords' return was removed by the Communist victory in the Civil War, dissatisfied peasants took up arms against the government. In the summer of 1920, peasants in the Tambov governorate rebelled against compulsory grain requisitions. This triggered a savage conflict between rebel peasant forces, led by the former SR, Aleksandr Antonov, and the Communist authorities and their supporters. Only after a year and tens of thousands of deaths was the rebellion quashed.

Peasant discontent also made itself felt in the cities. In February, strikes broke out in Petrograd. In March, sailors at the Kronstadt military base rose against the Communists, demanding 'soviets without parties.' The base, situated on the Neva River at the gateway to Petrograd, was critically important. Whoever controlled Kronstadt controlled Petrograd. The Kronstadt sailors of 1917, who had been a centre of revolutionary zeal and a strong base for the Bolsheviks, had left the garrison and gone to fight the Whites. Their replacements were new sailors, recently torn from the countryside, who had not been shaped by the experience of participating in the October Revolution. Their demands reflected their peasant origins: an end to grain seizures and the introduction of free trade in grain. Some of their demands represented real grievances that merited serious consideration.

The majority of Kronstadt sailors were by no means intent on bringing back the Whites. The Communist negotiating team certainly handled the situation badly. But, regardless of the intentions of many sailors, the success of their demand for 'soviets without parties' would have meant the collapse of the Communist government and a contest for power among its opponents. This would have led to a quick return of the Whites. The Whites certainly recognised their opportunity and channelled funds to the Kronstadt rebels. Facing the loss of the fortress and, with it, Petrograd, the Communist government sent the Red Army to storm it, resulting in many deaths.

Tambov and Kronstadt demonstrated that urgent measures were needed to address peasant grievances if the workers' state was to survive. The Tenth Party Congress, held at the very time that the Red Army launched its offensive on Kronstadt, was the occasion for a sharp change of policy. Lenin spelled out what was necessary if they were to go on to build socialism:

> Here industrial workers are in a minority, and the petty farmers are the vast majority. In such a country, the socialist revolution can triumph only on two conditions. First, if it is given timely support by a socialist revolution in one or several advanced countries... The second condition is agreement between the proletariat, which is exercising its dictatorship, that is, holds state power, and the majority of the peasant population.[7]

With these two issues in mind, the Congress introduced the New Economic Policy (NEP), ending grain requisitioning. Instead, peasants would be taxed and free to use whatever profits they could make. This effective reintroduction of the market pacified the peasants. The economy began to recover from its devastated situation in 1921. Grain began to flow into the cities, and manufacturing began to revive. The number of workers employed in large scale industry grew from 1.1 million in 1922 to 2.5 million by 1928, finally reaching the same figure as in 1917.

The NEP created something of a breathing space but could not halt the rise of a new state bureaucracy. This required the first of Lenin's conditions: an international revolution. The failure of the German Revolution in 1923 was a crushing blow to the Communists hanging on in Russia. Existing problems festered and grew more dangerous. The absence of a successful workers' revolution elsewhere in Europe ensured the defeat of the Russian Revolution. Rather than being overthrown from outside, the Revolution was destroyed from within – by the processes set in train by its isolation.

The NEP stabilised the economy and prevented further eruptions of peasant protest, but it also created opportunities for growing class differentiation. Opening up trade and commerce allowed the richer peasants (known as kulaks) and businesspeople in the city (soon dubbed NEPmen) the chance to make fortunes; but poverty was still widespread. Inequality soared in these years, and social ills such as prostitution and begging multiplied.

By the mid-1920s, the Revolution faced pressure on every side. The result was what Trotsky later called 'a long period of weariness, decline and sheer disappointment in the results of the revolution.' Those who had made the Revolution and survived the Civil War began to look for a quiet life, as did many who had joined the party since. As the spirit of self-sacrifice that had made victory possible subsided, 'pusillanimity and careerism' took its place.[8] Leading Communists began to make a virtue of the temporary measures limiting democracy that had been introduced in the desperate times of the Civil War and its immediate aftermath. This was the context in which Stalin was able to rise to power.

The troika emerges

Joseph Stalin joined the Bolsheviks in 1901 and served as a member of the Central Committee from 1912. In March 1917, as editor of *Pravda*, he was among the most prominent Bolsheviks to offer support for the Provisional Government. In the October insurrection in Petrograd, he barely figured. During the Civil War, he was assigned oversight of several military campaigns that led to large losses of Red Army soldiers. It was his election as general secretary at the Eleventh Party Congress in March 1922 that marked his emergence as a party leader of the first rank. From this position, he could directly influence the composition of party congresses, because appointment of delegates had replaced election by this stage. He was also able to use this post to reward favourites by assigning them plum posts and to punish opponents by sending them to remote regions far from the centre of power.

Although Lenin had supported Stalin's election as general secretary, he soon grew concerned by his high-handed treatment of his party comrades, including his 'Great Russian' chauvinism towards the Georgian Communists. Although he was of Georgian background himself, Stalin's arrogant behaviour towards the Georgian party members indicated his absorption of Tsarist colonial attitudes to the national minorities.

By the autumn of 1922, Lenin had decided that Stalin must be opposed. His ability to halt Stalin's rise to power was, however, seriously impeded by his own declining health: he suffered two strokes in that year which severely limited his political activities. Despite his diminished capacity for political combat, Lenin approached Trotsky in October 1922 to form a bloc to fight bureaucratic tendencies in both state and party, and, by the end of the year, had broken off personal relations with Stalin. Lenin now dictated a note calling for Stalin's removal as general secretary and began to prepare an offensive against him at the forthcoming Twelfth Party Congress. Lenin handed the note, known as his 'Testament,' to his comrade and partner Nadezhda Krupskaya and asked for it to be read out at the Congress.

Stalin, however, was busy building support within the Central Committee, forming a secret bloc – the 'troika' – with Zinoviev and Kamenev. The only common interest the three shared lay in blocking Leon Trotsky's rise to leadership on Lenin's death.

Trotsky stood second only to Lenin in the party. He had been one of the 1917 Revolution's chief propagandists and had led the Military Revolutionary Committee which carried out the October insurrection. He was then appointed Commissar for Foreign Affairs and negotiated the Treaty of Brest-Litovsk. Then, as Commissar for Military Affairs, Trotsky led the Red Army with distinction during the Civil War. Individually, none of the troika could match Trotsky for popularity within the party; collectively, they were a power. Zinoviev, with a strong base in Petrograd,[9] and Kamenev, with support in Moscow, believed that they could use Stalin as a prop for their own ambitions, not realising that it was they who would be used by Stalin.

Lenin's Testament gave Krupskaya and Trotsky a big opportunity to push back against Stalin at the Twelfth Party Congress. This took place in April 1923, one month after Lenin suffered a third stroke that removed him from any political activity. However, Krupskaya and Trotsky ducked the challenge at the Congress. Neither of them even revealed the existence of the Testament to delegates. Trotsky further failed to attack the bureaucratisation of the party, as Lenin had requested. He reprimanded his supporters who attacked the troika and left it to Bukharin and Christian Rakovsky to take up the fight against Great Russian chauvinism within the party.

Trotsky's unwillingness to confront the threat posed by the troika can be put down to three factors. The first was his lack of confidence in his authority in the party. Between the 1905 Revolution, when he first emerged as a significant figure as Petrograd Soviet president, and August 1917, when he joined the Bolsheviks, Trotsky had frequently sparred with Lenin. Lenin had accused Trotsky of trying to paper over the differences between the Mensheviks and Bolsheviks, preventing the necessary revolutionary clarification. In 1920–21, disputes between the two broke out again when Trotsky proposed that trade unions be absorbed by the state. The troika seized on Lenin's criticisms of Trotsky to undermine his credibility. Launching a fight against the troika while Lenin was still alive, a step that would only have been seen as a bid for leadership by Trotsky, would have magnified these criticisms tenfold.

Secondly, Trotsky did not appreciate the magnitude of the threat posed by Stalin, regarding him as a mediocre nonentity; in his view, Zinoviev was the main threat and the subject of his criticisms at the Twelfth Congress.

The most important factor, and something that would hamper Trotsky in the fight over the following years, was his belief that the main threat to the revolution came from foreign invasion or capitalist restoration through the NEPmen and kulaks. He did not fully understand that the revolution would ultimately be destroyed by forces internal to the party itself, in the bureaucracy of the party-state that looked to Stalin for leadership.

Stalin took advantage of Trotsky's reluctance to fight. He stacked the Congress with his supporters and had his supporters elected to numerous important positions. Trotsky was comprehensively outmanoeuvred, and only three of his allies were elected to the Central Committee: Rakovsky, Radek and Georgy Piatakov.

The summer of 1923 saw an upsurge of working class struggle in Russia. This was reflected inside the party in the formation of the 'Workers Group.' In October, prominent members of the party published the 'Statement of the 46,' demanding more party democracy, including an end to the ban on factions, as well as industrial planning to restore the economy and rebuild the working class. Trotsky, however, would not sign the Statement, not wanting to be accused of factionalising, even while he was gathering supporters around him as the head of a new Left Opposition. The troika was able to snuff out the challenge from the 46 by making some minor compromises while not giving ground on anything significant. The defeat in Germany in October signalled that a revival of revolutionary wave across Europe was no longer in sight, and this too helped the troika as representatives of 'stability.'

In late 1923, Trotsky came out more openly in opposition to the troika in a series of articles published in *Pravda*, known as *The New Course*. In these, Trotsky vigorously attacked bureaucratisation of the party and pushed for a renewal of party democracy, arguing that, unless this was done, the party and the revolution itself were at risk of degeneration. He also demanded, as a counterweight to the growing influence of private trade in agriculture, a more systematic approach to state planning and state industry 'as the keystone of the dictatorship of the proletariat and the basis of socialism.'[10]

Trotsky published *The New Course* as an intervention into the debate at the Thirteenth Party Conference in January 1924. Unfortunately, Trotsky was too sick to attend the conference. A supporter, the brilliant economist Yevgeny Preobrazhensky, led the charge for the Opposition, using the 'Statement of the 46' as a manifesto for reform. But, by now, opposition to the troika had been weakened and the demands for party reform were heavily defeated.

Lenin's death on 21 January 1924 left the way clear for Stalin and Zinoviev to launch a campaign against Trotsky. They attacked Trotsky for his supposed 'underestimation of the peasantry' as a revolutionary force and 'lack of faith in the leaders of Bolshevism,' especially Lenin. All were different ways of presenting Trotsky as hostile to Bolshevism and the Russian Revolution. To 'Trotskyism,' the troika counterposed 'Leninism,' another invented term never recognised by Lenin in his lifetime and whose meaning was defined by the troika as whatever would help them to beat their opponents.

The troika used Lenin's death to undertake a mass recruitment campaign, the 'Lenin Levy' – 250,000 mostly raw and inexperienced new members whom the troika mobilised to strengthen their hand. The result of this campaign and other manoeuvres was that, at the Thirteenth Party Congress in May, Trotsky had only one ally, Preobrazhensky, in a conference of over 1,000.

Zinoviev carried the fight against 'Trotskyism' into the Fifth Comintern Congress in June–July 1924. Zinoviev's main goal was to defeat Trotsky's supporters. The troika had reasons to worry. In January, the Polish Communist Party Central Committee had signed a statement in defence of Trotsky; his name, they declared, 'was indissolubly bound up with the victorious October revolution, with the Red Army, with communism and the world revolution.' Sections of the French and German parties also registered protests against attacks on Trotsky.

In the period leading up to the Fifth Congress, Comintern chairman Zinoviev rallied his supporters. He used the ultra left trio of Fischer, Maslow and Scholem. to throw Brandler and his supporters out of the KPD leadership and, by the time the Congress opened, Zinoviev had most delegates in his pocket. The German, French, British and US parties announced their wholehearted support for the Russian leadership. They argued that the opposition, consciously or not, was acting not only against the Russian Central Committee but:

> by imperilling the dictatorship of the proletariat in the union of Soviet Republics and by weakening the Russian Communist Party, which alone is capable of maintaining this dictatorship, it attacked the legacy of Lenin which is dear to every communist throughout the world.

The Fifth Congress resolved that supporters of the Russian opposition were 'a right-opportunist deviation,' while the platform of the opposition was 'petty bourgeois.'[11]

Zinoviev's attack on 'Trotskyism' at the Fifth Congress went hand in hand with 'Bolshevisation,' a term invented by Zinoviev which had at its heart a policy of stamping out democracy and imposing a monolithic, repressive political culture in the Comintern's sections. 'Bolshevisation' meant that the Comintern was henceforth to be, said Zinoviev: 'a strongly cemented, monolithic, centralised organisation which in a friendly and brotherly manner eradicates all differences in its ranks.'[12] This was more aspiration than reality, since debates continued to rage within the various national sections for several more years, but it showed that the troika was willing to impose a parody of 'Leninism' on the Comintern. As time went on, successive purges of Comintern parties rendered them steadily less capable of developing leadership within their own ranks. Submission to Moscow and unquestioning acceptance of its policy twists and turns became the key to advancement.

Zinoviev also used the Fifth Congress to engineer a 'left' shift in the Comintern, driven by his desire to avoid responsibility for the failure of the German October. He now promoted the idea of a 'united front from below,' meaning rallying Communists, social democratic and other workers under Communist party leadership. This was a fundamental distortion of the united front tactic. As Trotsky had explained in his 1922 statement on the united front, if Communists could win over social democratic workers by a direct appeal, there was no need for a united front. If that was not the case, however, the appeal for joint action must instead be directed to the reformist leaders, not the rank and file.

As part of the shift to the 'left,' Zinoviev also introduced a concept that was to have devastating consequences for the Comintern in later years – that social democracy was simply the twin of fascism:

> That is why it is historically incorrect to talk of a 'victory of fascism over social democracy.' So far as the leading strata are concerned, fascism and social democracy are the right and left hands of modern capitalism.[13]

Following the Fifth Congress, the newly installed KPD ultra left leaders set about witch-hunting alleged 'Trotskyists' in the party. Because there were so few of them, they had to invent another crime of 'Luxemburgism,' supposedly the fetishisation of spontaneity and hostility to party building. They used it to eliminate members who would not buckle down and support the line coming from Moscow. But those whom Moscow could raise up, they could also tear down. Just 15 months after being installed as KPD leaders, Fischer and Maslow were replaced. They had served their purpose in eliminating Brandler, but they also had an independent base of support in the KPD. Their replacement, Ernst Thälmann, owed his position entirely to Moscow and, unlike Fischer and Maslow who were genuine ultra lefts, the new leader could be trusted to swing either to the left or right – depending on Moscow's requirements.

A similar shift was imposed on the French PCF. Albert Treint, a discredited former leader, hoisted himself back into his position with the help of Zinoviev, simply by wielding the accusation of 'Trotskyism' against his opponents. The outcome was devastating. Treint expelled prominent leaders Rosmer, Monatte, Boris Souvarine and others. In the reorganisation that followed, almost three-quarters of the party left, replaced by malleable political novices.

Zinoviev's 'Bolshevisation' gradually squeezed the democratic spirit out of the Comintern. It was a way station to the triumph of Stalin, who took it over and used the Comintern as an organ of Russian foreign policy responsible to the needs of the new Russian ruling class, not those of the international working class and world revolution.

The troika splits

The counter-revolution took another step in December 1924, when Stalin announced that the Communist Party's new project was to build 'socialism in one country.' This was not a call to hold on until the international revolution came to Russia's rescue, but a reactionary, anti-Marxist utopia. It required the party to renounce the idea that the fate of the revolution in Russia depended on the victory of revolutions in the West. It represented a complete reversal of longstanding party policy of internationalism and opposition to national chauvinism and formed the foundation stone for the ideology of the rising bureaucracy.

Despite the fact that it ran directly contrary to Marxism, socialism in one country was quickly embraced by the Russian party. It appealed to the broad layers of lower and middle bureaucrats wary of the renewal of international revolution for fear of what it might do their own positions. It also fitted the mood of many workers looking for stability after years of turmoil.

'Socialism in one country' split the troika. Zinoviev and Kamenev retained enough of their revolutionary principles to understand that it represented rejection of all they had fought for. They broke with Stalin towards the end of 1925. While they continued to polemicise against Trotsky, they adopted much of the content of Trotsky's *The New Course* as a weapon in the fight against their former factional ally. 'Socialism in one country' may have lost Stalin the support of Zinoviev and Kamenev, but it won him Bukharin's loyalty. The former ultra left in the period 1918 to 1921, an advocate of revolutionary war to spread the revolution into the heart of Europe, had by the mid-1920s swung to the right. Socialism would only come 'at a snail's pace,' Bukharin now declared, and his message to the peasants and NEPmen was: 'Enrich yourself!'

The new lines of division in the leadership became obvious at the Fourteenth Party Congress in December 1925. Zinoviev and Kamenev demanded curbs on the kulaks, a more aggressive campaign of industrialisation and state planning, renunciation of the policy of socialism in one country and publication of Lenin's Testament. Trotsky, not for the first time, refused to seize the opportunity presented by the split in the troika to advance his arguments. In his eyes, it was all just a squabble among his enemies. He thereby granted Stalin and Bukharin total victory, with only Zinoviev's base in the former Petrograd – now renamed Leningrad – voting in his support. This was the last party congress where the party leadership faced open opposition. Henceforth, nothing but unquestioning loyalty was accepted.

Stalin now used the same punitive methods he had used against Trotsky to destroy his former allies. Zinoviev was forced from his position as leader of the Leningrad party apparatus by Stalin. Again, Trotsky stayed silent, failing to understand the significance of the struggle between the former allies.

In the spring of 1926, Zinoviev and Kamenev joined forces with Trotsky and his supporters in the Left Opposition to form the United Opposition. The new Opposition published a declaration signed by 13 Central Committee members, including Lenin's widow Krupskaya, Preobrazhensky and Piatakov. It identified the Opposition as that of the Bolshevik left, defending the interests of workers against the kulaks, NEPmen and bureaucracy. It demanded more democracy, increased wages for workers, higher taxation on the rich peasants and NEPmen, and more rapid industrialisation to build the working class and alleviate material hardship.

The Stalin–Bukharin Central Committee majority rejected all the United Opposition's demands. The Opposition was now forced to take the fight to the broader party. It made little headway, however, because of the situation at home and abroad. Calls to revive the revolution appeared out of kilter with the reality of capitalist stabilisation, and the mass of Russian workers were indifferent to the United Opposition's calls for change. In Leningrad, where Zinoviev could once have mobilised thousands of party members in his support, just a few hundred now backed their former leader. Where the Opposition tried to hold meetings, Stalin sent supporters to break them up. In October 1926, with Zinoviev leading the retreat, the United Opposition was forced to suspend its campaign. Fearing the breakup of the United Opposition, Trotsky went along with this decision.

Things moved quickly thereafter. On 18 October 1926, the *New York Times* published Lenin's Testament. Stalin and Bukharin accused the United Opposition of sanctioning its publication. Trotsky now mounted his most strident attack on Stalin, condemning the general secretary as 'the gravedigger of the revolution.' He was immediately removed from the Political Bureau, followed soon after by Zinoviev and Kamenev. At the Fifteenth Party Conference at the end of October 1926, the Opposition was routed and suffered defections to Stalin – including that of Krupskaya. In November, Zinoviev was replaced as chair of the Comintern by Bukharin. The Comintern

Executive endorsed the offensive against the United Opposition and approved the expulsion of Zinoviev and Trotsky's supporters from the international Communist movement.

While most of his fellow Oppositionists, fearing expulsion, kept their heads down following the Fifteenth Party Conference, Trotsky was convinced that a fight to the finish with Stalin was necessary in order to save the Russian party. He was confronted by the exhaustion of older comrades and a barrier of bewilderment, if not hostility, from the younger party members who did not comprehend the issues at stake. Developments in China in the first half of 1927 broke the logjam. Stalin and his envoys had instructed the Chinese Communist Party to tail Chiang Kai-shek's bourgeois Nationalists in the fight to rid the country of imperialist domination (Chapter 7). The Chinese Communists opposed this instruction but acquiesced under protest. Chiang demonstrated that the local Communists were right to have resisted when he repaid their loyalty by massacring thousands. The United Opposition revived and declared that Stalin's incorrect policies in China were connected to the degeneration of the Revolution at home. But, at this very moment, the British Government broke off relations with Russia, and Stalin used the threat of a British attack on Russia to crack down on the Opposition. Hundreds were arrested, and repression continued throughout the summer.

In preparation for the forthcoming Fifteenth Party Congress, the United Opposition drafted a platform which followed in many respects the lines of Trotsky's *New Course* and the 'Statement of the 46' but was more comprehensive than the earlier documents and much more critical of the party bureaucracy. It called for the restoration of party democracy and championed the cause of the working class against the kulaks, the NEPmen and the party bureaucracy. Concrete proposals included an increase in wages, freedom to negotiate wages through free trade unions, heavier taxation on the middle and rich peasants and NEPmen, voluntary collectivisation of the farms assisted by state credits and mechanisation, faster industrialisation and introduction of rigorous economic planning.

For several weeks in the run-up to the Fifteenth Party Congress, the Opposition organised meetings in Moscow and Leningrad to build support for their platform. Twenty thousand members attended such meetings to hear the Opposition's case. Support for the Opposition was reported not only in the biggest cities but also in regional centres in the Ukraine and Siberia, as well as in the universities and central government offices and among officers in the Red Army who had served under Trotsky and remained loyal to their former commander.

To rally their supporters, the Opposition called for independent contingents on the official commemorative demonstration to mark the tenth anniversary of the October Revolution. Stalin caught wind of the plan and raided the homes of prominent Oppositionists, scaring many away from their cause. The result was that the processions led by Trotsky and Zinoviev in Moscow and Leningrad were only of modest size and were attacked by police and right wing thugs. One week later, in the last display of public opposition to Stalin's counter-revolution, 10,000 Opposition supporters attended the funeral of Trotsky's ally Adolf Joffe, who had committed suicide in protest at Trotsky's expulsion and the counter-revolution now gathering pace.

The main problem the Opposition faced was that, while Stalin and Bukharin only aroused the enthusiasm of a minority of the party, that was also true for themselves. Most members were passive. In these circumstances, Stalin was destined to win. Ten thousand party members voted with the Opposition on the eve of the Fifteenth Congress in December, but this was a tiny number compared with the total membership of more than 700,000. The result was that the United Opposition was not able to count on the support of a single one of the 1,600 delegates who attended the party Congress. Nonetheless, Stalin was still vulnerable. As the Congress met, significant domestic unrest among peasants and workers was apparent. If Stalin did not root out the Opposition, they might emerge as leaders of this unrest. The Stalin-Bukharin axis therefore engineered the expulsion of 75 leading Oppositionists at the Congress, on top of other oppositionists already expelled or imprisoned. The United Opposition, always an unstable combination, broke apart. Trotsky and many of his followers refused to abandon their principles. Mass arrests took place and Trotsky was exiled, initially to Central Asia and then to Turkey. The majority of Oppositionists, however, including Zinoviev and Kamenev, were incapable of withstanding the pressure to recant and capitulated to Stalin.

The culmination of the counter-revolution

Stalin had crushed the Opposition, but he still faced serious problems. Foremost was the escalation of military tensions on Russia's borders. Through the summer and autumn of 1927, Britain appeared to be building a European coalition to attack Russia. With its industry still in poor shape, Russia was ill equipped to wage war.

Severance of relations with Britain also had economic consequences. Russia was now cut off from British capital, which it desperately needed for economic reconstruction. The other main source of foreign capital was grain exports. The regime therefore had to extract bigger grain deliveries from the countryside to generate foreign exchange. The problem was that, far from growing, grain deliveries were falling. Foreign currency earnings were threatened, and so were food supplies to Russia's towns and cities. A bad harvest in the autumn of 1927 and chronic shortages in the types of goods sought by the peasants in return for their grain (agricultural implements, construction material, cloth and consumer goods) were the main culprits. The peasants had little incentive to bring their grain to market if nothing could be bought.

This was the context for the announcement of Stalin's first Five Year Plan in 1928. The purpose of the Plan was to dramatically increase industrial production to allow Russia to build the weapons necessary to resist the threat of invasion. While the Russian economy had grown under the NEP, the gap with the advanced industrial nations was greater than in 1913. Russia had to make good this gap, as Stalin explained in a speech to factory managers in 1931:

> We are fifty or a hundred years behind the advanced countries. We must make good this distance in ten years. Either we do it, or we shall be crushed.[14]

Stalin's program of crash industrialisation meant that Russian workers and peasants had to be super-exploited. Stalin needed to extract the biggest possible grain deliveries from the rural areas to generate the foreign exchange to buy the imported machinery needed to drive industry and also to feed the cities where the new factories would be built. At the same time, millions of peasants had to be forced from the land into the cities to provide the necessary labour force to work the machines. Forced collectivisation – herding millions of peasants into big state-run collective farms at the point of a gun, while driving others into the cities – was the method. War on the peasantry was accompanied by war on the urban working class; Stalin's project of industrialisation could only work if workers' living standards were squeezed.

Under the NEP in the mid to late-1920s, economic growth had been accompanied by improvements in living standards. Under the first Five Year Plan, with heavy industry absorbing a record share of national income, wages and social spending were slashed. The few lingering gains of the Revolution that had survived in the factories were eliminated, and the unions lost any rights in the appointment of personnel.[15] Forced labour was employed on a mass scale, entire populations were uprooted, and millions died in the state terror used to carry the project through. It was as though the period of primitive accumulation – the expropriation of the peasantry, chattel slavery and other such horrors – prior to the Industrial Revolution in Britain was condensed in Russia into a period of several years instead of a few centuries. Carried out in the name of 'socialist construction,' this was actually nothing other than state capitalism: accumulation for the sake of accumulation, driven by the demands of competing in the world capitalist system.

Stalin's state capitalist project was by no means unique, even if it was at the extreme end of the scale. During World War I, Bukharin had written a pioneering work, *Imperialism and World Economy*, which pointed to the growing tendency towards 'statification' of the advanced economies. Imperialist competition forced each country with ambitions to regional or world leadership to marshal its resources in big monopolies. Only by centralising capital in this way could governments build vital industries – coal, steel, rubber, oil, machine tools, chemicals – of sufficient size to produce the warships, the tanks and the explosive shells to succeed on the battlefield against rival imperialist powers. This required bringing workers with the necessary skills together in big factories. Workers and peasants in uniform – millions under arms – had to be recruited, trained and equipped. Building what would later be called the 'military-industrial complex' was the prerequisite to national success, even survival, among the world's leading industrial powers. Those that did not succeed would be forced to capitulate to those that did. Just like every capitalist project, it was workers who would pay – in the form of pay cuts, longer hours, speed-ups and the destruction of collective organisation, both in the military sector and in civilian industries.

Every government knew that rearmament was far too important to leave to blind capitalist competition. They must step in. In every country, there emerged a tendency for the state to intervene, to take the lead in building military capacity. With governments collaborating with, sometimes even taking over, private industrial companies and banks, there began a new phase of what Bukharin called 'state monopoly capitalism' – the fusion of state and capital. Stalin's Five Year Plan, in which the state diverted the majority of the country's resources to building heavy industry, was only one example of this world historic process. In every country, there were *tendencies* towards state capitalism at this time, more profound in some than others. Nazi Germany saw government spending as a share of the economy rising from 18 percent in 1913 to 42 percent in 1938. In Japan and Britain, the government share rose from 13-14 percent to 29-30 percent and in France and Holland, from 8-9 percent to 22-23 percent. Even in the home of 'free market capitalism,' the United States, the government share of the economy grew from 8 percent to 20 percent[16] in this quarter century. World War II would see these figures rise even higher. The political framework within which state capitalism grew differed from country to country – Stalin triumphed on the back of a defeated workers' revolution, Hitler through fascist barbarism and Roosevelt through parliamentary elections – but, whatever form the political framework took, state capitalism was not socialism. Nor, despite the claims of their supporters, were Stalin's Five Year Plans immune to the anarchy of the world market which produced regular economic crises in every country.

The first Five Year Plan marked Stalin's emergence as undisputed party leader. Bukharin favoured concessions to the peasants to encourage them to sell their grain; Stalin favoured compulsory seizure of grain. Stalin's policy prompted peasant rebellions which spread across the country in the spring of 1928. Stalin could not risk Bukharin using his position as Comintern president to rally opposition within the international Communist movement. The campaign to break the rural crisis in Russia therefore necessitated a campaign against Bukharin. Having allied with Bukharin against the United Opposition, Stalin now turned on him, reducing him to a mere lackey within the Comintern.

By the early 1930s, nothing of the Revolution remained. The working class was politically weak, hamstrung at the workplace by the introduction of incentive schemes such as piece work and bonuses and driven to exhaustion by speed-ups in the factories and mines. Because consumer goods industries took second place to heavy industry, despite rapid growth of production of machinery and railways, shortages were endemic in housing, food, clothing, and other household essentials. Peasants suffered terribly from the destruction of their family farms. The Ukraine was plunged into a grave famine, and millions died. Russification, the forcible suppression of national minorities, saw the people of what had now essentially become a new Russian empire driven off their lands and their languages suppressed.

The position of women, which had advanced despite great difficulties in the early years of the Revolution, was driven backwards. The new ruling class wanted Russian women to take on the jobs the government would not – caring for children, the sick and the elderly. It encouraged women to have large families to supply the future needs of industry and the military. It also wanted to strengthen conservative attitudes associated with the 'natural' authority structure of the family. Early campaigns to encourage women to take a big role in public life were reversed, with marriage and motherhood now upheld as the natural purpose of women. In 1934, homosexuality was made a criminal offence, punishable by up to eight years of imprisonment. In 1935, a tax for divorce was established. In 1936, legal abortion was abolished except in very restrictive circumstances. In 1944, the government made divorce virtually impossible and reintroduced the legal concept of 'illegitimacy,' where children born out of wedlock were stripped of their right to claim support or inherit from their father.

Terror became government policy, apparent on several fronts. There was widespread persecution of the broad population. Article 58 of the penal code, introduced in 1927 to target 'counter-revolutionary crimes,' was used to charge and jail Russian civilians, commonly on no more solid basis than testimony by vindictive state officials or neighbours seeking payback for personal squabbles. Stalin destroyed those Communist leaders who remained from the October Revolution. One by one, virtually all of the Communists who had played a leading role in 1917 – even those who had capitulated to Stalin, such as Zinoviev, Kamenev and Bukharin – were accused of collaboration with fascist powers and executed after farcical show trials between 1936 and 1938. Trotsky was assassinated in Mexico in 1940 by one of Stalin's agents. Other elements of the state machine were also targeted. Thousands of factory directors and engineers who had met all the major plan targets required of them were nonetheless killed by Stalin on the spurious charge of participating in counter-revolutionary conspiracies. Thousands of Red Army officers and military specialists also fell victim to Stalin, and not even the secret police and state prosecutors were exempt.

All told, between the winter of 1936 and the autumn of 1938, approximately three-quarters of a million Russians were summarily executed.[17] More than a million others were sentenced to lengthy terms in labour camps. The exact number of victims of Stalin's terror regime over the whole period from 1927 to 1940 is hotly contested by historians. Estimates of those imprisoned in jails, labour camps or labour colonies range from two to 10 million; whichever estimate is used, the impact was horrendous.[18] Even as jails filled and firing squads carried out their merciless work, the cult of Stalin, with its busts and statues and paeans of praise, grew to new heights. The counter-revolution, with Stalin at its head, had definitively triumphed.

Could the counter-revolution have been halted?

Stalin's rise to power had catastrophic consequences for workers, both in Russia and outside its borders. It represented the victory of counter-revolution within Russia and the transformation of the Comintern into a tool of Stalin's foreign policy. It had nothing to do with any supposedly inherent feature of revolutions or Bolshevism; Stalin was not the logical successor to Lenin but a break from Bolshevism. Historian Ronald Suny summarises some of the features of Stalin's project:

> While appropriating the mantle of Lenin and much of the rhetoric of Bolshevism... Stalin revised, suppressed, and even reversed much of the legacy of Lenin. Internationalism turned into nationalism; the smychka [alliance] between the workers and the peasants was buried in the ferocity of collectivisation; radical transformation of the family and the place of women ended with reassertion of the most conservative 'family values.' And in the process almost all of Lenin's closest associates fell victim to the self-proclaimed keeper of the Leninist flame.[19]

If, as the Revolution's enemies claim, Stalinism arose as the consequence of dictatorial features of the Bolshevik Party, why did Stalin have to destroy the party's historical leadership? In fact, Stalin had to deny, debauch and overturn every Marxist tradition of the party in order to consolidate his bureaucratic rule.

What if Trotsky had won the internal fight? Might history have been different?[20] The Russian state was not a vehicle that could be steered in either direction depending on the whims of the driver. The defeat of the Revolution arose from much broader issues than the personality or courage of its leadership. These were the exhaustion of the Russian working class and the absence of international revolution. Stalin won, not because he was right, nor because he was more politically astute than others, but because the revolution was isolated, and the working class broken.

The objective circumstances were the necessary and sufficient condition for the rise of the bureaucracy under Stalin to the position of the new ruling class. But mistakes by Trotsky also eased the process. The most important of these was his misunderstanding of what was taking place. Firstly, he believed that Stalin was not the leader of the counter-revolution but representative of a centrist tendency, pulled between the workers – whose interests the Left Opposition represented – and the capitalists in the form of NEPmen and kulaks, represented by Bukharin, the leader of what Trotsky called the 'right.' Stalin and his allies were a vacillating layer within the party, Trotsky argued, and could still be won for socialism if put under enough pressure by workers.

In practice, Stalin did not vacillate. He and his supporters, not Bukharin, were the *real* right, the chief counter-revolutionary force. Stalin turned first on the left, represented by Trotsky, and then on Bukharin and his followers. He established himself as state leader at the head of a big bureaucracy, crushing the workers, the kulaks and the NEPmen alike. The party-state bureaucracy was not like the union bureaucracy, mediating between organised labour and the capitalist class, an analogy Trotsky used. Rather, it was a new ruling class, in charge of a state apparatus that by 1929 became, in the absence of a class of big capitalists or of workers' control, the de facto owner and controller of the major means of production and the employer of the workers. Trotsky's failure to understand the depths of the counter-revolution engineered by Stalin is hardly surprising, given the novelty of the process, but it was nonetheless harmful because it prevented him from seeing that the Communist Party had moved from the camp of revolution to that of counter-revolution, both within Russia and outside.

These factors combined to create impossible barriers to any consistent policy of opposition. Because Trotsky believed that the Communist Party could still be saved through internal reform, he argued for the continuation of the one-party state, even the banning of factions when the situation instead called for the formation of a revolutionary faction within the party and, if the Left Opposition were expelled, the re-founding of a revolutionary workers' party to fight the Communist Party, difficult though that would have been. At no point prior to 1933, when the Comintern proved unwilling to fight Hitler's rise to power, did Trotsky call on workers to rise up against the Communist Party. Worse: at times, the Opposition supported the party against workers in Russia when they struck in large numbers in 1928.

Even if Trotsky had called for workers to rise up against Stalin, it is very unlikely that he could have galvanised the numbers necessary to resist the counter-revolution, given the prevailing political passivity in the working class. Nonetheless, such a call by Trotsky would, at least, have oriented his supporters to the fact that the Communist Party was no longer salvageable for the revolution.

Because of his belief that the revolutionary ethos of the Russian Communist Party could still be revived, Trotsky's attacks on the rising bureaucracy were always hesitant rather than full blooded. If the party was still the only place for revolutionaries, and if factions were out of the question, as Trotsky believed, he had no alternative but to retreat time and again, to protect party unity. By making repeated concessions, he demoralised his supporters: how to keep them going without going on the offensive? In a letter addressed to Trotsky on the eve of his suicide, Joffe spelled out the problem:

I have never doubted that the way pointed out by you was the right way... But I have always been of opinion that you lack the inflexibility and firmness of Lenin, that determination to stick to the path recognised as right, even if wholly isolated, trusting in a future majority and a future recognition of the entire rectitude of your way.[21]

Trotsky's failure to join the Bolsheviks until 1917 counted against him. Unlike Lenin, Trotsky had not built a coherent revolutionary party but had spent the years prior to the Revolution trying to mediate between the Bolsheviks and Mensheviks. He therefore did not develop the same tactical skills as Lenin for building a party on firm revolutionary grounds. Hypothetically, had Lenin been in Trotsky's shoes in the mid to late-1920s, it is likely that he would have fought harder for a sharper break within the Russian Communist Party and pulled larger forces with him to build a new revolutionary party when he was expelled. It is also likely that, in such a situation, Lenin would have abandoned the project of trying to reform the Comintern much sooner than 1933. But this can only be speculation.

Whatever Trotsky's mistakes, any honest assessment of his revolutionary career after the death of Lenin must be overwhelmingly positive. The situation was absolutely unprecedented. How to make sense of a revolution that was degenerating, not under the impact of foreign invasion or capitalist restoration at the hands of the landlords and capitalists, but through foreign isolation and internal decay? That was a task no Marxist had ever had to confront. Trotsky may not have concluded that the counter-revolution had triumphed across the board in Russia, with a new ruling class in charge; he may have held faith for too long that the Comintern could be salvaged; but he was consistently scathing in his critique of the Stalinist regime and its imposition of counter-revolutionary policies on the Comintern. At a time in the 1930s when not only Stalinists but liberals and social democrats in the West were lauding Stalin as a great figure, beloved by the Soviet people, and when Stalinism presented itself to the world as the legitimate heir of the Revolution, winning the allegiance of millions of workers, Trotsky kept up his attacks on Stalin's betrayals of socialism.

Trotsky's personal bravery is not in doubt. He was driven from Russia and lived thereafter in exile, moving from country to country only one step ahead of assassins sent by Stalin to execute him, until one finally succeeded. He was denounced as an agent of German and Italian fascism, as was anyone who associated with him. All his allies who did not surrender to Stalin, and some who did, were imprisoned or executed. His four children all died before him, murdered or driven to despair by Stalinist persecution. Yet, Trotsky kept hammering away at the fundamental point: that Russia was not socialist, and Stalin was 'the gravedigger of the revolution.'

Trotsky's literary endeavours included such works as the *History of the Russian Revolution,* still an essential resource for anyone serious about learning the lessons of the Revolution. Nor did he restrict his efforts in exile to the study. Having witnessed the betrayal of the Second and Third Internationals, he dedicated his efforts after 1933 to the establishment of a Fourth. Even with tiny numbers of followers, he persevered, trying to build revolutionary parties wherever he could find an audience.

Most importantly, in works such as *The Revolution Betrayed*, Trotsky analysed the defeat of the Russian Revolution and the rise of Stalinism from a Marxist standpoint. During the Cold War, an entire academic industry developed attacking the Stalinist regime in Russia, but such works were written from a liberal or conservative standpoint. Without Trotsky, people coming to socialist politics in this period would have had to start a critique of Stalinism from scratch. Thanks to Trotsky, Marxists looking for an alternative to the idea that Russia was communist, that Stalin was the leader of world socialism, had a body of work to begin with and to build on in the light of changes since Trotsky's death. This meant that, when the realities of Stalinist rule became obvious to more and more socialists in the postwar decades, there were those who could stand up against the widespread tendency to give up or, worse, to embrace the West as superior.

Trotsky was incapable of holding back the counter-revolution in Russia; no single figure, however brilliant, could have done so. But he did leave behind a legacy that encouraged and guided future generations to build communist organisations to lead the next successful workers' revolution. None has yet succeeded; when they do, they will be in Trotsky's debt.

FURTHER READING

T. Cliff, *State Capitalism in Russia*, London, Pluto Press, 1974 [1955].

T. Cliff, *Trotsky: Fighting the Rising Stalinist Bureaucracy 1923–1927*, London, Bookmarks, 1991.

J. Geier, 'Zinovievism and the degeneration of world Communism', *International Socialist Review*, no. 93, 2014.

M. Haynes, *Russia: Class and Power 1917–2000*, London, Bookmarks, 2002.

J. Molyneux, *Leon Trotsky's Theory of Revolution*, Brighton, Harvester Press, 1981.

M. Reiman, *The Birth of Stalinism: The USSR on the Eve of the 'Second Revolution'*, London, I.B. Tauris, 1987.

J. Rees, 'In defence of October', *International Socialism*, no. 52, 1991.

L. Trotsky, *The New Course*, London, New Park Publications, 1972 [1923].

L. Trotsky, *The Platform of the Joint Opposition (1927)*, London, New Park Publications, 1973 [1927].

L. Trotsky, *The Revolution Betrayed: What is the Soviet Union and Where is it Going?* London, New Park Publications, 1973 [1936].

6.

THE BRITISH GENERAL STRIKE

The 1926 British General Strike was one of the greatest setpiece working class battles of the 20th century and a decisive turning point in British history and the class struggle internationally. At its high point, more than 2.5 million workers responded to the call for action in support of the hundreds of thousands of coal miners who had been locked out. They were callously sold out by their leaders.[1]

The General Strike was a classic example of a bureaucratic mass strike and an illuminating case study in the role of the trade union bureaucracy, particularly its left wing, in propping up capitalism. The left officials joined the right in betraying the strike, destroying the hopes of millions of workers and leaving workers wide open to a sustained employer onslaught in the period that followed. The Communist Party failed to prepare workers for this eventuality and so bears partial responsibility for the outcome.

The defeat of the General Strike followed the 1923 defeat in Germany and other setbacks for the working class movement. These left the Russian Revolution increasingly isolated and contributed to the conditions that allowed Stalin to triumph.

Class struggle in Britain after the war

The 1926 General Strike was the climax of a series of struggles in Britain that began with an explosion of strikes at the end of World War I. A range of industrial, social and political issues came together to fuel the wave: resentment at the sacrifices workers had endured during the war; profiteering by well-connected capitalists and politicians; and the growing realisation that 'the land fit for heroes' promised after the war was a lie. Workers understood that they had to fight to stand still. Many were inspired by the Russian Revolution, and government figures expressed their fear that the Bolshevik 'virus' was infecting workers and soldiers.

The postwar strike wave began in Glasgow on 27 January 1919. The Clyde Workers' Committee, an elected rank and file organising body born out of wartime struggles in the engineering industry, called a strike for the 40-hour week; 100,000 workers answered the call. The four-day strike was well organised, with roving mass pickets of up to 5,000 and the publication of a daily strike bulletin. Solidarity action spread elsewhere in Scotland and to Belfast, but the government was able to isolate the strikers and sent in soldiers backed by tanks and field guns to crush them.

Military force was one way to beat strikes, but the ruling class had another weapon at its disposal: the union bureaucracy. Time and again, during the postwar strike wave and extending through to the 1926 General Strike, it is the union bureaucracy that comes to the rescue of the ruling class. Conservative Party leader Bonar Law suggested that: 'the trade union organisation was the only thing between us and anarchy, and if the trade union organisation was against us, the position would be hopeless.'[2]

The defeat of the Glasgow strike was a blow, but it by no means ended strikes. Engineers, railway and transport workers, miners and cotton workers all took action in 1919. The union leaders shifted their rhetoric to the left in an attempt to keep on top of the situation. They revived the Triple Alliance, originally formed in 1914 in response to the rise of radical syndicalist forces in the British labour movement. This was made up of three of the most powerful unions in the country: the National Union of Railwaymen (NUR), led by Jimmy Thomas; the Miners' Federation, led by Robert Smillie and Frank Hodges; and the National Transport Workers' Federation, led by Ernest Bevin. With the imposition of government control of industry during the war, the union leaders put the Alliance into cold storage but, when strikes revived at war's end, they gave it fresh life. Ostensibly a solidarity pact to bring out the big battalions in defence of each other, it was actually a means to stifle strikes. If the three unions must move ahead as one body, no group of workers could take action independently. If the government struck a deal with one union, the other two must pull back. As Thomas explained to London Underground workers on the brink of striking in February 1919, they must consider their wider duty to the trade unions and forgo 'sectional claims.'

The coal miners lay at the heart of the postwar challenge to the British establishment. The industry employed 1.2 million workers, 5 percent of the country's workforce. The Miners' Federation was one of the country's most powerful unions, with 800,000 members. Its power was based partly on its history of struggle, which had created strong traditions of solidarity and militancy, but also on strategic positioning. Coal accounted for 95 percent of all domestic and industrial energy use. Britain was also a major coal-exporting nation, although its position was under threat from German producers, who were rapidly mechanising the industry while British miners were still using pickaxes. Undercutting by German producers was eating into the profits of British coal owners.

Because of coal's centrality to British capitalism, the industry's woes were an issue for the government and wider economy. Britain had won the war, but at great cost. It was slipping further behind the US as an industrial powerhouse. Germany, the defeated power, was recovering rapidly on the basis of modern technology. The British empire, once a source of competitive advantage, supplying cheap raw materials and markets, was becoming a drain, and several colonies were in open revolt. The British bourgeoisie had to inflict a decisive defeat on the working class if it was to push through the necessary restructuring of industry and remain a leading international power. Wage cuts and increased working hours in the mining industry were critical in that project, and that meant defeating the Miners' Federation.

Coal miners were as anxious as other workers to make gains in 1919. In January, they voted six to one to strike for a 30 percent wage increase, a six-hour working day and nationalisation of the industry under workers' control. The Miners' Federation announced plans for an unlimited national stoppage. Because the industry was still under wartime government controls, responsibility fell on the shoulders of Lloyd George's Coalition Government, which, given the militant mood among the miners, was in no position to reject the miners' claim out of hand. Instead, Lloyd George opted to delay, appointing Justice John Sankey to head a Commission of Inquiry into the state of the industry, whose terms of reference would include the possibility of nationalisation. The Miners' Federation leaders used this to call the strike off, buying the government much-needed time.

On 23 June, the Sankey Commission produced its report, recommending nationalisation of the mines. But, with the strike threat over, the Government was under no pressure to implement the Commission's recommendations and, in August, flatly rejected nationalisation. The Miners' Federation leaders appealed to its Alliance partners for help in pressing their claim, but they agreed only to lodge the issue of nationalisation of the mines at the forthcoming conference of the Trades Union Congress (TUC) in September. This Congress passed the issue further on, to a Special TUC conference in December. There the idea of a national strike over nationalisation was replaced by an 'educational campaign.' In March 1920, the TUC finally buried the strike.

Manoeuvring by the union bureaucracy, combined with concessions on wages and hours by employers, saw off the threat to the bosses from the 1919 upsurge. But conditions in the coal mining industry meant that fresh disputes would soon break out. In the autumn of 1920, coal miners struck for two weeks and won a temporary wage increase. Within a few months, however, a deep economic slump had set in, and the mine owners went on the offensive. In April 1921, they locked out the workforce and tried to force through drastic wage cuts. The Miners' Federation turned to their Triple Alliance partners for support. Initially, they agreed to call out their members, but they abandoned the miners on the appointed day. 'Black Friday', as it became known, was a massive defeat for workers. The miners were left to fight alone and succumbed to defeat in July. This was followed in 1922 by a big lockout in the engineering industry which lasted for 13 weeks and ended in total defeat. Union membership fell sharply, and many militants were victimised during the employer offensive.

A modest economic upturn in 1923-24 and improving prospects for the coal industry saw a revival of action. The Miners' Federation was able to mount a limited offensive and secure small wage rises. Further, the tide in the broader working class was now flowing strongly leftwards, with a strike wave accompanying the election of Britain's first ever Labour Government in January 1924.

Workers' increased fighting spirit was reflected in the election of A. J. Cook as Miners' Federation secretary. A noted radical, Cook had twice been jailed for left wing agitation. An influential group of left officials emerged on the General Council of the TUC: Alf Purcell of the Furnishing Trades, Alonzo Swales of the Engineering Union and George Hicks of the Building Trades Union. Purcell was TUC chair in 1924, Swales in 1925. These officials were well versed in left speechifying. Purcell told the 1924 TUC Congress:

> Workers must organise specifically and universally in direct opposition to capitalism and its political methods... Europe industrially organised – Russia, Germany, Britain and France and the rest – is the first step towards the complete destruction of warlords, market riggers, national and international reactionaries, racial and political strife promoters, in short, all working class exploiters. Our patriotism must be that of loyalty, unashamed and unflinching, to our class the world over.[3]

But the left officials were also loyal to Ramsay MacDonald's Labour government, whose early betrayals of election promises were already angering militants. In order to cover their left flank, the union leaders welcomed closer links with the Russian Government. In September 1924, a delegation of Russian trade unionists attended the TUC Congress and in early 1925, British unionists visited Moscow, where they established an Anglo-Russian Trade Union Committee for international trade union unity. While this flew in the face of virulent anti-Communist coverage in the British press, the formation of the Committee was a cynical exercise by both partners. With the TUC General Council on its side, the rising bureaucracy in Russia hoped to reduce the prospect of a British attack on Russia, and it was on that basis that many militants in Britain supported the initiative. However, by shoring up Stalin, the Committee only helped undermine what remained of the revolutionary forces in Russia. It was also a good bargain for the lefts on the TUC General Council. The Committee required only that the left leaders make a few statements expressing international solidarity, in return for which they were able to cloak themselves in a left aura which they then used to destructive effect in the 1926 General Strike.

The role of the British Communist Party

The Communist Party of Great Britain (CPGB), formed in 1920, had only a few thousand members in its first few years. It was overshadowed by the Labour Party, which retained the loyalty of millions of workers. Nonetheless, it had attracted to its ranks hundreds of the best known and seasoned union militants and, around them, a much larger periphery of veteran unionists. This enabled the CPGB to play a role far in excess of its size. What the party did, in these years leading up to the General Strike and during the General Strike itself, mattered.

In 1923, in an attempt to win greater influence in the unions, the CPGB established the Minority Movement, a bloc between rank and file activists and some left officials, to fight defensive battles.[4] The Minority Movement was not a rank and file movement, seeking to lead strikes independently of the officials; instead, it sought to organise solidarity with struggles called by the left officials. It supported the left in union elections and occasionally ran candidates. It propagandised for a fighting stance and intervened in trades councils to move left motions. It won its greatest influence in the Miners' Federation, where it worked closely with Cook (who had briefly been a Communist). By 1926, the Minority Movement claimed the support of trade union bodies representing nearly a million workers.

There was nothing inherently wrong with the CPGB's approach in principle. However, it did pose serious challenges for a party that was not clear theoretically, particularly on the all-important questions of union politics and the correct approach to the Labour Party. The confusions in the CPGB had their roots in the party's origins. A number of prominent party leaders, such as J. T. Murphy, had played a leading role in the wartime shop stewards' movement and had been members of the Socialist Labour Party. Influenced by syndicalism, they formed the left of the CPGB. But larger numbers came from the British Socialist Party, who pursued a more opportunist approach of capturing union official positions rather than building a rank and file movement. The CPGB in its early years was influenced by these different approaches.

The confusions in the CPGB could have been sorted out with a clearer lead from the Comintern. However, the Russian Communists had little experience in relating to Western unions with their entrenched bureaucracies and intimate links to mass reformist parties. Their advice, although given with the best of intentions in the early years, was not always helpful. The situation became much worse with the degeneration of the Russian party, which increasingly adopted an opportunist approach to foreign relations – as with the Anglo-Russian Trade Union Committee. The CPGB was initially sceptical of the Committee; the *Workers' Weekly* made the point that 'Unity that is based upon political agreement among leaders is useless unless backed up by mass pressure.'[5] But scepticism soon gave way to enthusiasm, because the leaders of the CPGB, one of the weaker Comintern sections in Europe, were in awe of the Comintern and slavishly followed Zinoviev's directions. Zinoviev was motivated primarily by his desire to maintain an alliance with the TUC General Council which, he believed, could be used in the interests of Russia. When viewed from the perspective of Russian foreign policy, the CPGB was inconsequential; its main job, in Zinoviev's eyes, was to avoid doing anything that might antagonise the General Council. This approach was to have devastating consequences.

The CPGB position on the Labour Party became an increasingly important question once Labour formed government in 1924. The syndicalist shop stewards' movement had had an ultra left, sectarian approach to Labour. Lenin correctly argued against them, most famously in *'Left Wing' Communism*, and urged the CPGB to apply for affiliation to Labour. Whether this was an appropriate tactic is debatable. In practice, it never came to fruition, because Labour denied the CPGB affiliation and eventually, at its 1925 party conference, banned CPGB members. But, for a period, Labour was not able to enforce its ban, and the CPGB took advantage of the opportunity. CPGB members in the

Labour Party set up the National Left Wing Movement in an attempt to draw Labour Party members into the orbit of the Communists. At one level, this was highly successful. The Left Wing Movement had influence in 50 Labour branches which refused to expel CPGB members. Its paper, the *Sunday Worker*, regularly sold 85,000 copies, a readership well beyond the ranks of the CPGB. However, the initiative came with heavy overheads. The National Left Wing Movement was meant to be a bridge to draw Labour members to the CPGB; in practice, it had the opposite effect. Just like the old British Socialist Party, which affiliated to the Labour Party and adapted to its host, CPGB members sent into the Labour Party also made concessions. Communists fighting to reform Labour inevitably created the illusion that Labour could be transformed into a party that fought for workers' interests. It is one thing for revolutionaries to intervene in a leftward shifting movement that emerges organically within the ranks of social democratic parties, but quite another for communists to form and lead one. The creation of the National Left Wing Movement inevitably meant pressure to stay in the Labour Party and fight and, consequently, to accommodate to the Labour lefts. This is exactly what happened; the bridge meant to carry radicals from Labour to the CPGB saw traffic move in the opposite direction.

The prologue to the General Strike

In November 1924, the Conservatives regained power under Stanley Baldwin. The new prime minister was determined to drive down workers' living standards, and he had the miners squarely in his sights. If they could be defeated, the path would be cleared to attack wages more generally. One of the government's first measures was to return Britain to the gold standard, forcing up the value of sterling on international markets. The stronger currency hit coal exports hard. On 30 June 1925, the financially pressed mine owners gave mine workers four weeks' notice of termination of the national wages agreement, foreshadowing significant wage cuts and a lengthening of the working day.

The Miners' Federation called on the TUC for support. On 30 July, under significant rank and file pressure, the combined union executives declared an embargo on the movement of coal. The mine owners had mistimed their move. Stocks of coal were low and a stoppage at the pits would cause industry across the country to grind to a halt. The Baldwin government was forced to back down, and the mine owners withdrew their ultimatum. Trying to buy time, Baldwin announced a nine-month subsidy for the coal owners and the establishment of a Royal Commission into the industry. Baldwin hoped to use the

Commission in the same way Lloyd George had used the Sankey Commission – to retreat, the better to advance. The union leaders, however, described this as a great victory: 'an enormous stimulus to every trade unionist.' The Labour paper, the *Daily Herald*, declared the day 'Red Friday' in banner headlines.

But this was only a breathing space before a decisive showdown. Baldwin was determined to force through wage cuts, for miners and the entire working class, 'to help put industry back on its feet.'[6] The government used the next nine months to prepare for battle and drew up elaborate plans to break a strike. It enrolled tens of thousands of middle class special constables and encouraged forces on the hard right of the political establishment, who set up the Organisation for the Maintenance of Supplies (OMS) – a body of middle class volunteers, to assist the authorities in keeping industries running. For their part, the mine owners built up coal stockpiles, overcoming the shortage that had forced the government to retreat on Red Friday. The government also came down hard on the CPGB, ordering the arrest of the entire party leadership on charges of sedition. The CPGB leaders were found guilty of incitement to mutiny, for urging soldiers not to shoot strikers, and they were sentenced to terms of between six and 12 months' imprisonment.

The TUC General Council recognised that the government and the employers were preparing for a confrontation, but they did nothing to prepare workers for battle. This was as true for most of the left officials as it was the right. Fiery rhetoric was not lacking; the September 1925 TUC Congress saw a string of left wing motions passed about the coming class battles. Conference resolved to empower the TUC to call a general strike in defence of the miners. It denounced the British empire. Indeed, nothing less than the overthrow of capitalism was on the agenda. In his presidential address, Swales told delegates:

> It is the duty of all members of the working class so to solidify their movements that, come when the time may be for the last final struggle, we shall be wanting neither machinery nor men to move forward to the destruction of wage slavery and the construction of a new order of society based upon coordinated effort and work with mutual good will and understanding.[7]

Despite rhetoric about 'the last final struggle,' the General Council sought negotiations with the government. From left to right, union leaders hoped that the government would back down again. There was no national strategy and little in the way of political preparation and agitation among union members.

The CPGB tails the left officials

The CPGB understood that Red Friday was merely a delay of the inevitable; an all-out struggle would soon take place. The *Workers' Weekly* declared:

> Behind this truce and the industrial peace talk which will accompany it, the capitalist class will prepare for a crushing attack on the workers. If the workers are duped by the peace talk and do not make effective counter-preparations, then they are doomed to shattering defeat.[8]

But who was to make these preparations? The TUC General Council? The left of the General Council? Or must preparation take place independently of the officials? These were the crucial questions in the nine-month period between Red Friday and the General Strike.

The shift to the left by the union bureaucracy over this period opened up opportunities for revolutionaries, who could demand that the left leaders prepare for confrontation – and use their calls for action to build the necessary organisation on the ground, ready to take things forward when the left bureaucrats inevitably pulled back. Instead, the CPGB placed its trust, and encouraged its periphery of militants to place their trust, in the left officials. This was a disgraceful decision. The left leaders were not unknown quantities. They had mostly been involved in the radical wing of the union movement before the war but had subsequently moved up the union hierarchy and become part of the union establishment, its left face. Some had even joined the CPGB on its formation but dropped out within a year or two when the party began to place demands on them. CPGB leaders would have known that such figures could not be relied upon. Indeed, in October 1924, a leading figure in the party, J. R. Campbell, correctly wrote:

> It would be a suicidal policy for the Communist Party and the Minority Movement to place too much reliance on the official left wing. It is the duty of the Party and the Minority Movement to criticise its weakness relentlessly and endeavour to change the muddled and incomplete left wing views of the more progressive leaders into a real revolutionary viewpoint.[9]

But, less than a year later, there was no sign of relentless criticism, only capitulation. The CPGB described the left officials as 'a leadership which is approaching more and more full recognition of the class struggle'[10] and heaped praise on them for their speeches at the September 1925 TUC Congress, giving them left cover. That the left officials could not be trusted was only confirmed when they failed to raise their voices to defend the CPGB when Labour confirmed its ban on the CPGB just two months later at its annual conference.

Advice from the Comintern only made things worse. The CPGB had argued in 1923 and 1924 for more power to the General Council, to unite the union movement and overcome sectionalism, but only if this was accompanied by measures to bring it under the influence of rank and file workers raised into activity through local action committees. Even this policy placed too much trust in the union apparatus rather than building rank and file power. But in 1925, under the direction of Moscow, the CPGB simply asserted: 'All power to the General Council!' and no longer linked it to any program of transformation for this body. This left workers disarmed in the face of a government which was determined to inflict a decisive defeat on the unions.

The Comintern's advice was not unchallenged. Trotsky was alarmed by the situation and called on the CPGB to break with the left officials and to take an independent line. In January 1926, he argued:

> The more left the [TUC] Congress decisions are, the further away they are from immediate practical tasks... To think that the leaders of the Scarborough Congress could become leaders of a revolutionary upheaval would be lulling oneself to sleep with illusions.
>
> The left faction of the General Council is distinguished by its complete ideological shapelessness and is therefore incapable of organisationally assuming the leadership of the trade union movement.[11]

The CPGB, however, stood solidly behind Stalin and Bukharin and was unwilling to listen to Trotsky's warnings. When the bankruptcy of the left officials became too blatant to be completely ignored, the CPGB made excuses for them or argued that the force of circumstances or the demands of the struggle would force the left officials onto the right path. In the face of the failure of the left officials to fight Labour's anti-Communist witch hunt, the party simply stated that they had acted 'very foolishly' and that their error could be attributed only to a lack of 'self-confidence.'

By the beginning of 1926, it was abundantly clear that the left officials were simply tagging along behind the right on the General Council. The CPGB was fully aware of the stakes. It knew that the Government was preparing to use all the resources of the state to inflict a heavy defeat on the unions and that the right wing leaders on the General Council had a proven record of treachery. The party also knew that the left officials were doing nothing to expose the treachery of the right. But it did nothing to sound the alarm. Only in the aftermath of the strike was the CPGB willing to condemn the left officials, but by then it was too late. The damage had been done.

Countdown to the strike

The government and bosses used the period leading up to May 1926, when the subsidy to mine owners would expire, to prepare their defences. By spring, everything was in place. The government would now neither back down nor defer a reckoning with the unions. It was determined to force the TUC to call a strike so that it could decisively defeat the unions in battle. It was not out to totally destroy the unions but to force them into a confrontation, knowing that they would retreat at some point, as they had in 1921. Unlike the CPGB, the Tory government had the measure of the union bureaucracy and made maximum use of that understanding.

On 10 March 1926, Baldwin's Royal Commission presented its report. It recommended reorganisation of the industry but not nationalisation, no continuation of the subsidy, and wage cuts. Mine owners immediately demanded 13 percent pay cuts and an eight-hour day, up from the current seven-hour day, starting on 1 May. The union leaders failed to respond in kind to this offensive. The TUC's Industrial Committee, a subcommittee of the General Council chaired by Swales, merely called for negotiations. Arthur Pugh, who had succeeded Swales as TUC chair, and Bevin, the dominant figure on the General Council, were privately in favour of acceptance of the Royal Commission recommendations. The leaders of the Miners' Federation stuck to their guns publicly, demanding no pay cuts and no lengthening of hours. But behind the scenes, Cook was undermining his executive by looking for a compromise involving wage cuts for some members.[12]

The problem for the TUC and the Federation leadership was that the coal owners were not going to back down. With coal stocks replenished and with the full support of the government, they brought matters to a head, announcing a lockout to take effect on 1 May. The General Council now had little choice. It did not want to strike but had been forced into a corner by the government and mine owners. It was also under pressure from workers: if it did not call a strike, more radical elements in the unions might seize the initiative and provide an alternative leadership. So the General Council called a special conference of all union executives for 29 April. Publicly, the union leaders defiantly opposed the lockout and wage cuts. Privately, they pressed the Miners' Federation to make concessions on hours and wages. The Federation leaders refused to accept wage cuts without assurances that their other demands would be considered. The mine owners were not prepared to agree. The meeting of union executives therefore had no alternative but to call a general strike for Monday 3 May. But, even with the date set, the General Council did little to prepare workers, seeing in the strike declaration only a bargaining chip to force the government and owners to give ground. But there was no mood for concessions. On 1 May, the coal owners locked out 800,000 miners, and on 3 May, the General Strike began.

The strike unfolds

Although their leaders had done little politically to prepare workers for the General Strike, workers responded to the call enthusiastically, far beyond the unions' initial expectations. Cook described the workers' reaction:

> What a wonderful response! What loyalty! What solidarity! From John O'Groats to Land's End, the workers have answered the call to arms to defend us, to defend the brave miner in his fight for a living wage.[13]

The railways were out almost to the last worker; on the last day of the strike, 99 percent of engine drivers were out. No London tramcars were in operation. Dockers were completely solid, as were building workers, iron and steel workers and those in the metal and chemical industries. There were exceptions. In some places, an almost normal bus service ran, and road haulage was another weak spot. However, trades councils in most areas, which brought together local representatives of all unions and formed the basis of the strike committees, reported that the strikes were solid. In many cases, non-unionists joined in when their workmates went out – sometimes even before them!

The workers were solid, but the General Council was determined to maintain tight control and to keep them passive. It refused to call for an all-out strike, instead calling for workers to take action in waves – a succession of partial strikes. Strategically important groups, such as engineering workers and shipbuilders, were told to work for the first few days. Others, including post and telecommunications workers, gas workers and naval dockyard workers, were completely exempted. This strategy of only partial struggle ran completely against the instincts of workers and meant that the strike was less effective. Newly established strike committees flooded the TUC with telegrams reporting their difficulty in holding back those who wanted to strike.

While reining in sections of workers, the General Council failed to provide the strike with any central direction. It left it to each union executive to decide how to implement its broad guidelines, leading to widespread confusion. At a time when the state was marshalling all its resources and tightly centralising decision-making over its strikebreaking measures, strike organisation was slapdash, resulting in multiple disputes about which sections were to come out and when. Many workers and local union branches defied the advice and went out anyway. Engineering workers, in particular, struck in big numbers days before being authorised by the General Council.

Union leaders were extremely anxious about losing control of the strike to Communists and other militants. The longer the strike went on, the more that anxiety grew. Charles Dukes of the General and Municipal Workers Union explained afterwards:

> Every day that the strike proceeded, the control and the authority was passing out of the hands of responsible Executives and into the hands of men who had no authority, no control and wrecking the movement from one end to the other.[14]

The idea that radicals were seizing control of the strike committees was far off the mark. Most committees were led by district officials and branch officers of the main unions who saw their role as little more than carrying out the General Council's instructions. However, the TUC feared that the committees might develop into something more. Thomas told the House of Commons in the aftermath:

> If by any chance it should have got out of the hands of those who would be able to exercise some control, every sane man knows what would have happened... That danger, that fear, was always in our minds, because we wanted at least, even in this struggle, to direct a disciplined army.[15]

The General Council's desire to keep the strike committees on a tight leash explains its refusal to set up workers' defence groups, even when picket lines were attacked by police. It forbade effective picketing, allowing the government to control the movement of food supplies and much else. It urged workers to 'keep smiling,' to take time with the family and to 'do your best to discountenance any ideas of violent and disorderly conduct.'[16] Church attendance was encouraged.

The TUC constantly sought to downplay the full significance of the strike. When the Baldwin government and the media sought to rally conservative support by accusing the unions of challenging the authority of parliament, the General Council insisted that it was only an industrial dispute with no political connotations. Acknowledgement that a general strike is, by its very nature, both an industrial and a political challenge to the state would have run counter to union leaders' enthusiastic involvement in a wide range of state-sponsored conciliation bodies and, in the case of some, their own parliamentary positions. Firmly attached to the state apparatus, they strongly rejected any idea that they were threatening it. On the fifth day of the strike, Thomas said bluntly: 'I have never disguised that in a challenge to the constitution, God help us unless the government won.'[17]

The left officials, just a few months earlier, had been promising to challenge the entire wage system. Now, they occupied their time striking out supposedly 'inflammatory' language in local strike bulletins. The editor of the TUC's official publication, the *British Worker*, saw his task as to 'keep the strikers steady and quiet.'[18] The General Council forbade publication of any other newspaper, including trade union-sponsored newspapers, allowing it to dominate coverage of the strike within the trade unions at a time when the government-run *British Gazette* was distributing anti-strike propaganda to every corner of the country. Such was its fear of being seen as in any way subversive, the TUC, still the British representative on the Anglo Russian Trade Union Committee, even refused money donated by Russian unions. The Labour Party played its part. None of its leaders offered any support for the strike. Only small numbers of Labour-run local councils denied facilities for the recruitment of scabs.

The union leaders were not always successful in keeping a lid on local activism. In the Newcastle and Durham area, the joint strike committee was able to force the government's Civil Commissioner to recognise its control over the movement of goods and the unloading of cargoes on the docks. The Royal Navy, which had sent ships to intimidate strikers in the area, was forced to withdraw, and the OMS was compelled to pull out scab truck drivers. In many towns, the issuing of permits by strike committees to allow business owners to move their goods without obstruction saw normal relations between bosses and workers turned upside down. One metal worker wrote to his union journal:

> Employers of labour were coming, cap in hand, begging for permission...to allow their workers to return to perform certain customary operations. 'Please can I move a quantity of coal from such and such a place' or 'Please can my transport workers move certain foodstuffs in this or that direction.' Most of them turned empty away after a most humiliating experience, for one and all were put through a stern questioning, just to make them realise that we and not they were the salt of the earth.[19]

In East Fife in Scotland, workers set up a 700-strong workers' defence committee after they were attacked by police. While this was an isolated experience, confrontations between strikers and scabs and police became more violent as the strike grew longer; the police hardened up their tactics and began making mass arrests. In Leeds, a scab bus driver was halted by strikers armed with guns. Scabs were too scared to run buses in London's East End. In Edinburgh, unionists impounded vehicles that did not have union permits. The number of workers involved and the effects of the strike grew as key industries were forced to shut down.

Betrayal

On 12 May, the ninth day of the General Strike, the General Council called it off. The Baldwin government and the bosses registered an historic victory. The General Strike was defeated, not because of any lack of determination by the strikers or the strong arm of the state. In fact, much of the strikebreaking machinery was ineffective: few of the thousands of middle class scabs who signed up for strikebreaking duties were of any use in keeping industry turning, and few of the nearly 250,000 special constables saw much action. The strike was defeated because the union leaders feared winning. Winning would have required granting much greater freedom for rank and file initiative, and union leaders feared the loss of control that this would have involved.

The union leaders had not wanted the strike in the first place and were horrified by its effectiveness. Even while proclaiming that the strike would continue until victory, they did their best to end it. From the very start, Thomas was busy making overtures to coal owners and big industrialists. Through these intermediaries, Thomas let the prime minister know that the General Council was keen to call off the strike and that the coal miners would accept wage cuts. Labour leader MacDonald secretly approached Baldwin to press for a settlement, including a 10 percent wage cut. Some members of the General

Council were not made aware of the details of these communications, and nor was the Miners' Federation. Publicly, the General Council announced that the strike would be escalated, but only with a view to putting pressure on the government and coal owners to make some modest concessions that would allow the Council to end the strike as quickly as possible.

The only obstacle to a hasty surrender by the General Council was the Miners' Federation, which adamantly refused to accept wage cuts. Unable to gain the Federation's support, the General Council simply decided to call the strike off. Not a single left official on the Council spoke or voted against the decision. Rubbing salt into the wound, the General Council told the miners that they were being unrealistic in rejecting a wage cut and that their obstinacy was causing pain for millions of striking workers taking action in solidarity with their cause.

The General Council, with the agreement of all but the Federation's representatives – and without consulting with the Federation – then voted to end the strike. Work would resume at midnight on Thursday 13 May.[20] The Miners' Federation immediately distanced themselves from the decision, stating that they were 'no party in any shape or form' to calling off the strike. The TUC's public announcements ignored this fact, creating the widespread impression that the Federation had agreed to it.

The Baldwin government rammed home its advantage. When TUC representatives trooped off to 10 Downing Street to formally inform the government of its decision to call off the strike and to attempt to secure agreement that no unionists would be victimised, the prime minister bluntly told them that he was there simply to confirm their surrender, not to negotiate. The pleading of the mighty men of the TUC was contemptuously ignored. One of Baldwin's Cabinet members noted that their surrender was 'so humiliating that some instinctive breeding made one unwilling even to look at them.'[21] The *British Gazette* made the reality of their situation plain:

> Unconditional withdrawal of notices by TUC. Men to return forthwith. Surrender received by Premier in Downing Street.

That evening, Baldwin broadcast a speech on the radio stating that the strike had ended without the government entering into any conditions.

The union leaders tried to excuse their treachery by saying that strike observance was deteriorating and that it was better to end the strike after nine days than face a rout. In fact, the numbers on strike were still increasing when it was called off. Indeed, on the day after the strike officially ended, there were more on strike than on the first day. Many workers, bewildered by the turn of events, simply stayed out, with the result that the strike continued into its tenth day. Attempts by the bosses to immediately force wage cuts simply encouraged workers to stay out longer. Big unions which had agreed to end the General Strike now instructed their members to hold out for re-employment on the old terms. In the localities, militants did their best to keep the struggle going. The CPGB issued a call for emergency meetings of strike committees and councils of action to continue the struggle.

Nonetheless, even if there were some holdouts, the General Strike was now over. The bosses had a field day. Thousands of unionists were sacked; tens of thousands of rail workers had still not been taken back on five months after the strike's end. Union leaders issued grovelling apologies to the bosses for having struck. The end of the strike meant that the miners were abandoned and left to fight on alone. After a gruelling six-month struggle, they were starved back to work amid widespread victimisations and much reduced conditions of employment, along with the destruction of their national agreement.

The right wing officials had behaved entirely as might have been expected. Not a single militant had any faith that the NUR's Thomas could be trusted to fight for the workers. It was the left officials who played the most damaging role, acting as a cover for the right. The CPGB had made the distinction between left officials and right officials the central factor in its approach to the union bureaucracy, but the officials themselves understood that far more united them than divided them. Ben Turner, the right wing president of the textile workers' union, wrote to the CPGB newspaper *Sunday Worker* in the aftermath of the strike:

> I don't think you were just to the General Council in dividing us into left and right wingers…the absolute unanimity of the General Council in declaring the General Strike off did not divide us into left wingers and right wingers.[22]

The leaders of the Miners' Federation were only partially an exception to this general pattern. The Minority Movement had its greatest support in that union and was therefore able to mount some pressure on the leadership. Thus it was that, when Cook initially accepted the need for wage cuts in the days leading up to the strike, he was pulled into line by his executive. But during the strike itself, Cook never went over the heads of the General Council to argue for rank and file solidarity. Even when the General Council was urging workers to go back to work, leaving the miners isolated, Cook offered no alternative.

While disparaging behind the scenes negotiations between the General Council and the government, Cook held meetings with industrialists without his members' knowledge.

Cook was largely responsible for the fact that the TUC General Council escaped censure for its treacherous role. In the immediate aftermath of the General Strike, when criticism of the General Council was widespread, Cook agreed to defer a special meeting of union executives to discuss the dispute. At the TUC's request, he also withdrew *Nine Days*, his damning account of the General Council's role. At the TUC Congress in September, with the lockout still in force, Cook played the main role in heading off an attempt by Minority Movement supporters to force a debate on the General Council's decision to call off the strike. By the time the issue was finally debated, at a conference of union executives in January 1927, the delay and the rising sense of hopelessness within the unions meant that those gathered overwhelmingly backed the General Council's report on the handling of the strike. The Federation opposed it, standing virtually alone.

The aftermath and lessons of the strike

The defeat of the General Strike was a terrible blow for the working class movement in Britain. Since 1911, the class struggle had been broadly on the upswing, and the General Strike raised hopes among millions of workers of a decisive breakthrough. But these hopes were dashed by the actions of the union leaders. Demoralisation now set in. Union membership collapsed from a peak of eight million to below five million. Many unions disaffiliated from the TUC.

The union leaders now swung sharply to the right. At the 1927 TUC Congress, the militant talk from 1925 was abandoned. Class collaboration was the order of the day. George Hicks, now TUC chair, gave a speech calling for 'a direct exchange of practical views' with the bosses. The subsequent Mond-Turner talks, named after the main representatives of the bosses and unions respectively, set the scene for decades of close collaboration between union leaders and bosses. A string of wage cuts resulted. The unions' drift to the right meant that the economic slump of the 1930s, which generated determined and militant resistance in many countries, produced only despair in Britain.

The Labour leaders, who had done nothing to help the coal miners and who had opposed the General Strike, benefited from its defeat. Workers turned to Labour, looking for salvation through the ballot box. At the 1929 election, Labour nearly doubled its parliamentary representation and formed its second minority government. Two years later, this collapsed when Prime Minister MacDonald, facing internal opposition to cuts to unemployment benefits, defected to form a National government with the Conservatives. At the subsequent elections, MacDonald and Thomas joined Baldwin and Samuel as leaders of the National coalition and won 497 seats, with Labour losing 235 seats.

The events leading up to the General Strike and the strike itself were ample confirmation of Trotsky's incisive analysis of the cowardice of the leaders of the British labour movement.[23] He wrote in 1930:

> If there were not a bureaucracy of the trade unions, then the police, the army, the courts, the Lords, the monarchy would appear before the proletarian masses as nothing but ridiculous playthings. The bureaucracy of the unions is the backbone of British imperialism. It is by means of this bureaucracy that the bourgeoisie exists not only in the metropolis, but in India, in Egypt and in other colonies. The Marxist will say to the British workers: 'The trade union bureaucracy is the chief instrument of your oppression by the bourgeois state. Power must be wrested from the hands of the bourgeoisie and for that, its principal agent, the trade union bureaucracy, must be overthrown.'[24]

How to orient to the left officials, such as Purcell, Swales and Hicks in 1926, remains one of the major questions for revolutionary socialists today. This is particularly the case in advanced capitalist countries, where union leaders have had more than a century of experience in talking out of both sides of their mouths. But it is also a vital question when unions are relatively new; for example, in the independent unions in South Africa and South Korea formed in the 1980s, there is now a long history of militant-talking leaders capitulating to the bosses. That far more unites than divides left and right union officials, who join forces at the workers' expense at all key moments, is something that revolutionaries have had to learn and, too many times, relearn, often through bitter experience.

The priority for revolutionaries at all times is to consider what is needed to build the strength of rank and file organisation. Sometimes that means rejecting any cooperation with the union officials. Sometimes it means working with the left officials, where this might help to move workers into action. But, in every case, it means being ready to act independently when the officials become a drag on the movement. This is not a simple operation, but it is vital for revolutionaries to grasp when they are working in countries with well-established union apparatuses that are committed to the maintenance of capitalism – like Australia.

The CPGB failed the British working class during the General Strike because it put its trust in the left union leaders. Many CPGB members played an admirable role during the General Strike. Although the party started the strike with just 5,000 members and with much of its leadership in jail, Communist militants played a disproportionate role in the strike. They were responsible for an enormous amount of local organising and were a visible presence in the strike committees in South Wales, Scotland, Merseyside, Manchester, Middlesbrough and London. The party's duplicated strike bulletin, produced in the face of constant police harassment, reached a circulation of 20,000 by the end of the strike and was probably read by closer to 100,000, because local branches reproduced its content in strike bulletins. As a result of its tireless activity, CPGB members bore the brunt of state and employer repression: 1,200 members were brought before the courts, most on charges of 'incitement' or 'sedition,' and the judges sentenced many to jail. Some were sentenced to hard labour for offences as trivial as chalking 'seditious' slogans on the pavement or issuing a leaflet urging workers not to become special constables. Hundreds were subsequently blacklisted by the bosses. The party's efforts drew to it thousands of new recruits, and it more than doubled in size in 1926.

Set against this honourable record, however, is the failure of the party to pursue an independent class struggle approach during the lead up to, and during, the General Strike. This meant that, when the General Council sold out the strike, the CPGB had done nothing to politically prepare worker militants for this situation, adding to the immense demoralisation and bewilderment. This applied even to its own members. When the sellout came, CPGB militants were left to do what they could to maintain the strike and were forced to improvise structures from scratch. Even after the strike, the party never critically examined the approach it took during the nine months between Red Friday and the General Strike. It retained the slogan 'All power to the General Council' for months after the dispute, although the General Council had been the vehicle for defeat.

Could the CPGB have pursued any other strategy with better results? Clearly, its small size affected its ability to decisively turn things around. But if the Minority Movement had maintained an independent stance critical of the left officials, the CPGB might have been able to provide a semblance of an alternative leadership during the General Strike. At the very least, it would have been in a position afterwards to draw to it those layers of militants seeking a coherent explanation of what went wrong. The party could have come out of even a defeated general strike considerably strengthened and better placed to play an important role in the class struggle in the following years. But the CPGB was too identified with the left officials it promoted to have any credibility in attacking them now. It was, therefore, incapable of providing any concerted opposition to the sharp shift to the right in the working class movement that followed the betrayal of the General Strike. The CPGB itself suffered in this process; its membership collapsed from 10,700 in October 1926 to 3,200 by March 1928.[25]

The Comintern shares the blame for the CPGB's disastrous strategy. In its search for supposed allies to defend Russia, it had courted the TUC left officials in a totally opportunist fashion. A few weeks after the strike collapsed, the Comintern Executive correctly assessed the weakness of the strike:

> The 'left' leaders, who had a majority on the General Council, put up no resistance whatever to the deliberate traitors like Thomas, but marched all the time under the right-wing orders. In fact, Thomas and Co. ran the General Council throughout the course of the strike. Thus the 'left' objectively played an even more shameful role.[26]

This denied the Comintern's own role in the betrayal. The Executive had consistently advised the CPGB to support the TUC, in particular the left officials, in order to maintain the Anglo-Russian Trade Union Committee. For the sake of unity of the union bureaucrats – a unity which proved spurious when the TUC abandoned the Anglo-Russian Committee in September 1927 – the Comintern sacrificed a revolutionary attitude and policy for diplomatic evasions and opportunism. This practice of pressuring Comintern sections to abandon class struggle in favour of the needs of Russian foreign policy was to have a disastrous impact in the years to come.

FURTHER READING

M. Armstrong, 'Socialist trade union strategy in the Bolshevik era', *Marxist Left Review*, no. 6, 2013.

T. Cliff and D. Gluckstein, *Marxism and Trade Union Struggle: The General Strike of 1926*, London, Bookmarks, 1986.

D. Hallas, 'The Communist Party and the General Strike', *International Socialism* (first series), no. 88, 1976.

C. Harman, *The General Strike, May 1926*, St Albans, Panther Books, 1974.

C. Harman, 'The General Strike', *International Socialism* (first series), no. 48, June–July 1971.

7.

THE CHINESE REVOLUTION

The gathering pace of the counter-revolution in Russia had a disastrous impact on the class struggle in Britain. The effect was greater and far bloodier in China. Waves of worker and peasant struggle swept the country in the 1920s.[1] The workers at times held the fate of Hong Kong, Guangzhou and Shanghai in their hands. The peasants drove out the landlords and took over the land. But they were defeated. The property owners, foreign and local, fought back, using police, soldiers and criminal gangs to try to wipe out the insurgents. The result was not a forgone conclusion; the counter-revolutionary forces only succeeded because of Stalin's machinations.

Prior to the invention of 'socialism in one country' in 1924, it had been universally accepted in the Comintern that the survival of the Russian Revolution depended on international revolution. Lenin had declared that the Soviet Union must make 'the greatest national sacrifices for the overthrow of international capitalism.'[2] The adoption of socialism in one country turned this on its head. Henceforth, under Stalin, survival of the Russian *bureaucracy* required *counter-revolution* outside its borders. Over time, this transformed the Comintern from a revolutionary agency to a counter-revolutionary instrument of Moscow. The last thing Stalin wanted was revolution in Europe or on Russia's eastern borders; that could have jeopardised his attempts to forge alliances with foreign governments and reignited working class unrest inside Russia itself. The outcome of Stalin's intervention was the destruction of the movement in China and the elimination of the young Communist Party's forces in the cities.

Imperial collapse and the birth of popular politics

At the beginning of the 20th century, China was mired in political and economic backwardness. The Qing dynasty, which had ruled since the 17th century, was unwilling to modernise the nation for fear of the social forces this would unleash. The big landlords and their retinues dominated the countryside. Big imperial powers occupied 'concessions,' colonial trading and manufacturing zones in the coastal and river cities. They controlled China's foreign trade and plundered its wealth, limiting the ability of Chinese-owned businesses to expand. Eighty percent of the population were peasants, often living in extreme poverty. Chinese backwardness was brought home vividly to millions in 1895 when the country was routed by Japan after a brief war, resulting in the loss of Taiwan and the payment of an enormous indemnity to the victor. Further humiliation followed, with the suppression of the anti-imperialist Yihetuan Movement (Boxer Rebellion) in Beijing 1900 and the occupation of the capital by imperialist armies. Popular resentment at the situation was captured in this roadside poster:

> THE FOREIGN TROOPS COME TO OUR TOWN,
> IN FLAMES THE HOUSES TUMBLED.
> INDEMNITIES ARE HUGE;
> WE COMMON FOLK MUST PAY THEM…
> IMPERIAL LEVIES WEIGH HEAVY NOW,
> OFFICIALS GRAB LIKE HUNGRY WOLVES.
> WHO DARES STRAY NEAR THE IMPERIAL ROAD,
> IS FINED THREE THOUSAND SILVER TAELS.
> AND ALL ALONG AND BY THIS ROAD,
> RAZED ARE THE HOUSES AND ANCESTRAL TOMBS.[3]

Following the Russo–Japanese war of 1904-05, Japan made further inroads, occupying South Manchuria and taking steps to absorb Korea, formerly a Chinese tributary.

In 1911, having thoroughly rotted out from within, the Qing dynasty collapsed and was replaced by a republic led by the Nationalist People's Party, the Guomindang (GMD), under Sun Yat-sen.[4] The new republic was weak and incapable of solving any of the country's social and economic problems and lacked any serious military forces of its own. Sun was quickly replaced as leader and sent into exile by one of his former allies, Yuan Shikai. After Yuan's death in 1916, the country disintegrated as warlords fought for power and established rival fiefdoms. In 1917, Sun returned from exile to set up a GMD government in the southern city of Guangzhou.[5] The ruling group in Guangzhou was little more than a feuding collection of members of the rural and urban gentry, military officers, landlords and capitalists. Although Sun was nominally in charge, real power lay in the hands of warlords. For the common people, everyday life worsened rapidly under the new republic; warlords fought over territory, landlords imposed ever higher rents, and taxes rocketed.

The end of World War I brought further political turmoil in China. Negotiations at Versailles over the spoils of war provided the spark for revolt. China had anticipated that the resource-rich Shandong province, controlled by Germany before the war and then seized by Japan, would be returned to China. Instead, the Entente rubber-stamped Japan's annexation of Shandong. Rather than fight, the Chinese government simply accepted the outcome. This, the latest of many humiliations at the hands of foreigners, was too much for politically aware Chinese to bear. On 4 May and in subsequent days, student demonstrations denouncing the theft of Chinese territory swept the major cities in what became known as the May Fourth Movement. In Shanghai, students were joined by tens of thousands of workers who struck for five days in the city's textile plants, print shops, metal works, public utilities, shipping concerns, paper mills and tobacco factories. Merchants and business owners grouped in chambers of commerce also supported the movement.

The May Fourth Movement is best understood as an extension of the New Culture Movement that had been taking hold among progressive young Chinese since 1915. This was China's first mass popular political movement in the cities, as opposed to the peasant revolts of earlier times. Its supporters unapologetically attacked everything associated with an imperial order based on Confucianism, which emphasised social order and hierarchy. Its leading forces included two prominent writers: Chen Duxiu, dean of Peking University, the country's most prominent centre of teaching and research, and founder of the most influential Chinese journal of the day, *New Youth*; and Li Dazhao, chief librarian at the University. They argued that China had to break with feudal tradition and embrace modernisation.[6] The New Culture Movement championed the rights of the downtrodden social classes and women. It saw itself as defending Chinese territorial integrity against onslaughts by the imperialists and their local collaborators. Many of its adherents were influenced by anarchist ideas from Japan and Europe and attempted to escape the crushing conformity of the old social order, particularly its restrictions on women, by setting up communes where adherents could attempt to lead liberated lives.

The working class and the nationalist movement

The May Fourth Movement saw the working class tentatively step onto the Chinese political stage. China had a long tradition of craft guilds, but in 1918 the first unions for factory workers and labourers were formed. The working class was growing rapidly. In 1916, there were nearly one million industrial workers; by 1922, this number had doubled, with foreign-owned workshops and factories blossoming in Guangzhou, Hong Kong and particularly Shanghai, the biggest city of all and home to half the country's industrial workers, including tens of thousands of women textile workers.

The first wave of mass working class struggle exploded in January 1922. Thirty thousand Hong Kong seafarers and waterside workers struck for eight weeks for union recognition and higher wages to bring their pay into line with that of Europeans. It was a bitter and bloody battle that soon drew in workers from a range of industries. The strike ended with the bosses granting pay rises of 20 to 30 percent and recognising the union. The seafarers' strike was of historic importance: it marked the arrival of the working class as a social force in China. Over the next five years, China experienced a dramatic acceleration in the tempo of class struggle. Development that took Russian workers three or four decades to experience and learn from, and British workers a full century, was compressed in China into five years. Two organisations came to dominate the workers' movement: the GMD and the Communist Party.

The GMD had led the seafarers' strike and experienced an influx of several thousand recruits. However, the party was still weak and disorganised, little more than a series of disputing factions. Its leader, Sun, attempted to centralise power in his own hands but was incapable of doing so. The GMD had few effective fighting forces of its own and could not impose its rule on the fractious warlords in Guangdong, still less pose as a government of the whole of China. Sun's slogans – democracy, people's welfare and nationalism – represented an attempt to cohere all classes around his banner. There were some shifts to the left in the party's rhetoric following the Russian Revolution and the May Fourth movement, but the GMD was still run in the interest of capitalists and warlords.

The May Fourth Movement and Russian Revolution also gave a mighty impetus to the formation of a communist party in China. By 1920, the anarchist-influenced politics that had informed many of the activists in the May Fourth Movement had exhausted itself. The attempt to form communes based on new, liberated ways of living had experienced great difficulties, demonstrating the limits class society imposed on individual solutions. The most radical students and intellectuals were looking for new answers. The emergence of an urban working class pointed to Marxism as an alternative road. The Russian Revolution, followed by the Bolshevik government's announcement that it would withdraw Tsarist-era territorial and financial claims on China, enthused students to turn their attention to Marxism. By the end of 1918, Li had established the Marxist Research Society at Peking University, consisting of a dozen students and faculty members who met on campus to study *Capital*. In the autumn of 1919, Li and Chen published a special issue of their journal on Marxism, in which Li wrote the most serious analysis of class struggle and the workings of capitalism that had yet been published in China. Students and intellectuals across the country who were groping for new ideas seized on this article, which brought Marxism to a new audience, although Li's Marxism was not yet thoroughly worked out.

The arrival of Comintern agents Grigori Voitinsky and Yang Mingzhai in the spring of 1920 gave the process another nudge. In August 1920, together with Chen, Li and several other emerging figures, they established a branch of the Comintern in China. They used the new Moscow-financed newspaper, *Shanghai Chronicle*, to disseminate Marxist propaganda. Chen moved to Shanghai and set up the Socialist Youth League, which soon grew to 30 members. The League gathered together the most serious students of their generation, those looking to do more than discuss and debate, but their knowledge of Marxism was meagre, and many were still influenced by anarchism. The intervention in these early years by Comintern emissaries such as Voitinsky and, later, the Dutch Communist Henk Sneevliet was crucial to clarifying the distinctions between anarchism and Marxism. Elsewhere, under the direction of Mao Zedong, a communist group was founded in Hunan, and other groups formed in Hubei and Beijing. Communism also found a following among Chinese students studying in Japan and France, including, Zhou Enlai and Deng Xiaoping, later to become national leaders.

In July 1921, in the absence of the unavailable Li and Chen, and with Voitinsky having left the country, new Comintern representative Henk Sneevliet convened the first Congress of the Communist Party of China (CCP) in Shanghai.[7] Chen was elected secretary-general of the party. The Congress was tiny, bringing together only 12 delegates. Membership of the new party stood at just 50, with another 350 in the more loosely defined youth group. The party was based on a clear call for workers' revolution and declared its sympathies with the Comintern. It was still in an embryonic stage, because of its small size and because of continued conflicts within its ranks over what attitude to take to the GMD. Finances were tight. Only at the CCP's Second Congress in July 1922, held in the aftermath of the Hong Kong seafarers' strike, was the party founded on a solid basis with the help of Russian financial assistance. Even now, however, it had only 195 members, not including those overseas. They were overwhelmingly students and intellectuals with no experience in the workers' movement.

The Chinese Communists looked to the Comintern for guidance, in particular concerning relations with the GMD. While the Second International had given only the briefest attention to the colonial world and never defended the right of the colonies to independence, the Third International openly championed the rights of the oppressed nations, including China. These nations, Lenin told the Comintern's Second Congress, constituted 70 percent of the world's population.[8] Their struggle for freedom was therefore of enormous importance to the Comintern. As Lenin told a congress of the Communist Organisations of the Peoples of the East in Moscow in November 1919:

> The socialist revolution will not be solely, or chiefly, a struggle of the revolutionary proletarians in each country against their bourgeoisie – no, it will be a struggle of all the imperialist-oppressed colonies and countries, of all dependent countries, against international imperialism... The civil war of the working people against the imperialists and exploiters in all the advanced countries is beginning to be combined with national wars against international imperialism.[9]

There was a direct connection between the struggles in the oppressed and oppressor nations. In his 1916 book *Imperialism: the Highest Stage of Capitalism*, Lenin had argued that the ruling classes of the imperialist powers derived immense wealth from their colonies and their prosperity depended on this continuing. Anti-colonial struggles, by disrupting this flow of profits to the imperialist metropoles, could plunge them into economic crisis, thereby opening the door to revolution. Indian Communist M. N. Roy, Lenin's collaborator on the Comintern Commission charged with looking into the issue, told the Second Congress that:

> The breakup of the colonial empire, together with the proletarian revolution in the home country, will overthrow the capitalist system in Europe. Consequently, the Communist International must widen its sphere of activities. It must establish relations with those revolutionary forces that are working for the overthrow of imperialism in the politically and economically subjugated

countries. These two forces must be coordinated if the final success of the world revolution is to be assured.[10]

An additional reason why Communists in the oppressor nations must champion the right of oppressed nations to self-determination was to combat the national chauvinism of their own working classes. Radek urged British Communists attending the Second Congress to make common cause with independence movements in Ireland and India. Failure to do so would only set their own struggles back:

> If the British workers, instead of confronting the bourgeois prejudices, support or passively tolerate British imperialism, then they are working for the suppression of every revolutionary movement in Britain itself. It is impossible for the British proletariat to free itself from the yoke imposed on it by capitalism unless it steps into the breach for the revolutionary colonial movement.[11]

There were two reasons why this was so. Firstly, Radek argued, any workers' state that took power in Britain would need food from Ireland, India and Egypt. If workers and peasants in the colonies saw British workers as their comrades rather than accomplices of imperialism, they would be more likely to offer support for the new workers' state. A more immediate reason was that, so long as workers in the imperial powers retained chauvinist and racist attitudes towards the nationally oppressed peoples, so they bound themselves hand and foot to their own rulers. In 1914, Lenin had had cause to take up this issue in relation to Great Russian chauvinism:

> Let us consider the position of an oppressor nation. Can a nation be free if it oppresses other nations? It cannot. The interests of the freedom of the Great-Russian population require a struggle against such oppression. The long, centuries-old history of the suppression of the movements of the oppressed nations, and the systematic propaganda in favour of such suppression coming from the 'upper' classes have created enormous obstacles to the cause of freedom of the Great-Russian people itself, in the form of prejudices, etc.[12]

Such nationalist prejudices encouraged the Great Russian workers to believe themselves members of a superior civilisation, one duty-bound to rule over the inferior. This only encouraged them to identify with Tsarism and in particular its most reactionary military wing. Russian workers convinced of the glories of the empire were more likely to accept that higher taxes were required to sustain the army, more likely to volunteer their sons for military service, more likely to salute the army as it massacred striking workers. Russian communists were obliged to fight such sentiments. Lenin explained:

> The proletarian revolution calls for a prolonged education of the workers in the spirit of the *fullest* national equality and brotherhood. Consequently, the interests of the Great-Russian proletariat require that the masses be systematically educated to champion – most resolutely, consistently, boldly and in a revolutionary manner – complete equality and the right to self-determination for all the nations oppressed by the Great Russians.[13]

Such arguments applied with equal force to every Communist party in the imperialist countries. The Second Congress therefore determined that each such party must offer its wholehearted support to the national movements in the colonies, not just in word but in deed.

As for Communists in the oppressed countries, where they existed, they must wholeheartedly support the revolutionary liberation movement in the colonies. But this did not mean uncritical support. The CCP in particular faced the pressing question of how to relate to the bourgeois GMD which led the national movement in China but, being capitalist, was hostile to the prospect of seriously mobilising the peasantry for their own class demands. This was a general phenomenon, Lenin noted. The bourgeoisie in the oppressed nations shared with the colonial powers a deep hostility to the liberation of the peasants and workers. Lenin explained to the Congress:

> There has been a certain rapprochement between the bourgeoisie of the exploiting countries and that of the colonies, so that very often, perhaps even in most cases, the bourgeoisie of the oppressed countries, while it does support the national movement, is in full accord with the imperialist bourgeoisie, that is, joins forces with it against all revolutionary movement and revolutionary classes.[14]

Having pointed to the perfidious nature of the bourgeoisie in the colonial world, Lenin continued:

> We, as communists, should and will support bourgeois liberation movements only when they are genuinely revolutionary and when their exponents do not hinder our work of educating and organising in a revolutionary spirit the peasantry and the masses of the exploited.[15]

But where was such a bourgeois liberation movement to be found? The whole experience of class struggle since 1848 had demonstrated that bourgeois movements will *inevitably* resist the demands of the 'masses of the exploited.' The issue prompted a debate at the Second Congress between Lenin and Roy. The latter advanced another set of theses which emphasised the class divisions within the colonies and the need to prioritise building communist parties to foster 'the mass action of the poor and ignorant peasants and workers for their liberation from all forms of exploitation.'[16] The theses adopted by the Congress about the tasks of the communists in the colonial world bore the stamp of both Lenin and Roy's contributions:

> A resolute struggle must be waged against the attempt to clothe the revolutionary liberation movements in the backward countries which are not genuinely communist in communist colours. The Communist International has the duty of supporting the revolutionary movement in the colonies and backward countries only with the object of rallying the constituent elements of the future proletarian parties – which will be truly communist and not only in name – in all the backward countries and educating them to a consciousness of their special task, namely, that of fighting against the bourgeois-democratic trend in their own nation.
>
> The Communist International should collaborate provisionally with the revolutionary movement of the colonies and backward countries, and even form an alliance with it, but it must not amalgamate with it; it must unconditionally maintain the independence of the proletarian movement even if it is only in an embryonic stage.[17]

The critical point for the CCP was that, while collaborating with the 'revolutionary movement,' *the party had to maintain its independence.* How exactly that would be done became the subject of continued controversy for the CCP and the Comintern emissaries sent over to help the young party.

A brief survey of the contending classes in China provides some sense of the environment faced by the CCP. The social structure of China bore some similarities to Russia at the time of the big debates among Russian Marxists in the late 19th century; however, the country was much more economically backward, the working class was much smaller and politically untested, and China, unlike Russia, was nationally oppressed by the imperialist countries. Despite these differences, Trotsky's arguments in his 1906 work, *Results and Prospects* (see Chapter 1), help to shed some light on the tasks facing Chinese revolutionaries in the 1920s, although Trotsky himself made no attempt at that point to generalise his findings beyond Russia.

The Chinese bourgeoisie, made up of several intermingled and heterogeneous layers, was no more revolutionary than the Russian capitalists had been prior to 1917. The fortunes of many of them were tied directly to foreign interests who dominated finance and industry in China. This layer certainly had no interest in throwing out the imperialists. Others did resent imperialist domination and looked to the GMD to promote their interests with respect to the foreign capitalists. Some of them rallied behind the May Fourth Movement, hoping to use it to extract concessions from the imperialists. But they needed access to a mass force to give their demands weight.

The peasantry provided an obvious battering ram for any social class interested in challenging the status quo. But the Chinese peasantry would never rise up around the question of 'the Chinese nation,' which meant nothing to their daily lives. Land was the crux of the matter and 'land to the tillers!' the only demand that meant anything to them. But such a demand was anathema to the capitalists in the cities, many of whom had invested their fortunes in land. 'Land to the tillers!' meant ruin for them. Nor could the capitalists call on workers to rise up behind their banner, because the interests of the working class directly challenged their own. Many Chinese capitalists chafed at the high-handedness of the foreigners who lorded it over them. They wanted more political liberties for themselves but were terrified by the prospect of militant mass mobilisation by Chinese peasants and workers; that had the potential to go beyond opposition to the imperialists, to challenge exploitation across the board. The capitalists were therefore incapable of leading a national movement against foreign occupation.

If the capitalists would not lead the fight, the peasantry could not. The Chinese peasants had an even longer and more heroic record than the Russian peasantry of mass struggle against their exploiters. And yet the conclusion to every such struggle was the installation of a new ruler on the imperial throne or defeat at the hands of the incumbent.

Only the working class, capable of transforming social relations, destroying the old state and erecting a new one on its ruins, could release the peasantry from this vicious historical cycle by cancelling their debts and granting them land. The working class had to ally with the peasantry – but also to *lead* it in struggle against both the imperialists and the domestic exploiters. It must not, under any circumstances, abrogate its leading role to the 'democratic capitalists' who sought only to throw out the foreigners in order to grab greater control for themselves.

Trotsky and Lenin had argued for the central role of Russian workers in the fight against the Tsarist autocracy. They could point to the rapid advancement of capitalism in the countryside and cities. They could point particularly to the struggles by factory workers, which took on mass dimensions for the first time in the 1880s and continued thereafter. By the 1890s, Marxists had set up study circles which drew in many workers. Russian Marxists also avidly followed debates in the Second International and were familiar with the chief tendencies in the European workers' movement. The problem for young Chinese Marxists was that they could point to no such traditions when their party was founded. The Chinese workers' movement was virtually non-existent outside the craft guilds, and Marxism was unknown among leading worker militants – the *Communist Manifesto* was not published in Chinese in its entirety until 1920. The CCP had to build a brand new political tendency in a class that was still in its infancy.

Comintern representative Sneevliet had recently helped form the Communist Party of Indonesia and sought to transfer his methods to China. Sneevliet had urged Indonesian communists to join *Sarekat Islam* (Islamic Union), a 400,000-strong nationalist Islamist movement challenging Dutch colonialism. Sneevliet now urged the Chinese Communists to enter the GMD as individuals to wage Marxist propaganda within it and to organise Communist caucuses within the GMD-dominated trade unions. This became known as the 'bloc within' tactic.

Chen and his comrades hotly opposed Sneevliet's proposal. They argued that the GMD was a capitalist party and aimed to lead Chinese capital and landlords, not the working class. For Communists to join the GMD as individuals would entail their subordination to this capitalist party. Any alliance with the GMD should therefore be temporary, be based on specific issues and ensure the continuing independence of the Communists. At its Second Congress in July 1922, the CCP adopted a manifesto which endorsed a 'democratic united front' with the GMD, while warning that:

> The proletariat's support of the democratic revolution is not [equivalent to] its surrender to the capitalists. The CCP is the party of the proletariat. Its aims are to organise the proletariat and to struggle for [the establishment of] the dictatorship of the workers and peasants, the abolition of private property, and the gradual attainment of a Communist society... The working class must not become the appendage of the petit bourgeoisie within this democratic united front but must fight for their own class interests.[18]

Chen repeated his opposition to the 'bloc within' tactic at the Fourth Comintern Congress in November, arguing that, while cooperation with the GMD was necessary in the fight for democracy and national unification, it was vital for the CCP to retain its independence.

Whether Sneevliet was right – that, for a small group, entering the GMD offered more opportunities than remaining outside – cannot be definitively judged, but the tactic was not itself a matter of *principle*. The Communists were permitted to enter the GMD while retaining their own organisation with its strictly centralised apparatus. The critical issue was when entry led to political *subordination*. That would soon occur, when distortions of Russian foreign policy began to come to the fore in the Comintern.

The civil war was over, but Russia was still isolated, under threat of invasion and eager to find allies. From Moscow's perspective, a stable nationalist government in China, led by the GMD and friendly with Russia, could relieve pressure from Japan. The Russian Communists also judged that the new CCP, with just 300 members in 1923, was in no position to bid for power any time in the near future; the GMD was a much more likely prospect. Russian interest in the GMD was reciprocated. Russia's success in beating back the White armies during the Civil War had attracted international attention. The GMD was an organisational shambles and had little military strength; Sun looked to Russia to remedy these deficiencies. In January 1923, following months of meetings between Sun and Sneevliet, Sun and the Russian emissary Adolph Joffe signed an agreement confirming cooperation between the Russian government and the GMD. The statement declared that communism was off the agenda in China and that the CCP's efforts should henceforth be devoted to supporting the GMD's bid for national unification and independence. Russia offered to assist the GMD in the formation of an army, with weapons and military training. The decision to do so aroused considerable controversy on the Comintern Executive, with Voitinsky and G. I. Safarov, head of the Eastern Section of the Comintern, both opposing Russian assistance to the GMD and accusing Sneevliet of covering up the true politics of the GMD.

The CCP's Third Congress in June 1923 saw another heated debate as Sneevliet again insisted that the CCP enter the GMD. CCP leaders remained reluctant to do so, but loyalty to the Comintern eventually prevailed. Delegates endorsed a manifesto stating that the:

> GMD should be the central force of the national revolution and should assume its leadership... We hope that all the revolutionary elements in our society will rally to the GMD, speeding the completion of the national revolutionary movement.[19]

In January 1924, Communists were admitted to the GMD, pledging loyalty to the organisation and its leadership. Henceforth, as CCP members led the most radical workers' struggles, they increasingly did so under the blue and white banner of the GMD and moved towards a class collaborationist perspective.

While Sneevliet's instruction for the tiny CCP to enter the GMD was controversial, he was at least motivated by a desire to build the forces of communism in China. By 1925 at the latest, the Comintern under Zinoviev had abandoned this project in favour of its alliance with the GMD, which made the CCP expendable. The Comintern had thrown in its lot with a party devoted to the interests of the capitalists and landlords at the expense of a party devoted to the victory of the proletariat. The Chinese Communists were now to hold the workers back if ever they should threaten the GMD and the class interests it represented. This was little more than warmed-over Menshevism – or worse, because at least the Mensheviks had never advocated joining the Cadets and submitting to their orders, which would have been the Russian equivalent of the Comintern's instructions in China. American journalist Harold Isaacs, who spent several years in China in the 1930s, spelled out the significance of the Comintern's new perspective in his classic work, *The Tragedy of the Chinese Revolution*:

> The course thus laid before the Communists led directly and unavoidably to the idea that the national struggle against imperialism preceded or temporarily postponed the struggle between the classes. The very idea that classes with opposing interests could unite in a single party was based on the assumption that imperialism temporarily welded the interests of the various classes instead of deepening the antagonism between them. It

assumed that the bourgeoisie could and would play not only a revolutionary role, but the leading role in the national revolutionary movement. This was a radical shift from the broad line of strategy laid down by Lenin at the Second World Congress of the Comintern, for it immediately canalized the Nationalist movement on to bourgeois-democratic lines and put an end to the political and organizational independence of the Communist Party.[20]

The class struggle advances

The first wave of working class struggle, kicked off by the Hong Kong seafarers' strike, was brought to an end in the winter of 1923 when a northern warlord smashed a strike by railway workers, killing 35 and wounding many more. Other bosses took advantage of the railway workers' defeat to go on the offensive. Workers soon hit back in 1924 with massive May Day marches in Guangzhou and Shanghai, and a peasant movement began to spread across the country the following winter.

In May 1925, a second wave of struggle broke out when textile workers in Shanghai struck in the city's Japanese-owned cotton mills. In picket line fighting, security guards killed a young worker. Several thousand students and workers marched in protest on 30 May. British police stationed in the city's international concession fired on the demonstration, killing 12 and wounding many more. Two days later, the General Labour Union, newly formed by the CCP, launched a general strike in Shanghai against foreign capitalists; within a fortnight, 160,000 workers in foreign-owned businesses across the city were on strike. What started as a dispute about wages and a protest against imperialist injustice began to develop into a political battle for national liberation. This combination of economic and anti-imperialist demands characterised the popular struggle in the following years.

Nowhere was the link between economic and political demands clearer than in Hong Kong and Guangzhou. On 21 June, workers in the two cities struck in protest against the 30 May massacre. On 23 June, as striking workers and students in Guangzhou marched past the foreign concessions, British and French police opened fire, killing 52 and wounding more than 100. Word of the massacre spread rapidly to Hong Kong, where workers in the British colony went on strike and initiated a boycott of British goods.

To avoid being forced back to work, many Hong Kong strikers moved to Guangzhou. There they set up a strike committee of 13, responsible to a delegate conference of 800 which met twice a week. The strike committee became known as 'Government Number Two,' a rival to the GMD government in Guangzhou. It was, as Isaacs describes it, 'the first embryo of workers' power in China.'[21] The strike committee supervised the feeding, housing and entertainment of the strikers. It requisitioned the gambling dens and opium houses and reopened them as dormitories, rest rooms and education centres. The strike committee published a weekly newspaper and organised schools for adult workers and their children. It set up an army of 2,000 uniformed and armed pickets to blockade Hong Kong and Shamian Island (home to foreign capitalists and embassies in Guangzhou) and established courts to ensure civil order. It even maintained a fleet of gunships to apprehend river smugglers. With British businesses in Hong Kong losing £250,000 a day as a result of the strike and boycott, the colony's governor complained: 'An attack has been made upon us, as representing the existing standards of civilisation, by the agents of disorder and anarchy.'[22]

The Chinese capitalists were also alarmed by developments in the southern cities. They had encouraged the May Thirtieth movement in its early days, calculating that they could benefit from British losses; but they were increasingly concerned about the grip of the strike committee over the life of Guangzhou and Hong Kong. Their concern grew when strikes broke out across the country in the summer of 1925. Workers flocked to trade unions. Peasants seized land, forming peasant associations which operated in many villages as embryonic soviets, complete with armed militias. The CCP, which had thrown itself into the struggle, grew rapidly: from just 1,000 members – most of them students and unemployed workers – at the start of 1925 to 10,000 at the time of the May Thirtieth Movement and to 20,000 by the end of 1926, with workers now constituting two-thirds of the membership. The CCP played a leading role in the new mass unions, with the leaders of the Hong Kong seafarers joining the party. Communists also won support in the old craft guilds, weakened by rapid industrialisation in the big coastal cities and open to new leadership.[23] The CCP's newfound strength once again posed the question: how much longer must it submit to Comintern orders to tail the GMD?

With Russian help, the GMD also began to build its forces. Sneevliet had returned to Moscow in 1923 and been replaced by Mikhail Borodin, whose main responsibility was not to advise the CCP but to work with the GMD. He fell to this task with gusto, transforming the GMD from a weakling to a significant political and military authority. Very soon, the Russian emissary was attending meetings of the GMD central executive. In January 1924, Borodin convened the GMD's First Congress and wrote the major documents. It was he who won the GMD's support at this Congress for the entry of CCP members into the party as loyal members abiding by its rules, and he arranged for three CCP members to be elected to the 41-strong central executive.

The pages of the CCP's journal began to fill with articles extolling the merits of the GMD. No longer was the GMD denounced as a capitalist and landlord party. It was now, supposedly, a 'bloc of four classes' – workers, peasants, patriotic businesspeople and intellectuals – that could lead the fight to throw off warlord and imperialist oppression and establish a true People's Republic. The CCP's role was to build a left wing within the GMD to combat feudal elements in its ranks and to guide its leadership onto a revolutionary path. CCP cadres under Borodin's direction spent much of their time building GMD branches, recruiting workers directly to the GMD. The result was that the GMD became a centralised party for the first time, with a mass membership in all areas of society. Sun, needless to say, refused to be 'guided' by the CCP and threatened Communists with expulsion if they criticised his leadership.

Russian funding and military support were just as important for the GMD's development. In 1923, Moscow forwarded the CCP 12,000 gold rubles in quarterly instalments to pay for the party's expenses. By contrast, Russia earmarked two million gold rubles for the GMD, nearly 200 times as much. Much of this money went to setting up a GMD military academy at Whampoa. Chiang Kai-shek, hailing from a wealthy merchant family and with extensive connections to the criminal underworld, was appointed commander of the academy. The CCP's Zhou Enlai was nominal second in command. Russia's arms shipments and military training transformed the GMD's puny military forces into a professional army. By 1926, the Whampoa academy had trained 3,000 men from landed gentry families to form the officer class of the new Nationalist Army; these were to become Chiang's counter-revolutionary shock troops.

Sun died in March 1925, and Chiang Kai-shek took over the GMD leadership. Now a mass party and with military capability growing rapidly, the GMD attracted those who saw in it the potential for a strong centralised government capable of protecting the property of the wealthy. For the first time, the GMD began to extend its authority beyond Guangdong into neighbouring provinces. In June, it proclaimed itself the Government of China.

In January 1926, the GMD's Second Congress appeared to register success for the CCP and its energetic involvement in the GMD. Delegates who identified with the CCP and the left GMD accounted for a majority. The Congress passed left wing resolutions and elected leftists to senior positions. Moscow played up the GMD's left credentials in its greetings:

> To our party has fallen the proud and historic task of leading the first victorious proletarian revolution... We are convinced that the Kuomintang will succeed in playing the same role in the East.[24]

One month later, with only Trotsky voting against, the Comintern Executive approved the admission of the GMD as an associate party and elected Chiang as an honorary member of the Executive. Trotsky later wrote of this episode: 'In preparing himself for the role of an executioner, he [Chiang] wanted to have the cover of world communism – and he achieved it.'[25]

The attempt to paint the GMD red was a cynical ploy by Stalin, who was coming to dominate in Moscow. In terms of forces on the ground, as opposed to conference votes, it was the right, based in the landlord families whose sons were undertaking military training at Whampoa, which dominated the GMD. The GMD right were confident class warriors and were now on the offensive against the CCP. Led by Chiang, they openly opposed strikes, the peasant leagues and the very presence of the CCP in the GMD. At the GMD Second Congress, Chiang secured an obligation by the CCP to limit its membership of GMD committees to one-third and to submit a list of Communists in leading GMD positions to the leadership. The CCP protested, but the Comintern forced it to comply.

On 20 March 1926, Chiang tightened the screws in Guangzhou, putting the city under martial law and arresting his Russian advisers, along with CCP leaders and the strike committee. Having been repeatedly assured by Borodin of Chiang's reliability, the CCP was caught off guard by Chiang's coup. Borodin again instructed the Communists not to fight but to submit to still more humiliating GMD orders, including that the party hand over a list of all party members, remove all Communists from GMD leadership positions and apologise to Chiang for 'misdemeanours' – the party's failure to crawl abjectly to the GMD leader.

CCP leaders demanded for the third time to be allowed to break from the GMD and appealed to Borodin for arms to defend themselves. Borodin rejected their plea, telling them: 'The present period is one in which the Communists should do coolie service for the Kuomintang.'[26] Walking away from the GMD, Borodin argued, would be abandoning the 'revolutionary GMD' to the bourgeoisie; besides, the workers were too weak to lead the revolution. In Moscow itself, where the Stalin–Bukharin axis was under threat from the United Opposition led by Trotsky, Zinoviev and Kamenev, the leadership simply pretended that all was well in China and that any talk of a split in the 'revolutionary alliance' of the CCP and GMD was an imperialist lie.

The Northern Expedition and the Communists' bloody defeat

Late in the summer of 1926, Chiang's Nationalist Army struck out from its base in the south to conquer China. Chiang's Northern Expedition was accompanied by an explosion of rural uprisings and land seizures, because peasants believed that the hour of liberation had come. Railway workers took control of railway lines to secure the movement of Chiang's army and prevent the movement of its enemies. Strikes surged, and union membership soared. The CCP was to the fore in organising the revolts

The Comintern Executive, now led by Bukharin after Zinoviev's dismissal, became alarmed by the peasant and worker uprising in China, fearing that it would sow divisions in the united front with the GMD. The Executive ordered the CCP to target only 'reactionaries, militaries and compradores and those landlords and gentry who are waging civil war against the Kuomintang National Government.'[27] Other landlords and capitalists were to be left untouched. There was, therefore, a constant tension in the operations of the CCP between the natural instincts of the party and its supporters – to urge the struggle on – and the instructions from Moscow to hold it back.

The Nationalist Army swept all before it. By January 1927, Chiang's forces were advancing on Shanghai – still in the hands of warlords and imperialists. Ostensibly, the Northern Expedition was a joint GMD–CCP operation to free China from such forces, but Shanghai gave the lie to this. The GMD, the warlords, the imperialists and the Chinese capitalists all had a common enemy in the militant working class in Shanghai and its Communist leadership. They conspired to destroy it. In late November 1926, Zhang Zuolin, the warlord who controlled Beijing, had mobilised an army of 150,000 to march south to attack the advancing Nationalist Army; he then suddenly countermanded the order, allowing Chiang's army to advance on Shanghai unobstructed. Japanese forces also stood back to allow Chiang free passage.

Chinese factory owners and bankers in Shanghai also threw their weight behind Chiang. Like their colleagues in Guangzhou, they had initially welcomed the workers' movement as an opportunity to squeeze concessions from the imperialist powers. Now, they grew alarmed by the insurrectionary movement. At the end of 1926, the head of the Shanghai Chamber of Commerce offered Chiang substantial financial support. The big bosses also held discussions with the chief of Chinese detectives in the French concession. He was a major underworld figure in close contact with the Green Gang, the city's biggest secret society and controller of its prostitution trade, gambling rackets and opium distribution. The purpose of these discussions was to ensure that squads of armed thugs would be on hand to attack the working class when Chiang's army entered the city.

As the counter-revolutionary forces were being drawn together, the Comintern instructed the CCP in Shanghai to treat Chiang's troops as comrades-in-arms. To greet their arrival, the CCP-run General Labour Union called a general strike for 19 February. Workers in their hundreds of thousands heeded the call and seized control of large areas of the city. Shanghai's police, warlords and gangsters rallied their forces and fought back, inflicting heavy casualties. Frightened that his own soldiers would join the striking workers and fraternise with the Communists if he allowed them to march into the city, Chiang held his forces back 40 kilometres from the city and allowed the slaughter to proceed.

Although the first strike was beaten, workers were not decisively crushed. On 21 March, Chiang's forces began to move closer to the city, and the General Labour Union launched a second general strike and an armed insurrection. Again, the workers seized control of the city. Isaacs states:

> Practically every worker in Shanghai came out onto the streets. Their ranks swelled when they were joined by shop employees and the hordes of the city poor. Between 500,000 and 800,000 people were directly involved.[28]

Workers cut power and telephone lines, seized police stations and occupied railway stations, often after heavy fighting. New unions were created, and union membership ballooned in the insurrectionary atmosphere. On 27 March, 1,000 delegates representing 300 union branches attended the General Labour Union conference. According to the GLU, there were now 499 unions in the city, representing more than 800,000 workers. There was also a 2,700-strong workers' militia, well armed with weapons seized from police stations and military depots. The CCP grew by leaps and bounds, reaching 58,000 by April, a threefold increase in less than four months.

On 26 March, Chiang himself arrived in Shanghai. CCP members were instructed to greet the GMD army with banners 'Hail the National Revolutionary Army! Welcome to Chiang Kai-shek!'[29] and to hand the city over to the GMD boss. But Chiang did not return the CCP's warm wishes. Instead, he hurried to meet the representatives of Shanghai's capitalists and underworld gangs to put the final touches to their plans to massacre the workers.

The GMD had made no secret of its intentions towards the CCP and the worker militants it led. The Nationalist Army had murdered workers and broken unions in town after town as it marched down the Yangtze River to Shanghai. The Comintern leadership, whose emissaries followed in the train of Chiang's forces, covered up these attacks or simply attributed them to 'right GMD' forces. To have revealed the truth would have wrecked the united front between the CCP and GMD, and that would have undermined Stalin's authority in Moscow. Trotsky had begun to argue that Chiang was preparing a coup against the workers and peasants, something fiercely denied by the Comintern Executive: 'A split in the GMD and hostilities between the Shanghai proletariat and the revolutionary soldiers are absolutely excluded right now.'[30] Stalin told an audience of 3,000 Red Army officers in Moscow that:

> Chiang Kai-shek was submitting to discipline, the KMT is a bloc, a sort of revolutionary parliament, with the right, the left and the Communists.[31]

Although Chiang was no revolutionary, Stalin argued, the GMD leader had no option but to turn his guns on the imperialists. Stalin said that Chiang could be used by the Communists and then 'squeezed out like a lemon and then flung away.'[32]

But Stalin ensured that it was the Communists who were squeezed. Step by step, the CCP, acting on Moscow's orders, weakened the revolutionary forces in Shanghai in order to ensure GMD control of the city. The General Labour Union ordered workers to rein in strikes and continued to argue for the united front with the GMD. The CCP gradually wound back the city's provisional municipal government after the city's capitalists boycotted it. While CCP leader Chen Duxiu urged worker militants undertaking picket duties to retaliate if attacked by right GMD forces, he rejected the Communist Youth League's appeal for workers to be armed with wooden staves, on the grounds that it would encourage 'hooliganism.' And when the commander in charge of Chiang's forces in Shanghai, General Xue Yue, approached the CCP with an offer to arrest Chiang and to bring his men over to the Communists, the party leaders baulked at the offer, because it would have resulted in a split in the united front. Chiang took advantage of the CCP's refusal and ordered General Xue's First Division out of the city, replacing it with loyal units untouched by the revolutionary virus.

The CCP's instincts were often to fight, but Stalin repeatedly pulled them back. When the CCP Central Committee sent a telegram on 31 March, saying that Chiang 'has already begun a coup in Shanghai,' the Russian politburo replied on the same day: 'Do not for a moment, engage in open battle…do not give up arms, hide them if necessary.'[33]

The CCP's kowtowing to the GMD did not save them. In the first week of April, piecemeal attacks against the CCP and its offices began. On 12 April, Chiang delivered his *coup de grace*. Paramilitary forces of gangsters, with the support of imperialist security forces and Chiang's troops, attacked the headquarters of all the large unions, killing union leaders, arresting hundreds of unionists and disarming pickets. Under orders from Moscow, the CCP allowed its members to go like lambs to the slaughter, not even appealing to Chiang's soldiers to turn their guns on their officers. Having been told that the GMD were allies in the revolutionary war to drive out warlords and imperialists, many workers were completely unprepared for this murderous turn of events. Between 2,000 and 5,000 Communists and worker militants were killed in Shanghai and thousands more were arrested or fired from their jobs. CCP membership in the city collapsed, from a peak of 8,000 members in March to just 1,200 by late July. Having crushed the working class in Shanghai, Chiang extended his anti-Communist purge to other cities, massacring thousands more.

First time as tragedy, second time as farce

Chiang's coup in Shanghai forced the Comintern to change course. It switched support to the supposed left GMD government in Wuhan, led by Wang Ching-wei, who had split from Chiang. Even now, however, the Comintern Executive could not admit that its instructions to the CCP had been wrong. Quite the opposite – Bukharin doubled down, stating baldly that the Comintern's strategy up until Chiang's coup in Shanghai had been completely correct. That phase of the revolution had now closed, Bukharin argued. The Comintern Executive now sought to prettify the left GMD, describing it as a new revolutionary bloc of three classes, the proletariat, peasantry and petit bourgeoisie, the bourgeoisie having joined the 'feudal-imperialist alliance.' Bukharin instructed the CCP to 'take a most energetic part' in the work of what he called the Wuhan 'provisional revolutionary government.'[34] The CCP leaders again swallowed their reservations and delegated two members to serve as Ministers for Agriculture and Labour. While the Comintern did its best to play up their appointment as a step forward for the revolution, Isaacs describes the situation more accurately: the ministers were 'hostages and compliant agents of Kuomintang policies.'[35]

The provinces over which the Wuhan government nominally ruled were in revolutionary ferment. The peasantry, particularly in Hunan, had risen up. The GMD's nationalist rhetoric against the imperialists did not move the peasants. Their enemies were much closer to hand: the landlords and their hired thugs who had terrorised and exploited their families and villages for generations. Rather than wait helplessly for the Wuhan government to give them land – which would never happen, given the GMD's ties to the landlords – the peasants seized it themselves. They formed peasant associations, drove out the landlords and asserted democratic rule over villages. They set up popular courts and dispensed justice. They took over temples and converted them to schools and meeting places. Superstitions and entrenched habits, in particular the severe oppression of women, were challenged. Foot-binding was abolished. Women cut their hair short and demanded rights. Rent to landlords was abolished. Loans outstanding at usurious rates of interest were declared cancelled. The peasant associations also cracked down on opium smoking and gambling dens. Under peasant control, the villages knew such peace and justice as they had never experienced before.

The landlords and their thugs initially fled the villages but soon gathered their forces and counterattacked, torturing and murdering thousands of peasants. The peasant associations demanded the protection of the Wuhan government and, if that could not be provided, rifles to defend themselves. The government did nothing to help them. Far from arming the peasants, the CCP Minister for Agriculture turned his back on them, condemning land seizures as threatening good relations with the landlords.

In late May, the counter-revolution was ratcheted up further. General Xu Kexiang, the Nationalist commander of the garrison in Changsha, capital of Hunan, mounted an all-out attack on the revolutionary forces in the city. Xu's soldiers ransacked the left GMD offices and the quarters of the many workers', peasants' and students organisations, arresting and shooting everyone they found. Wholesale slaughter of civilians followed. Once begun at the provincial capital, the terror spread throughout the province. During the next few months, an estimated 20,000 people were killed. When local peasant leaders in Hunan province mobilised an army of several thousands to march on Changsha to put down the reactionaries, the CCP Central Committee in Wuhan ordered them to retreat 'in order to avoid further friction' with the GMD.[36] The result was a bloody reign of terror in the province, forcible reappropriation of land that had been seized, the arrest of thousands of activists and many hundreds of executions. The CCP did its best to pretend that none of this was happening.

By July, Wang, the leader of the left GMD government in Wuhan, had patched up his differences with Chiang and turned on the CCP in Hubei province. By the end of the month, thousands more lay dead, and all unions and peasant associations were declared illegal.

The disaster in China had an effect inside Russia. Trotsky had begun to campaign against the Comintern line on China in the spring of 1927, arguing that Wang could not be trusted; peasants should be organised to form soviets and provided with arms to fight the threat of counter-revolution. Stalin and Bukharin denounced the suggestion, arguing that the establishment of soviets would challenge the 'revolutionary government' in Wuhan. Even at the time that this 'revolutionary government' had declared war on the peasants, Stalin and Bukharin instructed the CCP to hold fire.

On 6 July, when the CCP had been decisively defeated, Bukharin suddenly announced a sharp change of Comintern line: the Chinese Communists should fight the GMD. This was followed one week later by a fresh Comintern statement saying that, although the GMD had joined the counter-revolutionary camp, the CCP should nonetheless remain within it. Stalin and Bukharin pinned the blame for the debacle in China on the hapless CCP leaders, although they had done nothing other than loyally follow Comintern instructions. On 7 August, Chen was deposed as party leader on the grounds of his supposed 'right opportunism.' The CCP now abandoned its strategy of urban insurrection and emphasised instead using the party's militias to capture cities from without.

In early August, the CCP's armed forces, now badged the Red Army, seized the city of Nanchang in Jiangxi province. They were soon driven out by the GMD and forced to retreat hundreds of kilometres east to the wilderness of Fujian province.

In September, Stalin ordered the remnants of the CCP to mount a series of revolts, known as the 'Autumn Harvest Uprisings.' Four regiments of the Red Army, led by Mao, attacked strategic towns in Hunan. At a time when the priority should have been defensive consolidation of the CCP's forces, this was sheer adventurism. Each rising, horribly isolated, went down to defeat; most of the party units were quickly wiped out. Mao now pulled the party's remaining forces out and sought refuge in the mountainous area of Jiangxi province, indicating another important shift in CCP strategy – from attacking big cities to building in the rural areas.

Stalin needed a victory in China to help dampen criticism in Russia of his disastrous policies. In November, he ordered the CCP to launch an insurrection in Guangzhou, timed to coincide with the Fifteenth Congress of the Russian party. The CCP military commanders in Guangzhou, the last remaining area of party strength in the cities, knew that this adventure stood no chance of success but, again, agreed to do Moscow's bidding. On 11 December, several thousand ill-equipped Red Guards, completely isolated from the organised working class but taking advantage of the element of surprise, seized the city. Within two days, much larger numbers of well-armed Nationalist troops moved into the city and crushed the insurgents. The Communists suffered heavy casualties, with 6,000 killed and an equal number missing. One day after the Guangzhou uprising was crushed, with Chiang no longer needing Stalin's support to put down the insurgency, the GMD broke off relations with Moscow. It was the CCP and the Comintern, not Chiang, who turned out to be the lemon that was squeezed and then thrown away.

Stalin's suicidal venture in Guangzhou destroyed what was left of the CCP's urban base and the party's leadership in the south. Between March 1927 and June 1928, the GMD and warlords killed more than 26,000 Communists. Party membership collapsed to just 10,000. Trade unions and peasant associations were outlawed or disbanded.[37]

The CCP's withdrawal to Jiangxi province enabled the party to survive but fundamentally changed its character. From being an overwhelmingly proletarian mass party in early 1927, it became a party dominated by professional guerrilla fighters. Military power, not workers' social power, was now key to the party's future advance. Mao announced:

> One of the Party's mistakes in the past was that it neglected the military. Now we must pay sixty per cent of our attention to the military movement. We must seize and build political power by means of the gun.[38]

This conception formed the basis of Mao Zedong's later rise to leadership, signifying the party's abandonment of working class revolution. Chapter 16 will explain how the CCP's change of strategy coloured the later struggle for power.

The Comintern and the Chinese defeat

In 1931, Trotsky described the Chinese Revolution of 1925-27 as 'the greatest event of modern history after the Revolution of 1917 in Russia.'[39] But it ended in tragedy. One perspective holds that the Chinese working class and peasantry were doomed to fail. US historian Lynda Shaffer argues that the objective conditions were against the young CCP: any notion that workers in Shanghai could have seized and held power was 'a fantasy.'[40] The working class was too small and the warlords too powerful. Even if the CCP had received the best advice from the Comintern's emissaries, Shaffer argues, they could not have held on to the power they had seized in the cities and would still have been wiped out. British historian Steve Smith draws similar conclusions, based on his assessment of the situation in Shanghai. The Communists lacked their own military force and were too weak to challenge Chiang and his Nationalist Army; the largely migrant working class of the city was too riven by particularistic loyalties based on native place and clientelist ties with supervisors, labour contractors or informal brotherhoods and sisterhoods; and Shanghai's citizens saw Chiang as a liberator, not a counter-revolutionary, so could not be roused to fight him.

Modern CCP accounts of the Communist defeat in 1927 attribute it to three factors: the 'superior strength and political experience of the combined imperialist and feudal forces'; Chiang's 'sudden betrayal' and surprise attack' on the CCP; and the 'Right capitulationist errors' of Chen Duxiu.[41]

There can never be any guarantees of success for any revolutionary movement. But Stalin's support for the GMD *ensured* defeat for the Chinese working class. Two elements of the Comintern's intervention were crucial. Firstly, it transformed the GMD from a weak outfit, badly organised, ill equipped and militarily impotent, into a powerful mass party with a strong leadership and military capacity – which it used to crush the revolution. Had Moscow instead provided the CCP with substantial funding, weapons and military specialists, the balance of power would have been fundamentally different.

Secondly, the Comintern lied about the GMD, describing what was actually a party of the landed gentry, urban business owners and Nationalist army officers as a 'workers' and peasants' party,' thereby covering up its counter-revolutionary role. This fundamentally misoriented Chinese Communists and the militant workers in their periphery. This error was not the result of Chen's 'right capitulationism' but of the Comintern's own directives, which were informed not by, as the CCP now puts it, the Comintern's 'failure to understand the actual conditions in China,' but its desire to maintain Russia's pact with Chiang.[42] Had the CCP instead relentlessly criticised Chiang, rather than providing him with left cover, Shanghai's workers would have kept up their guard as the Nationalist Army marched into the city. Had the Communists appealed to Chiang's foot soldiers to switch sides, there was at least a chance they could have won them over, dividing the Nationalist forces which were thinly stretched and, as the case of General Xue indicated, not entirely reliable. By giving the GMD a 'left face,' the CCP also undermined its opportunity to force a split in the ranks of the GMD itself. There were tensions within the GMD that could have been exploited by the CCP if it had maintained a clearly independent political line fighting for a working class program. However as the CCP slavishly followed first Chiang and then the 'left GMD,' it lost any possibility of decisively winning over the peasants and workers under left GMD influence to communism. Telling the truth about the GMD and splitting it were, however, the last things on Stalin's mind.

Many CCP leaders wanted to fight the GMD. They knew far too much of Chiang's record to have possibly been 'surprised' by his attack on the party, as the CCP now dishonestly claims. On 1 April, shortly before Chiang's coup in Shanghai, the party's leader in the city, Luo Yinong, called a meeting of district secretaries, telling them to recruit thousands of new members to the party with the aim of overthrowing Chiang. Five days later, at a meeting of CCP activists, Luo told those assembled that Chiang could not be trusted and was 'the focus of all reactionary forces.'[43] Chiang was preparing a coup against the CCP, Luo said, and therefore on no account should the comrades hide their weapons. This much the CCP leaders understood from their practical experience with the GMD. But they lacked theoretical clarity about the counter-revolutionary nature of the GMD, and this undermined them in their criticisms of the Stalin-Bukharin line. The result was that they flip-flopped between urging resistance to Chiang and political accommodation to him, or criticising him privately but never in public. The mass of Shanghai workers were therefore never to hear the CCP's warnings.

Trotsky's fight against Stalin and Bukharin only came to public attention in 1928, after the slaughter of Chinese Communists.[44] Immediately, hundreds of Chinese Communists declared their support for the Left Opposition. Opposition was particularly widespread among CCP members attending the Comintern training institution in Moscow, the Sun Yat-sen University. Stalin retaliated. He sacked director Karl Radek, who had invited both Trotsky and the now-sidelined Bukharin to lecture to students, and replaced him with Pavel Mif and his Chinese lieutenant Wang Ming – who went on to serve as Stalin's stooge in the CCP in the 1930s. Stalinist thugs harassed the Chinese Left Oppositionists in Moscow and, in late 1929, scores were arrested by the GPU, the Russian political police. Some were imprisoned and then deported if they agreed to recant; some were sent to labour camps in Siberia or the Arctic Circle; some were shot. Fewer than a dozen of those who refused to capitulate to Stalin managed to get back to China, where they helped to set up Left Opposition cells.

Some of Trotsky's supporters believed that the disaster in China might undermine Stalin and his project of socialism in one country. Defeat, however, only made his project more appealing. Trotsky wrote in 1930 about the impact of the Chinese debacle:

> The fact that our forecast [of catastrophe] had proved correct might attract one thousand, five thousand, or even ten thousand new supporters to us. But for the millions the significant thing was not our forecast but the fact of the crushing of the Chinese proletariat. After the defeat of the German revolution in 1923, after the breakdown of the English general strike in 1926, the new disaster in China would only intensify the disappointment of the masses in the international revolution. And it was this same disappointment that served as the chief psychological source for Stalin's policy of national-reformism.[45]

Henceforth, 'socialism in one country,' Stalin's 'national-reformism,' was seen as the only way forward by most of those attracted to communism. Stalin secured his absolute power on the bones of thousands of Chinese workers and peasants who lost their lives because of the Comintern's criminally destructive leadership.

FURTHER READING

J. Chesneaux, *The Chinese Labor Movement 1919–1927*, Stanford, Stanford University Press, 1968.

Communist International, 'Theses on the National and Colonial Question Adopted by the Second Comintern Congress', 28 July 1920, in J. Degras (ed.), *The Communist International, 1919–1943, Documents, Volume I 1919–1922*, 1955.

J. Fenby, *The Penguin History of Modern China*, London, Penguin Books, 2013.

N. Harris, *The Mandate of Heaven: Marx and Mao in Modern China*, Chicago, Haymarket Books, 2015 [1978].

C. Hore, *The Road to Tiananmen Square*, London, Bookmarks, 1991.

H. Isaacs, *The Tragedy of the Chinese Revolution*, Chicago, Haymarket Books, 2009 [1938].

S.A. Smith, *A Road is Made: Communism in Shanghai, 1920–1927*, London, Routledge, 2000.

L. Trotsky, 'III. Summary and Perspectives of the Chinese Revolution: Its Lessons for the Countries of the Orient and for the Whole of the Comintern', in *The Third International after Lenin*, Pathfinder, 1996 [1928].

THE COMINTERN'S ULTRA LEFTIST TURN

1928 to 1933

8.

'SOCIAL FASCISM': THE PATH TO NAZI VICTORY IN GERMANY

The Third Period

The degeneration of the revolution in Russia was reflected in a series of gyrations in Comintern policy. After pursuing a right turn in the period of the British General Strike and Chinese Revolution, with the Comintern ordering Communist parties to attach themselves to trade union leaders and bourgeois nationalists respectively, the Comintern Executive superficially reversed direction. In 1928-29, it embraced an ultra left perspective that led to the entirely avoidable disaster of Hitler's triumph in Germany – the worst horror ever to befall the working class.

The ultra left turn had its roots in Stalin's program of crash industrialisation and forced collectivisation of agriculture as embodied in the first Five Year Plan. This required an offensive against the wing of the Communist party represented by Bukharin. Bukharin gave voice to the interests of the NEPmen and wealthy peasants, advocating continuation of the NEP and 'socialism at a snail's pace.'

Such an approach was incompatible with Stalin's program in which the rich peasants were not to be cosseted but expropriated. The ultra left turn was the political stick Stalin used to beat Bukharin and the social layers he represented, while also providing him with left cover against Trotsky, whose attacks on Stalin were hitting home with some in the party. The ultra left policy also had a subsidiary benefit. Although it was not designed consciously in this way, the policy effectively isolated the Communist parties from the working class movement, rendering them abstentionist and passive. These parties therefore proved no threat to their ruling classes, and in particular the German ruling class, with which the Russian bureaucracy hoped to conduct more foreign trade – in particular, import of industrial machinery and export of Russian raw materials, on which the Five Year Plan depended.

The first element of the ultra left turn was proclaimed at the Sixth Comintern Congress of July 1928. The Executive Committee announced the end of the 'second period' of 'capitalist stabilisation' and the arrival of:

> the third period...a period of intense development of the contradictions in the world economy...of the general crisis of capitalism...a fresh era of imperialist wars among the imperialist states themselves; wars of the imperialist states against the USSR; wars of national liberation against imperialism; wars of imperialist intervention and gigantic class battles.[1]

This assessment bore no resemblance to the world economy at this time, which was still growing and would continue to grow for another year. Had the Comintern Executive been a revolutionary body, the formulation could have been corrected at a subsequent meeting if necessary. The Executive, however, was no longer a revolutionary body. It was developing its program not on the basis of the needs of the working class but those of Stalin and the emerging Russian ruling class. This became clear when it doubled down on the 'Third Period' with the suicidal policy of 'social fascism.'

'Social fascism' was not new to the Comintern. In the aftermath of the defeat of the German October, Zinoviev had argued: 'The leading strata of the German Social Democrats are at the present moment nothing else than a fraction of German fascists under a socialist mask.'[2] Stalin followed, asserting:

> Objectively, Social Democracy is a moderate wing of fascism.
> They are not poles apart but immediate neighbours.[3]

Misleading formulations such as these continued to circulate in the Comintern in the mid- to late 1920s, particularly in the KPD. In July 1929, with Bukharin having been replaced as Comintern leader by Stalin's protégé Vyacheslav Molotov, the Executive announced social fascism as the new Comintern orthodoxy:

> In this situation of growing imperialist contradictions and sharpening of the class struggle, Fascism becomes more and more the dominant method of bourgeois rule. In countries where there are strong Social-Democratic parties, Fascism assumes the

particular form of Social-Fascism, which to an ever-increasing extent serves the bourgeoisie as an instrument for the paralysing of the activity of the masses in the struggle against the regime of Fascist dictatorship.[4]

It was true that social democratic parties played a role in paving the way for fascism, both directly, as in the SPD's creation of the Freikorps during the November Revolution, and indirectly, because they supported capitalism. But there was much more to the argument than that. Third Period Stalinism stated not just that social democracy could not hold back fascism, but that reformist parties had become, or were well on the way to becoming, fascists themselves, 'social fascists.' Social fascism was held up as a *worse* threat to workers than fascism, with the left wing of the social democrats, the 'left social fascists,' *the most* dangerous of all.

'Social fascism' was ultra left lunacy. With fascism on the march in Europe, the idea that social democrats were the main enemy of the working class was completely irresponsible. This was not a genuine, organic ultra leftism, usually associated with impatient, newly radicalised workers and students, such as afflicted the KPD in its early years. It was a cynical policy adopted by Stalin to hammer the Bukharinist wing of the party in order to force through the transformation of the Russian economy. Those party leaders who opposed the new line were condemned as soft on social fascists, objectively allies of the main enemy confronting workers. They were replaced by yes-men, lackeys for Stalin.

The 'social fascism' policy had terrible consequences for the international working class. Nowhere was this clearer than in Germany, where it paved the way for the fascist victory.

The social base of Nazism

The Great Depression had a devastating impact on Germany.[5] Industrial production dropped by more than 40 percent between 1929 and 1931. Workers suffered mass unemployment, which rose sharply to three million in 1929 and to more than six million by January 1932. Poverty became widespread.

The middle class was also ravaged. Small business owners went to the wall, and their children could not get jobs. University graduates could not find work. Small peasants were hit hard by the lower prices they received for their produce. Many formerly 'respectable' middle class people were thrown into the ranks of the lumpen proletariat. Desperate, they offered themselves to the capitalists as strikebreakers and thugs for hire.

Economic distress exacerbated the longstanding sense of grievance among current and former non-commissioned army officers, who continued to complain bitterly about being 'stabbed in the back' by 'subversives' on the home front during the Great War and humiliated by the Versailles Treaty. Thousands of police also resented the breakup of the old imperial order. Provincial mayors and business owners yearned for the return of 'order.' By the early 1930s, many in the middle class had lost all their remaining faith in the Weimar Republic. They lashed out in both directions, at big capitalists above them and workers below. Driven mad by the crisis, they believed that an amalgamation of big business, Jewish bankers, parliamentary democracy, the SPD-led coalition government and communism was conspiring to ruin them.

Unable to find a way out of their crisis, the middle class sought a higher authority to rescue them. That was the appeal of Hitler and his Nazi party. He was the powerful, authoritarian leader, rhetorically hostile to big capital, progress and modernisation, which they held responsible for their plight. Fascism differs from traditional reaction in that it is not simply a movement from above, directly controlled by the ruling class or a section of it (e.g. a military coup), although of course it did have some early bourgeois backers. The Nazis built a genuine mass movement of middle class elements driven into hopelessness. The Nazis appealed to the middle class to unite behind them, not primarily on the basis of anti-Semitism, but on the grounds of strong government, law and order, extreme nationalism and fear of and resentment towards the working class.

The Nazis picked up a lot of support among the middle classes in the traditional Protestant areas of eastern Germany, which had been strong bases of support for nationalist parties for many years. They also won votes in Bavaria, where the defeat of the short-lived council republic in 1919 weakened and demoralised workers and scared the middle class about the prospect of future working class agitation. The Nazis also grew in smaller centres where nationalist middle class forces were a big presence. And, once they had demonstrated their power, elements of the liberal middle class also came over to them, seeing them as a force for order.

It is important to emphasise that the middle class was the mass basis of fascism, because some scholars try to emphasise its appeal across all classes, including the working class. In fact, the Nazis grew disproportionately in rural areas and small towns where the social weight of organised workers was weakest. By contrast, the Nazis only ever won 15 percent of the vote in Berlin, one of the centres of proletarian strength, and that vote was concentrated in well-off areas and in suburbs with very high levels of unemployment, where the working class had been pulverised and broken politically.

The Nazis did win some support amongst workers, most obviously those who had previously voted for conservative, nationalist parties or liberal parties. They also attracted the desperate unemployed disillusioned with the ineffectiveness of the SPD and the KPD. But the Nazis won relatively few votes away from working class parties or from those Polish and other Catholic workers who voted for the Catholic Centre Party. They had even less success with working class activists; less than 1 percent of works council members were Nazis in 1931.

If the Nazis were a mass counter-revolutionary movement of the desperate middle class, not simply a bourgeois conspiracy, they could only come to power with the support of the bourgeoisie. While many capitalists had thrown their support behind the Nazis by the early 1930s, the bulk of the bourgeoisie and the military top brass hesitated until the last minute before doing so, partly because of their fear of provoking working class resistance, but also because they did not control the Nazis. Yet, they understood that this mass movement could, in the right circumstances, be even more effective than the police and army in wiping out the unions and the workers' parties. When the bourgeoisie saw that their reliance on the SPD and the union bureaucracy to hold workers in check was no longer a viable option, they overcame their reluctance. Fascism gave them the opportunity to settle accounts with the entire legacy of the November Revolution. After Hitler's victory, Trotsky wrote:

> The Nazis call their overturn [coup] by the usurped title of revolution. As a matter of fact, in Germany as well as in Italy, fascism leaves the social system untouched. Taken by itself, Hitler's overturn has no right even to the name counter-revolution. But it cannot be viewed as an isolated event; it is the conclusion of a cycle of shocks which began in Germany in 1918. The November Revolution, which gave the power to the workers' and peasants' soviets, was proletarian in its fundamental tendencies. But the party that stood at the head of the proletariat returned the power to the bourgeoisie. In this sense the Social Democracy opened the era of counter-revolution before the revolution could bring its work to completion. However, so long as the bourgeoisie depended upon the Social Democracy, and consequently upon the workers, the regime retained elements of compromise. All the same, the international and the internal situation of German capitalism left no more room for concessions.

> As Social Democracy saved the bourgeoisie from the proletarian revolution, fascism came in its turn to liberate the bourgeoisie from the Social Democracy. Hitler's coup is only the final link in the chain of counter-revolutionary shifts.[6]

The response of the workers' parties to the rise of the Nazis

The SPD was thoroughly committed to the Weimar Republic at a time when the ruling class was preparing to dispense with it and the middle class had lost all faith in it. The SPD believed that they could win the middle class away from fascism by moderation and constitutionalism. So long as the police, the army and the courts were loyal to the Weimar Constitution, all would be well. This was a delusion.

The SPD-led coalition government of Herman Müller collapsed in March 1930 after a revolt against plans to cut the dole. It was replaced by, but offered its support to, a minority coalition government led by Heinrich Brüning of the Centre Party. With a weak base in parliament, Brüning ran the country by presidential decree for the next two years. His government was no protection against fascism: Brüning refused to use the police and army against the Nazis because many of them had joined the fascists. The Chancellor also understood that an attack on the Nazis would give workers time to regroup and to resume mass struggle; the entire ruling apparatus, including the president, the arch reactionary General Hindenburg, still feared working class struggle far more than fascism. In May 1932, Hindenburg sacked Brüning, replacing him with his puppet, Franz von Papen.

The SPD's moderation was simply the worst option from the perspective of holding back the fascists. The middle class could only be won away from fascism if the working class parties offered a serious alternative to the Weimar Republic and solutions to their economic distress. This was a possibility; considerable sections of Nazi supporters – especially those in the Brownshirts – were attracted to anti-capitalist rhetoric. They could have been won over to the working class parties by a fighting stance. The SPD was not interested in such a stance. By affirming its loyalty to the bankrupt Weimar Republic, the SPD, with its huge party machine, its mass membership, extensive press and control of state and municipal governments all over the country, only tied itself to a doomed regime, incapable of imposing itself on society. Better, thought many in the police, the army and civil service, to side with the Nazis who well may be our bosses tomorrow; they at least, unlike the SPD, were serious about imposing their authority on the state and broader society.

The Third Period line of the KPD under Stalin's appointee, Ernst Thälmann, was no less disastrous. Millions of unemployed workers were on the defensive and not in a position to go on the kind of revolutionary offensive envisaged by the Third Period. The working class needed to first go into battle around partial demands in order to rebuild its confidence and fighting capacity. But the KPD was not interested in such a scenario. It simply asserted that a breakthrough for the party was imminent and ignored other evidence. At the September 1930 Reichstag election, the Nazis increased their vote from 2.6 percent to 18.3 percent, jumping to second largest party behind the SPD. The SPD vote fell from 29.8 percent to 24.5 percent, while that of the KPD rose from 10.6 percent to 13.1 percent. Rather than focus on the threat posed by the rapid rise of the fascists, the KPD hailed the outcome as a victory and the 'beginning of the end' for the Nazis.

The KPD treated social democracy and fascism as two sides of the same coin. In May 1931, the Central Committee declared:

> The fascist dictatorship does not in any way represent a contrast in principle to bourgeois democracy under which the dictatorship of finance capital is also carried out…it is simply a change in the forms, an organic transition.[7]

Conflating the two rendered the KPD complicit in the rise of fascism.

The KPD also broke with Lenin's *'Left Wing' Communism* on the question of trade unionism. In the 1920s, the KPD had worked within the established unions to win a hearing among workers. Under the Third Period, however, the KPD attempted to create separate or parallel organisations, attacking the existing unions. This further isolated the party from the working class.

In a situation calling for unity against fascism, the KPD helped to divide workers and embittered SPD workers against it. In August 1931, the right wing nationalist parties, including the Nazis, initiated a referendum to bring down the SPD government in Prussia, the largest German state and an SPD stronghold. On Comintern orders, the KPD campaigned *alongside* the Nazis to bring down the SPD government. Although what the KPD misleadingly called the 'Red Referendum' failed, it still attracted 10 million votes in support. The KPD hailed this as a blow by workers against social democracy, but it seriously poisoned relations with the SPD rank and file.

Another element of the KPD's degenerate politics was its attempt to appropriate German nationalism. In the 1930 election, it called for the 'national and social liberation of the German people' and condemned the Versailles Treaty in nationalist terms.

Trotsky urges a united front

The situation was extremely perilous for a working class saddled with abysmal leadership. Trotsky, in exile in Turkey, wrote furiously about the situation. His analysis and strategy to beat back the Nazis represent some of his most valuable thinking.

Trotsky's main objective was to divert the KPD from its disastrous path, taking aim in particular at the social fascist line. Workers could not be ambivalent between social democracy and fascism, Trotsky argued. Fascism meant, first and foremost, the destruction of working class organisation:

> Fascism is not merely a system of reprisals, of brutal force, and of police terror. Fascism is a particular governmental system based on the uprooting of all elements of proletarian democracy within bourgeois society. The task of fascism lies not only in destroying the Communist vanguard but in holding the entire class in a state of forced disunity. To this end the physical annihilation of the most revolutionary section of the workers does not suffice. It is also necessary to smash all independent and voluntary organisations, to demolish all the defensive bulwarks of the proletariat, and to uproot whatever has been achieved during three-quarters of a century by the Social Democracy and the trade unions.[8]

The incompatibility of fascism and social democracy was the basis for a united front between the KPD and SPD. Trotsky explained:

> At present the strength of the National Socialists lies not so much in their own army as in the schism within the army of their mortal enemy. But it is precisely the reality of the fascist threat, its growth and proximity, the consciousness of the necessity of averting it at any cost, that must inevitably push the workers toward unity in the name of self-defence. The concentration of the proletarian forces will take place all the more quickly and successfully, the more reliable the pivot of this process, the Communist Party, is shown to be. The key to the situation still rests in their hands. Woe to them if they lose it![9]

The united front, Trotsky emphasised, was not a trick:

> To fight, the proletariat must have unity in its ranks. This holds true for partial economic conflicts, within the walls of a single factory, as well as for such 'national' political battles as the one to repel fascism. Consequently, the tactic of the united front is not something accidental and artificial – a cunning manoeuvre – not at all; it originates, entirely and wholly, in the objective conditions governing the development of the proletariat.[10]

The urgency of the situation should be clear to the working class:

> Worker-Communists, you are hundreds of thousands, millions; you cannot leave for anyplace; there are not enough passports for you. Should fascism come to power, it will ride over your skulls and spines like a terrific tank. Your salvation lies in merciless struggle. And only a fighting unity with the Social Democratic workers can bring victory. Make haste, worker-Communists, you have very little time left![11]

A successful united front could hold back the fascist movement and inflict some blows on it. Some victorious defensive struggles could have broken Hitler's momentum and prepared the ground for workers to go on the offensive, thereby becoming a pole of attraction for sections of the middle class and the unemployed. The point of a united front was not to prop up the Weimar Republic. That was no longer a real option; the status quo could not prevail. The crisis of the Great Depression, the ruling class's desire to crush the working class and the radicalisation of the middle classes all meant that Germany had reached a fork in the road. Only through a united front could the mass of workers loyal to the SPD be won to a revolutionary program. Only through a combative revolutionary party could a section of the radicalising middle classes be pulled to the left. Only under these conditions would it be possible to crush the fascist threat.

Times were difficult, but the correct leadership could have defeated the Nazis. The combined KPD and SPD vote, 37 percent of the total, held up at the two general elections in 1932, with the KPD making ground on the SPD. While the Nazi vote increased dramatically in July, from 18.3 percent to 37.4 percent, it fell back in November to 33.1 percent, giving the workers' parties a slight edge. The Nazis experienced increasing internal strife and faltering morale and met worker resistance wherever they campaigned. Joseph Goebbels wrote in his diary about his tour of the Rhineland, Germany's manufacturing heartland:

> Now we travel in disguise... We have to take a side-street to keep from falling into the hands of the Communists who have occupied all the other entrances... In Elberfeld, the Red press has called the mob into the streets. The approaches to the stadium are blocked off completely... I must leave my own native city like a criminal, pursued by curses, abuse, vilification, stoned and spat upon.[12]

And the SPD still had a mass membership, much of which supported actively fighting the Nazis. Had the SPD been persuaded to fight, the two parties might have moved millions into action. Most importantly, workers still had social power. The Nazis may have received many votes, wrote Trotsky:

> But in the social struggle, votes are not decisive. The main army of fascism still consists of the petty bourgeoisie and the new middle class: the small artisans and shopkeepers of the cities, the petty officials, the employees, the technical personnel, the intelligentsia, the impoverished peasantry. On the scales of election statistics, a thousand fascist votes weigh as much as a thousand Communist votes. But on the scales of the revolutionary struggle, a thousand workers in one big factory represent a force a hundred times greater than a thousand petty officials, clerks, their wives, and their mothers-in-law. The great bulk of the fascists consists of human dust.[13]

But neither workers' party was willing to lead a united resistance. SPD leaders mostly resisted appeals for united action, arguing that the Nazis and Communists were both enemies of the Republic. They dreaded the prospect of socialist revolution and consistently played down the threat posed by Hitler. They limited their opposition to Hitler to non-violent, lawful means, and they expelled or disciplined members preparing for a battle with the Nazis. The union leaders were even more miserable. They tried to keep their heads down. They could potentially be pressured into supporting united action, but that would have required the missing element: the correct approach by the KPD.

Although its vote and membership were growing, the KPD was too small to lead alone. It had many young, inexperienced and unemployed members and a high rate of member turnover. It lacked the deep roots that the SPD enjoyed among organised factory workers. This was obvious in the poor response to the KPD's repeated calls for general strikes. They only advertised the KPD's weakness. Lacking the ability to lead on its own initiative, the KPD needed to approach the SPD to form a united front.

A united front did not in any sense mean accommodation to the SPD. The KPD had to propose a united front in the full knowledge that social democracy had prepared the way for fascism. Even if the SPD leaders agreed to some united action, they could not be relied upon. The united front tactic was motivated by the need for joint defensive action, but it was also a way of testing the SPD leaders, said Trotsky:

> We must understand how to tear the workers away from their leaders in reality... This stage cannot be skipped. We must help the Social Democratic workers in action – in this new and extraordinary situation – to test the value of their organisations and leaders at this time when it is a matter of life and death for the working class.[14]

Trotsky was not proposing an electoral bloc with the SPD but practical agreements for combating a common enemy:

> Election agreements, parliamentary compromises concluded between the revolutionary party and the Social Democracy serve, as a rule, to the advantage of the Social Democracy. Practical agreements for mass action, for purposes of struggle, are always useful to the revolutionary party.[15]

The united front might appear to be an agreement to suspend hostilities between the two parties, but it was in part a tactic to undermine the hold of social democracy on German workers:

> The front must now be directed against fascism. And this common front of direct struggle against fascism, embracing the entire proletariat, must be utilised in the struggle against Social Democracy, directed as a flank attack, but no less effective for all that.[16]

The only way of carrying out this struggle effectively was by guaranteeing the full independence of the KPD and its right to criticise the SPD:

> No common platform with the Social Democracy, or with the leaders of the German trade unions, no common publications, banners, placards! March separately, but strike together! Agree only how to strike, whom to strike, and when to strike! Such an agreement can be concluded even with the devil himself, with his grandmother, and even with Noske and Grzesinski. On one condition, not to bind one's hands.[17]

The tragedy was that Trotsky's forces in Germany were tiny. Few socialists were aware of his warnings. The KPD leadership maintained its ultra left line to the end, making defeat inevitable. Trotsky wrote:

> For us, the Communist Party is the subjective factor; the Social Democracy is an objective obstacle that must be swept away. Fascism would actually fall to pieces if the Communist Party were able to unite the working class, transforming it into a powerful revolutionary magnet for all the oppressed masses of the people. But the policy of the Communist Party since the September [1930] elections has only aggravated its inconsistencies: the empty talk of 'social fascism,' the flirtations with chauvinism, the imitation of genuine fascism for the purpose of petty market competition with it, the criminal adventurism of the 'red referendum' – all this prevents the Communist Party from becoming the leader of the proletariat and of the people.[18]

Just as Lenin had argued in *'Left Wing' Communism*, the KPD's ultra leftism only strengthened social democracy. Trotsky noted: 'By its convulsions, its mistakes, its bureaucratic ultimatism, the Stalinist bureaucracy preserves the Social Democracy, permits it again and again to regain its foothold.'[19] Trotsky's arguments were in line with the united front policies adopted by the Comintern Third Congress and confirmed by the Fourth. By now, however, the Comintern had renounced its revolutionary heritage. Thälmann declared that united action with reformists was:

> the theory of an utterly bankrupt Fascist and counter-revolutionary. This is indeed the worst, the most dangerous, and the most criminal theory that Trotsky has construed in these last years of his counter-revolutionary propaganda.[20]

The KPD's sectarian approach meant that it was incapable of appealing to workers loyal to the SPD. When the KPD proposed in July 1932 that the two parties organise a general strike to oppose Chancellor von Papen's attempt to sack the SPD government in Prussia, the SPD leaders were under no pressure from their members to agree. The KPD issued a call for a general strike; as usual, the call fell flat. For too long, the KPD had slammed the SPD as 'social fascist.' Now, there was no reason for workers loyal to the SPD to listen to the KPD's call for action.

Hitler seizes power

The final weeks of the Weimar Republic exposed both the pathetic leadership of the SPD and the KPD's criminal social fascism policy. Following the November 1932 election, at which the Nazi vote fell, President Hindenburg appointed Hitler Chancellor. With control over the key ministries, the Nazis began a reign of terror against the workers' movement, deploying tens of thousands of Brownshirts and SS. They stormed and destroyed the KPD's head office in Berlin and banned its newspaper. Worker activists were forced to go underground in fear for their lives.

The SPD tried to dampen down alarm at Hitler's appointment, even describing it as 'constitutional.' Again, the KPD called a general strike; again, it fell flat. Even facing an actual fascist takeover, the KPD continued to speak of a rising revolutionary mood, directing its attacks primarily at the SPD. Chair of the KPD's Reichstag faction, Ernst Torgler, said of a proposal to form a united front against the Nazis:

> It doesn't enter our heads. The Nazis must take power. Then in four weeks the whole working class will be united under the leadership of the Communist party.[21]

Four days later, following the burning of the Reichstag building, which the Nazis blamed on the KPD, Hitler declared a state of emergency, arresting Thälmann and 4,000 KPD leaders and members. The entire party press was outlawed, the party was deprived of its parliamentary representation, and its legal organisations were smashed. Even then, there was potential for resistance, as the Weimar Republic's last elections showed. With Hitler in power, the KPD banned and widespread rigging of the electoral process by the Nazis, the working class parties still recorded 12 million votes in the March election. But the KPD's sectarian politics had ensured that the willingness of workers to resist the Nazis was wasted. On 24 March, the Reichstag, with the support of all parties except the SPD (KPD representatives having been arrested), passed a *Law to Remedy the Distress of the People and the Reich*, known as the Enabling Act. It suspended the constitution and gave Hitler dictatorial authority.

Even as KPD leaders were being thrown in jail, the KPD remained delusional, comforting its followers with the slogan: 'After Hitler, our turn.' The SPD union leaders were outright traitors, preferring to crawl to the Nazis rather than fight them. Union leaders joined in Hitlerian 'National Day of Labour' celebrations on 1 May. The next day, they were rounded up and sent to concentration camps.

With Hitler's seizure of power, the German working class, the best organised in the world, suffered a catastrophic and entirely avoidable defeat. The KPD refused to acknowledge the massive setback and continued to argue that the social democrats were the main buttress of capitalism. The Comintern Executive backed the KPD leaders to the hilt, declaring:

> The policy carried out by the Executive Committee of the Communist Party of Germany, with Comrade Thälmann at its head, up to and during the time of the Hitlerite coup, was absolutely correct.[22]

How could they claim otherwise, when this debacle was their doing? Stalin played down the enormity of the defeat. The Comintern Executive further declared:

> The establishment of an open fascist dictatorship accelerates the tempo of the development of a proletarian revolution in Germany by destroying all democratic illusions of the masses and by freeing them from the influence of the Social-Democracy.[23]

Had the German workers driven fascism back, they would have been in a position to go on the offensive, opening the road to revolution. They could even have sparked off a fresh revolt in Russia, given the social discontent there, posing a mortal threat to the new ruling class. Instead, as with the failure in China, defeat in Germany reinforced the idea that Russia was the only hope for international socialism. Stalinism and Nazism fed off each other's successes, both products of the destruction of workers' power.

FURTHER READING

T. Cliff, *Trotsky: The Darker the Night, the Brighter the Star*, London, Bookmarks, 1993.

D. Gluckstein, *The Nazis, Capitalism and the Working Class*, London, Bookmarks, 1999.

L. Trotsky, *For a workers' united front against fascism*, 1931.

L. Trotsky, *Germany, the key to the international situation*, 1931.

L. Trotsky, *What next? Vital questions for the German proletariat*, 1932.

L. Trotsky, *What is National Socialism?* 1933.

9.

COMMUNISM IN AUSTRALIA DURING THE GREAT DEPRESSION

The effects of the the Comintern's ultra leftist turn were felt in the Communist Party of Australia (CPA).[1] Although Stalin's tactic did not open the door to fascist barbarism in Australia, as it did in Germany, it did impede the project of building a revolutionary party to rival the reformist Australian Labor Party (ALP). It ensured that many workers searching for an alternative to social democracy at a time of enormous social and political polarisation were repelled by the CPA because of its sectarian 'social fascist' line and inoculated from anything bearing the stamp of 'Communism.'

The CPA in Australia

The CPA had struggled since its formation in 1920. It was small, no more than a few hundred members. It was formed only after the wave of militancy that swept Australia during and after World War I had subsided and shortly before a swing to the right in society between 1922 and 1928 – a period of relative capitalist prosperity and declining worker militancy. Internal problems compounded the effects of the rightward drift in society. In the first half of the decade, NSW Labor Council secretary Jock Garden led the party. Garden and his fellow union officials, known as the 'Trades Hall Reds,' were deeply embedded in the official union apparatus. They sought to establish the party as little more than a faction of the ALP. Following the Comintern Fourth Congress's adoption of the united front approach, the Comintern Executive had instructed the CPA to enter the ALP, with the (extremely overblown) aim of capturing it. Under Garden's leadership, this approach simply took the form of liquidating the CPA into the ALP, a practice which the Comintern Executive did nothing to challenge.[2] The party paid the price for Garden's unprincipled manoeuvring. When the ALP voted to expel CPA members in 1924, many of Garden's supporters in the union bureaucracy in Sydney, faced with the prospect of an abrupt halt to their careers, chose to quit the CPA. The defection of the union officials – and the subsequent expulsion of Garden from the CPA in 1926 for refusing to publicly affirm his CPA membership – was no great loss to the party. If the CPA was ever to become more than a ginger group on the fringes of the ALP, it needed a leadership prepared to forge an independent identity for the party. But Garden's strategy mistrained many rank and file members who also abandoned the party when forced to choose between the ALP and CPA. The whole experience had set the CPA back years; an enormous amount of party time and resources had been spent pursuing a fruitless campaign for ALP affiliation rather than pursuing other channels to build the party.

Garden's replacement as party chair, Jack Kavanagh, inherited a party in bad shape.[3] Under Garden, CPA membership had shrunk substantially, leaving an activist core of just a few dozen. Membership turnover was rapid, party education was weak, and the finances were in dire straits. So poor did the party's prospects seem that party co-founder Guido Baracchi proposed dissolving the party. Kavanagh strove to put the CPA on an even keel. He steered the party to a more independent stance towards the ALP and placed greater emphasis on political education and cadre development. The CPA threw itself into industrial work, playing an important role in the 1927 North Queensland sugar workers' strike and the accompanying statewide railway lockout. As the spokesperson for the NSW Labor Council's Disputes Committee, Kavanagh played a significant role in the nine-month timber workers' strike in 1929. He also did much to encourage debate within the party, carrying out an open fight with Garden in the pages of the party paper *Workers' Weekly*.

Kavanagh faced a series of problems. First was the Comintern's continued loyalty to his predecessor. The NSW Labor Council, the most significant union body in the country, had affiliated to the Red International of Labour Unions under Garden's leadership, and he remained leader of the Labor Council and was central to the Australian Council of Trade Unions' (ACTU) affiliation to Moscow's Pan Pacific Trade Union Secretariat, an international union body linking unions across the Asia-Pacific. Successive Comintern leaders Zinoviev and Bukharin cared more for these connections than for the fortunes of the tiny CPA, so the Comintern instructed the party not to antagonise Garden after his expulsion from the CPA. This hindered the CPA's attempt to build its new united front union formation, the Militant Minority Movement (MMM) which it established in 1928 to enhance the party's influence in the unions. To avoid conflict with the Labor Council, the CPA was forced to sideline the MMM in

Sydney, one of the party's main areas of activity. During the timber workers' strike, for example, during which Kavanagh worked for the Labor Council, the MMM played no role. Only in the coal mining industry was the MMM seriously encouraged. Because the Miners' Federation was not affiliated to the NSW Labor Council, there was no risk of a clash between MMM activists in the industry and Garden and his Labor Council allies. The MMM quickly established itself as a force, with groups in all the major mining centres, which gave it influence among delegates to the 1928 Miners' Federation convention. In 1929, its call for a total shutdown of the industry in NSW during a lengthy lockout won support among rank and file miners.

The main obstacle to the party's growth under Kavanagh remained the broader economic and political situation. It was hard going for a party declaring itself committed to overthrowing the entire political order. Although the CPA grew under Kavanagh's leadership to about 300 members, it was only able to sink roots in the working class in a few restricted areas.[4]

The ultra left turn proclaimed at the Comintern's Sixth Congress in 1928 ushered in a dramatic shift in the CPA's politics. An opposition emerged, led by Lance Sharkey, Bert Moxon and Queensland leader, Jack (J.B.) Miles, demanding that the party aggressively oppose the ALP, both in propaganda and electorally. Their motivations varied. Moxon was a committed ultra leftist who naturally took to the Comintern's more aggressive approach to the ALP. Sharkey, however, was an opportunist, arguing in 1927 for a stepped up campaign for ALP membership, in line with Comintern demands at that time, but just two years later, aware of the changes afoot in Moscow, attacking Kavanagh for being too soft on Labor. The opposition received support from CPA members inclined to ultra leftism, including some who had attended Moscow party schools and returned home as Stalin's loyalists. Kavanagh himself was sympathetic to the Comintern's new perspective and, by any objective measure, a genuine leftist, but he sought to moderate its application for local circumstances. For this, he was attacked as promoting 'Australian exceptionalism.' Kavanagh pushed back, suspending Sharkey and Moxon from the central executive. At the CPA's Eighth Conference in December 1928, Kavanagh held a narrow majority.

Stalinist takeover of the CPA

The dispute within the CPA came to a head in late 1929, when the opposition appealed to the Comintern Executive for support. The Comintern obliged, sending a lengthy letter denouncing Kavanagh. It described the central executive's opposition to running candidates at the October 1929 federal election as 'a glaring example of right deviation deserving the severest condemnation.'[5] Under pressure from both the Comintern and the internal opposition, Kavanagh and his supporters began to lose ground. At the CPA's Ninth Conference in December 1929, Sharkey, Moxon and Miles defeated Kavanagh and his allies and formed a new leadership, sending a telegram to Moscow:

> Annual conference greets Comintern. Declares unswerving loyalty new line.[6]

With the party now committed to the Comintern ultra left line, the new leadership quickly moved to crush Kavanagh and his supporters who dominated in the Sydney district, the party's largest. Moxon, the new party chair and one of those who had visited Moscow in 1928, appealed to Moscow for help. In April 1930, Comintern emissary (later revealed as an FBI agent) Herbert Moore arrived from the US and took control of the party, transforming the CPA leadership, program and constitution.[7] Moore had cut his teeth in the US CP, squeezing out the 'right' leadership of Jay Lovestone. Moore was now put to work fighting 'rightist deviation' in Australia. He rewrote the CPA's program, took over the party paper, *Workers' Weekly*, and initiated the 'social fascist' line with gusto. By the middle of 1930, when the Comintern began to tone down some of its ultra left excesses, headlines in Moore's *Workers' Weekly* still read: 'Down with the socialist fascist bureaucrats' and 'Eradicate social fascist defeatism.' Moore broke up the Sydney district leadership, relocating them to more distant cities. Kavanagh was forced out of the party. He was readmitted in 1931 but expelled again three years later for Trotskyist sympathies.[8] Moore turned on Moxon next; he had suited Moscow's needs in deposing Kavanagh, but he showed independence of mind, making him unsuitable for Stalin's purposes.

Moore left Australia in July 1931, handing over the reins to a new leadership: Miles, Sharkey, Richard Dixon and Jack Blake. Over the following four years, the process of Stalinising the party was completed. The new leadership crushed a series of rebellions that took place against the new regime, reprimanding or expelling members and replacing district leaders. They had few scruples, in one instance using *Workers' Weekly* to draw attention to the irregular immigration status of an oppositionist. They slammed dissenters as 'Trotskyite wreckers,' an allegation that removed any sympathy for the victims during the international campaign of vitriol against Trotsky.

In the name of 'democratic centralism', the CPA established a monolithism unprecedented in the Australian labour movement. The CPA's Tenth Congress[9] in 1931 was little more than a stage-managed exercise with no genuine debate. Annual Congresses were abolished and only two more were held by the end of the decade. Party leaders followed Moscow's instructions without question. Whether they genuinely believed the line from Moscow or were cynically carrying it out simply to remain in Stalin's favour, the effect was the same. Just as Stalin was building a cult in the Russian party, CPA propaganda increasingly foregrounded Miles and Sharkey, creating cults of personality around them. Moore introduced the practice of 'self-criticism,' which became standard practice. Internal critics of the leadership had to abase themselves, reducing the space for critical thinking.[10] Local party units followed the national lead, expelling members for minor infractions of party discipline, suspected political opposition or failure to carry out tasks. Eventually, the mania for expulsions forced the leadership to rein in the local units. The result of this internal transformation, writes Stuart Macintyre, was that 'an organisation that had once allowed vigorous debate and open discussion of differences was reconstituted as a conventicle of rigid conformity.'[11]

Whatever its errors and problems, the CPA under Kavanagh had sought to build a base for socialist ideas in the working class and to take the class struggle forward. The tragedy was that the party was not given the opportunity to test itself as a revolutionary force in the new period opening up in the tumultuous 1930s. The Stalinisation of the party decisively ended any such prospect.

The Depression sets in

It was as a party that was rapidly absorbing Stalinist politics and methods that the CPA sought to intervene in the class struggle during the Great Depression. The agenda of the ruling class at the outset of the Depression was clear: to shift the burden of the economic crisis onto the shoulders of the working class. With the economic downturn gathering pace in 1928, bosses attacked waterside workers, timber workers and coal miners in turn, using lockouts, the Arbitration Court, police violence and scabs to destroy workers' conditions. On the Melbourne waterfront, police injured many workers; at least one later died of his wounds. In the NSW Hunter Valley, police clubbed and shot at a demonstration of thousands in the mining town of Rothbury, killing one miner and wounding dozens.

The bosses' offensive opened up schisms within the union movement. As the disputes lengthened in the timber industry and in coal mining, a divide developed between union leaders looking for a settlement and workers becoming more militant. Rank and file workers increasingly sought to take charge of the disputes but were isolated from other groups of workers by union officials determined not to spread the action. All three groups – the wharfies, timber workers and coal miners – suffered bad defeats. The bosses and industrial tribunals seized the opportunity and slashed wages and conditions.

Defeated industrially, workers looked to the ALP to save them. The Scullin Labor government was elected in a landslide in October 1929. It was sworn in just two days after the Wall Street Crash, and the international economic collapse formed the backdrop for the government's two years in office. Very quickly, the Scullin government, backed by state premiers – four of whom were also Labor – capitulated to the capitalists' demands for sharp cuts in public spending and attacks on workers. The Arbitration Court cut the Basic Wage by 10 percent, and this flowed through to wage cuts across the board. Ignoring an election promise, Scullin did nothing to reinstate the locked-out NSW coal miners. Unemployment of union members climbed steadily to 29 percent by 1932. Tens of thousands were evicted from their homes. State Labor governments followed the Scullin government in slashing spending and making workers work for a pittance dole payment in relief camps that were places of misery and destitution.

Political polarisation

Faced with mass unemployment and industrial defeat, many workers gave way to hopelessness, but a minority shifted to the left. The radical mood quickly found its way into the NSW ALP and cohered around Premier Jack Lang. Lang had led the ALP to victory in NSW in November 1930, on a populist election platform, blaming the Depression misery on British bankers. Lang vowed not to make interest repayments on loans from British banks. He attacked the Scullin government for its austerity measures. In 1931, tensions between Lang and the federal ALP came to a head and the premier took his followers out, the great majority of party members and voters, to set up the Lang Labor Party. Lang's outdoor rallies in Sydney drew tens of thousands. He also had considerable support outside NSW, especially in the South Australian and Victorian branches. While Lang at times used left rhetoric, he did his best to crush the left inside the party. This was clearest when it came to the Socialisation Units.

The Socialisation Units were set up after the 1930 NSW ALP conference to promote the socialisation plank of the ALP platform, which called for 'the democratic socialisation of industry, production, distribution and exchange, to the extent necessary to eliminate exploitation and other anti-social features in these fields.' This plank had been adopted in 1921, but party leaders had done nothing to implement, or even promote, it. In 1930, amid capitalism's worst ever crisis, many members concluded that it was time to put socialism into practice. The Socialisation Units spread very rapidly. By Easter 1931, there were 97 Units, and, by the end of 1932, 178. In the early days of the Units, before the ALP barred CPA members from joining, membership was open to all. Before long, many Units were much larger than the ALP branches to which they were attached.

The Socialisation Units established a statewide newspaper, *Socialisation Call*, and undertook mass propaganda for socialism in working class communities. At their height, there were five inner city socialist education classes in Sydney and another 15 in the city's suburbs. With membership peaking at 50,000, the Units represented the biggest left wing current in ALP history. In order to burnish his credentials as a populist champion – and to act as a foil against the CPA, which he loathed – Lang initially backed the Units.

At the 1931 NSW ALP conference, the Units succeeded in passing a motion committing Labor to introduce socialism within three years. This was a step too far for Lang: generalised motions stating the desirability of socialism were one thing, but this motion placed demands on his government. On the following day, using a combination of skilful manoeuvre, bluster and threats, Lang had the motion recommitted and defeated on the conference floor.

As the Socialisation Units grew, they became more radical. In August 1931, a report written for the Units by Tom Payne, who was close to the Communist Party, called for 'the complete expropriation of the capitalist class' and the setting up of 'the dictatorship of the working class.'[12] Many ALP members and supporters rallied around these forthright demands. However, close Lang allies and reformist socialists, who were a majority in the Units' leadership, rejected the Payne report and blocked its adoption.

Despite this defeat of the more radical wing, Lang still regarded the Socialisation Units as a threat and used his immense popular authority to marginalise them. At the 1933 state conference, Lang won a majority to dissolve the Units. The weakness of the Units was now starkly revealed. Most of their members had illusions in Lang, and so were not prepared for this turn of events. Very soon, most of them abandoned politics and within months, the Units were a spent force.

After successfully smashing the left threat, Lang still faced a serious enemy on his right. The ruling class regarded Lang as the focus for worker resistance to austerity and was determined to crush him. There were several elements to their offensive. The first was the mobilisation of militant right wing 'grassroots' forces. These had existed in various forms since the 1910s. They were spurred on by the emergence of Labor as a party of government, the World War I anti-conscription campaigns and the Russian Revolution, which together conjured up a 'Bolshevik threat' to the conservative middle classes. Supported by wealthy Establishment figures in business and the military, various groups sprang up to galvanise these forces. The most significant was the Old Guard, a Protestant, monarchist paramilitary group based in Sydney's prosperous northern suburbs. The Old Guard had the Lang Government squarely in its sights. In 1931, however, the Old Guard split; the more adventurist and less bourgeois New Guard embraced openly fascist ideological perspectives. Its leader, Eric Campbell, was a supporter of Hitler and Mussolini. The New Guard quickly recruited tens of thousands of members, many under arms. New Guard thugs launched numerous attacks on the left, breaking up meetings of the ALP, CPA and trade unions, assisting the police in anti-eviction struggles, bashing unemployed activists, and even assaulting Jock Garden in his own home.

In Victoria, the far right rallied to a group called the White Army. Bolstered by generous donations from business and society circles, and with the encouragement of the police (the commander of the White Army, Major General Thomas Blamey, was also Victorian Police Commissioner), paramilitary bodies flourished. In March 1931, the White Army staged armed uprisings across rural Victoria, aimed at forestalling what they saw as an imminent revolution by the combined forces of Irish Australians, Communists and the unemployed.[13] When the Unemployed Workers' Movement (UWM) organised meetings in regional Victoria and NSW, far right thugs rallied farmers to attack them.

Alongside the openly and aggressively right wing organisations, business figures and army officers in Sydney also formed the All for Australia League (AFAL), which aimed to channel widespread anti-unionist and anti-socialist sentiments into a supposedly apolitical 'citizens' movement.' AFAL grew very quickly, encouraged by Keith Murdoch's newspapers, Rotary Clubs, Returned Services Leagues, charitable societies and an advertising campaign funded by employer organisations. By April 1931, just three months after its formation, AFAL claimed a membership of 130,000, with 84 branches in Sydney alone. In May, it merged with the Victorian Citizens' League (VCL), founded by the former president of the Victorian RSL and richly endowed with business donations. The VCL claimed a membership of 80,000 at the time of the fusion. AFAL did much to focus blame for the Depression on 'reckless' Labor governments. It was a conduit for right wing individuals to join the New Guard and White Army.

In April 1931, the various conservative organisations, citizens' leagues, former Nationalist Party politicians and business owners, along with future prime minister Robert Menzies, agreed to merge all the anti-Labor forces under one banner, the United Australia Party (UAP). Its first leader was Joe Lyons, Scullin's Treasurer until he quit the party, frustrated by its refusal to implement even more savage budget cuts. At the December 1931 election, the UAP heavily defeated the Scullin government and Lyons became prime minister.

Despite the right's success in winning government nationally, the Lang government was still a thorn in its side. It now mobilised to throw it out of office by unconstitutional means. The New Guard made a trial run at a coup, but police were still loyal to Lang, and the coup was brutally smashed.

In May 1932, the Old Guard was on the verge of mobilising its tens of thousands of heavily armed members to attack the Lang government. The army top brass, businessmen and senior public servants backed it. On the eve of the planned coup, however, another coup took place. On 13 May, using the reserve powers of the British crown, NSW Governor Sir Philip Game sacked the Lang Government and appointed UAP leader Bertram Stevens in his place. Incensed workers flocked to a huge rally of 250,000 to protest against Lang's dismissal. Fearful of the consequences of calling on workers to fight for his reinstatement, Lang simply accepted his dismissal and walked away. At the subsequent election, the UAP, in coalition with the Country Party, won a handsome majority.

By the end of 1932, conservative parties held office federally and in most states, and this helped to allay any anxieties of the mainstream elements of the far right about incipient Bolshevism in Australia. The new conservative government in NSW, stuffed full of members of far right groups, struck hard against Communists and other agitators The regular police, many sympathetic to the far right, continued to smash meetings and rallies of the left. By 1933, the Old Guard, New Guard and the White Army had faded into the background as independent bodies, their purpose accomplished.

CPA work among workers and the unemployed

The economic crisis and social and political polarisation of the early 1930s form the backdrop for the CPA as it was being transformed into a counter-revolutionary party. The CPA of course did not trumpet its counter-revolutionary agenda. Party policy may have been decided in Moscow, but CPA leaders knew that a tiny party irrelevant to the working class was of no use to Moscow. The Russian ruling class wanted Comintern parties big enough to allow it to exercise influence in the country concerned. The CPA could only build such a party by appealing to workers who wanted to fight capitalism and were attracted to socialism. Some leaders undoubtedly genuinely believed that the CPA could be the vehicle for socialism in Australia and were willing to devote their lives to advance that project.

The CPA sought to advance on a range of fronts. One was in the unions. In 1931, the CPA revived the MMM, renamed the Minority Movement (MM), to agitate in the unions. The MM built a following over the following years in North Queensland among wharfies, rail workers, metal miners and meat workers. It also established a presence in the Victorian railway workshops. The MM had its biggest success by far in the NSW coal industry. During the 15-month lockout of 1929–30, the CPA boosted its membership among miners in the Northern district, heart of the dispute, from less than one dozen to 100. In 1933, sustained work in the coal industry resulted in the election of MM national secretary Bill Orr as Miners' Federation general secretary, followed in 1934 by the election of Charlie Nelson as Federation president.

The unemployed were the focus of CPA attention during the Depression. In April 1930, the party set up the Unemployed Workers' Movement (UWM) in NSW. The UWM grew quickly. It held its first conference in the middle of the year, bringing together local branches, most from metropolitan Sydney but some from the coalfields and regional towns. Later, branches were established interstate. By the end of the year, the CPA boasted that the UWM had 30,000 members nationally. Wherever they were established, CPA members, although usually only a small minority, were the driving force of the UWM.

Economic distress was now biting hard. With no dole, it was difficult for working class families to pay rent, and the number of evictions rose sharply. The UWM vowed to resist. Initially, it relied on public meetings and sent deputations to landlords and agents, in which it was made clear to them that evictions would invite retaliation. Such threats were usually enough to get landlords to back off or to reduce rents. In late February 1931, however, the UWM upped the ante, setting up pickets inside houses and holding daily meetings of local residents outside houses. In some cases, these meetings involved hundreds of unemployed parading through the streets. This combination of tactics was so successful that the UWM in Sydney won every eviction battle it took on in the first five months of 1931.

Frustrated by the UWM's success, the courts began to direct police to enforce eviction orders. Bloody battles ensued between UWM activists, occupying the homes of tenants, and police sent in by the Lang Government to turn them out. In mid-June, two big fights in Bankstown and Newtown (Sydney) brought things to a head. Police shot at anti-eviction squads, who fought back with rudimentary weapons. While the number of supporters involved in Bankstown was small, in Newtown, a crowd reported as several thousand gathered outside the house to jeer at the police and cheer for those arrested. They only held back from physically attacking the police when officers brandished guns. These battles forced the Lang government to introduce tenant protection legislation and a moratorium on evictions in the depths of the Depression.

The UWM was also in the thick of the fight for a better deal for those on sustenance programs (work for the dole) and government relief works. The unemployed were forced to line up for charity or ration bags, funded by state governments but distributed by local charities. Charities freely discriminated between the 'deserving' and 'undeserving' poor. In the first half of 1931, as unemployment shot up, outbreaks of unrest broke out against this kind of humiliating treatment, with the UWM to the fore. On 10 January, the UWM led a march of 2,000 unemployed workers behind a red flag to the Treasury Building in Adelaide, demanding that the state Labor government overturn its decision to remove beef from their rations. Police attacked savagely, but the crowd fought back with batons and other weapons. On 6 March, a demonstration by the unemployed outside government offices in Perth escalated into a riot. On 10 May, the 'South Coast dole riot' saw NSW police fire on unemployed workers protesting outside the ration depot in Bulli.

One of the first acts of the Lyons government was to scrap award rates of pay for those employed on government relief works. The CPA used the Relief and Sustenance Workers' Union, which it set up after dissolving the UWM late in 1931, to lead the fight for better wages and conditions on sustenance and relief works programs, involving strikes and bans. These included an eight-week stoppage of workers employed on sustenance jobs in Melbourne in 1933, which forced an increase in dole payments; and a statewide strike in Victoria in 1935, involving 17,000 sustenance workers, which pushed up the dole a second time.

The CPA used the Depression to make propaganda about the failures of capitalism and the glories of Stalin's Russia. Branches determinedly built the party's profile wherever they could find an audience. They held public meetings, sold the *Workers' Weekly* and made stump speeches to crowds at the Yarra Bank in Melbourne, the Sydney Domain and King Street in Newtown. They faced constant harassment from councils which refused to grant the party venues to hold meetings or permits to hold rallies or sell papers. The police regularly arrested and bashed Communist agitators, and right wing thugs were given a free hand to assault Communists, especially in rural and regional areas. Many Communists served time in jail. The Lyons government also censored the party press, preventing it from being distributed by post, and blocked imports of Communist literature.

At a time when the union leaders were inert and Labor governments usually ready to smash resistance to austerity, the CPA stood out during the Depression for its willingness to fight. The party drew to its ranks many hundreds of workers who refused to surrender their dignity at a time of immense working class hardship. Illusions in Stalin's Russia and the legacy of the Russian Revolution were another important drawcard. CPA membership, less than 300 at the start of the Depression, stood at 2,400 by 1934, when the worst of the Depression began to pass.

The cost of bureaucratic ultra leftism

The CPA's adoption of 'social fascism' did not prevent it from growing. But it did render the party incapable of winning over much greater numbers of workers during the biggest crisis Australian capitalism had experienced, or adjusting tactics quickly when these proved mistaken.

One example of a mistaken tactic that followed adoption of the Third Period perspective of ascending revolutionary struggles was the MM's advocacy of general strikes without reference to the balance of class forces in Australia. The demand for general strikes did not fit the situation in Australia. The industrial defeats, the mass sackings and the rapid growth of unemployment had put workers on the defensive. The number of strikes declined dramatically during the Depression, and most strikes were defeated. The MM repeatedly calling for general strikes only demonstrated how out of touch the party was.

The CPA's wild Third Period rhetoric encouraged the party to engage in more adventurist tactics when workers refused to respond to its call for general strikes. During the coal lockout, Moxon proposed taking over the mining town of Cessnock, arms in hand. The party claimed that it had established a Workers' Defence Corps to protect picket lines in the northern coalfields, with 2,000 armed workers, but this was fanciful. At the conclusion of the coal lockout, Central Committee member Esmonde Higgins was instructed to use any means, including violence, to prevent union officials ('social fascists') from addressing the final mass meeting in the Northern district. Higgins wisely disobeyed, knowing that he would have had the support of only a tiny minority of the workers.

The CPA's ultra left tendency only grew more extreme following Moore's arrival. Under his leadership, the party secretariat discussed seizing Broken

Hill, including the police and railway stations, and went on to entertain the idea that the CPA might be in a position to take power across the entire country 'in the course of the next period.'[14] The CPA's Workers' Defence Corps – an absurd notion for a party with a few hundred active members – attracted some former Irish Republicans. Little more than gangsters, they boasted about planning to shoot police, as they had in Ireland. During the anti-eviction campaign in Sydney, more attention was given to small groups of party members securing properties than to mobilising working class sympathisers in the neighbourhood; the Newtown battle was a rare exception. In Port Adelaide, three CPA members were arrested and charged with possession of automatic pistols, ammunition and gelignite.

Even where members were not brandishing guns or planning to brandish guns, the CPA's readiness to resort to physical violence isolated it. Having faced repeated attempts by union leaders to destroy it, the UWM stormed a meeting of the Victorian Trades Hall in August 1931. A wild brawl erupted. Union officials called police to evict the radicals. Subsequent meetings also ended in uproar until the officials closed the chamber to non-delegates. The CPA engaged in similar antics in Sydney, Brisbane and Adelaide, with the same results. Some UWM branches rejected such tactics, defecting to rival unemployed councils set up by the ALP. Substantial numbers of party members suffered constant and vindictive police harassment; many were jailed. Recruitment to the UWM fell sharply, and the Central Committee wound it up at the end of 1931. Twelve months later, party secretary Miles himself recognised: 'The workers got the impression that in order to get into the UWM you had to bash or be bashed.'[15]

The CPA had relentlessly portrayed union leaders as 'social fascists.' This had a deleterious effect on the ability of party members to intervene effectively in their unions. In 1932, the Sydney MM complained that party members tended to treat trade union work as 'a joke' or in 'a light-hearted manner.'[16] In retrospect, the CPA recognised the problem: 'There was a marked tendency to seize upon the rank and file movements as alternative forms of organisation to the trade unions instead of as supplementary forms.'[17] But the CPA leadership had itself helped to create this culture.

Rhetorical radicalism but political passivity

The Comintern's 'social fascist' rhetoric also explains the CPA's failure to pick up more recruits from among those Labor supporters disgusted by the sellouts by federal and state Labor governments. The CPA was incapable of appealing to this audience because it dismissed the ALP – not just as a dead-end for the working class, which it was, but as fascist. The party's Tenth Congress in December 1931 unanimously resolved that:

> The various social democratic and labor parties throughout the world have become the worst enemies of the working-class, the most effective weapon in the hands of the bourgeoisie for crushing the working class.... Lang and the Left Social fascists constitute the most dangerous enemies of the working class.[18]

Workers who might be winnable were simply presented with an ultimatum:

> No honest worker can remain in the Labor Party, except at the price of becoming an open enemy of his class...he has now the choice: – with the Communist Party to the workers' revolution, or becoming an open social fascist defender of capitalism and all its crimes.[19]

That attitude could not enable the party to build a bridge to workers loyal to the ALP. A united front approach – making demands on the ALP and union leaders in order to test them in the course of a defensive struggle – was impossible. The CPA said that it sought a 'united front from below' with rank and file ALP members, but it made no effort to rally ALP members to join them in the eviction battles of 1931. At the 1932 May Day rally in Melbourne, the party organised a separate march through the city which culminated in CPA members storming the stage. Victorian ALP president Don Cameron and Deputy Premier Tom Tunnecliffe were thrown to the ground, punched and kicked. The Central Committee condemned this wild behaviour, but it was the natural consequence of the CPA's social fascist line.

The damage caused by social fascism became obvious during the campaign to defend the Lang Government against ruling class attacks. The CPA should have been throwing itself into the campaign, to demonstrate to rank and file Labor supporters that the CPA were the more determined fighters. But it refused to, airily dismissing the premier's repudiation of interest to British banks as of 'no concern to the working class.' When the NSW Governor sacked Lang in May 1932, hundreds of thousands of workers turned out to defend him – only to see him capitulate. This was a golden opportunity for the CPA to try to convince Lang's supporters why their faith in the premier was misplaced. Instead, the CPA only distributed leaflets denouncing Lang as 'the chief force holding the radicalised workers in check and keeping them from the path of struggle against capitalism.'[20] The party had nothing to offer Labor militants who wanted to fight Lang's sacking.

The CPA had the same dismissive attitude to the Socialisation Units. Historian of the Units, Robert Cooksey, says: 'Never before or since have so many rank and file branch members been activists – or socialists.'[21] The CPA had the opportunity to win thousands of them away from Labor and was well aware of this fact:

> It is very important that our party should understand that in the elements which are emerging from the 'socialisation nuclei' we have new cadres for our party, workers who are the best elements of the Labor Party, energetic and active. If we succeed in drawing them in to the party, we shall acquire the best elements that we need.[22]

For this reason, CPA members in some areas secretly entered the Units, hiding their party cards.

But the CPA was no longer interested in fighting for socialism, now pursuing only a counterproductive strategy imposed on it by the Kremlin. By condemning the Socialisation Unit leaders as left social fascists, the party repelled 'the best elements of the Labor Party' whom it aimed to recruit. Empty rhetoric replaced a strategy to connect the propaganda orientation of the Units with struggles by workers and the unemployed:

> McNamara's [the secretary of the Socialisation Committee] clownish talk of socialisation of industry through Parliament is, if anything, a key to fascism... Every worker, and particularly every Labor Party worker, must decide between proletarian dictatorship or fascist dictatorship. The Communist path to socialism or the Labor Party path to fascism.[23]

Stalinism or reformism was now the choice faced by workers. Had a genuine socialist party been built, taking some of the commitment and courage displayed by CPA members but embedding this in principled socialist politics, it could have provided a home for those radicalised during the Depression and an alternative to the dead-end choice that confronted them. A few who had quit or been expelled from the CPA in the late 1920s and early 1930s did gravitate to Trotskyism, including some of the main leaders of the UWM. They formed a tiny Left Opposition group of around two dozen in Sydney in 1933. But their small size meant that they were easily marginalised by the Stalinists, denounced as 'stool pigeons of the fascist bourgeoisie' and 'rats... filthy agents of capitalism, informers, spies, enemies of the Comintern and the Soviet Union, deserters' for whom there was one remedy: 'They must be ruthlessly destroyed and driven out of the working class movement. Place your heel on the head of these snakes.'[24] Some CPA members took these words literally and bashed the Trotskyist 'rats.'

Further, the CPA failed to build a useful cadre during the Depression. The majority of recruits were young unemployed workers who mostly churned through the party, quitting within a few months. Dedicated members who worked tirelessly for the party were the exception; in 1931, around three-quarters of members took no part in party activities. This level of turnover in party ranks and the lack of integration of members in the work of the organisation was clearly a weakness, but it actually served the new leadership well. Overwhelmingly, the opposition to the Stalinist takeover of the CPA at the outset of the Depression came from older members, those who commonly had histories in the socialist movement preceding the formation of the CPA and who recoiled at the imposition of Stalinism. With a few exceptions, this layer of members was purged in the early 1930s. Most of the Depression-era recruits were perfect raw material for an authoritarian party regime, because, lacking political experience, they had little authority to challenge the twists and turns of the party line. The fact that many of the new recruits were unemployed also helped the leadership impose the social fascist line because, not being held accountable by work mates, unemployed radicals could engage in ultra left stunts without being pulled into line. Social fascism could prevail because it was not subject to any real test within the working class. By the time that the CPA did begin to recruit more worker militants, in the mid-1930s, the leadership of Sharkey and Miles had converted it into a bureaucratic machine where a prerequisite for continued membership was submission to the leadership. The high rate of turnover of members and their lack of roots in the working class also served the interest of other groups: the police and surveillance arms of the state which infiltrated the CPA, undoubtedly encouraging the tendency to rash confrontations with the police, resulting in needless arrests and imprisonment of members.

Conclusion

Stalinism emerged triumphant in the Comintern on the eve of the Great Depression. Its first significant strategic 'turn,' the Third Period, was disastrous for workers in many countries. The case of Germany was most obvious:

far from blocking the rise of fascism, Stalinism eased it to power, with ghastly consequences for the world.

In Australia, Stalinism did not pave the way to concentration camps, but it nonetheless cut short a serious challenge to the betrayals of the Labor Party. The CPA grew during the Depression, but Stalinism prevented it from seizing the opportunity to win thousands more worker militants to genuine socialism out of the political polarisation of the time. Abusing Labor supporters as 'social fascists' and corrupting the meaning of socialism, Stalinism made 'communism' a dirty word, profoundly damaging the socialist cause off which it leeched. Many individual party members sincerely believed that they were fighting to advance working class interests; but the party as a whole had no such conception. It now owed its loyalty to Stalin and the Russian bureaucracy.

FURTHER READING

M. Armstrong, 'Between syndicalism and reformism: Founding the Communist Party of Australia', *Marxist Left Review*, no. 21, 2021.

T. Bramble and R. Kuhn, *Labor's Conflict: Big Business, Workers and the Politics of Class*, Melbourne, Cambridge University Press, 2010.

R. Cooksey, *Lang and Socialism: A Study in the Great Depression*, Canberra, ANU Press, 1976.

A. Davidson, *History of the Communist Party of Australia*, Stanford, Hoover Institution Press, 1969.

C. Fox, *Fighting Back: The Politics of the Unemployed in Victoria in the Great Depression*, Carlton, Melbourne University Press, 1996.

R. Gollan, *Revolutionaries and Reformists: Communism and the Australian labour movement 1920–1950*, Sydney, Allen and Unwin, 1975.

S. Macintyre, *Reds: The Communist Party of Australia from origins to illegality*, Sydney, Allen and Unwin, 1998.

POPULAR FRONT: GRAVEYARD OF STRUGGLES

1935 to 1945

10.

THE POPULAR FRONT IN FRANCE

The origins of the Popular Front

Starting in 1934, the Comintern shifted away from the Third Period and social fascism towards a new strategy: the Popular Front. During the Third Period, Communist parties had isolated themselves by their ultra left rhetoric, denouncing social democrats as worse than fascists. Now, the Popular Front saw them flip over and partner with social democrats and even with openly capitalist parties. Long gone was any idea of international revolution.

The Popular Front strategy dominated the practice of Communist parties for decades, until their eventual collapse. Like the 'left' turn of 1928, the 'right' turn represented by the Popular Front was to lead to a series of disasters for the workers' movement. This chapter and the following four analyse how the Popular Front derailed worker militancy in a range of countries in the 1930s and 1940s.[1]

The Popular Front was a product of shifts in Stalin's foreign policy. When Hitler took power in 1933, Stalin initially sought to maintain the peace treaty with Germany that had been in place since 1922, signing off on an extension of the treaty three months after Hitler's appointment as Chancellor. Stalin certainly had no principled objection to fascism; Russia had been on the best of terms with Mussolini's Italy for years. Only when it became clear in early 1934 that Hitler was not interested in renewing the peace treaty did Stalin give up on the alliance with fascist Germany. While Stalin's apologists at the time and since argue that the Russian dictator saved the world from fascism in the 1940s, Stalin did not object to fascist governments, only those that turned on Russia.

Relations with Germany having turned sour, Stalin then began to look for allies in Britain and France. They too were alarmed by the threat of a more aggressive Germany. Stalin's search for imperialist partners propelled Russia into the League of Nations (denounced by Lenin as a pack of imperialist robbers) in May 1934. In May 1935, Stalin forged a Mutual Security Pact with France, committing each nation to come to the other's defence in the event of a German attack.

Russia's new alliances produced a transformation in Comintern rhetoric. For years, the Comintern Executive had, correctly, denounced Britain and France as imperialist enemies of the working class and the oppressed of the world; now, it described them as forces for peace, stating by way of explanation:

> Today the situation is not what it was in 1914. Now it is not only the working class, the peasantry and all working people who are resolved to maintain peace, but also the oppressed countries and the weak nations whose independence is threatened by war. The Soviet Union, the invincible fortress of the world proletariat and the oppressed of all countries, is the focal point of all the forces fighting for peace. In the present phase, a number of capitalist states are also concerned to maintain peace. Hence, the possibility of creating a broad front of the working class, of all the working people, and of entire nations against the danger of imperialist war.[2]

The Popular Front policy was formally announced at the Comintern's Seventh Congress in August 1935, the first for seven years (and last). The Congress resolved that: 'The struggle for peace opens up before the Communist parties, the greatest opportunities for creating the broadest united front.'[3]

The Popular Front was to drag Communist parties far to the right. While the Third Period was a counter-revolutionary policy clothed in revolutionary rhetoric, the Popular Front policy much more clearly abandoned any claims to revolutionary authenticity. In order to secure and maintain alliances with the British and French ruling classes, Russia and the Comintern had to ensure that the Communist parties in those countries were not agitating for the downfall of their rulers. Peaceful relations between Russia and the Western imperialists must entail peaceful relations between the classes in the imperialist world. More accurately, the working class was to accept its subordination to the rulers of Britain and France in the name of People's Fronts of supposedly 'progressive' forces. Such forces included not just other workers' parties but any capitalist parties that were prepared to support close relations with Russia.

The Popular Front had nothing in common with the united front policy of the Comintern's earlier revolutionary years or the strategy Trotsky had argued for in Germany. The united front was a temporary alliance between working class parties in order to wage a defensive battle to secure the interests of the working class; the Popular Front incorporated openly bourgeois forces and required the working class to suppress its demands for fear of antagonising them. The united front constituted a practical agreement to fight for specific aims; the Popular Front involved a common electoral program and support for a bourgeois government. The united front, superficially a defensive tactic, contained an offensive element: to win over the working class supporters of reformist parties by demonstrating the superiority of Communist tactics over those of the reformists; the Popular Front ensured that Communists would tail behind reformist leaders. The united front required complete ideological independence and freedom of criticism for the Communists; the Popular Front ensured the Communists' subordination. The united front was a means of combating workers' reformist illusions; the Popular Front encouraged them. The united front encouraged workers to fight for concrete demands that could pull the desperate middle class away from the far right; the Popular Front involved alliances with the *parties* of the petit bourgeoisie, in practice serving the interests of the big bourgeoisie and driving the petit bourgeoisie into the arms of the far right.

The Popular Front was an inherently nationalist project. In imperialist countries, that meant an imperialist project. One of the most revolutionary features of the Comintern in its early days, as opposed to the national chauvinist Second International, was its solid stance against imperialism and for the independence of the colonies and oppressed nations (Chapter 7). In the 1920s, the British and French Communist parties had been at the forefront of agitation against colonialism and the huge military budgets necessitated by large empires. Under the Popular Front policy, this had to go. The new era of what was called 'collective security' between Russia and its Western allies compelled the British and French Communist parties to champion strong military and colonial rule, albeit with some minor liberal adjustments.

Socialist collaboration with capitalist parties was not new. Well before the Popular Front policy, sections of the socialist movement had been involved in alliances with bourgeois forces and entered bourgeois governments. But it had usually been the right wing of the socialist movement that engaged in these betrayals of workers' interests, and the left had roundly condemned them. Now it was the Communist parties, supposedly the left wing of the movement, championing a class collaborationist strategy. They provided a sophisticated theoretical defence for class collaboration, couched in Marxist rhetoric and liberally peppered with quotes from revolutionary icons – more thorough than SPD revisionist theoretician Eduard Bernstein had ever offered. This gave class collaboration new credibility with class conscious workers. The left wing intelligentsia also embraced the Popular Front and produced countless books and articles establishing it as the supposed centrepiece of revolutionary strategy. Such propaganda confused and disoriented generations of workers and students who saw themselves as Marxists.

It is vital for genuine revolutionaries to have a clear understanding of the problems with Popular Front politics. Their adoption demonstrated how deeply the rot had penetrated in the Comintern by the 1930s. When the Third Period was foisted on the Comintern in 1928 by Bukharin and his successor, Molotov, Moscow faced resistance from some sections of the International. The purges of the late 1920s and early 1930s brought leaders of the Comintern sections into line. Ordered now to adopt the Popular Front, many of the same leaders who had risen to their positions condemning social democracy as the biggest enemy of the workers' movement now embraced alliances with parties well to the right of social democracy. French PCF leader Maurice Thorez was one. The French Popular Front was the prototype, ending in tragedy for workers and paving the way for Marshal Pétain's semi-fascist regime to take power in 1940.

The Popular Front in France

Hitler's triumph in Germany sounded alarm bells throughout the working class in Europe and this made itself felt within the social democratic parties, whose leaders understood that the fascists would crush not only Communists but the entire independent workers' movement. The calamity in Germany impressed on workers the price to be paid for disunity among working class parties in the face of fascism. It fired a tremendous impulse towards unity. Radical tendencies appeared in the socialist parties, particularly their youth wings. There was talk of creating new Marxist parties that would unite revolutionary socialists and Communists. These factors were conducive to overtures made by the social democrats to the Stalinist parties. In February 1933, the successor to the Second International, the Labour and Socialist International, declared its readiness to open discussions with the Comintern to organise joint actions against fascism. Soon afterwards, the French SFIO, four times larger than the PCF, announced its readiness to do the same. In early 1934, the Spanish Socialist Party declared itself in favour of a Workers' Alliance and invited the Spanish Communists to join them.

Still adhering to 'social fascism,' the Comintern Executive initially scorned these approaches, repeating its claims that social democrats were the main prop of capitalism and that left social democrats were the most dangerous of all. The PCF replied to the SFIO's overture by repeating its repudiation of the 'united front from above' in favour of a 'united front from below' – the sectarian demand that social democratic workers must abandon their leaders before the Communist Party would work with them:

> More than ever do we fraternise with the Socialist workers, more than ever do we appeal to them for joint action with their Communist comrades. And more than ever do we denounce the Socialist leaders, the Socialist Party, lackeys of the bourgeoisie and last bastion of capitalist society.[4]

The PCF maintained this sectarian approach for the first few months of 1934, but it could not cut itself off entirely from the growing sentiment for unity in the working class. The Third Period had been a disaster for the PCF. Its vote fell at every election, as did its membership, barely 30,000 by 1932. By the spring of 1934, the Thorez leadership held to the social fascist line only because of loyalty to Stalin. Less inhibited was Thorez's rival for leadership, Jacques Doriot, mayor and parliamentary deputy for the working class suburb of Paris St Denis, who argued for collaboration with the SFIO to fight fascism. A mobilisation by the fascists themselves drove unity between the SFIO and PCF.

The Depression hit France later than most countries – in 1931 – but it then had a similar impact: bankrupting businesses, pushing down agricultural prices, cutting wages and driving up unemployment. As in Germany, layers of the middle class looked for a strong leader to protect them from ruin. Ex-soldiers flocked to the far right Croix de Feu, led by Colonel de La Rocque. Others from the middle class looked to the royalist Action Française. These layers scorned the bourgeois republican party, the Radicals, led by Édouard Daladier, which held government. The Radical Party had traditionally drawn most of its votes from the peasantry and urban petit bourgeoisie, but its support was now leaking to the right.

On 6 February 1934, fascists and monarchists organised a mass demonstration in Paris, demanding the resignation of the Daladier government amid allegations of massive corruption.[5] Thousands showed up and attempted to storm the National Assembly. Security forces drove them back and inflicted many casualties. The demonstration then turned into a virtual uprising by the far right, with several days of rioting and street fighting. By the time the fascist insurgency was over, 15 lay dead and more than 1,400 injured.

Daladier was driven from office and replaced by Gaston Doumergue, who was welcomed by fascists because his government was a clear half-step towards fascism.

The fascist mobilisation in Paris emphasised the importance of a united working class response. Thorez would not move without authorisation from Moscow, so Doriot seized the opportunity. He approached the SFIO leaders and the party's union federation, the CGT, for joint action against the fascists. They agreed. The CGT called for a strike and mass demonstrations on 12 February. After some delay, the PCF-aligned union federation, the General Confederation of Labour – Unitary (CGT-U), joined in, fearing that it would be left behind. Workers turned out in strength across the country: 4.5 million struck, a milestone, the first general strike in the history of the French working class. One million marched, in Paris, Marseille, Toulon, Toulouse, Rouen, Bordeaux and French colonial Algeria. In Paris, hundreds of thousands came out to the two demonstrations called by the CGT and CGT-U. When the demonstrations converged at the end, workers demanded 'Unity! Unity!' Socialist paper *Le Populaire* described the scene:

> Socialists, communists, members of the united workers' party [Parti d'Unité Prolétarienne], Trotskyists, all were fraternally united, arm in arm and with a single song rising from this great wall of chests, an invincible rampart against the enemies of the labouring class. It was L'Internationale, the song of a class in complete communion, sharing the same hope and the same desire for battle.[6]

Five days later, Socialist Party members took part in the funeral procession of Communist workers killed by police during the demonstrations against the fascist insurgency. The Thorez leadership, still clinging to 'social fascism,' stated that the Socialist presence at the funeral should not be taken as 'a realisation of the united front': while SFIO leader Léon Blum might call for defence of the Republic against fascism, Thorez argued, the Republic was already fascist.[7] Actual fascism marched on relentlessly. Just days after the mass demonstrations in Paris, the fascists in Austria seized power. Workers this time fought bravely until overcome.

On 31 May, the PCF's paper *L'Humanité* announced an abrupt turn, publishing an appeal to the SFIO for united action. Confirming that this initiative was at the behest of Stalin, that issue reproduced an article from the Russian Communist paper *Pravda*, dated 23 May, which approved joint Communist-Socialist action.

What had happened between February, when the SFIO was still being denounced, and the end of May, when the PCF opened the door to unity? The answer can be found in Russian foreign policy. In January, the German and Polish governments signed a pact. To Moscow, the pact signified an aggressive move against Russia, because Germany had been its ally until then. To Paris, the pact signified the breakdown of its system of anti-German alliances, including one with Poland, that had been patiently built up for years. Both the French and Russian governments began to see an advantage in closer relations to combat the Polish–German alliance. In May, the French Government proposed to Russia a Mutual Security Pact within the framework of the League of Nations, which Russia then applied to join. Within days, Moscow gave the PCF the green light to unite with the SFIO. Ironically, Doriot, who had advocated just such a step for many months, was expelled from the PCF in June for disloyalty.

One month later, on 27 July, the PCF signed an anti-fascist unity pact with the SFIO. On the 29th, Socialists and Communists joined forces in Paris in a big rally to commemorate the anniversary of the assassination of prewar socialist leader, Jean Jaurès. The immediate result of the pact was a rise in the electoral fortunes of both parties at the October local elections, reflecting workers' desire for unity.

Stalin, however, was not interested merely in seeing the workers' parties in France form a bloc. The whole point of the Popular Front was to involve the main bourgeois party, the Radicals, in order to secure a military alliance between Russia and France. In October, Thorez appealed to the Radicals to form a 'Popular Front for liberty, work and bread.' The Radicals saw the Popular Front as an opportunity to present themselves to the ruling class as the party that could discipline the working class; they would stabilise bourgeois rule more effectively than the parties growing in size and influence on the far right. They therefore agreed, in principle, to join an electoral Front of the three parties. The Popular Front was sealed in writing at a formal ceremony on Bastille Day, 14 July 1935, followed by a half-million strong demonstration. Contingents of all three parties marched. The French flag flew alongside the red flag, the *Marseillaise* was sung alongside the *Internationale*. The following month, the Comintern formally adopted the Popular Front policy at its Seventh Congress.

The prospect of unity to defeat fascism drew workers towards the two workers' parties. The PCF grew particularly rapidly: from 29,000 in 1933 to 42,000 in 1934 and to 90,000 by the beginning of 1936. Workplaces also reflected the shift to the left, with strikes growing throughout 1934 and 1935, even as the PCF called for 'calm' and 'discipline.' In February 1936, the momentum towards a

Popular Front picked up with the election of a Popular Front government in Spain. In March, the CGT and CGT-U reunified, resulting in an influx of new members to the combined CGT.

The PCF's priority was now the national elections, due in May. It went out of its way not to scare away its new allies, particularly the Radicals. The PCF now championed French military security; this met Russia's needs too, because the Mutual Security Pact required a strong French military if it was to be of any use to Stalin. Under the PCF's influence, the election platform of the Popular Front was extremely limited. It committed only to nationalisation of war industries, whereas the SFIO had wanted much wider nationalisation. It promised to pump money into the economy through public works, in the hope that this would lift the economy out of depression. It offered workers some reforms – the establishment of an unemployment fund, introduction of the 40-hour week, defence of trade unions and democratic rights and the dissolution of the fascist organisations; but Popular Front candidates were not bound to accept the program. All it offered the oppressed in France's colonial empire was a parliamentary commission to investigate their situation. Historians Danos and Gibelin write: 'All available evidence indicated that the mass of ordinary people were well to the "left" of this electoral programme,'[8] which was little different from the classical Radical program. The PCF went to the elections with the slogan: 'For a strong, free and happy France.'

The elections, held in two stages on 26 April and 3 May 1936, unmistakably reflected the polarisation of French politics. There was a sharp shift to the parties of the left. The SFIO triumphed with 149 seats, up from 97, and therefore provided the new prime minister, Léon Blum. The PCF saw its parliamentary representation rise from 10 to 72. The Radicals, traditionally the biggest party in the National Assembly, saw their tally of seats fall from 159 to 110. The Radical Party was saved from an even greater loss by the decision of Communists and Socialists not to run against it in the second round of voting in several seats. The three parties, together with a smattering of independent socialists, formed government with a majority of 162 seats in the lower house. Determined not to scare the middle and capitalist classes, the Comintern instructed the PCF not to take up the Cabinet positions to which it was entitled.

The Comintern was less elated by the workers' parties' strong showing than might have been expected. From Moscow's perspective, the only thing that mattered was the Mutual Security Pact. In that respect, the weak showing of the Radicals caused Moscow great concern. Russian Foreign Minister Litvinov told a French newspaper:

What is essential is that France should not allow her military strength to be weakened. We hope no internal troubles will favour Germany's designs.[9]

Workers, on the other hand, greeted the election result with jubilation. Leftists in the Socialist Party were exuberant. Marceau Pivert declared in *Le Populaire* on 27 May: 'Now everything is possible for those who are bold enough.' For him, that meant only pressuring the incoming government to deliver reforms. But workers were not going to wait. For them, Pivert's slogan meant that everything was now up for grabs.

The June 1936 working class revolt

The new government would take office on 4 June, but workers were not willing to wait for change. They welcomed the election result, seeing in it their own power, but they were also sceptical that a Popular Front government containing the hated Republicans would deliver them much. If they were to make progress, they must take matters into their own hands. Dockworkers in Marseille had already gone on strike against wage cuts in December 1935. On 1 May, coal miners struck in an action prepared many weeks beforehand. Once the election results were known, a veritable explosion of strikes followed. Historian of the Comintern Fernando Claudin writes:

> From the very first day, indeed, the movement bore the mark that is to be found at the beginning of every genuine revolution: spontaneous initiative by the broad masses, qualitative change in its state of mind, the joining together of millions of people in one single will to put an end to a certain order of things, the overflowing of habitual frameworks.[10]

On 11 May, strikes started sporadically in several regional cities. On 24 May, an unprecedented 600,000 people rallied to commemorate the martyrs of the 1871 Paris Commune. On 26 May, strikes began to take off. Communist militants had been preparing for this moment for months; now, their hard work building factory cells within their workplaces paid off.

The engineering, automotive and aviation industries moved first, because PCF unionists had a solid presence there. On 28 May, 35,000 workers at Renault downed tools and occupied their plant, inspiring others to follow their lead. By the 29th, occupations were underway at more than a dozen factories in Paris;

French workers were aware of the factory occupations in the US (Chapter 12) and took up the tactic enthusiastically. Historian Jacques Fauvet writes: 'the movement assumed a twofold revolutionary aspect, attacking both authority and property.'[11]

Building workers stopped work on big sites in Paris. By 30 May, more than 100,000 workers were on strike in manufacturing and construction. There was then a lull of a few days. Some groups of workers went back to work, but a new wave of strikes began on 2 June involving workers in chemicals, food, textiles, industrial design, furniture, transport and oil. By 3 June, 200 factories were occupied, with the red flag hoisted aloft at some. On 4 June, the day when the Blum Government was sworn in, strikes spread further, drawing in truck drivers, newspaper distribution, restaurants, hotels, printing, petrol distribution, pharmaceutical laboratories, tailoring, gas and farms. The movement spread across the country, from the Belgian border to the Mediterranean coast. Strikes also shut down the entire coal mining industry in the militant *départements* (provinces) of Nord and Pas-de-Calais and the whole of the Paris engineering sector.

The June strike wave was driven from below. At no point during the June days did the unions ever attempt a national general strike. Some strikes had even broken out in workplaces with no union members at all. To the extent that individual unions called industry-wide strikes, this was generally to try to hold the movement in check.

Against a tidal wave of strikes, the bosses' initial attempt at an intransigent united front gave way to panic and disintegration. As the bosses granted concessions in one factory, that served as a spur for other workers to come out on strike again to win the higher rates. There was no way out for the bosses apart from government intervention. In its first two days in office, the Blum Government had been forced to look on impotently. On its third day, the employer federations appealed to the government to convene talks to resolve the crisis. On the other side, the CGT leaders were also looking for a way to rein in a movement that was moving out of their control. Jacques Duclos, Thorez's right-hand man, stated:

> We are concerned about two things – first, to avoid any disorder, and second, to get talks going as soon as may be, with a view to a quick settlement of the conflict.[12]

On Blum's fourth day in office, 7 June, Blum sat down with representatives of the CGT and major employer groups at the prime minister's residence, the

Hôtel Matignon, to try to bring an end to the occupations. The only thing that could break the momentum was a big package of concessions by the employers and government, something that would allow union leaders to get back in front of their members – having only tailed them helplessly for the previous week.

The resulting Matignon Agreements, signed by the Blum Government, the CGT and the employers, granted significant concessions to workers, including the right to bargain collectively, the recognition of trade unions, wage increases averaging 12 percent and a system of factory delegates. The government promised to bring forward the introduction of the 40-hour week, paid holidays and nationalisation of war industries. These were the biggest gains ever made by French workers and reflected the pressure on the bosses.

Having signed their names to the Matignon Agreements, the union leaders now sought to bring the struggle to an end as quickly as possible. The condition for a return to work spelled out in the Agreements was that workers would end their action once their employer expressed willingness to abide by the decisions contained in the Agreements and readiness to begin negotiations for a local or regional agreement aimed at resolving specific workplace problems.

The PCF newspaper greeted the Agreements with banner headlines: 'IT'S VICTORY!' But the number of workers on strike grew, and many workers refused to end their sit-ins. Any number of local issues needed addressing. In many cases, negotiations opened up the issue of the extraordinarily low rates of pay received by some groups of workers. A 12 percent increase on these entirely inadequate rates was not satisfactory. And so, on 10 June, a meeting of 700 Paris engineering delegates refused to return to work, voting instead for a resolution that the employers should accept their demands within 48 hours, or their plants would be nationalised. On being presented with the workers' demands, the engineering employers gave in on the main points. The workers then insisted on more concessions.

In the north east, strikes spread from engineering to textiles, the coal mines and the docks. Engineers sent delegations to the textile mills to offer help, while rail workers organised to help the women guarding the gates outside their occupied plants. Not only blue collar workers were active; in Paris, workers at the big department stores stayed out and won public support by displaying their starvation wage rates on posters at the shop entrances. In the hotels, cafés and restaurants, 8,000 blue and white collar workers formed a series of processions through the streets of Paris. Those still working were pulled off the job; by the following day, virtually the entire industry in Paris was closed. Insurance staff walked off, with pickets and occupations at some enterprises. In Marseille, the number of strikers increased several days after the agreement was signed, with construction workers, print workers, chemical workers and shipyards all stopping work.

The workers were striking not just for a franc here or there, but against intolerable conditions and for the right to be treated by their bosses as humans and with dignity. In the early days of the strike wave, there were many cases of workers locking their bosses in their offices. The insurance workers' demands included not just the Matignon terms but the setting up of disciplinary committees, comprised of equal numbers of representatives of staff and management, which must give unanimous approval to any dismissals of established staff. No longer were they prepared to tolerate a situation where the managers walked among them as dictators. Women workers played an important role in the strikes, with the department stores seeing an intensive rush of organising among workers with few industrial traditions. They built unions where none had existed before. Union membership at the Bon Marché department store rose from 11 to 1,800 in June 1936. In many cases, where the bosses just gave workers the conditions in the Agreements without a strike, workers still walked off the job to be part of the national movement.

Simone Weil, a Christian with anarchist sympathies who had thrown in her teaching job to work in a Paris engineering factory, describes the atmosphere:

> The very act of striking is a joy. A pure and unalloyed joy.
>
> Yes, a joy. I have been to see my pals in the factory where I worked a few months ago... What joy to enter the plant with the smiling authorisation of a worker guarding the gate. What joy to find so many smiles, so many friendly words of welcome... Joy to roam freely through the shop where we were once chained to our machines ... Joy to hear music, songs and laughter instead of the pitiless din of machines... Joy to walk near the foreman with our heads held high... Joy to live the rhythm of human life in amongst the silent machines... Of course, the old hard existence will begin again in a few days, but no one is thinking about that now... At last, for the first time, different memories will haunt these heavy machines, souvenirs of something other than silence, constraint, submission. Memories which will keep a little pride in our hearts, which will breathe just a little human warmth into all this cold metal.[13]

Alongside this joy went determination to avenge past injustices. People sang and danced but also raised their fists and flew red flags. The fact that the struggle was not just a festival was particularly obvious to workers in France's colonies in North Africa. The agitation by Arab and Berber workers in Morocco and Algeria, whom the French regarded as little more than slaves, alarmed the colonial authorities and French settlers. Several workers were shot. Nonetheless, even in these conditions, workers were able to wrest concessions.

The Blum Government sought to push back on three fronts. They rushed the social laws – the 40-hour week, paid holidays and collective agreements – through the lower house in just three days. The second strategy was repression. Squads of riot police were already deployed to working class districts of Lille, in the industrial north east, and to regions affected by farm workers' strikes. Troops and riot police were now deployed in the Paris region. On 12 June, the government seized all copies of the Trotskyist newspaper *La Lutte Ouvrière* at the print works and announced legal proceedings against the leaders of France's tiny Trotskyist organisation. The third front, and the main game, was to use the Communist leaders to bring workers to heel. The Radicals certainly could not do this, and nor could Blum's Socialists; workers had gone on strike and occupied their factories without seeking Blum's permission, an implicit repudiation. Everything hinged on the PCF, the only party untainted by parliamentary wheeler-dealing and proudly proclaiming its revolutionary credentials.

Communist militants had helped organise many of the strikes, but their leaders sought to keep them within limits. PCF leaders argued that the new government should be allowed to carry out its program 'in order, calm, tranquillity and without a perfectly useless precipitation' which would only alarm the middle class and play into the hands of the fascists.[14] But the PCF leaders could not turn their backs on the workers without losing credibility. They had to keep the faith of the militants while bringing their action to an end.

Once it became clear that workers were raising new demands and carrying the struggle beyond the limitations of the Matignon Agreements, potentially leading to a challenge to the Popular Front government, the PCF turned strongly against the strikes, warning of 'outside forces' and 'suspicious elements' intervening to prolong the strikes. It raised the spectre that workers might lose the support of the middle class and the peasantry and be crushed, just as the Paris Commune, isolated from the peasants in the provinces, was crushed in 1871. The PCF leaders had firstly to bring the party's rank and file militants into line. On 11 June, Thorez told a meeting of worker militants:

> It is necessary to know when to end a strike once satisfaction has been obtained. It is necessary to know when to make a compromise

if all the demands have not been met, but if victory has been won on the most essential demands. All is not possible.[15]

PCF leaders argued that only the 'Trotsky fascists' wanted to continue the strikes. The bourgeois press greeted Thorez's speech warmly, and 'We must know when to end a strike' became the theme of PCF speeches.

The PCF's intervention was essential to derailing the strikes. The PCF had the membership, growing rapidly from 90,000 in February to 131,000 in May and 216,000 by July, overtaking the SFIO.[16] PCF members were well implanted in the key industries and soon came to dominate the new united union federation, which grew dramatically from 1.5 million to 5.5 million. PCF members also had the credibility among worker militants to bring the strikes to a halt. They had earned the respect of their fellow workers for their organising on the job in the years leading up to 1936. Because they still cloaked themselves in the aura of the Russian Revolution, they were seen as the genuine radicals. This gave them the ability to quickly take charge of the strike committees which emerged in hundreds of workplaces. The PCF also had the apparatus to take control of the strikes. Its success at municipal elections over the previous 18 months had given it control over councils in working class areas, which it used to collect funds and food supplies for strikers. The party leadership directed all these assets to breaking the strike wave.

The PCF played its cards cleverly, running to the head of the movement that it had not wanted, the better to reverse it. On 11 June, engineering workers had voted to refuse to return to work. On the 12th, the day after Thorez's speech declaring 'it is necessary to know when to end a strike,' a new delegate assembly voted almost unanimously to accept the terms on offer. Thirteen other collective agreements were signed on the 12th and seven more on the 13th, covering occupations as diverse as hairdressing and stonemasonry.

The PCF was not immediately successful in breaking all strikes; there were still plenty of workers with fight in them. Department store workers, for example, did not return until the 22nd. However, the tide was turning. By early July, most strikers had returned to work. Some workers kept fighting: workers in the St Nazaire dockyards were still occupying on 14 July; 800 hairdressers were still on strike in Marseille; and only on the 14th did building workers in that city end their strike after 32 days. While June was undoubtedly the peak of the strike wave, with 1.8 million workers and 12,000 strikes, a further 180,000 workers stopped in 1,750 strikes in July.

The PCF did its best to prevent workers from seeing the political implications of their actions – that the government and bosses were paralysed by the workers' offensive, that large numbers in the middle classes were being pulled behind the workers, and that workers had the capacity to be the masters of the situation. Rather, the PCF sought to focus workers' minds on making economic demands on the boss. The party failed to raise demands for the formation of factory committees to run the factories or for workers' councils to coordinate the workers in the 9,000 factories and workshops occupied in June–July 1936. The PCF never raised the demand for nationalisation of the big enterprises under workers' control; outside armaments, only the railways were nationalised by the Popular Front government, and only because the rail companies were collapsing under the weight of their debts. In short, the Communists failed to propose any steps to take the struggle forward to a new, higher, level. Why? Because the party feared that escalation of the struggle might give rise to an armed confrontation with the French state, thereby threatening French 'security' and undermining Stalin's new military partner. With PCF leaders thinking only of how to end the movement, the potential for a serious challenge to capitalism was thrown away.

The PCF now enjoyed a high profile in the National Assembly, the local councils and unions. It had become part of the political establishment, its leaders given access to the radio and capitalist press and treated as significant figures, not marginalised rebels. The party drew in significant numbers of middle class people, intellectuals and peasants for the first time. Where figures from professional milieux would not sign a party card, the PCF still assigned them leading positions in the various front groups that accompanied the Popular Front project – professional and intellectual associations and women's groups.

The worker militants the PCF recruited may have been attracted by the party's associations with 1917, but most quickly became apologists for class collaboration and nationalism. Revolution, if the PCF ever mentioned it, was now only for the far-off future. The patronage opportunities that came with holding dozens of parliamentary seats and control over local councils provided a reward for loyal party members and a stick to beat dissidents.

The bosses' counterattack

The class struggle never stands still. In the summer of 1936, the whole logic of the economic crisis meant either the workers had to advance, to encroach further onto the sacred rights of the capitalist class, or the bosses would counterattack and claw back the gains that workers had won. For workers to advance, they required a political leadership up to the task. The

PCF, putting the interests of the Popular Front government ahead of those of workers, was not that leadership.

In June, the bosses suffered heavy blows and were temporarily disoriented. But the PCF's success in ending the upsurge allowed them to regroup. Events in Spain further enthused them: on 17 July, General Francisco Franco led a coup against the Popular Front government in Madrid. Many French bosses, well aware of Hitler's success in crushing the German working class, began to look to the far right for a solution to their problems. Two parties emerged to fill the space. One, the Parti Social Français, emerged out of the Croix de Feu; the other, the Parti Populaire Français, was created by Doriot, who had veered hard to the right since his expulsion from the PCF.

The capitalists turned on Blum as his government began to introduce the reforms outlined in the Matignon Agreements. The right wing press used anti-Semitism to foster middle class hostility to the country's first Jewish prime minister. Many middle class people, pulled to the left by the impact of the strikes, now swung back to the right as workers were demobilised.

The PCF's reaction to these developments was to push the Popular Front further to the right, calling in August for a 'French Front' to include parties of the mainstream right. The proposal was stillborn. Neither the bourgeoisie, moving to the right, nor the Radicals had any interest. The PCF proposal, however, had a broader purpose. In preparation for an anticipated war with Germany, in which France would fight on the side of Russia, Stalin wanted to create a government of national unity in France capable of disciplining French workers to sacrifice for the war effort.

During the autumn of 1936, Blum came under fire on a range of fronts. The economy went backwards as the bosses pulled investments out of the country. Many capitalists could not afford further concessions to the working class; they mounted a propaganda offensive against implementation of the 40-hour week. Working class disillusionment with the government also grew. Unemployment barely budged, and inflation ate away at wage rises granted in the summer. Nonetheless, workers were not defeated, and strikes revived in September.

Rather than organise workers to resist the employer offensive, the PCF diverted the strikes into industrial arbitration procedures that had been introduced in the Matignon Agreement. Thorez and the PCF lulled workers to sleep with stories about their great victories during the summer. Blum, well aware of his government's dependence on loans from British and US banks, began to prepare a program of austerity.

In the latter half of 1936, the Spanish Civil War emerged as the cause of an ongoing dispute between the PCF and Blum and an opportunity for the

Communists to give themselves an unwarranted left gloss. Stalin did not want a revolution in Spain, but nor did he relish the prospect of a quick victory for Franco; that would throw another European country into the fascist camp.[17] The PCF therefore pushed the Blum Government to arm the Republican government in Madrid, the democratically elected authority. Blum, however, was anxious not to alienate the British Conservative government, many of whose ministers were Franco sympathisers. British bankers had lent substantial sums to Spanish capitalists, which might never be repaid if workers in Spain seized their assets. Blum also knew that a victorious workers' revolution in Spain would quickly spill over into France: the fate of the two workers' movements was tied. At a time when Germany and Italy were pouring in weapons and soldiers to support Franco, and when the sympathies of millions of French workers lay squarely with Republican Spain, Blum refused to supply French arms to the Madrid government. This created a running sore in relations with the PCF, but it also allowed the PCF to put itself at the head of support for the Republic, even as it preached moderation in France. The PCF helped to smuggle arms into Spain, and thousands of French Communists crossed the Pyrenees to fight, but the PCF would not do the one thing that could have tipped the balance in favour of the Republic – pursue a revolutionary policy in France. Organising workers in the munitions industry and the railways to manufacture and transport weapons to supply the Republican armies directly could have made all the difference. But urging workers to take over two major French industries would have created an immediate confrontation with the Radicals and thus wrecked the Popular Front.

Into reverse gear

Worker dissatisfaction with the Blum Government began to grow over the winter and spring of 1937, but the PCF continued to provide it with left cover. The party supported the government's use of special powers to increase public transport fares, postage charges and the price of tobacco. Inflation continued to erode workers' wages, while the conciliation and arbitration procedures tied worker militants up in useless tribunal hearings. In March, 8,000 workers, called out by the PCF and SFIO, protested against a fascist meeting in Paris authorised by Blum's Minister of the Interior. Police opened fire, killing five and injuring hundreds. Some factories held strikes the following day, and militants chased out known fascist sympathisers at the Renault factory. Blum's ministers blamed leftists for the deaths, saying that they had provoked the police. Rather than focus anger at Blum and his ministers for allowing the fascists the room to organise and defending the murderous police, the PCF made excuses for the ministers and called only for Blum to punish the police responsible and to ban the fascists.

After one year as prime minister, in the midst of a severe financial crisis and under intense pressure from the right wing controlled Senate, Blum resigned on 22 June, bringing an end to the first Popular Front government. Workers who had welcomed its accession to power with joy received the news of its dismissal with indifference; demoralisation and resignation were setting in. Blum was replaced by the Radical Party leader, Camille Chautemps, forming the second, much more openly pro-capitalist, Popular Front government. Under orders from Moscow, which feared that a government dominated by the right wing opposition parties would rip up the Mutual Security Pact, the PCF backed Chautemps.

Chautemps stepped up the pace of attacks on workers, provoking strikes and a new round of factory occupations in late 1937 and early 1938. Indeed, there were more strikes in 1937–38 than at any time before. But these were defensive strikes. Workers faced lockouts, mass sackings and police terror because the bosses were in no mood to make concessions. Defeats far outnumbered victories. Workers must either mobilise for a determined assault on the capitalists or go down to a terrible defeat. But such an assault would have destabilised the government, so the PCF had no appetite to lead it.

The PCF's enthusiasm to include the Radicals in the Popular Front was explained to worker militants as a means to draw the middle class behind the working class, to prevent them from succumbing to the lure of fascism. But, by 1936, many in the middle class were turning away from the Radical Party, seeing it as corrupt and responsible for their economic distress. They were looking for parties that could offer them bold policies that could address their many discontents. The PCF's willingness to tailor the program of the Popular Front to keeping the Radicals happy, far from drawing the middle class to the Popular Front, only alienated many in the middle class, pushed them into the camp of the fascists, who were seen to be challenging the corrupt political establishment they despised.

In March 1938, Blum briefly reoccupied the post of prime minister to form the Third Popular Front government. After four weeks, Daladier, who had now moved sharply to the right, replaced Blum. Daladier threw out the Socialists and appointed a new Cabinet, consisting mainly of Radicals and some figures from the parties of the Right. The Popular Front was dead. The Daladier government moved aggressively against the gains of 1936, in particular the 40-hour week. Regardless, the PCF continued to support Daladier, but it paid the price:

at its base, members were becoming demoralised by the party's right wing trajectory. Thousands resigned. Others reduced their level of involvement.

The PCF pulled its support from the Daladier government after six months, not because of its anti-worker policies, but because it signed the Munich Agreement with Nazi Germany. This agreement codified a realignment of alliances in Europe with far-reaching effects for the Comintern parties. In 1938, Germany demanded that Czechoslovakia surrender Sudetenland, an area with a majority German-speaking population. The Czech Government turned to its allies, Britain and France, for support. But neither had any appetite for a clash with Germany. The French ruling class was petrified at the prospect of war with Germany, fearing that it would create social upheaval of the type that it had experienced during and after World War I. Further, a substantial number of ruling class figures with fascist sympathies, including Foreign Minister Georges Bonnet, believed that, if France were to go to war, it should be as an ally of Germany against Russia. The attitude of Neville Chamberlain's British Conservative Government was that, so long as Germany did not infringe on the British empire, Hitler was welcome to territory. If Britain had to fight a war, better it be against Russia, not Germany. The result was the Munich Agreement of 30 September, in which France and Britain ratified Germany's seizure of Czechoslovakia.

Munich was a disaster for Stalin. His policy of 'collective security,' involving a Russia-Britain-France bloc against Germany, now lay in ruins. Stalin no longer had any need to support French imperialism, so the PCF pulled its support from the Daladier government.

The PCF now felt compelled to offer some opposition to Daladier's continuing offensive against workers. The CGT, now under Communist control, called a 24-hour general strike for 30 November. Unfortunately, with many sections of workers having already been beaten in local battles and with the government given plenty of time to prepare, the workers went into the strike in the worst possible state. Two million struck, including workers in many key engineering factories, construction sites, printing companies, mines and various other occupations. However, vital sections of workers did not come out, including those in war industries, railway workers, metal workers and other advanced layers of the proletariat. The strike ended in a bad defeat. The bosses now had a clear opportunity to hit hard, locking out workers, sacking hundreds of thousands and victimising thousands of militants. The government restored the six-day week, abolished penalty rates and scrapped limits on piecework. CGT membership collapsed to just one million. Most of the gains of June 1936 had been swept away, with paid holidays the only remaining advance.

The defeat of the November general strike was evidence that radical workers' movements do not keep growing organically in strength and consciousness. If the correct leadership is not provided, they inevitably start to subside under the impact of attacks by bosses, governments and reformist leaders. The PCF drained workers' energy by repeatedly blunting their ability to fight, tying up militants in time-wasting arbitration procedures, and turning the struggle on and off according to the needs of Stalin's foreign policy. The high hopes of June 1936 had given way to a mood of fatigue and despair by the end of 1938.

The end game

The Munich Agreement, by neutralising British and French opposition to German expansion, freed Hitler to turn his attention to Russia - which, because of Stalin's purges of the army high command, was in no state to fight a war. Stalin quickly abandoned all the anti-fascist rhetoric of the previous four years and switched course. On 23 August 1939, the foreign ministers of Russia and Germany signed the Molotov-Ribbentrop pact (also known as the 'Stalin-Hitler pact') which stated that neither government would ally itself to, or aid, an enemy of the other. A secret protocol which accompanied the pact allowed Russia and Germany to divide up Poland. The protocol also gave Russia the green light to take over Finland and the Baltic States, which it attempted over the following 12 months with mixed success.

The Molotov-Ribbentrop pact was a major blow to the PCF. The whole premise of the Popular Front had been that the French nation had to stand as one against the fascist threat; workers had had to trim their demands to maintain 'national unity.' Now, it all seemed to have been for nothing. The 'socialist motherland' had made peace with the Nazis. Thousands of members tore up their party cards in disgust over Stalin's deal with Hitler. Those who remained had the unpalatable task of explaining to their workmates why Stalin, whom the PCF had for years been praising as a god, was correct to sign a deal with the fascist devil.

It took some time for the PCF leadership to adjust to the real meaning of the Molotov-Ribbentrop pact. Still in a Popular Front mindset, it initially remained committed to French nationalism. When Britain and France declared war on Germany on 3 September after Germany's invasion of Poland, the PCF voted for war credits in the National Assembly, reprising the Socialists' treachery in August 1914. The Daladier government repaid the PCF's loyalty to French militarism by banning the party and driving it underground. In November, the Comintern Executive announced a policy somersault. For several years the

Comintern had promoted Britain and France's supposed peaceful intentions; it now declared that these were imperialist countries whose war efforts must be resolutely opposed by Communists:

> The ruling circles of England, France and Germany are waging war for world supremacy. This war is the continuation of the many years of imperialistic strife in the camp of capitalism... They want to divide anew, for their own advantage, the sources of raw materials, food, gold reserves and the huge masses of people in the colonies... The working class cannot support such a war. The communists have always been in opposition to such a war.[18]

PCF members who, only yesterday, had been told to fly the tricolour and swear their loyalty to the French fatherland, now had to decide whether or not to follow Moscow's latest instructions to fight their rulers. Some refused and quit, including 21 of the 72 parliamentary deputies, but party loyalty in the face of government repression ensured that many members obediently followed the new line from Moscow. The PCF had built up a hardened Stalinist apparatus and cadre over the previous five years, and they were able to carry the change of line in the ranks with few losses.

Conclusion

In June 1936, Trotsky declared that 'The French Revolution has begun.'[19] By the end of 1938, revolution in France was a remote prospect. The problem was, Trotsky explained:

> Recent history has furnished a series of tragic confirmations of the fact that it is not from every revolutionary situation that a revolution surges, but that a revolutionary situation becomes counter-revolutionary if the subjective factor, that is, the revolutionary offensive of the revolutionary class, does not come in time to aid the objective factor.[20]

This was the tragedy of France in 1936. The workers' upsurge came after years of defeat for the workers' movement, stretching back to Mussolini's victory in Italy in 1922, through the defeats in China and Britain in the mid-1920s, to the fascist breakthroughs in Germany and Austria in 1933–34. French workers had the potential to halt this string of defeats and move the working class back onto the offensive. Whether or not Trotsky's assessment – that a revolutionary situation existed in the summer of 1936 – was correct, there is no doubt that the working class had the potential to go much further than the gains won in the Matignon Agreements. But workers lacked a leadership committed to advancing the struggle beyond the program of the Popular Front government, still less to a revolutionary conclusion. The PCF drew to it tens of thousands of militants but cynically used them to defend the Blum Government. During the summer of 1936, with millions on strike and occupying their factories, the PCF did not fan the flames of the struggle but did its best to stamp them out.

The PCF's strategy was not informed by workers' best interests but by the foreign policy priorities of Stalin's government, the most important of which was to maintain a strongly militarised French state. To have placed more aggressive demands on the Blum Government might have frightened the Radicals and the big bourgeoisie, jeopardising the Franco–Soviet Alliance. When Stalin changed course in 1939 and abandoned Russia's alliance with France in favour of a pact with Hitler, the PCF somersaulted in line with Moscow's new orders.

The Popular Front offered no protection against fascism. Following the German invasion of France and the fall of Paris in June 1940, the majority of both the Radicals and the Socialists voted with the parties of the Right to grant full powers to the German puppet government of Marshall Pétain. Strikes were immediately banned, prices and wages frozen. Far from halting fascism, the Popular Front had paved the way for it. French workers were to pay for this failure in blood, repression and hunger for the next four years.

FURTHER READING

F. Claudin, *The Communist Movement: From Comintern to Cominform*, Harmondsworth, Penguin Books, 1975.

J. Danos and M. Gibelin, *June '36: Class Struggle and Popular Front in France*, London, Bookmarks, 1986 [1952].

D. Hallas, *The Comintern*, Haymarket Books, 2008 [1985].

T. Kemp, *Stalinism in France: Volume One*, 1984, London, New Park Publications.

L. Trotsky, 'Once again: Whither France, parts 1-5' and 'The French Revolution has begun', 1936.

11.

THE SPANISH REVOLUTION: ANARCHISM PUT TO THE TEST

The Spanish Civil War of 1936-39 was no ordinary war between ruling classes contending for power. It was a war between the Spanish proletariat, drawing sections of the peasantry behind it, and the ruling classes – the capitalists, the aristocracy, the generals, the landlords and the Catholic Church, all intent on crushing the fight for freedom.[1] Whether the parties always recognised it as such, it was a revolutionary war in which the working class at one point stood on the threshold of victory. If the working class had been victorious and imposed its rule on Spain, it would have dealt a blow to fascism, shaken the Western parliamentary democracies and challenged Stalin's grip on the international left. Instead, the working class suffered a terrible defeat, allowing the fascists to seize power, and so brought closer the onset of the second imperialist war.

The Spanish workers were primarily defeated, not because they lacked courage but because of the politics that dominated the workers' movement. The Stalinists played an openly counter-revolutionary role, but the anarchists also played a very damaging role. For all their talk of libertarian communism, the anarchists restricted the revolutionary impulse of Spanish workers and channelled it into a weak capitalist state that was incapable of resisting fascism. The Spanish Civil War offers important lessons about the need for a revolutionary party to fight for leadership of the working class and ensure that insurrectionary moments such as these are not thrown away.

On the eve of revolution

In the 1920s and 1930s, Spain exhibited all the features of what Trotsky called 'uneven and combined development,'[2] in which new economic and social forces born out of capitalism coincide and interact with the old forces with their roots in feudalism.

The mass of the population still lived in rural areas, in situations only one or two steps beyond feudalism. Most were landless labourers on big estates ('latifundia'), sharecroppers or owners of usually tiny, barely viable plots. Poverty was endemic. The big estates were owned by a combination of the old aristocratic semi-feudal landlords and capitalists based in the cities who used their fortunes to buy up land from the decaying aristocratic order.

Capitalist advance was even more notable in the cities. During and after World War I, capitalists and the state rushed to catch up with the more advanced European powers, promoting rapid industrial development. At the centre of this process stood Barcelona, the capital of Catalonia, which accounted for half of all Spanish industry by the 1920s. With industrial development came the growth of a working class, which doubled in size between 1910 and 1930. Nonetheless, the country was still one of the most backward in Europe. Even by the 1920s, workers were still only a small proportion of the population, with just two to three million industrial workers and miners in a population of 25 million. Because heavy industry was still little developed, workers in large factories were a still smaller component.

Spanish politics was dominated by several interwoven but frequently antagonistic elements: the landlords, old and new, the industrial and financial bourgeoisie, the officer corps, the monarchy and the Catholic Church. All held large rural estates and were ferociously anti-democratic. The bourgeoisie, which had driven political progress in France and Britain in earlier centuries, was tied to the aristocracy in Spain and acted as a force for political stagnation. The interests of these conservative forces were protected by General Miguel Primo de Rivera, who ruled as dictator from 1923 to 1930.

The Great Depression brought economic collapse and mass unemployment, sounding the death knell for the old regime. Rivera was forced out in 1930, having lost the support of the king and army. In 1931, the king himself was exiled. A republican parliamentary democracy was elected, under new Prime Minister Manuel Azaña, a member of the bourgeois liberal Left Republicans. But the new Republic was an extremely stunted parliamentary democracy. The Azaña government, with a Cabinet made up of Republicans and Socialists, was under pressure to respond to rising worker militancy and peasant demands for land reform. It was also loyal to Spanish capitalism and therefore incapable of meeting even the most modest demands for change. The government promised redistribution of land to the peasants but could not deliver, because every sector of the ruling class opposed the step. Azaña granted autonomy to the Catalans, but not the Basques, who had a stronger sense of national identity. The government promised higher wages and better working conditions for urban workers, but it could do nothing about the mounting unemployment caused by the Depression. And when workers repeatedly went on strike to obtain the promised reforms, they were beaten back to work by the army and the Assault Guards, a newly created paramilitary police force recruited predominantly from Republicans and Socialists.

In November 1933, the right drove Azaña out of office and ruled for two years. These were years of reaction. The largest party in the governing coalition, CEDA, was influenced by Mussolini and Austrian clerical fascist leader Dolfuss. The government viciously attacked peasants and workers. In October 1934, the class tensions exploded in response to the appointment of three CEDA politicians to the Cabinet. Spanish workers were well aware of the fate of German and Austrian workers at the hands of fascist dictatorships and determined to resist. Twenty thousand miners seized power in the northern state of Asturias, led by the Workers' Alliance, which brought together socialists, anarchists and dissident and orthodox communists. But they were isolated. In retaliation, the army executed 3,000 miners after they had surrendered and imprisoned 40,000 activists in the subsequent crackdown.

The workers' movement was far from obliterated by the defeat in Asturias, and strikes continued to break out through the course of 1935. Two forces of roughly equal size dominated the workers' movement. The Spanish Socialist Workers' Party (PSOE), with its union federation the General Union of Workers (UGT), had about 1.5 million members and was dominant in Madrid, among metal workers in the Basque country and among mine workers. Although the PSOE identified as a Marxist party, it was traditionally social democratic in orientation. Veteran union leader Largo Caballero had been a state councillor under Rivera and Minister of Labour in Azaña's government. As labour minister, Caballero devoted his time to building the UGT, at the expense of its anarchist rivals, and to stamping out strikes. Indalecio Prieto, from the party's right, served as Azaña's resolutely orthodox Finance Minister and was close to the premier's Left Republicans.

Following the fall of the Azaña government in 1934 and in response to the radicalisation of the masses, a significant section of the PSOE shifted sharply to the left and declared itself to be revolutionary. The UGT led the Workers' Alliance that organised the uprising in Asturias; it also benefited from an influx of 400,000 landless labourers whose hopes had initially been raised by the Socialist presence in the Azaña government. The youth section of the party was most affected by the leftward shift and grew rapidly. In response to these developments, Caballero shifted left and started to describe himself a revolutionary, cohering a substantial left behind him within the party, while Prieto retained the loyalty of the party executive and many leading cadres. By 1936, the *caballerista* and the *prietista* wings functioned essentially as two different parties.

The other force in the workers' movement was the anarcho-syndicalist CNT. Although equivalent in size to the UGT, the CNT was the more significant: it was based in Catalonia, home of the most advanced section of the class, and also covered Madrid's militant building workers. It was quite sectarian. Since 1927, the CNT had been under the control of the secretive Iberian Anarchist Federation (FAI). Under the FAI's leadership, the CNT expelled syndicalist and communist currents as reformist heretics, resulting in a mass exodus of members in 1931. In 1932-33, the CNT's armed wing engaged in several adventurist uprisings, without popular support. They were bloodily put down, with mass arrests. In 1934, when the right wing government in Madrid dispatched troops to crush Catalonia's special autonomy status, the CNT refused to mobilise its forces in defence of Catalonia on the grounds that its president, Lluís Companys, was a petit bourgeois nationalist. During the Asturias revolt, the FAI condemned as reformists the local syndicalists who had joined forces with the Socialists in the province to fight the right. The CNT usually abstained during parliamentary elections, giving the parties of the right an automatic advantage. In the factories and workshops, the CNT's attitude was 'you're either with us or against us.' It regarded workers who refused to join the CNT as scabs. While condemning reformism, the CNT's revolutionary rhetoric masked an essentially reformist practice, which became very clear during the Spanish Revolution.

The Communist Party of Spain (PCE) was far smaller than the Socialists and CNT, with at most 5,000 members in 1931 and with very little sway in the workers' movement. It was a thoroughly Stalinised party; its Moscow-trained leaders, José Díaz and Dolores Ibárruri, were installed by Stalin in 1932 and supervised by an Argentinian Comintern agent, Vittorio Codovilla. The new leaders dutifully followed the sectarian Third Period line, organising 'red unions' and denouncing the CNT as 'anarcho-fascists' and the UGT's Workers' Alliance as 'the rallying point of reactionary forces.' The PCE only joined the Asturias rising at the last moment on Stalin's instructions. Only with the upsurge in radicalism following the election of the Popular Front government in February 1936 and the merger with the Socialist Youth in April did the PCE become a mass force, with 30-50,000 members by the time of Franco's coup in July 1936.[3] In Catalonia, where the party had very little influence before 1936, its merger with three larger parties to form the 2,500-strong United Socialist Party of Catalonia (PSUC), which it quickly dominated, gave it a presence in the key province for the first time.

Finally, there was the Workers' Party of Marxist Unification (POUM), based in Catalonia. With a membership of 3,000 in July 1936, it was a touch larger than the PSUC. The POUM was formed in 1935 by the fusion of two groups led by 'communist-syndicalists' Andreu Nin and Joaquín Maurín, who had quit the CNT to help found the PCE but then split from the latter in response to Stalin's triumph in Russia. After leaving the PCE, Nin led the Spanish section of the Trotskyist Left Opposition, the Communist Left, while Maurín established the Workers and Peasants Bloc (BOC). The BOC was an ideologically heterogeneous oppositional communist group which, despite having broken with the Comintern, defended positions close to those of the Stalinists. The POUM which brought these two parties together was, from its birth, a classic centrist organisation – revolutionary in rhetoric but accommodating to non-revolutionary forces in practice. It condemned the Comintern's Popular Front strategy as class collaborationism, but it signed the Popular Front pact in 1936, albeit with reservations, and took seats in the Cortes. Although small, with a base in Catalonia, where the Communists and Socialists had historically been weak, and with several well-known worker leaders in its ranks, the POUM had an impact well beyond its numbers. Its union federation had 50,000 members, many organised in unions expelled from the CNT, and the anarchists regarded it as a competitor for influence in the Catalan working class.

Election of the Popular Front government

The elections of February 1936 saw the Popular Front under Azaña sweep into office. Like the French Popular Front government, this was not a workers' government but an alliance between bourgeois parties and workers' parties. The Front included Azaña's Republican Left, the Republican Union, another bourgeois party, the Communists and the Socialists. It was supported by Catalan and Basque nationalist parties and the UGT. The CNT refused to take part in the election because of its 'principled' position of abstaining from parliamentary politics, but it tacitly encouraged its members to vote for the Popular Front – under the influence of the syndicalists who had been readmitted to the CNT that month. The POUM signed the pact but would not offer the new government any political support. It believed that the electoral coalition would soon implode under the impact of the class struggle, opening the road to revolution.

The program of the Spanish Popular Front was extremely moderate, lacking any serious social and economic demands. In its only real concession to the left, the new government ordered the release of the tens of thousands of political prisoners incarcerated since the Asturias rising and the reinstatement of those workers who had been victimised by their employers. The Azaña Cabinet was made up entirely of ministers from the bourgeois Republican parties. Many senior figures in the PSOE, including Prieto, wanted to join the government. They were prevented from doing so by Caballero who, under pressure from the left within the party and well aware of the damage that Socialist participation in the first Azaña government had caused the party, refused to allow Socialist politicians to take Cabinet positions.

Moderation was the watchword of the government, but workers were impatient for change. They moved into action with a wave of strikes, storming prisons to free political prisoners and carrying out violent attacks on right wing parties, bosses and police. The five months after the elections saw 113 general strikes and 228 partial strikes. Revolutionary momentum was evident everywhere. The POUM's Luis Portela explained:

> [The workers] wanted to go forward, they weren't satisfied simply with the release of political prisoners and the return to their jobs of all those who had been sacked as a result of the revolutionary insurrection of October 1934. Instinctively, they were pressing forward, not necessarily to take power, not to create soviets, but to push forward the revolution which had begun with the Republic's proclamation.[4]

In the countryside, landless labourers and poor peasants seized the big estates, often attacking landlords and clashing with the Civil Guard. Strikes for better pay and working conditions spread from village to village until they covered entire districts, or even provinces. Angry over the reactionary role played by the Catholic Church, historically the monarchy's biggest supporters, workers and peasants burned or shut down churches and killed priests.

The reaction to the upsurge in struggle by the workers' parties was mixed. Caballero made grand speeches about the need for a dictatorship of the proletariat. The Socialist Youth cheered his radical rhetoric enthusiastically, chanting slogans demanding a 'workers' government' and a 'Red army' at the big May Day rally in Madrid. Caballero's revolutionary rhetoric was designed to scare the right into making concessions. A veteran bureaucrat, the UGT leader remained focused on manoeuvres between the parties rather than on fostering workers' councils; his concept of the dictatorship of the proletariat was a government led by the PSOE. Prieto and the PSOE right condemned strikes and 'disorder' as 'childish revolutionism' that would drive the middle classes towards fascism. The Communists echoed Prieto, denouncing a strike by CNT-led Madrid building workers as playing the bosses' game by giving them the pretext for a military coup. Foreshadowing the words of the French Communist Thorez in June (Chapter 10), the Spanish Communists stated: 'The moment has arrived to know how to end a strike.'[5]

Fascist coup meets workers' revolt

The ruling class was very alarmed by developments. Everything they held sacrosanct – private property, the unity of Spain, the church, the family – was threatened by this revolt from below. Middle class youth flooded into the fascist Falange, and armed clashes with the left on the streets became common. Spanish capitalism was in deep crisis as a result of the world economic slump. Only by smashing the working class could capitalism be put back on its feet in Spain. It was clear to the ruling class that the Republican parties were not up to the task.

The Spanish military had a long tradition of political interference and had been the mainstay of the Rivera dictatorship. High-ranking army officers, monarchists and fascists began to plot a coup, barely bothering to conceal their plans. The Popular Front government tried to play for time, because it could not directly attack the military without threatening the stability of the state.

On 17 July, the generals made their move. General Franco called on the Army of Africa, Spain's only professional army – garrisoned in Morocco – to rise up. Generals on the mainland did the same, deploying their soldiers against the civilian authorities. Even now, Azaña, who had by now taken up the presidency, did his best to play down the coup, initially even refusing to acknowledge its existence. The Socialists and the Communists supported Azaña, telling their supporters to wait for a call for action: 'The government commands and the Popular Front obeys.'[6] Of course, the call never came.

Only the resistance of workers saved the day. Backed in many cases by the Assault Guards, who for the most part remained loyal to the Popular Front, the workers stormed army barracks with makeshift weapons, seizing guns. In Malaga in Andalusia, workers held the insurgent soldiers at bay with hastily constructed barricades and a ring of gasoline-fired houses, forcing their surrender. Wherever the left went on the offensive, they beat back the coup. The landlords, bosses and priests were forced to flee for their lives from an armed population filled with revolutionary zeal. Where the left deferred to the Popular Front government or were unsure or unconfident, they were defeated – not through a lack of strength, but through a failure to move decisively enough against the generals.

Within three days, the initial fighting was over. Spain was divided into territorial and ideological camps: the industrial and commercial centres, in the hands of the Republicans; peasant Spain, in the hands of the Nationalists; and latifundist Spain, the poorest region in the south, divided between the two sides. The air force and fleet remained loyal; sailors shot their officers, declared for the Republic and anchored their ships off Tangier, preventing Franco from shipping reinforcements from Morocco to the mainland.

The revenge wrought by the generals on those identified as 'left' in the villages and towns that fell to them was pitiless. Thousands perished. This was a war to determine which class was to hold power. The generals were determined to teach workers and peasants a lasting lesson in ruling class terror. Workers and peasants responded in kind, killing judges, Civil Guards, priests, bosses, prison wardens, suspected informers and torturers.

Workers' power in Spain

Catalonia, particularly Barcelona, was the revolutionary centre where power passed furthest into the hands of CNT workers who had led the resistance to Franco. The bourgeois state had collapsed. Society was turned upside down, with workers taking initiatives in every sphere. At the Ford Iberia factory, a workers' committee abolished piece work, reduced the pace of work and raised compensation payments to injured workers. Workers on the trams, which employed 7,000, met in general assemblies and elected a control committee to oversee all operations. Much the same happened in the railways, with general assemblies, local committees and weekly meetings of militants. Everything from hotels and restaurants to the telephone exchange was organised collectively. Tourist hotels provided free meals for workers' families, militia fighters and the poor. A Communist railwayman, Narciso Julián, recalled:

> It was incredible, the proof in practice of what one knows in theory: the power and strength of the masses when they take to the streets. All one's doubts are suddenly stripped away, doubts about how the working class and the masses are to be organised, how they can make the revolution until they are organised. Suddenly you feel their creative power; you can't imagine how rapidly the masses

are capable of organising themselves. The forms they invent go far beyond anything you've dreamt of, read in books. What was needed now was to seize this initiative, channel it, give it shape.[7]

Having overrun the barracks during the early days of Franco's coup, the CNT in Barcelona had a vast armoury at its disposal. Public security now lay in the hands of the anti-fascist militias comprising 30,000 armed workers equipped to defend and patrol the city. The old police forces had all but disappeared; some joined the popular movement, others fled to join the fascists. Armed workers stood guard outside every public building and union headquarters. Even those heading to and from work slung a rifle over their shoulder in preparation for a renewed fascist attack. Workers' committees directed resources into military production to drive back Franco's forces.

Socialist red and anarcho-syndicalist red and black flags adorned government buildings in Barcelona, and popular music blared from loudspeakers. The poor reclaimed their possessions from pawn shops. Polite forms of speech, saturated with class privilege, disappeared. English writer George Orwell observed that waiters and shop staff looked customers directly in the eye and demanded to be treated as equals, challenging servile forms of speech, while the rich were forced to abandon their expensive suits and dresses for workers' attire. Orwell recalls:

> Above all, there was a belief in the revolution and the future, a feeling of having suddenly emerged into an era of equality and freedom. Human beings were trying to behave as human beings and not as cogs in the capitalist machine.[8]

Little wonder that women made strides towards equality in a society no longer dominated by the church. Women enthusiastically joined the militias and the neighbourhood committees. Women workers in department stores demanded an end to sexual harassment. Abortion was legalised, and birth control information became available. The CNT instituted a new form of civil marriage, 'uniting a man and a woman freely and without coercion.' Traditional ideas about female inferiority were challenged. In just a few months, women's position in society advanced beyond that of any other country in the world. The experience of the collective action of workers and poor peasants in defence of their own interests heralded a different morality. Socialist Maria Solana remembered:

> The war bred a new spirit in people, it was amazing. I was often sent round villages on propaganda missions with other party youth and there wouldn't be enough beds. I, the only woman, would sleep in the same bed with two or three youths and nothing would happen – absolutely nothing. There was a new sense of human relationships.[9]

The workers' committees soon took responsibility for controlling who could enter the liberated regions of Catalonia and Aragon, Catalonia's rural hinterland and the fighting front against Franco's forces. French union leader Robert Louzon recalls:

> As soon as you cross the frontier, you are halted by armed men. Who are these men? Workers. They are militiamen – that is, workers with their normal clothes – but armed with rifles or revolvers and with signs on their arms indicating their functions or the power they represent… They are the ones who…will decide… not to let you in or to refer it to the 'committee.'
>
> The committee is the group of men who are in charge… It is the committee who see to the normal municipal functions, who formed the local militia, armed it, and supplied it with food and lodging from the funds raised by a levy imposed on all the local inhabitants. They were the ones who give you permission to enter or leave the town, who closed down the local fascist shops and who carried out essential requisitions.[10]

In the towns and villages of Catalonia and Aragon, hundreds of collectives were established. Workers and peasants formed committees to control housing, manage public utilities and attend to education. They provided free health care and saw that orphans, widows and the infirm were looked after. They destroyed property records, abolished rent and did their best to foster equality. In some villages, the committees collectivised all the land and held everything in common; others took only the land that belonged to owners who had fled or who had fought in Franco's forces.

Catalonia and Aragon went furthest, but they were not alone. A right wing Republican observed that the well-to-do in Madrid were forced to adapt to the new reality:

> The appearance of Madrid was incredible: the bourgeoisie giving the clenched-fist salute... Men in overalls and rope sandals, imitating the uniform adopted by the [working class] militia; women bare-headed; clothes old and threadbare...[11]

Dual power prevailed in many Republican towns and regions over the summer and early autumn. The workers' committees and collectives, along with their militias and revolutionary tribunals, held power in a real sense. The Popular Front government still ruled nominally, because no other authority had replaced it, but it represented virtually nothing. The capitalists had abandoned the government when it became plain that it could not hold back the revolution. It represented, said Trotsky, not the bourgeoisie, but 'the shadow of the bourgeoisie.' This shadow took the form of Azaña, president of the Republic, and Lluís Companys, president of the Generalidad (provincial government) of Catalonia, described by Trotsky as 'insignificant debris from the possessing classes...political attorneys of the bourgeoisie.'[12]

How did this weak government, this shadow, roll back the revolution and eliminate workers' power within 12 months? The answer can be found in the role of those parties that *did* represent real social forces – the Socialists, the CNT and, as they grew more powerful, the Communists – who provided this government with genuine social weight. What was their response to the unfolding situation?

The anarchists

Just two days after Franco's coup, the working class controlled Barcelona. They were largely organised by CNT militants and, to a considerably lesser extent, those of the POUM. Official power, however, still rested in the hands of Catalan President Companys. The president had few forces at his disposal, but unless his administration was overthrown and a revolutionary state put in its place, he had an opportunity to build his forces. One side or the other had to prevail.

On 20 July, Companys convened a meeting with the CNT leaders. He started by acknowledging that they were 'the masters of the city and of Catalonia.' He then challenged them directly: did they want him to stay or to go?

> You have won and everything is in your hands. If you do not need me, if you do not want me as president, say so now... If on the other hand, you believe me when I say that I shall yield this

post to victorious Fascism only when I am dead, then perhaps with my party comrades, my name and my prestige, I can be of use to you.[13]

Companys proposed that the anarchists not seize power but instead participate in an 'Antifascist Militias Committee.' It would include all the Popular Front parties, plus the CNT, and would direct the revolution. The Companys government would remain in place.

The CNT representatives demurred, not having expected to be faced with such a clear choice: either the CNT would overthrow the Companys government and establish a revolutionary government, or it would have to collaborate with Companys and the Generalidad and risk seeing the revolutionary momentum fizzle out. The CNT leaders told Companys that they would have to discuss his proposition.

Three days later, the CNT regional committee convened in Barcelona. Delegates and visitors packed the hall for the momentous meeting. Would the CNT take power into its own hands?[14] Delegates from the most militant section of the federation insisted that the CNT reject Companys' proposal and 'move ahead with the revolution, and finish establishing libertarian communism.' Juan García Oliver, a leader of the CNT's armed militias in Barcelona, supported that course. Other CNT leaders pushed back. Federica Montseny argued that pressing ahead would entail establishing an 'anarchist dictatorship.' Catalan CNT secretary Mariano Vázquez opposed 'compromising the organisation in dictatorial practices,' i.e. taking power. Another said that Britain and France would abandon the Republic if the CNT took power in Catalonia.

None of the CNT speakers conceived of revolution as being about workers themselves taking power under their own direct organisations, like soviets in Russia in 1917. The only issue was whether the CNT itself would form government. In the end, the meeting overwhelmingly approved the motion to accept Companys' proposal to support his government and to allow him to remain president. The significance of the decision was clear. By renouncing power, the CNT had left it in the hands of the exploiters. The banner headline in CNT paper *Solidaridad Obrera* just three days previously, 'Only by making the social revolution will fascism be crushed,' was quietly forgotten. A sympathetic anarchist historian comments:

> Instead of undertaking a social revolution in conditions so favourable that they might well never recur, the plenum decided in effect that the Confederaçion [CNT] should commit itself

single-mindedly to waging war against the Nationalists – and defer to the indefinite future the issue of making a revolution.[15]

For several weeks, the newly formed Antifascist Militias Committees were hegemonic in Catalonia: nothing moved without their approval. But the committees were not soviets in the style of Russia in 1917.[16] They were not elected bodies subject to recall, acting democratically according to the will of the majority. They included representatives of the workers' parties and moderate Republican parties. None of these favoured using the committees to overthrow Companys and form a new revolutionary government. As the weeks went by, workers and peasants carried less and less weight in committees as the revolutionary battles and the direct exercise of power in the streets by armed workers faded into the past. The apparatuses of the parties and the unions took their place.

Meanwhile, in Madrid, the Republican parties had mostly disintegrated in the weeks following the coup. They were incapable of reconstructing the state apparatus that had been torn apart from both left and right. It would be the Socialists, the anarchists and the Communists who would take chief responsibility for this task. Their first priority was to select and authorise a new prime minister following Azaña's resignation in May. During the summer, a couple of stand-ins had occupied the post, but Caballero was the only figure with any credibility among the militants. During August, all sides of Republican Spain entreated him to take the job. The Communists flattered him as the 'Spanish Lenin.' The Russian embassy, by now intervening openly in Spanish politics, also lent its support to Caballero. In truth, Caballero was a 'revolutionary' until confronted with a live revolution, at which point he revealed his true colours. On 4 September, Caballero accepted the post, forming a new Cabinet in which he dispensed with the Right Republicans and replaced them with figures from the PSOE, the PCE and the Left Republicans. The CNT at first refused to take ministerial posts but supported the Caballero government from the outside.

The CNT soon demonstrated that its 'revolutionary abstention' had its limits. In the Basque country, the CNT had already joined the Basque regional government, dominated by middle class nationalists. In Catalonia, CNT leaders decided that they must sacrifice the Antifascist Militias Committees if Republican Spain were to have any hope of receiving arms from Britain and France. This was a very significant step. Whatever their weaknesses, the Antifascist Militias Committees were a genuinely revolutionary power. Their legitimacy arose purely out of the insurrection and the power of the workers' parties who had taken control of production and formed militias in Catalonia.

To abandon the Committees was to formally give up on any attempt to counter the authority of the Companys government.

On 26 September, the CNT entered the Companys government. Three of its leaders were appointed ministers. Just days later, Companys instructed the Antifascist Militias Committees to disband; the CNT printed the Generalidad's decrees in its newspapers without comment. All the most important committees were dissolved into the Generalidad structures, with the local committees liquidating into municipal councils.

Having joined the Catalan Government, there was no principled reason for the CNT not to join Caballero's government in Madrid as well. Caballero was certainly keen to have them. Without the CNT's involvement, his government lacked a mass base among militants in Catalonia. On 4 November, four CNT representatives, including García Oliver and Montseny, were brought into the Cabinet. The CNT rationalised its decision to join the government on the grounds that it was no longer a capitalist government:

> The CNT has always been, by principle and conviction, anti-statist and the enemy of every form of government... But circumstances... have changed the nature of the Spanish government and state... The government has ceased to be a force of oppression against the working class, just as the state is no longer the entity that divides society into classes. Both will stop oppressing the people all the more with the inclusion of the CNT among their organs.[17]

This was just a cynical cover for the CNT's decision to halt the revolution.

In the weeks that followed, Caballero gradually wound up the revolutionary apparatus that had emerged over the summer. The CNT, which had once had a powerful presence on the back of workers under arms, was reduced to minority status in the municipal councils. The counter-revolution had taken a step forward – because the CNT allowed it. Once a workers' organisation rejects the goal of working class seizure of power through insurrection, it inevitably becomes a reformist political force, whatever its formal ideas are; and the CNT's ideas were an incoherent mishmash that incorporated plenty of semi-reformist conceptions of political change and political power.

In later years, Montseny recalled the effect of the CNT joining the Caballero government:

> As a consequence, the state recovered the position it had lost, while we revolutionaries, who formed part of the state, helped it to do so.

That was why we were brought into the government. Although we did not enter it with that intention, we were in it, and therefore had no alternative but remain imprisoned in the vicious circle.[18]

Far from transforming the capitalist state, the anarchists soon adapted to their new positions. CNT Industry Minister Juan Peiró asserted: 'We say: first the war and then the Revolution. It is the government that is in command.' Minister for Justice García Oliver told officer cadets: 'Your soldiers…cease to be your comrades and must take their place as cogs in our Army's military machine.'[19]

These statements show clearly how the anarchist leaders had fallen in line behind the Popular Front argument that anti-fascists had first to win the war before pursuing revolution. That line might appear logical at first glance. If Franco's forces won, what would be left of the revolution? But the situation was more complex. It was not a matter of war *or* revolution, but *what kind of war*? A conventional war, embraced by the Popular Front parties, in which the Republic fielded conventional armies at the front and restored capitalist rule in the rear? Or a revolutionary war, such as the Red Army waged in Russia, with workers fighting the capitalists by using revolutionary means? Choosing the first option ensured that anti-fascist forces lost both the war and the revolution.

'First, win the war' meant taking responsibility for Spanish capitalism and preserving good relations with Britain and France, whose capitalists were significant investors in Spanish land and industry. That prevented the Popular Front from taking the measures needed to win the war. For example, the navy, whose sailors remained loyal to the Republic, had succeeded for the first two weeks of the Civil War in blocking Franco from moving his 40,000-strong Army of Africa to the mainland. Had they held fast, the balance of military forces would have been more favourable to the Republic. Only with the help of the German and Italian air forces was Franco able to transport a limited number of these troops to join the fight. But under pressure from Britain and France, both alarmed at the prospect of leftist Spanish sailors controlling access to the Mediterranean and thus to their colonial possessions, Azaña ordered the sailors to lift their blockade, enabling Franco to land his troops in Spain. Franco thereafter had no problem drawing on troops or material from Morocco, assisted by reinforcements from Italy and Germany, which gave him a marked military advantage over the Republican forces.

The Popular Front could also have broken Franco's army by granting independence to Morocco, as Moroccan nationalists urged. Such a move would have given the Moorish troops, who were the mainstay of Franco's fighting forces, an incentive to switch sides. But granting independence would also have angered France and Britain, with significant interests of their own in North Africa. By refusing to do so, in the hope that the two big imperialist powers would arm the Republic, the Popular Front government gave the Moorish soldiers no reason to fight against Franco and for the Republic.

Revolutionary initiatives at home could also have strengthened the fight against the fascists. The foot soldiers of the Nationalist armies raised on the mainland mostly came from small villages or regional towns. Many of them shared an objective interest in breaking up the big rural estates and winning a better deal for workers. But the Popular Front government refused to support land seizures or the formation of workers' councils, giving Franco's Spanish soldiers no incentive to switch sides or desert.

The Republican government could also have nationalised industry and banking and confiscated the fortunes of industrialists, bankers and landowners. It would then have been in a stronger position to stop the capitalists sabotaging the Republican war effort. Given that virtually every big capitalist had joined the counter-revolution, there were definitely military grounds to do so. But the Popular Front project of protecting capitalist interests prevented it from taking steps to threaten them.

Finally, the Popular Front made no attempt to utilise guerrilla warfare against the fascists in Nationalist-controlled territory, because such tactics would have subverted its efforts to build a conventional army and to disband the militias that had sprung up in the early months of the war.

It was these political calculations that ensured that the Popular Front was condemned always to fight with one arm tied behind its back.

The Communists

The Communists were horrified by the radicalism that had swept Spain following the election of the Popular Front. The PCE took its orders from Stalin, whose foreign policy hinged on an alliance with Britain and France against Germany. Stalin was determined to ensure the Comintern parties did nothing to threaten this alliance. A workers' revolution in Spain was an anathema because it would have wiped out significant British and French investments in Spanish businesses. It would have encouraged French workers to push their mass strikes much further (Chapter 10). It would have threatened the French and British empires. On no account, therefore, should the PCE try to advance the revolution. As one of Trotsky's US followers put it:

'Socialism in a single country had revealed its full meaning as "no socialism anywhere else".'[20] Nor did revolution in Spain suit Stalin's interests within Russia. The economic chaos caused by the crash program of industrialisation in the first Five Year Plan had created much discontent, and Stalin feared that a figure might emerge within the Comintern to give a voice to this discontent. The show trials and purges of 1936-38 were designed to crush any such threat. Revolution in Spain, reviving memories of 1917, would have threatened Stalin's counter-revolutionary project. To prevent this, Stalin sent dozens of well-funded Comintern agents and Russian advisers to sabotage the Spanish Revolution.[21]

Such considerations explain the Spanish Communists' resolute hostility to revolution. Instead of workers' revolution, they spoke in the language of stabilisation and national unity. In the party's paper, *Mundo Obrero*, PCE leader and Education Minister in the Caballero government Jesús Hernández Tomás wrote:

> It is absolutely false that the present workers' movement has for its object the establishment of a proletarian dictatorship after the war has terminated. It cannot be said that we have a social motive for our participation in the war. We Communists are the first to repudiate this suggestion. We are moved exclusively by a desire to defend the democratic republic.[22]

Defending 'the democratic republic' meant defending private property. Party secretary, José Díaz Ramos, told the party's Central Committee:

> If in the beginning the various premature attempts at 'socialisation' and 'collectivisation'...might have been justified... at the present time, when there is a government of the Popular Front, in which all the forces engaged in the fight against fascism are represented, such things are not only not desirable, but absolutely impermissible.[23]

The Stalinists became *the* champions of 'order' in Spain. As a party committed to private property and ending the 'excesses' of the early months, the Communists began to draw in middle class elements, better-off peasants, small employers, army officers and careerists looking for government posts. The party took up their cause and championed their grievances against big capitalists and workers alike and on this basis grew rapidly.

Two other factors helped the Stalinists to emerge as a powerful force. One was the failure of the existing leadership of the workers' movement, the PSOE and the CNT, to lead workers to victory in the crucial summer months. Their evident failure created the space for a rival to emerge. The other was the PCE's connection to Russia – particularly Russian arms. This connection was vital in determining the balance of forces within the anti-fascist camp during the Battle of Madrid. On 8 November, Franco's armies launched a fresh offensive to seize the capital, having failed in July. Caballero, his ministers and union leaders abandoned the capital and fled to Valencia. The CNT, which had just joined Caballero's government, remained in the city, as did the PCE.

At first sight, the prospects for a successful defence of the capital looked dim. While the workers' militias in the capital outnumbered the fascists two to one, many were poorly armed and lacked basic training. But the workers of Madrid did not surrender. They hastily gathered arms and headed to the outskirts of the city to fight the fascist offensive. For two weeks, workers pushed the fascists back, fighting street by street, house by house, showing incredible heroism. Men and women often went to the front unarmed, waiting to relieve someone or waiting for a comrade to fall in battle and free up a weapon. Franco's armies failed to gain more than a tiny foothold in the outskirts of the city, at a cost of 5,000 casualties. They withdrew. The Popular Front had won its first significant victory of the war.

The Communists played a significant role in the defence of Madrid. Although Stalin had planted his men and women in the leadership of the PCE, he had done nothing to help the Republic in the first few months of the Civil War. The contingents of foreign socialists and anarchists who arrived from France, Italy, Poland, Germany and elsewhere to fight Franco did so without any encouragement from the Russian leader. But Stalin wanted neither a workers' revolution nor a quick fascist victory in Spain. A fascist win would have freed Hitler to turn his attention east to Russia. Starting in early October, Stalin began to send military aid to the Republic. This was not an act of international solidarity; Republican Spain had sent the country's entire gold reserves to Moscow for safe keeping and so paid for every gun it received. The weapons Russia supplied were enough to prevent the immediate collapse of the Republic but not enough to ensure outright victory.

With Stalin's blessing, the Communists joined the CNT in forming the Madrid Defence Council to direct the resistance, although it refused to work with the POUM. The PCE did its best to evoke the atmosphere of the revolutionary defence of Petrograd in the Russian Civil War. Posters proclaimed:

MADRID WILL BE THE TOMB OF FASCISM. No pasaran! Every house a fortress, every street a trench, every neighbourhood a wall of iron and combatants. Emulate Petrograd! 7 November on the [River] Manzanares must be as glorious as on the Neva![24]

The arrival on 8 November of 2,000 International Brigade volunteers, largely Communists from Italy and Germany sent by Stalin and eager to fight fascism, reinforced the revolutionary atmosphere in Madrid. Eventually, the International Brigades grew to 30,000 men and women under arms, workers and intellectuals who were desperate to halt fascism after its victories in Europe. Tragically, the International Brigades were used mainly as propaganda to further Stalin's aim of stifling the revolution, regardless of the aims of the fighters themselves.

The PCE's defence of Madrid paid off. Membership rose to 100,000 by the end of 1936, augmented by several hundred thousand supporters in the party's youth section and the UGT. But the PCE failed to use the popular victory in Madrid as the precursor to a revolutionary war to drive back the fascist onslaught. It actually did all it could to destroy the revolutionary energy of workers and peasants. Bit by bit, the Communists quashed the popular committees in the cities and rural areas. In the name of creating a 'people's army,' the PCE liquidated workers' militias into the remnants of the old regular army and appointed Communist political commissars to oversee the 'people's army.' The commissars ensured that 'socialism' and 'revolution' were expunged in favour of 'patriotism' and 'discipline.' In January 1937, the PCE's Fifth Regiment and the international brigades were merged into this army to reinforce Russian domination. Those in the popular movement who insisted on pursuing the revolution were attacked as fascists. When POUM leaders protested the PCE's decision to bar them from the Madrid Defence Council, the Russian consul-general in Barcelona denounced the party's paper *La Batalla* as part of 'the press that has sold out to international Fascism.' Stalin's Spanish propagandists simply regurgitated rhetoric from the Moscow Trials:

> Trotskyism is not a political party, but a gang of counterrevolutionary elements. Fascism, Trotskyism, and the unruly elements are the three enemies of the people that must be eliminated from political life, not only in Spain, but in all civilised countries.[25]

This was no idle threat. The PCE's death squads, under the command of Russia's Alexander Orlov, an NKVD major sent by Stalin, hunted down, jailed, tortured or killed militants from parties to its left, including Trotskyists, independent socialists and anarchists. The Communists were creating a quasi-Stalinist authoritarian regime. On 17 December, *Pravda* drew the links with the Moscow Trials:

> In Catalonia, the elimination of Trotskyists and Anarcho-Syndicalists has already begun; it will be carried out with the same energy as in the USSR.[26]

The POUM

The POUM could have fought to take the leadership of the working class away from the PCE and CNT. It stood out for its consistent argument that the revolution needed to go forward in order to defeat fascism. It supported workers' councils taking power and grew rapidly to 40,000 members on the basis of its radical platform. Within months of Franco's coup, the POUM militia had 10,000 men and women under arms. To break through, however, it had to win over substantial numbers of CNT members. While the POUM made formally correct criticisms of the CNT, it tailed the CNT leaders rather than challenging them. POUM leader Nin sought to influence the CNT leaders with personal arguments and ended up accommodating to their reformist political project.

Rather than being a revolutionary pole of opposition to the Popular Front, the POUM moved to become its extreme left wing. It used its influence among Catalan workers to sow illusions in the Popular Front when an independent fighting stance was needed. It joined the regional government in Valencia and then followed the CNT in joining the Companys government in Catalonia, with Nin appointed Minister of Justice. The POUM argued to its supporters that, by joining the ministry, it could secure proletarian power. Its main concern, however, was that to refuse to join Companys would isolate it from the CNT. It did not join the Caballero government, not because of any principled opposition but because the PCE blocked it. In November, the Communists, with the support of the CNT, kicked the POUM out of the Catalan Government, but the POUM still refused to break politically from the Popular Front coalition of workers' and bourgeois parties.

Even though the POUM was formally in favour of winning the war through spreading the revolution, in practice, it fell in behind the Popular Front strategy, arguing that the revolution had to take second place. Luis Portela, the head of the POUM in Valencia, used words that could have come from the PCE: 'We could win the war without making revolution, but we could not make the revolution without winning the war.'²⁷ This was completely misleading: as the prospects for revolution were quashed, so too were the chances of a working class victory in the war.

The May days in Barcelona

The defeat of the immediate fascist threat to Madrid at the end of 1936 opened up growing conflicts between the contending forces on the Republican side. The Stalinists had succeeded in ending workers' control and peasant land seizures in most parts of the country, but some elements of dual power still remained in Catalonia, although confidence had ebbed. There were also growing signs of opposition, particularly from youth, to the compromises by the Popular Front government. Dissatisfaction grew over falling living standards, food shortages and rampant corruption among the well connected. Constant demands by the government parties and unions for sacrifice by workers were greeted with scepticism and bitterness. On 14 February, more than 14,000 young people attended a meeting organised in Barcelona by the CNT and POUM to form a Revolutionary Youth Front. This new organisation mobilised thousands of young workers to defend the revolution. It set up a network of local committees and began to form joint militia columns.

In order to 'normalise' the situation, to snuff out the last vestiges of the revolution, the PCE had to put an end to this nascent opposition in Barcelona. In March, police patrols reappeared in the city. In April, police tried to disarm the CNT militias that still existed. Fierce fighting broke out and, under intense pressure from their members, the CNT ministers briefly withdrew from the Companys government, declaring 'No more concessions to reformism!' On 1 May, such was the tension in the city following two weeks of fighting between the CNT and the police that the Companys government, with Communist support, banned the traditional May Day march. Two days later, the crisis broke. Three truckloads of Assault Guards, under the personal command of a Communist minister, evicted the CNT-led workforce from the city's telephone exchange. The exchange had been under CNT control since the July uprising and was the most visible remaining symbol of workers' power in the city.

The Stalinist attack led to an eruption of resistance. A general strike swept Barcelona and barricades went up all over the city. The workers won the street fighting, seizing the entire city except for the central area. Similar resistance by workers in other Catalan towns disarmed the police and took over Communist party offices and government buildings. The Stalinists were in disarray. This could have been a turning point, an opportunity for the revolutionary forces to halt the retreat. There was no guarantee that an uprising in Barcelona would have gained support outside Catalonia; but, if Barcelona fell to the Stalinists, the revolution would not recover. Dual power can survive for a comparatively long time in a revolution for so long as neither side feels strong or confident enough to break the other. It cannot survive a test of arms, however. Revolution or counter-revolution were the only two options. The POUM representative saw the significance of the situation, telling regional CNT leaders at a meeting on the first night: 'Either we place ourselves at the head of the movement to destroy the enemy within or the movement fails, and that will be the end of us.'[28]

With CNT militants organising the resistance on the barricades, their leaders worked for surrender, supporting Companys when he appealed for calm and urging their supporters to lay down their arms. The CNT newspaper refused even to report the news that the whole city was covered with barricades. When appeals by local CNT leaders proved insufficient, Montseny and García Oliver flew to Barcelona and repeatedly urged workers to dismantle the barricades and return to work. Some anarchists, organised as Friends of Durruti (named after the anarchist militia leader Buenaventura Durruti killed in the defence of Madrid), argued for the overthrow of the government and the formation of a revolutionary junta based on the CNT and UGT – precisely what the CNT should have done the previous July. The CNT leadership repudiated them in the harshest terms. In disgust, workers burned bundles of CNT newspapers at the barricades and shot at their radios when they heard their leaders' appeal on air. The CNT also ordered back a column of its fighters marching from the front to Barcelona to reinforce the resistance. Lacking the support of their leaders, CNT militants eventually retreated in frustration and disgust. As the barricades came down, 5,000 Assault Guards sent from Valencia, officered in many cases by Communists, swept into the city like a conquering army.

The POUM played a weak role, despite its tens of thousands of members in Catalonia. It understood the counter-revolutionary implications of the Stalinist attack and correctly called for the formation of Committees for the Defence of the Revolution in neighbourhoods and workplaces. It demanded the creation of a Revolutionary Workers' Front with the anarchists, to defend the gains of the revolution. It reiterated its call for a government of workers' organisations to save the revolution and push it forward. Some of its members, particularly the youth, fought heroically. But when the CNT leaders refused to take any action that might involve a breach with the Popular Front, the POUM leaders gave up. On the fourth day of fighting, they called on their fighters to abandon the barricades and ordered back the POUM militia column marching to Barcelona. The POUM leaders could only express their 'reservations' about the CNT policy of surrender to the Stalinists. Their ongoing anxiety not to open a breach with the CNT leaders meant that they tailed behind them. To cover their surrender, the POUM leaders declared that workers had 'defeated a counter-revolutionary provocation' and 'won a great, partial victory.'[29] The POUM's Barcelona committee was not taken in. It denounced Nin and accused the leadership of capitulation in the face of the counter-revolution. Whether or not the POUM could have relaunched the revolution in Catalonia in May, as Trotsky argued later that year, is an open question; regardless, it was the last gasp of the revolution, and the POUM gave it up without a serious fight.

Having put down the resistance in Barcelona, the right within the Popular Front, including the PCE, now went on the offensive against any remaining traces of radicalism. Caballero had served his purpose as the left face of the counter-revolution. On 17 May, the PCE and the right Socialists under Prieto joined forces to drive Caballero and his entire Cabinet, including the three CNT ministers, out of office. His replacement was the more reliably pro-Moscow right Socialist, Juan Negrín. The remnants of the popular militias were disbanded. All demonstrations were banned. Workers were subjected to military rule. Any criticism of the government was deemed treachery. The POUM was outlawed, its leaders kidnapped, and some of them, including Nin, shot by the Russian secret police. In July, the Italian Comintern leader, Palmiro Togliatti, arrived in Spain to take charge of the purges of socialists and anarchists. All told, the PCE and Russian agents tortured or killed several thousand opponents of Stalinism over the following 12 months.

With the revolution from below defeated, workers' and peasants' bold defiance and willingness to risk everything also vanished. What was there now to fight for? The outcome of the war now hung on technical contingencies: who had more troops and better training, more guns, more planes, more tanks. This guaranteed that Franco would win. The supplies he received from Germany and Italy were far superior to those flowing from Russia to the Republicans. In January 1938, when the fascists attacked Barcelona, the former revolutionary citadel gave up without much of a fight. The final act in the tragedy came in early 1939 when the remnants of the Republican government, now led by General Segismundo Casado, surrendered to Franco.

The consequences of Franco's victory were devastating. Over the course of the Civil War, Franco's forces executed tens of thousands of Republican supporters. Postwar repression also claimed the lives of tens of thousands more. Another 200,000 died of hunger and disease during the first years of Franco's rule, and hundreds of thousands fled the country. The Spanish dictator ruled until his death in 1975, casting a pall of reaction over Southern Europe. More, Franco's victory emboldened fascists across Europe. The Civil War had provided the German and Italian military with a testing ground for methods of warfare against a civilian population that they were soon to unleash on a much broader front.

Conclusion

The triumph of fascism in Spain was a catastrophe for Spanish workers and peasants and, ultimately, for the international working class. In 1936, leftists across the world were enthused by the fight against fascism in Spain. In the context of strike waves in France and elsewhere, Spain was a big opportunity to change the balance of forces in favour of the working class. It was the last of the great inter-war revolutions. But instead of it being the start of a revival for the workers' movement, the Revolution's defeat helped lay the basis for World War II.

Fascism triumphed in Spain, not because workers were unwilling to wage revolutionary struggles, but because the existing organisations of the left betrayed them. The Comintern and the local Stalinists played a thoroughly cynical and counter-revolutionary role. Trotsky explained:

> By setting itself the task of rescuing the capitalist regime, the Popular Front doomed itself to military defeat. By turning Bolshevism on its head, Stalin succeeded completely in fulfilling the role of gravedigger of the revolution.[30]

By smashing the Spanish Revolution, Stalinists paved the way for fascism. They also, however, enhanced their authority on the international left. Stalin's supply of arms and the activity of the International Brigades gave Russia the unearned reputation of being a bulwark against fascist aggression, especially compared with Britain and France, which failed to support the elected government in Madrid. Once the Republic fell, all that appeared to stand between Europe and fascism was Stalinist Russia. Many who might have had reservations about Stalin shelved their hesitations and embraced the Russian dictator, even as he was executing thousands of suspected opponents.

Anarchism received its greatest test in Spain. It was a decisive failure. The CNT served as the loyal opposition to the Popular Front and left the workers leaderless in the face of the Stalinist takeover. Its decision to join both the Companys and the Caballero governments was opposed in anarchist circles at the time, both at home and abroad. But what alternative did these anarchist critics offer? They could not wish away the capitalist state. Unless the anarchists abandoned their political program and fought for the establishment of a workers' state based on soviets, they could only adapt to the existing state machine. While they renounced taking power in Barcelona on the grounds that this would only result in an 'anarchist dictatorship,' this was a cover for the fact that they had no conception of the workers taking power themselves. This led them inexorably to a position of supporting the existing capitalist state – even when the capitalists had abandoned it. Trotsky argued: 'In opposing the goal, the conquest of power, the Anarchists could not in the end fail to oppose the means, the revolution.'[31] Failing to pursue revolutionary goals, the CNT paved the way for Franco's triumph.

The revolution also highlighted the failure of the POUM. The leadership agreed with workers' power at a formal level but failed to build a party that would seriously fight for it; it went soft on the anarchist and reformist political forces in the heat of the struggle. A revolutionary Marxist party of some size could have made all the difference. It could have told the workers the truth about the counter-revolutionary intentions of the Republic, put forward a revolutionary strategy to defeat fascism, exposed the betrayals of the Stalinists and laid bare the bankruptcy of the CNT. It would have had to show in practice what opposition to the Popular Front meant, instead of making abstract objections or 'reservations,' as the POUM did. The strategy and tactics put forward by such a party would have to take reality – the existence of workers' committees, peasant committees and a workers' militia – as its starting point for a strategy to crush Franco and lead the workers and peasants to power.

FURTHER READING

R.J. Alexander, *The Anarchists and the Spanish Civil War*, volume 2, London, Janus Publishing, 1999.

G. Bailey, 'Anarchists in the Spanish Civil War,' *International Socialist Review*, no. 24, 2002.

B. Bolloten, *The Spanish Civil War: Revolution and Counterrevolution*, 1987.

P. Broué and E. Témime, *The Revolution and the Civil War in Spain*, Cambridge, MIT Press, 1972.

A. Durgan, 'Trotsky and the POUM,' *International Socialism*, no. 147, 2015.

R. Fraser, *Blood of Spain*, New York, Pantheon Books, 1986.

J. Molyneux, *Anarchism: A Marxist Critique*, London, Bookmarks, 2011.

F. Morrow, *Revolution and Counter Revolution in Spain*, New York, Pathfinder Press, 1974 [1938].

G. Orwell, *Homage to Catalonia*, London, Penguin Books, 2013 [1938].

12.

SIT-DOWN FEVER! U.S. WORKERS' STRUGGLE AND THE ROOSEVELT ADMINISTRATION

President Roosevelt's New Deal administration in the 1930s looms large in the popular imagination in the United States.[1] In Democrat mythology, a Democrat president, backed by an array of progressive forces, including trade unions, small farmers, students and intellectuals and enlightened business owners, introduced reforms which improved the lives of ordinary people, apparently proving that the party can be used as a vehicle for social reform.[2]

But Roosevelt and the Democrats were not friends of workers and the poor. Roosevelt's objective in office was to rescue capitalism from the twin threats of economic collapse and working class insurgency. The crucial factor driving his reforms was the mass strikes which radicalised broad swathes of the population and in which radical socialists, not Democrats, played a leading role. Employers, accustomed to running their factories like personal fiefdoms, were forced onto the defensive by these strikes and had to make concessions. Roosevelt briefly tacked left, to capitalise electorally on this explosion of strikes, but only with the aim of defusing militancy and directing it into safe channels. Once this had been achieved, with imperialist tensions rising, Roosevelt swung hard to the right and pursued policies virtually indistinguishable from Democratic presidents before and since.

The 1930s industrial upsurge demonstrated the explosive potential of US workers and the cynical response by Democratic politicians. It also revealed the treacherous role of union leaders. Some turned their backs on the strikes and factory occupations; the more astute rode the tiger, capitalising on worker militancy to build their organisations, talking left to protect their left flank, but snuffing out the challenge in the end, thereby securing their own positions and good standing with employers and the White House.

The Communist Party of the United States of America (CPUSA) played a vital role in allowing Roosevelt and the union leaders to quash the upsurge in militancy. The party earned its stripes among militants during the Depression by organising the unemployed in the face of tremendous hardship and brutal repression. During a modest economic recovery in 1933-34, CPUSA militants threw themselves into building fighting trade unions. But with the switch to Popular Front politics, the party used its credibility among workers to divert the explosion of struggle from below into bureaucratic trade unionism. The CPUSA dismissed the chance to build a national labour party, ensuring that the impulse for independent working class political organisation was channelled back into the Democrats.

The militancy and radicalisation of US workers in the 1930s demonstrated three things: that it was possible to create militant industrial unions, based on shopfloor union organisation, that could fight for workers' rights; that it was possible to launch an independent labour party with substantial electoral representation and a mass membership; and that there was an opportunity to cohere a revolutionary socialist workers' organisation of some tens of thousands. The dead hand of Stalinism ensured that these opportunities were lost.

After the Depression

The Great Depression was a catastrophe for millions of US workers. Unemployment rose to one-quarter of the workforce – fully half of the workforce in many industrial cities. Millions were evicted from their homes to tramp the streets. Shanty towns of tin sheets and cardboard became homes for millions of working class families. Employers took advantage of the situation, imposing savage wage cuts. Bosses played divide and rule, splitting the skilled from the unskilled, Blacks from whites and immigrants from the native-born, and organised them to scab on each other. They combined this with brutal repression to smash union organising drives. Big companies such as General Motors (GM) employed private armies and controlled the police, the magistrates and local government in company towns. The administration of Republican President Herbert Hoover, who had taken office in 1929, had nothing to offer workers and the unemployed. The bosses ignored the administration's piecemeal labour reforms. With dole queues lengthening, most workers pulled their heads in and survived as best they could.

Some fought back. Unemployed workers went on hunger marches. Unemployed organisations drove out bailiffs trying to evict families from their homes. Food riots and raids on delivery trucks were common. Landlords, employers and authorities hit back hard. In 1932, Detroit police attacked a hunger march of 3,000 current and former Ford workers, killing four and injuring 60 more. More than 30,000 marched in the funeral procession.

Communists and socialists were frequently at the centre of these struggles. The CPUSA had been a weak party at the onset of the Depression, having struggled in the 1920s due to severe state repression and serious internal disputes. By 1929, membership was only 6,000 in a population of 120 million. In 1930, Stalin installed Earl Browder as national secretary. Browder immediately implemented the Comintern's sectarian 'social fascist' line, whose targets included liberals, non-Stalinist socialists, the American Federation of Labor and African American organisations whose leaders were attacked as 'traitors' and 'scab herders.' Nonetheless, in a situation where few other organisations were willing to take up the challenge, the CPUSA formed the backbone of many struggles.

The Communists campaigned vigorously against racism. In Alabama in the Deep South, the CPUSA organised Black sharecroppers and fought the Ku Klux Klan. In Harlem in New York, the biggest urban concentration of African Americans in the country, Communists organised against unemployment, demonstrated against racist hiring policies and protested against lynching. The CPUSA championed the case of the Scottsboro Boys, nine Black youths sentenced to death in 1931 by an all-white jury on a trumped-up charge of gang rape. Such initiatives enabled the party to recruit hundreds of African Americans in the early 1930s, a stark contrast to the record of much of the US left. The party's reputation in the African American community at this time was crucial in affording it access to Black factory workers in the years to come. The CPUSA also picked up members by trumpeting lies about the supposed achievements of Stalin's Russia at a time when the West was mired in Depression. Radicalised students also flocked to the party. By 1933, the CPUSA had more than doubled in size to 14,000, still a tiny number in a large country, but becoming more of a force.

What of the union movement? The established unions organised in the American Federation of Labor (AFL) were ill equipped to defend workers during the Depression. Coverage was extremely low; membership fell to just three million in 1933, down from its 1920 peak of five million. Whole sections of the workforce in the rapidly developing mass production industries, such as rubber, steel and autos, were completely unorganised. The AFL showed no signs of trying to break into these industries beyond their traditional constituency, skilled workers in craft unions. The AFL leaders despised unskilled and semi-skilled workers, calling them 'riffraff' and 'garbage' and relegating them to second class status, driving many to quit soon after they joined.³

The AFL made no effort to challenge the bosses' divide and rule tactics. Millions of African Americans escaping the Jim Crow South were pouring into factory jobs in the northern cities, but the AFL craft unions did little to welcome them. Some unions refused to sign up Black workers. while others recruited them but did nothing to break down segregation of union locals (branches) and meetings and refused to respond to pleas to organise Blacks.

The CPUSA and other socialist agitators and radicals did their best to overcome the bureaucratic lethargy at the top of the union movement. Although most workers were cowed by high unemployment and the bosses' offensive, desperate coal miners were prepared to fight. Coal was the source of 90 percent of US energy needs, which gave miners tremendous leverage. The United Mine Workers of America (UMW), however, was in bad shape, with membership down from its peak of 400,000 in 1920 to just 75,000 by 1930 in a workforce of 600,000. The mine owners were viciously anti-union, but the more significant problem was the anti-communist and anti-strike union president, John L. Lewis, who presided over the UMW like a tyrant. The CPUSA had, with other radicals, fought Lewis during the 1920s, but in 1928, in line with the Comintern's 'red union' strategy, the party abandoned the UMW, setting up the National Miners Union (NMU). During the Depression, the NMU and other independent socialist oppositionists to Lewis tapped into a deep vein of dissatisfaction with Lewis's leadership among coal miners. In 1929-30, numerous spontaneous strikes erupted. In 1931, several large strikes saw 20,000 coal miners coming out in Pennsylvania, 20,000 in West Virginia, 40,000 across three states and 10,000 in Harlan County, Kentucky.

The NMU recruited from these strikes, but, as was generally the pattern with the Comintern's 'red unions,' was unable to hold the new recruits and never became a serious challenger to the UMW. But the organising efforts of the NMU and other socialists and radicals did give the bosses and conservative union leaders a fright. The employers began to seek out the UMW to sign backdoor contracts, and UMW membership revived rapidly. In 1932, there was a new wave of strikes in the mines, most often led by rank and file militants but now under UMW auspices, involving perhaps as many as 100,000 miners.

Not only coal miners were on the move. Garment workers struck in 1932-33, boosting union rolls by thousands. In the first half of 1933, auto workers at multiple companies in Michigan heralded the biggest strike wave in the industry since the early 1920s. Workers struck not primarily for wages or working hours but against what Mike Davis calls 'the petty despotism of the workplace incarnated in the capricious power of the supervisors and the inhuman pressures of mechanised production lines.'[4] One contemporary observed:

> Early in 1933 hell began to pop. Strike followed strike with bewildering rapidity. The long-exploited, too-patient auto slaves were getting tired of the game.[5]

Radical activists were at the heart of this strike wave. They included implanted revolutionary cadres, primarily CPUSA members, particularly those from the party's immigrant cultural organisations; skilled mechanics who rejected the AFL's exclusivism and elitism; and second generation migrants employed in semi-skilled blue collar jobs. These came together in industrial shop committees and rebel locals. The radicals were able to give voice to the accumulated resentments of workers.

The significance of these disputes is that they challenge the conventional wisdom that favourable legislation introduced by Roosevelt gave the spur to union organising. All these disputes took place *before* Roosevelt's 1933 labour reform. Campaigns led by radicals and communists actually provided the initial impetus for union organising in basic industries. And the growth of the UMW prepared this union to play an outsize role in resourcing the organising efforts in other industries in coming years.

The first New Deal

Popular hatred of the Hoover administration saw the Republican president lose the 1932 election in a landslide to Roosevelt. In contrast to the popular image today, the incoming president was no progressive. His election platform focused on balanced budgets, differing little from the Republicans. There was no mention of labour rights. Roosevelt headed a party centred on important factions of the capitalist class. In the North, these included property developers, immigrant capitalists and small business owners. The party monopolised power in many big northern cities using clientelist 'Tammany Hall' politics rooted in working class immigrant communities, including Italians, Irish, Poles and Jews. In the South, the Democrats ('Dixiecrats') ruled as the party of unbridled white supremacy. Jim Crow laws and lynchings were used to terrorise Blacks and exclude them from any political power. Such was the power of the Dixiecrats that Roosevelt refused to back anti-lynching legislation or any laws to restore the voting rights of African Americans or challenge segregation of public facilities in the South.

Faced with the severe economic crisis and the risk that unemployed riots might intensify, Roosevelt was forced to shake up the existing power blocs within the party and unleash forces that were to remake US society. The *National Industrial Recovery Act 1933* (NIRA) aimed to put capitalism back on its feet by encouraging big firms to take over small firms, allowing them to dominate their markets and boost their profits. Attempting to quieten agitation by the unemployed and workers, the Act also provided for minimum wages and maximum hours, eliminated child labour and, in a sop to Lewis, recognised the right of workers to organise and bargain collectively.

There were real limits to the NIRA for workers. It excluded workers in domestic service and farm workers. The National Labor Board, established to oversee union recognition elections, had no enforcement mechanism. Workers had to fight to win the right to a union. Nonetheless, militants were encouraged by the easing of Depression conditions and a fall in unemployment. The number of strikes doubled from 841 in 1932 to 1,695 in 1933, and the number of strikers quadrupled from 324,000 to 1.2 million.

Roosevelt may have called for industrial peace, but the bosses were determined to fight the incursion of independent unions. Rather than recognise AFL unions, they set up company unions – allowed under the NIRA. Membership of these fake 'unions' shot up from 1.3 million to 2.5 million between enactment of the NIRA and May 1935, when the NIRA was struck down by the Supreme Court. This was more than twice the growth of AFL union membership. The bosses also unleashed wholesale violence against organised labour. The American Civil Liberties Union reported of the first six months of the NIRA that: 'at no time has there been such widespread violations of workers' rights by injunctions, troops, private police, deputy sheriffs, labor spies and vigilantes.' More than 15 strikers were killed, 200 injured and hundreds arrested.[6]

Repression played its part in defeating many strikes in 1933. An AFL hierarchy uninterested in fighting to win was also responsible. Radical agitators were busy building new locals, new unions on the ground, and the AFL feared their development into mass industrial unions outside AFL control. Their solution was to corral them within the AFL. In late 1933, AFL leaders began to set up 'federal locals,' local unions directly attached to the AFL rather than to an affiliate, ruled by the AFL top officials. These were designed to draw in semi-skilled workers in the basic industries: rubber, chemicals, automotive, electrical and steel. Federal locals were to be a temporary measure: AFL leaders planned to divide the newly-organised workers in the federal locals among the numerous craft unions claiming jurisdiction over the various types of work done by members in the same workplace. The

AFL steered the rising demand for militant, democratic union organising on an industrial basis into a series of squalid deals with the employers. The initial influx of members into the federal locals soon gave way to an exodus. Workers could see that the leaders were not serious about fighting.

1934: a watershed

Three strikes in the spring of 1934 demonstrated workers' willingness to press their demands. They were led not by the established union leaders, who actively opposed them, but by self-proclaimed revolutionaries who had cut their teeth organising the unemployed at the height of the Depression and now threw themselves into the industrial struggle.

The great strike wave began in Toledo, Ohio, on 12 April, when 4,000 workers at Auto-Lite, an automotive components company, walked off the job in protest at their employer's refusal to negotiate over a pay increase and recognition of their newly-organised federal local. For the first few weeks of the strike, management used scabs to keep the plant going, and the AFL leaders did nothing to stop them. The workers looked set for defeat.

In early May, radicals stepped in to turn the situation around. A. J. Muste was a Marxist whose American Workers Party had organised the local unemployed in the Lucas County Unemployment League. He now rallied the city's unemployed against scabbing and in support of the strike. Muste brought 1,000 unemployed to the picket on the first day, 4,000 on the second, and 6,000 on the third. The pickets were mostly peaceful until 23 May, when management used security guards armed with tear gas bombs, iron bars and clubs to break up the picket line. Picketers fought back with bricks in what became known as the Battle of Toledo. Even the arrival of the National Guard, which fired on the strikers, killing two and injuring dozens, did not break the picket. Strikers and their unemployed supporters fought the National Guard for six days. Finally, on 31 May, the company agreed to close the plant and the National Guard was removed. The workers and their supporters came out in huge numbers the following day, with 40,000 demonstrating outside the courthouse to protest the arrest of 200 strikers. Of Toledo's 99 local unions, 98 pledged to call a general strike in sympathy with the workers. Within days, the company capitulated, granting exclusive recognition to the federal local and agreeing to rehire the strikers. This was the first breakthrough in the auto industry. By the end of the year, the Toledo auto workers had organised another 19 auto plants. Before the end of 1935, auto workers had begun their assault on GM, a bastion of anti-unionism.

On the other side of the country, the CPUSA swung into action to support a strike by 14,000 West Coast waterside workers. At the centre of the walk-off was a strike committee in San Francisco led by Harry Bridges, a seafarer who originally hailed from Melbourne and had for years identified with the Wobblies before drawing close to the CPUSA. In 1933, ahead of the party as a whole, the California district of the CPUSA had abandoned the red union approach – which had only isolated them among the state's waterside workers – in order to focus on organising within the AFL affiliate, the International Longshoremen's Association (ILA). The CPUSA leader in California, Sam Darcy, contacted Harry Bridges and other syndicalist wharfies and formed a committee of militant waterside workers to fight the conservative ILA leadership. This committee was able to channel the radical traditions and increasing militancy of San Francisco wharfies and win control of the local, drawing in a flood of new recruits. In February 1934, a convention of ILA rank and filers met in San Francisco and endorsed the formation of a West Coast Waterfront Federation to bring together all the craft locals in each port. They elected a rank and file committee to begin negotiations with ship owners independently of notoriously corrupt national ILA officials. Delegates voted to strike on 23 March, demanding a pay rise, shorter hours and union control over hiring. The strike was sabotaged by the ILA officials following Roosevelt's intervention to have it called off. The dispute was shunted off to a mediation board hearing which dragged on for weeks.

Fed up with the delay, 1,500 members of the San Francisco local resolved to strike on 8 May. On that day, 14,000 wharfies up and down the West Coast struck, from Portland to San Diego. A strike committee was set up in San Francisco, and Bridges was elected president. The committee organised daily mass meetings and round-the-clock pickets, up to 1,000 strong. The picketers appealed successfully for solidarity. Within a week, the local teamsters (truck drivers) refused to haul cargo, and 25,000 seafarers were on strike along the entire coast. After eight weeks, the San Francisco mayor sent the police in to break up the picket. A bloody fight ensued; cops killed four workers and injured hundreds more. Workers met this challenge with a four-day San Francisco general strike involving 130,000 workers, with Communists, Socialists and Wobblies all to the fore. A sympathetic journalist records the scene:

> The paralysis on the morning of July 16 was effective beyond all expectation. To all intents and purposes, industry was at a complete standstill. The great factories were empty and deserted. No streetcars

were running. Virtually all stores were closed. The giant apparatus of commerce was a lifeless, helpless hulk.[7]

City authorities lashed out, deploying police, the National Guard and vigilante gangs to attack strikers. Police raided the offices of the Communist and Socialist parties. The dramatic political polarisation and escalation of the struggle frightened the West Coast ILA leaders, who saw the dispute escaping their control. They pushed the strike committee aside and fought to bring the strike to an end, surrendering key demands and limiting the strike to fewer and fewer workers. After four days, in the teeth of opposition from the strike committee, the AFL leadership terminated the strike before a decisive victory had been secured. Nonetheless, within weeks, the employers agreed to grant effective union control over hiring as well as significant wage and working conditions improvements, transforming the ILA into the most powerful union on the West Coast. The CPUSA's role in the strike earned it leadership of the union for decades to come and significantly heightened its national profile. Party membership doubled from 14,000 to 27,000 between 1933 and 1935. Success in San Francisco, along with shifting sentiment in Moscow, also saw the CPUSA formally ditch 'red unionism' and enter the AFL federal locals in earnest by the end of the year.

The third big strike in 1934 involved teamsters in Minneapolis in spring. Daniel Tobin, a typical AFL leader – implacably opposed to strikes and internal democracy – led the national union. The union was divided on craft and industry lines, perpetuating internal divisions and ensuring industrial weakness. In the early 1930s, a small group of Trotskyists began to organise in Local 574 in Minneapolis. They were members of the tiny Communist League of America, expelled from the CPUSA in 1928 after declaring their support for Trotsky. Local 574 was in dire straits at the time with only 75 members – barely surviving. The city was a notorious 'open shop' town, where the bosses fired active unionists on the spot. However, it had a tradition of industrial militancy and was home to many former Wobblies, Socialist Party loyalists and workers bringing socialist traditions with them from their homelands in Germany and Scandinavia. The Trotskyist leaders of Local 574 won a hearing among these layers of workers, bringing together a fusion of native-born and immigrant labour militancy.

In 1933, the Trotskyists and their allies had their first breakthrough, organising coal drivers on strike. The coal drivers won. On the basis of this victory, Local 574 began to pull in not only truck drivers but warehouse workers and others involved in trucking. This strategy was anathema to the AFL, with its policy of keeping workers split up into disconnected unions. Local 574, now with 3,000 members, began to prepare for the next strike. They rented strike headquarters, organised a women's auxiliary and sought support from local farmers and the unemployed.

On 16 May 1934, thousands of teamsters struck in Minneapolis. Within two days, most of the commercial transport in the city was shut down. Oversight of the strike was in the hands of a 75-member rank and file strike committee, with the Trotskyists playing a leading role. The committee organised roving pickets to enforce the strike. It held nightly mass meetings of all striking workers and published a daily strike paper. The strike headquarters incorporated an infirmary, to treat strikers bashed by police, and a kitchen that fed thousands of strikers and supporters. By the end of the first week, hundreds of picketers armed with clubs brawled daily with police and deputies organised by a local bosses' organisation, the Citizens' Alliance. The picketers got the better of the police and deputies, pushing them back. In a dramatic escalation, 35,000 building workers walked off the job in support of the teamsters, followed by taxi drivers. After nine days, the bosses and the union signed an agreement that gave workers all their main demands – union recognition, reinstatement of strikers, seniority and no victimisations. By now, Local 574 had grown to 7,000 members.

In mid-July, bosses reneged on the agreement. Roosevelt's National Labor Board did nothing to bring them into line. The strike resumed, but the city police were now better prepared. After three days, police fired round after round of buckshot at point blank range, cutting down dozens of picketers, killing two and injuring 67. Local 574 responded, immediately calling out union taxis, ice, beer and gasoline trucks. Forty thousand marched in the subsequent funeral procession. The Minnesota Governor, elected as a progressive, declared martial law, bringing 4,000 National Guardsmen onto the streets to allow thousands of scab trucks to operate freely. The union maintained flying pickets to harass them where they could. The leadership of Local 574 also had to fend off continued attacks from national president Tobin, who was determined to drive them from the union.

Eventually, the bosses were forced to settle, accepting the union's chief demands. Teamsters Local 574 was now famous across the country. They had turned a non-union town into a union stronghold. Subsequently, they extended the gains from Minneapolis across wide swathes of the upper Midwest. Thousands of workers in other industries flocked to join unions, helped by Local 574. It was a victory for the Communist League of America, which grew to 100 members in Minneapolis alone and hundreds more nationally.

The three strikes in Toledo, the West Coast and Minneapolis demonstrated that left wing radicals in local branches could step in when national union leaders would not mobilise workers and the unemployed to fight for their rights. This frightened the union leaders. Many responded to the developing mood of militancy by doing their best to smash it. Others could read the writing on the wall: unless union leaders took charge of the millions of new and predominantly semi-skilled workers flooding into the factories and mines, these workers might fall under the sway of radical forces. In 1935, Lewis seized the moment and established a new union federation, the Committee for Industrial Organizations (CIO). Lewis was a staunch anti-communist who had backed Hoover in 1932, but he understood where the future of unionism lay: not with the small minority of skilled workers, whose future was coming under increasing threat from mechanisation and mass production, but with the semi-skilled and unskilled, whose strength lay not in their exclusiveness but in their numbers and their ability to bring big factories to a halt. These workers had to be organised on industrial lines, with unions open to all, regardless of skill or race. Lewis poured UMW money into this venture. His gamble paid off. Auto workers, electrical workers and rubber workers, who were at the forefront of the new militancy, rushed into the new federation and built it from the ground up.

Roosevelt and the second New Deal

The upsurge of militancy in 1934–35 saw big business begin to abandon Roosevelt, jeopardising his plans for re-election. A hostile Supreme Court struck down the provisions for unions to organise. Roosevelt needed to rally workers and their unions behind him in order to defeat the capitalist mobilisation. It was more than simple electoral expediency. The extreme social and political polarisation frightened liberal reformers in the government concerned to preserve social stability. They were alarmed by the threat posed by radicals in the labour movement. Liberal Senator Robert La Follette Jr used the big strikes of 1934 to warn his colleagues of the risk of 'open industrial warfare.'[8] Unless some way could be found to support the AFL, the capitalists might have on their hands a genuinely left wing union federation led by radicals. The default position of many big US capitalists – intransigent opposition to labour reform – was only fuelling radicalisation and undermining the conservative AFL leaders. Roosevelt's electoral considerations and the need to dampen radicalisation worked together to underpin the passage of a wave of progressive laws.

Roosevelt's second New Deal contained several elements. The *National Labor Relations Act 1935* (the Wagner Act) was more far reaching than the administration's first round of labour legislation. The Wagner Act outlawed company unions, declared traditional anti-union practices illegal, legalised union organising efforts and established the National Labor Relations Board (NLRB). The aim was to channel the burgeoning labour unrest into formal processes of orderly collective bargaining, backed up by compulsory mediation and arbitration processes. The *Social Security Act 1935* created old age pensions, unemployment insurance and aid for widows with dependent children. *The Fair Labor Standards Act 1938* would establish a minimum wage. The new Works Progress Administration set up public works programs for the unemployed.

The second New Deal was designed to soothe class tensions. However, more intransigent capitalists saw in it the threat of socialism. They immediately appealed the Wagner Act, preventing its enforcement until the Supreme Court upheld its constitutionality in the spring of 1937. Most workers, by contrast, greeted the reforms warmly. The second New Deal, more than anything, is responsible for the Democrats' reputation as a 'progressive' party. But Lewis and his fellow CIO leaders were the most enthusiastic of all, seeing in the Wagner Act the potential to recruit members to new industrial unions *en masse* while diverting militant strikes into arbitration. Although the Wagner Act was not enforced for nearly two years, union leaders were grateful that its provisions intended to make them 'labour statesmen' rather than outlaws.

Enthused by Roosevelt's reforms, CIO leaders threw themselves behind the president's 1936 re-election campaign. Lewis established Labor's Nonpartisan League, dedicated to getting the vote out for Roosevelt and the Democrats. The CIO raised $750,000 for Roosevelt, offsetting the loss of corporate donations, and diverted the resources it had allocated to organising the steel industry to Roosevelt's re-election. For his part, Roosevelt swung left during the election campaign, attacking the large corporations and calling for a 'people's government.'

While Roosevelt was garnering support from the CIO, many working class radicals remained sceptical about the Democrats. They had seen Democrat governors using the National Guard to smash strikes. Even if they wished Roosevelt well, they did not trust the Democrats, and they were well aware of the limitations of the second New Deal: domestic workers and farm workers, overwhelmingly African Americans, along with retail workers, were excluded from old age pensions and unemployment insurance and the protection of the Wagner Act. Radical unionists, along with the American

Civil Liberties Union, opposed the Act's restrictions on the right to strike and its bias towards the AFL.

In increasing numbers, radicalising workers began to demand the formation of a national labour party, independent of the Democrats. The creation of such a party would have been a definite advance, breaking the stranglehold of two big bourgeois parties funded and run by the capitalist class and their close allies. While not breaking from capitalism, a labour party could have loosened the grip of bourgeois politics and helped to cohere the working class as a political force in US society. The labour movement did not break from the Democrats, largely because of the CIO.

In 1936, several important unions endorsed resolutions supporting a national farmer–labour party. This initiative was actively counterposed to support for Roosevelt in some cases, but not all. At the 1936 convention of the United Auto Workers (UAW), a newly formed international union that had emerged out of the organising efforts of radicals in the industry, socialists won a vote to support the formation of a national farmer–labour party and voted down a motion endorsing Roosevelt. The CIO jumped into action. One of Lewis's lieutenants threatened to cut off CIO funding to the UAW. The following day, the convention reversed its position. In the clothing workers' union, the union president and CIO co-founder Sidney Hillman successfully quashed an attempt by the union's class conscious and radical Jewish members in New York, who had long voted Socialist, to set up the American Labor Party – potentially a rival party to the Democrats. Such blocking moves by the CIO ensured the stillbirth of a labour party when the potential for such a formation was at an all-time high.

Sit-down fever

Mike Davis describes the working class upsurge of the mid-1930s as 'the high-water mark of the class struggle in modern American history.'[9] The zenith of this movement was 1936–37. Strikes went through the roof. Young, left wing rank and file activists, communists and socialists of various stripes, seized upon new methods of organising or recalled organising methods used by the Wobblies in earlier years. Lewis gave them their head. In just two years, these activists made historic gains in unionising the mass production industries, overturning decades of obstruction by America's biggest and most powerful corporations. All of this took place before the Wagner Act came into effect. It was class struggle that built US unions, not the Roosevelt administration.

Rubber workers in Ohio led the way with a wave of strikes and factory occupations, dubbed sit-down strikes, in the first half of 1936. Auto workers were next to move: numerous strikes broke out across the industrial Midwest. Detroit and Flint in Michigan, home to the country's biggest car factories, were the centre of the action. The most famous of the strikes was at GM Fisher Body Plant #1 at Flint, where thousands of auto workers, most having just joined the UAW, occupied their factory. Occupation gave the workers an important bargaining chip and prevented the bosses from bringing in scabs.

The Flint sit-downs were a model of workers' collective action and democracy. The strike committee, where communists and socialists, including Trotskyists, played leading roles, ensured that security, food and entertainment were all provided for on a collective basis. Daily mass meetings gave strikers the opportunity to discuss tactics. Alongside the strike committee, 350 strikers' wives organised the Flint Women's Emergency Brigade to mobilise women to defend the sit-downs against police attacks. One woman activist wrote:

> A new type of woman was born in the strike. Women who only yesterday were horrified at unionism, who felt inferior to the task of organising, speaking, leading, have, as if overnight, become the spearhead in the battle for unionism.[10]

GM refused to negotiate with the UAW, in clear defiance of the Wagner Act. Instead, it tried to freeze and starve the workers out of the Fisher Body Plant, cutting off heat and food deliveries and securing an injunction to have them evicted. Soldiers with machine guns patrolled the perimeter. But the company could not beat the workers' resolve. The sit-down strikers sent a telegram to Governor Murphy, a New Deal Democrat and Roosevelt ally:

> Unarmed as we are, the introduction of the militia, sheriffs, or police with murderous weapons will mean a bloodbath of unarmed workers… We have decided to stay in the plant. We have no illusions about the sacrifices which this decision will entail. We fully expect that if a violent effort is made to oust us many of us will be killed, and we take this means of making it known to our wives, to our children, to the people of the state of Michigan and the country that if this result follows from an attempt to eject us, you are the one who must be held responsible for our deaths.[11]

The next morning, a call for solidarity brought 5,000 supporters, including veterans of the Toledo Auto-Lite strike, Akron rubber workers and Pittsburgh coal miners, to their aid. They encircled the factory, fought a pitched battle with security guards and police and forcibly reopened the gates to allow food deliveries. With the Women's Emergency Brigade smashing windows at another GM plant to divert police and security, workers seized the nearby Chevrolet #4 plant, which produced the company's engines.

The Flint sit-down became the focus of national attention and something of a test case: would the UAW be able to insist on its right to exclusive recognition, as spelled out in the Wagner Act, or would the bosses be able to ignore the legislation? The company's intransigence elicited widespread public sympathy for the workers. Although he had played no role in organising it, Lewis backed the sit-down, stating that he would take his place alongside the occupying auto workers if the police were sent in to evict them. Faced with the threat of massive retaliation by the rapidly growing CIO, the Michigan Governor pulled back on his threat to send in the police and National Guard. The company was forced to back down and sign a six-month contract with the UAW, the first in the company's history. The UAW quickly followed its victory at GM with the occupation of nine Chrysler plants. Within four weeks, Chrysler buckled and signed a settlement. Sit-down strikes now spread like wildfire in the auto industry, with GM alone recording 170 sit-down strikes in the spring of 1937.

The breakthrough in the auto industry opened the floodgates for unionism across the country. Rubber workers in Ohio finally won union recognition at Firestone, Goodyear and Goodrich. In the spring of 1937, 400,000 workers took part in 477 sit-downs. Labour historian Sidney Fine records:

> The sit-downs involved every conceivable type of worker – kitchen and laundry workers in the Israel-Zion Hospital in Brooklyn, pencil makers, janitors, dog catchers, newspaper pressmen, sailors, tobacco workers, Woolworth girls, rug weavers, hotel and restaurant employees, pie bakers, watchmakers, garbage collectors, Western Union messengers, opticians and lumbermen.[12]

Police were virtually powerless to break them up; of the 1,000 sit-down strikes recorded in 1936 and 1937, only 25 were broken by police.

The initials CIO at this time struck fear into the hearts of bosses and AFL leaders alike but conveyed to US workers a genuine sense of liberation. Daniel Guérin writes:

> The union became the nerve centre of all these human-beings, bowed and defrauded as they had been for so long... The American workers, whom capitalist society had made into self-interested individualists and cynics, suddenly discovered that unknown treasure: comradeship. It was as if a new world, a new existence has begun. The women, doubly exploited, as workers and as women, were doubly delivered.[13]

A very significant element of the working class upsurge in mass production industry was its multiracial character. By the end of the 1930s, half a million Black workers had joined the CIO, a significant achievement in challenging racism within the working class. Even in Richmond, Virginia, still a Jim Crow stronghold, hundreds of Black tobacco workers, men and women, struck for increased wages, the 40-hour week, union recognition and the right to be treated with dignity. White women workers in the CIO's Clothing and Textile Workers Union walked the picket lines in support of the striking tobacco workers, shocking segregated Richmond society.

The sit-down tactic was not confined to unions. Protesters sat down in unemployment relief offices, employment agencies and against evictions. Prisoners adopted the tactic. Even children sat down in cinemas to protest against program cuts.

By the end of 1937, nearly half a million workers had taken part in a sit-down, and nearly two million had gone on strike – the second largest number since records began in 1881. Frequently, sit-downs were organised without the approval of union leaders. After GM signed a contract with the UAW, Lewis told auto workers that they had no further need for sit-downs. Any CIO representative who authorised strikes without the approval of the union head office would be dismissed. Regardless, plenty of workers were willing to press their demands. In the four months after the first GM contract, auto workers engaged in at least 200 'quickie' strikes without union approval.

Following the win at GM, many big corporations capitulated to the CIO rather than face a strike. The previously impregnable US Steel Corporation was one. The sit-down strikers also brought the anti-union Supreme Court to heel. One month after the union win at US Steel, the Supreme Court was forced to recognise the new industrial reality, upholding the Wagner Act and so ratifying what workers had already won by striking.

The CIO was now a major force. At its August 1937 conference, the federation claimed four million members, outstripping the AFL. Even the AFL was inundated with workers demanding union coverage, boosting rolls by one million.

The role of the Communist Party

As the Comintern began to inch away from 'social fascism' and before it embraced the Popular Front, the CPUSA enjoyed some freedom to manoeuvre. Lacking instructions from Moscow to tack hard to the 'left' or 'right,' the party reverted to some of the united front tactics it had adopted in the 1920s before being Stalinised. These tactics had been very effective in the West Coast waterfront strike in 1934. The party now used the same approach in the AFL federal locals; alongside other socialists and radicals, it strove to convert them into militant, democratic, industrial unions. This strategy was tremendously successful, most notably in auto; by 1936 the CPUSA had built a fraction of 630 members, and its factory cells pulled in a much larger periphery of sympathisers. CPUSA members played a leading role in the strikes that swept the electrical and machinery industries plants in 1936. Charlie Post suggests that, without the CPUSA's 'pragmatic united front policy' at this time, the CIO would probably never have been born. The AFL bureaucrats would have dissipated worker militancy as they had in 1933, and Lewis and his collaborators would not have been moved to break with the AFL.[14]

By late 1936, this interregnum was ending. Stalin had identified the US, Britain and France as partners in a bloc against Germany, Italy and Japan. Moscow ordered the CPUSA to cultivate good relations with the supposedly 'progressive' wing of the US ruling class. Every organisation that did not openly avow fascism was now an ally or potential ally, including liberal sections of the bourgeoisie and the Catholic Church hierarchy.[15] This prompted a political reorientation by Communists in the US, one element of which included embracing the Democratic Party. The CPUSA played an important role in stifling moves to build an independent labour party. During the 1936 presidential election, only fear that the Republicans would seize on Communist support for Roosevelt stopped the party publicly backing the Democratic candidate. At a time when Roosevelt was tacking to the left, vowing to crush the 'economic royalists,' the CPUSA ran Browder as its candidate under the extremely conservative slogan 'Communism is Twentieth Century Americanism.' Within a year, with Roosevelt re-elected, the CPUSA was openly praising his administration as a partner in the supposed anti-fascist popular front.

The CPUSA underwent a similar shift in its approach to the CIO bureaucracy. In the first months of 1937, the party swung hard behind Lewis, who was no longer described as a fascist but as a democratic ally. To some extent, they had a common project. Both wanted to build industrial unionism, but neither wanted wildcat strikes – Lewis because they threatened his control over restive workers, and the CPUSA because continued industrial rebellion might undermine Roosevelt and the New Deal coalition of middle class and bourgeois forces they were promoting. On the basis of this mutual understanding, Lewis employed hundreds of CP members as CIO organisers and staffers, not to advance the class struggle but to rein it in.

The right wing turn by the CPUSA became evident after the flurry of sit-downs in the winter and spring of 1937. CPUSA organisers began to position the party as advocates of industrial order. In response to media claims that the strike upsurge was all the work of 'the Reds,' Browder protested: 'The Communist Party is not stirring up strikes.' The *Daily Worker* ran a statement by the party's Michigan secretary, declaring:

> unequivocally and emphatically that the Communists and the Communist party had never in the past and do not now in any shape, manner or form advocate or support unauthorised and wildcat action and regard such strikes as gravely injurious to the union's welfare.[16]

No longer trying to appeal to militant workers on the basis of socialist (in reality, Stalinist) politics, the CPUSA wound down many of its factory cells and newspapers, ending independent propaganda among workers.

The capitalist counteroffensive and the transformation of the CPUSA

Roosevelt had tacked to the left in 1936 because the capitalist class had deserted him. Workers responded by giving him another big majority. From autumn 1937, with the economic recovery beginning to slow and with imperialist tensions rising in Europe and the Pacific, Roosevelt shifted sharply to the right. Instead of offering support to those tipped back into poverty and unemployment by the renewed economic downturn, Roosevelt slashed relief and public works programs. He also began to cultivate CIO leaders who were happy to follow the White House – sidelining Lewis, who opposed the president's drive to war.

A defeated steel strike did much to prepare the way for Roosevelt's shift to the right. While the big steel companies had signed CIO recognition agreements, the smaller companies, known collectively as Little Steel, tried to hold the federation at bay. They prepared for a confrontation, recruiting vigilantes and accumulating stockpiles of weapons. The CIO leaders demonstrated no such determination and lulled workers into a false sense of security, telling them that Roosevelt and the Democrat mayors and governors would protect their interests. The CPUSA echoed that line.

The strike at Little Steel broke out in May 1937. At its height, 80,000 workers, including coal miners who struck in solidarity, were involved. But this was a very bureaucratically run strike, a far cry from the Flint sit-down strike. The CIO instructed workers not to occupy the steel mills. The CPUSA simply tailed Lewis. The workers were set up for a loss. Democrat governors sent the National Guard from one steel town to another to break picket lines. The bloodiest episode took place on 30 May, Memorial Day. On the orders of Chicago's Democrat mayor, one of the major figures in Roosevelt's New Deal coalition, police viciously attacked strikers and their families marching to the gates of the Republic Steel plant in South Chicago. Labour historian Art Preis describes the scene:

> The police charged with swinging clubs and blazing guns, beating down or shooting every laggard. In a couple of minutes, ten lay dead or fatally wounded – every one shot in the back. Another 40 bore gunshot wounds – in the back. One hundred and one others were injured by clubs – including an eight year old child.[17]

During the Little Steel strike, 18 workers were killed. Roosevelt turned his back on the workers, saying that both sides were to blame for the bloodshed. The CIO attempt to break into Little Steel went down to defeat, breaking the federation's momentum, emboldening more right wing elements in its leadership and hardening the resolve of anti-union bosses.

The CPUSA's newfound enthusiasm for industrial order brought it into conflict with militants in its own ranks who were keen to maintain the fight against the bosses that had drawn them to the party. The stage was set by the September 1937 UAW national executive meeting, which voted unanimously – CPUSA members included – to inform GM that it could fire any workers engaged in 'unauthorised strikes.' In October, the *Communist* magazine confirmed that the party was against such strikes. The issue came to a head during a five-day struggle at a GM factory in Pontiac, Michigan. Five hundred workers occupied the plant in response to the sacking of four union activists for leading a wildcat strike. One of them, George Method, was a CPUSA member who led a substantial party cell in the plant. The sit-in was condemned by the Democrat Governor and by Lewis. The UAW leadership tried to persuade the strikers to leave the plant but failed. It was the CPUSA which tipped the balance. The party had initially supported the sit-in; but, with the Democrat establishment, including the *New York Times*, turning the screws on the party and alleging that the CPUSA was stirring up industrial lawlessness, the CPUSA capitulated. Browder personally ordered the CPUSA auto work fraction to end the occupation. Method convinced the workers to vacate the plant. Within an hour, they were out, the strike lost. The *Daily Worker* argued that such strikes 'only play into the hands of the bosses.'[18]

By 1938, some CPUSA militants had quit in disgust at the party's turn away from class struggle. But most remained. The party had tripled in size to 84,000 members and had become a powerful force in the labour movement, with members in mid-level and leading positions in important unions. Many militants saw no feasible alternative to the CPUSA. The Trotskyists had grown in the 1930s but were only a small fraction of the size of the CPUSA, and the Socialist Party's electoral orientation made it irrelevant as an industrial force. There was also a real pull on many Communists: the lure of a job in the CIO bureaucracy for those who toed the party line. Outside the maritime industry, the CPUSA's union presence was now less dependent on mass membership strength than on control over the union machinery, resulting in what Mike Davis calls the 'paradoxical process of simultaneous growth and relative "deproletarianization"' of the party.[19]

Popular Front politics drove other changes in the party's orientation. In African American struggles, the CPUSA abandoned its orientation to poor and working class Blacks and focused instead on middle class Blacks. Those prepared to swallow the twists and turns of the party line went from being militant champions of sit-down struggles to cogs in the Democratic Party machine. The CPUSA had championed women's economic independence and sexual equality; now it proclaimed itself 'staunch upholders of the family.' The CPUSA once rhetorically proclaimed its internationalism (although contaminated by loyalty to Stalin's Russia). Now it wrapped itself in the Stars and Stripes. Communists such as Harry Bridges, who had once led heroic strikes, now advocated no-strike agreements. The CPUSA began for the first time to recruit significant numbers of middle class professionals who were attracted by its new respectability and its claim to be the party of collective defence against fascism. Professionals who found CPUSA membership a step too far formed a significant periphery of fellow travellers prepared to contribute financially or to write for party journals.[20]

Following the outbreak of World War II, before the US enlisted as a combatant, the CPUSA continued to lead strikes. After Russia's entry into the conflict in June 1941, the party dramatically changed course; it now took to breaking strikes and pushing speed-ups. There was no working class principle the CPUSA would not abandon in its enthusiasm for the war. It backed the FBI prosecution of the leaders of the Trotskyist Socialist Workers Party (SWP), including those who had led the Minneapolis strikes in 1934, on charges of sedition and conspiracy to overthrow the federal government. It cheered the internment of tens of thousands of Japanese Americans as a potential 'enemy within.' At war's end, the CPUSA backed the atomic bombing of Hiroshima and Nagasaki. To emphasise its patriotism, Browder renamed the party the American Communist Party. He then dissolved the organisation into the 'Communist Political Association,' which was meant to operate as a ginger group on the periphery of the Democrats. In an attempt to ingratiate itself with the White House, the CPUSA proposed at the end of the war that the CIO continue its wartime no-strike pledge. This sharp jag to the right alienated wide layers of militant workers and allowed politically conservative forces, such as the Association of Catholic Trade Unionists and the UAW's Reuther brothers, once Socialist Party members but now themselves shifting to the right, to outflank the CPUSA in their support for strikes during and after the war.

After the war, with a Cold War atmosphere developing rapidly, the CPUSA fell victim to the very forces that it had spent years cultivating. With the tide in society running strongly to the right, the CIO purged Communists from its ranks, banning them from holding official positions. Thousands of party members, along with socialists of all descriptions, were sacked from their jobs and hounded to the margins of political life. In 1949, the CPUSA leaders were prosecuted and jailed under the same sedition laws that they had supported when they were used against the SWP. Because the CPUSA had lost the goodwill of many thousands of militants during the war in its strikebreaking role, it found few militants prepared to defend it now that it too was under the hammer. The left in the US labour movement, unlike the Western European or the Australasian, was more or less wiped out as a result, a situation from which it has still not recovered many decades later.

Conclusion

Contrary to Democrat mythology, the gains won by US workers in the 1930s did not originate in the goodwill of the Roosevelt administration. It was mass disruptive working class action, under the leadership of radicals, combined with the fear that US capitalism could be destabilised by a revolt from below, that underpinned Roosevelt's reforms. These reforms were designed to save the system, not to threaten it; not to stimulate workers' struggle, but to dissipate it. They aimed to replace the picket line by arbitration, the wildcat strike by orderly collective bargaining, and the demand for worker control on the shopfloor by a few dollars extra in the pay packet. By the late 1940s, the project had been successful. CIO leaders happily took their allotted place as 'labour statesmen' in the new environment of formal 'dispute resolution' procedures which snuffed out any element of rank and file insurgency and union democracy.

The experience of the 1930s demonstrates that the US working class is not irredeemably right wing. It also demonstrates the need for a political leadership prepared to take the mounting radicalisation among substantial numbers of militants as far as it can go. Workers won some reforms – but far fewer than a more thoroughgoing anti-capitalist offensive could have yielded. The political situation in the US in the 1930s was not one where revolution was on the cards, but workers owed their inability to move their struggle beyond a certain point to the CPUSA. The party was willing to fight, but only to the point where class struggle ran up against the interests of the Democrats. Then, it threw the struggle into reverse gear for the sake of its Popular Front allies. When the opportunity came for a serious industrial and political breakthrough, the CPUSA held it back. The party was certainly larger and more influential by the end of the decade, but it used the authority it had won in the class struggle in the first half of the decade to wind struggle back, sacrificing rank and file organising to the project of building a political bloc with the Roosevelt administration. Internationalism was abandoned for nationalism. The CPUSA helped to give the US ruling class a new lease of life after one of its biggest frights in many decades.

FURTHER READING

M. Davis, *Prisoners of the American Dream*, London, Verso, 1986.

D. Guérin, *100 Years of Labor in the USA*, London, Ink Links, 1979.

D. Milton, *The Politics of US Labor: From the Great Depression to the New Deal*, New York, Monthly Review Press, 1982.

C. Post, 'The New Deal and the Popular Front: Models for contemporary socialists?', *International Socialist Review*, no. 108, 2018.

A. Preis, *Labor's Giant Step: Twenty Years of the CIO*, New York, Pathfinder, 1972.

S. Smith, *Subterranean Fire: A History of Working Class Radicalism in the United States*, Haymarket Books, 2006.

13.

SALUTING THE FLAG: AUSTRALIAN COMMUNISTS DURING WORLD WAR II

The Communist Party of Australia, like the CPUSA, enjoyed a brief interregnum between the abandonment of 'social fascism' and the adoption of the Popular Front.[1] For a period, the CPA took advantage of a more favourable industrial climate in the early to mid-1930s to engage in united front work in the trade unions and to build up a profile for its members as serious militants. The introduction of Popular Front, however, saw the party swing sharply to the right. With the signing of the Stalin–Hitler pact in 1939, the CPA moved back to the 'left' again. Two years later, that switch was again reversed and an even more right wing version of the Popular Front was imposed. The CPA now enthusiastically backed the war it had just been denouncing and used its influence in the unions to try to smash strikes that threatened Australia's war effort.

No part of the CPA's cynical, right-left-right zigzagging in the 1930s and 1940s had anything to do with the needs of workers in Australia or internationally. It was the Stalinist bureaucracy in Moscow that was pulling the CPA's strings. The party drew to it many thousands of worker militants in this period, many of them sincere socialists who believed that the CPA stood in the traditions of the Russian Bolsheviks, and abused their trust. The CPA turned their class conscious instincts against them and trained them to jump to Stalin's orders.

Communists in the unions in the 1930s

As Australia began to pull out of the Great Depression in 1933–34, CPA activists who had earned valuable political experience organising the unemployed now began to find jobs. The mood in the working class also began to lift;

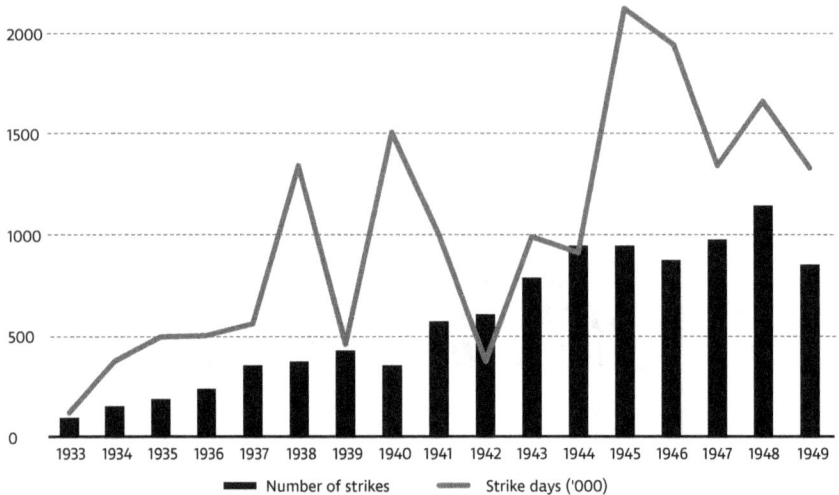

Figure 1. Strikes in Australia, 1933 to 1949. After S. Deery and D. Plowman, *Australian Industrial Relations*, Sydney, McGraw-Hill, 1985, p. 57.

as the lines of the unemployed grew shorter, workers began to lift their heads again and strikes started to rise (Figure 1).

The CPA made its first breakthrough in the coal mines, a traditional hotbed of industrial militancy. Following the union's heavy defeat in 1930, the Miners' Federation leaders hunkered down during the Depression, hoping only to survive. Strikes plunged. But some in the union wanted a more aggressive policy. This was embodied in the rise of the Militant Minority (MM), particularly in Lithgow in the Federation's NSW Western District, where Communists Bill Orr and Charlie Nelson won a high profile for fighting for the miners.

Consistent work by the MM also saw it recruit coal miners in the South Gippsland town of Wonthaggi in Victoria. In 1932, MM activist and CPA member Idris Williams won the vice presidency of the 1,300-strong branch. Local Communists readied themselves for a big fight with the Liberal state government, which owned the mine through the Victorian Railways. The fight came in March 1934. Mine management had already sacked hundreds of workers during the Depression; now, they dismissed still more and threatened further wage cuts. The workers struck, demanding reversal of the dismissals and the introduction of pit committees to stop management sacking workers at will.

The Wonthaggi strike, which lasted more than four months, was a model of rank and file organisation. The workers set up a strike committee to control the dispute. Many of the committee's 60 members were MM members, and CPA member Tom Currie was elected secretary. Two hundred miners were drawn into strike organising. The strike became a beacon for militants across the country who understood that a victory at Wonthaggi could begin to turn back the tide of years of defeats and retreat. In the fourth month of the dispute, with Orr threatening a national strike, Robert Menzies, Victorian Attorney General, gave way. The workers did not win everything, but the outcome was a big step forward. For the first time in years, a union had emerged from a strike stronger. The MM swept the polls in the subsequent union elections, and the CPA established a strong branch in the town.

The win at Wonthaggi was a springboard for further advances in the Miners' Federation. Under the leadership of Orr and Nelson, who had taken the top two spots in the national union, the Federation was revived as a fighting force. A big industrial campaign in 1937–38, including a six-week strike, won sweeping gains unprecedented in any other industry, including abolition of Saturday morning shifts, 10 days' annual leave and a 40-hour week for underground workers.

The MM also campaigned vigorously among cane cutters and mill workers in the North Queensland sugar industry. Sugar workers faced opposition from the bosses, the industrial court, the Forgan-Smith Labor government and the right wing AWU, which worked hand in hand with the bosses to stamp out militancy. The MM set up branches in all the region's sugar towns and called its first conference in Innisfail, aiming to bring rank and file activists together. The issue that fired up the workers was the sugar bosses' refusal to burn the cane fields to kill rats, which carried deadly Weil's disease. This infection afflicted hundreds of cane cutters and had killed at least 15. In 1934, the MM branches in the sugar industry led workers out on strike, first in Ingham and then in other towns, forcing the bosses to burn the cane. One important element of the strike was the MM's willingness to combat the racist tactics of the bosses, who had long played the Italian and British workers off against each other. The AWU had done nothing to combat this. The MM, by contrast, emphasised the need for workers' unity and provided translators at meetings. All workers were informed and involved.

In 1935, the battle in North Queensland between the MM and AWU resumed when the sugar bosses reneged on an earlier agreement and refused to burn the cane. The MM took up the fight, again organising strikes by cane cutters and mill hands and mobilising supporters in the sugar towns to provide food and supplies for the strikers. Alarmed at the strike's success, the bosses arranged to have the state government send hundreds of extra police to the region. The bosses also sent scabs to work the sugar mills and evicted the cane cutters from their barracks. The Forgan-Smith government rushed through laws making it an offence to 'incite' anyone to take part in an illegal strike. With scabs breaking the pickets under police protection, the strike committee eventually recommended a return to work to limit victimisation, and the strike ended after two bitter months. However, the bosses had been warned that any further refusal to burn the cane might lead to a revival of unrest. In 1936, the Arbitration Court ordered the bosses to burn the cane from then on.

During the Comintern's ultra left phase, the CPA had routinely denounced the union leaders as 'social fascists.' As the party began to abandon ultra leftism, however, another problem emerged – opportunism. The union leaders, the CPA now began to argue, could be won over:

> The Communists must learn to be more flexible, to adopt better tactics... And to exert every effort to win to our side the union officials who are honest and sincere, but who, maybe are still steeped in a whole series of reformist illusions, habit and customs.[2]

What of those who were not 'honest and sincere'? The solution was for the CPA to throw them out and take their place. Richard Dixon told the Central Committee at the end of 1934: 'The trade unions are the key to the whole present situation in Australia and we can capture a number of trade unions in this country.'[3] Success in the Miners' Federation revealed a genuine opportunity to do this in the mid-1930s. Workers were keen to take advantage of falling unemployment, demanding pay rises. A generation of older officials were retiring, allowing Communist candidates to garner rank and file support and win leadership positions in several important unions. In 1934, Lloyd Ross was appointed secretary of the NSW branch of the Australian Railways Union (ARU). Two years later, Tom Wright was elected secretary of the Sheet Metal Workers' Union. Ernie Thornton won the position of Federated Ironworkers' Association (FIA) general secretary. In 1937, Jim Healy was elected general secretary of the Waterside Workers' Federation (WWF). E. V. Elliott rose to become Queensland branch secretary of the Seamen's Union (and general secretary in 1941). J. J. Brown became Victorian ARU secretary in 1942. Communists made inroads in the NSW Teachers Federation. By 1937, 29 Communists held full-time union posts, and one-quarter of the party's national membership held executive or local union positions. In five years, the CPA's position in the unions had been transformed.

Transformation of the CPA's position in the unions affected its internal life. CPA coverage of industrial issues increasingly focused on the exploits of union leaders. The party abandoned the MM, aiming now to build a 'majority movement' – but on a passive, mostly electoral basis. The party no longer called incessantly for general strikes; the approach now was more geared towards industrial arbitration, peaceful resolution of disputes and 'bread and butter' demands. In pursuing 'pragmatism,' the new CPA union leaders several times – in the Miners' Federation and the Waterside Workers' Federation – came up against rank and file militants with the bit between their teeth. This tendency to conservatism was much exaggerated by the party's Popular Front turn in 1936.

Collective security and the CPA

Historically, the CPA had maintained that war was caused by capitalism and was used to turn the workers of the combatant nations against each other. Ralph Gibson told an audience in Melbourne in 1933: 'When we are called on to fight for King and Country we are called on to follow our enemies and shoot our friends.'[4] The CPA should, therefore, seek every opportunity to turn an imperialist war into a civil war, with soldiers turning their guns on their officers. The capitalists had to be overthrown and an Australian Soviet Republic established. That rhetoric suited Stalin's needs at that time. In the mid-1930s, however, with Moscow seeking an alliance with Britain against Germany, 'collective security' was the need of the hour. Initially, this was expressed as a desire for peace. Very quickly, it became converted into a demand that Australia prepare for war with Germany. The ruling classes of non-fascist countries such as Australia were now regarded as potential allies (even if a significant minority were sympathetic to fascism).[5] The British empire, whose bloody crimes the CPA had long highlighted and campaigned against, was now described as a force for peace.

Populism now predominated. Gone were references to class war against exploitative Australian capitalists; in came the struggle by 'the Australian people' against a small clique of robbers. The problem, the CPA determined, was 'the monopolies' or 'the twenty families' that owned Australia, a small clique of super rich. Against these, the CPA now ranged not only the working class but the 'progressive and democratic people,' estimated by the party as 90 percent of the population and including farmers, shopkeepers, small businessmen, teachers, civil servants and other professionals.

Class peace changed the CPA's attitude to the ALP. During the Depression, the party had denounced Labor as social fascists. At the 1937 federal election the CPA campaigned heavily for Labor, issuing three million leaflets and putting up 150,000 posters in support of Labor's candidates. Unlike the Communists in France and Spain, the CPA was far too small to actually bring a 'people's government' to power, so it sought to push the ALP into forming a government that included a wide range of middle class and capitalist parties. Richard Dixon named them as: 'groups in the Country Party which are in opposition to the reactionary groups which betray the farmers' and 'the middle classes in the cities and the towns and their organisations and also groups in the UAP who are discontented with their leadership.' The main obstacle to bringing the Popular Front to fruition, the CPA complained, was the unhelpful attitude of some ALP figures, who 'instead of taking the course of working to achieve agreement with the malcontents of the UAP and the Country Party, set out to abuse them and prevent agreement.'[6]

During the Third Period, the CPA had claimed to be the embodiment of the revolutionary aspirations of the working class, even as it pursued policies that directly prevented their realisation. The Popular Front saw such claims consigned to history. At the party's Twelfth Congress in 1938, Sharkey declared the CPA's support for the 'parliamentary road to socialism':

> Thereby, the Communist Party declares its faith that the majority of the Australian people can be won for the defence of democracy, for the struggle for the interests of all toilers, for the defence of peace and finally for the great change from capitalism to socialism through democratic means.[7]

'Let it be known definitely once and for all,' Victorian state secretary Jack Blake told the Congress, 'the Communist party is not and never has been an advocate of force and violence.'[8]

Working through 'democratic means' – the Australian state – inevitably meant adopting Australian nationalism. The CPA, its leaders boasted, had become an 'Australian party par excellence, the real inheritor of the true Australianism of the spirit of the fathers of democracy' – a category that included the reactionary Henry Parkes, 19th century liberal parliamentary reformers, the Anzacs and the Eureka rebels! The working class was no longer brothers and sisters of no country but 'the only consistent champion of patriotism.'[9] Class rhetoric was junked: Victorian paper *Workers' Voice* became the *Guardian*, while the national paper *Workers' Weekly* was rebadged *Tribune*, 'the people's paper,' with its hammer and sickle shorn from the masthead.

As was the case with the other Western Communist parties during the

Popular Front years, the CPA began to cast its net wider, attracting middle class liberals who had steered clear of the party when it was widely seen as an outlaw outfit, membership of which would involve social ostracism and an end to career ambitions. Sharkey made this pitch to them:

> You will not be asked to expose yourself to victimisation, nor have to spend all your time on Party work. The Party is 'growing up' and the old harmful 'leftism', as it will, in inner-Party life of the past, has been largely abolished.[10]

While some in Sharkey's target audience of professors and church leaders would join, most would not. The party nonetheless cultivated them as 'fellow travellers,' sympathisers who could play a useful role in broadening the appeal of the CPA's various front groups and helping to create pro-Russian sentiment in Australia. As middle class layers drawn to 'order,' they admired what they saw as the planned nature of the Russian state, where the state directed citizens to strive for collective goals. Some of them toured Russia and, having been exposed to a highly selective experience, enthused about the achievements of the new order on their return. They even expressed approval of the Moscow show trials. The party became more attractive to this layer at this time because it rested on the laurels of 1917 while burying its revolutionary lessons.

While the CPA advocated peace with 'progressive capitalists' and good relations with middle class professionals, it ferociously attacked Stalin's enemies, anyone who would not bend to Moscow. CPA leaders had already used the 'Trotskyite' label to demonise those within the party who would not fall into line. Now, with the Moscow Trials underway and the Comintern instructing sections to drive out the 'Trotsky-fascist menace,' the CPA turned up its abuse of real and alleged Trotskyists. It faithfully transmitted the Moscow line about world events. In May 1937, as the PCE and Russian agents smashed the POUM in Barcelona and executed its leaders, *Workers' Weekly* headlined its coverage: 'Barcelona crushes Trotsky fascists.' It alleged that the POUM was in league with Franco. In 1938, a new constitution was drawn up which barred members from maintaining any political or personal friendships with confirmed Trotskyists.

The CPA zigzags on the war

When war between Britain and Germany broke out in September 1939, the CPA received no instructions from Moscow. Left to its own devices, it followed its Popular Front instincts, calling for the victory of the 'democratic powers' against fascism and urging the dispatch of an Australian expeditionary force to Europe. The Stalin–Hitler pact made this position untenable, since Germany was Stalin's new ally. In October, Moscow imposed a change of line: Comintern sections in the Allied countries were to stridently oppose the war. The CPA quickly switched tack and declared the war in Europe 'an unjust, reactionary imperialist war.'[11] It condemned the suggestion (advocated a mere three weeks earlier) that Australian troops be sent to help Britain. By the beginning of 1940, the new line was well established. Dixon stated:

> To this war the working class can have only one attitude – that of resolute determination to seize upon every opportunity to hasten the overthrow of the capitalist system and the establishment of socialism.[12]

From praising the peace-loving British empire, the CPA reverted to denouncing its crimes, vowing that Australian workers should not shed one drop of blood for Britain's war ambitions. The CPA's new position superficially resembled Lenin's internationalist position during World War I – that communists must campaign to turn the imperialist war into a civil war against the capitalists. However, it was not motivated by internationalism, but by Russia's desire to undermine the Allied war effort against Germany and promote its own imperialist bid for territory. The CPA cast Russia's seizure of territory in Finland, Poland and Romania as 'self-defence.' Some members found this too much and quit the party in disgust; others, who continued to object to the Stalin–Hitler pact, were expelled.

Although the CPA's opposition to the war was adopted for cynical reasons of Russian realpolitik, it resonated with the working class. Workers had bitter memories of the terrible sacrifices endured during World War I and the years of hardship during the Depression. Few workers had starry-eyed notions of martial glory or faith in a better life at war's end. There was also a strong nationalist and isolationist sentiment in the labour movement, a belief that wars in far-off Europe on behalf of the British empire were of no concern for Australia – particularly not for Irish Australians, who formed the bedrock of Labor's support base. Worker militants knew that the Menzies federal government's anti-fascist pretensions were just that – pretensions. This attitude underpinned the NSW Labor Council decision on 7 September 1939 to support the declaration of war but to express no confidence in the government:

> The present Government which supported the appeasement

policy, encouraging Hitler fascism to develop its aggression leading to the present war, cannot be entrusted with the task of conducting this war in the interests of Australian democracy.[13]

Opposition leader John Curtin, who had been jailed in World War I for opposing conscription, enthusiastically supported the new war, but met opposition from within the federal Labor caucus. At Easter 1940, the NSW state Labor conference declared for an immediate end to hostilities. Two weeks later, FIA leader Ernie Thornton moved a similar motion at the ACTU Congress and saw it fail by just two votes. Such was the social climate in the first months of the war, and enlistment in the armed forces was accordingly slow.

The demand for military supplies drew workers off the dole queues and into jobs. Workers took advantage of the new conditions. The number of strike days rose sharply (see Figure 1). In March 1940, coal miners undertook a two-month strike and achieved the 40-hour week that had been promised after the 1938 strikes. Waterside workers were next to mobilise, striking against an adverse Arbitration Court decision by Justice Beeby, the same judge who had savaged their conditions in 1928. The wharfies were successful this time around. Iron workers, like the coal miners and waterside workers led by CPA officials, went on strike repeatedly. Textile workers followed. Attempts by the press to turn the public against the strikers, on the grounds that they were jeopardising the war effort, had little success.

In June 1940, the Menzies government charged the CPA leadership with sedition and banned the party, along with the Trotskyist Communist League. It suppressed the CPA's publications and raided its offices and members' homes, driving the leadership underground. Many party members resisted state persecution valiantly. They saw in Menzies the personification of the fascist threat to the working class, and they were not alone in this view. Dissatisfaction with the Menzies government saw CPA parliamentary candidates fare quite well, winning many thousands of votes at the September 1940 federal election and March 1941 Queensland state election. In May 1941, when two Communists, Horace Ratliff and Max Thomas, were sentenced to internment for printing leaflets denouncing the war, 50,000 workers in Communist-led unions struck for a day in their defence. The party suffered some losses after being declared illegal but very soon began to grow steadily.[14]

Once Germany invaded Russia in June 1941, the CPA did another U-turn. No longer was it an imperialist conflict; it was now a just 'people's war.' The *Communist Review* asserted:

> The greatest battle of all history has been joined! The battle of darkness against light, night against day, death against life.

The CPA's duty was now to throw all its efforts behind the war: 'To achieve this victory [of Russia], every nerve must be strained, all else must be subordinated.'[15]

Rank and file party members were not enthusiastic about the change of line, which sounded like warmongering and support for imperialism. Historian Beverley Symons argues: 'It was not easy to overcome the problem of the CPA's virulent opposition to the war for the last year and a half.'[16]

Workers' attitudes towards the war shifted from the middle of 1941 because of three factors. The first was the accession to office of the Curtin Labor government in October 1941. Labor had advantages over the hated Menzies government in winning working class support for the war. Curtin had been an anti-war activist during World War I and was not tainted by pro-fascist sympathies. Labor's connections with the unions meant that workers were far more likely to trust Curtin than Menzies. The second factor was Japan's attack on Pearl Harbour in December 1941, quickly followed by its capture of Singapore and bombing of Darwin. Aware that workers had not been particularly concerned by conflicts in Europe, the Curtin government turned to the red herring of a Japanese invasion to convince the population to support the war effort. There was little in this propaganda about fighting fascism; the 'yellow peril' was the theme, a trope deeply entrenched in the country's history as a white colonial settler state in Asia. The Curtin government ran newspaper advertisements declaring of the Japanese: 'We've always despised them, now we must smash them.'[17] Australian Imperial Force (AIF) commanding officer General Blamey, who appeared in Chapter 9 as Victorian Police Commissioner and leader of the White Army during the Depression, called the Japanese soldier a 'subhuman beast' and described the Japanese nation as representing a cross between human beings and apes.[18] The third factor that shifted working class attitudes to the war was Russia's entry into the conflict and the sympathy that still existed among many workers for Russia: it now seemed that Australia was fighting a war alongside Russia against fascism.

The Curtin government took full advantage of this stirring of enthusiasm for the war within the working class. It introduced conscription for service outside Australia, something that the Menzies government had not dared to attempt. With prominent leftist Eddie Ward as Minister of Labour, the Curtin government was able to persuade unions to agree to work intensification and dilution of skilled labour. In the short term, the strike rate dropped. The bosses producing military supplies for the armed forces made money hand over fist on cost-plus contracts.

Debunking the myths about the war

What was wrong with the CPA's support for the Allied war effort? World War II is popularly believed to have been the 'Good War,' a war for democracy, often contrasted with the previous major imperialist war – a tragic waste of human life with no redeeming features. One reason for this popular support for World War II is that the Left at the time backed it and, for the most part, continues to do so. The 'Good War' argument suggests that the threat posed to the world democratic order by the fascist and militarist Axis powers was so great that the Left had no alternative but to rally around the flag and back the war effort.

The case for the 'Good War' does not stand up to close scrutiny. It was not a war for democracy; this is very easily demonstrated by the disregard most of the Allied powers had for it. Britain and France possessed vast empires whose subjects had very few or no democratic rights, including most obviously the right to decide who governed their country. The US may not have run a formal empire, but it dominated whole swathes of Central and Latin America and the Caribbean, along with the Philippines. The US propped up dictatorships and regularly invaded countries in its sphere of influence to enforce its interests; in the case of the Philippines, this resulted in one million deaths. At home, the US ruling class ran a reign of terror against Blacks in the South. During the war, the Roosevelt administration interned 120,000 Japanese Americans in concentration camps. Russia, Britain's ally after June 1941, was run by a bloody dictatorship that had spent the previous decade wiping out any remnant of democracy. Chiang Kai-shek's Chinese government, another Anglo-American ally, was so corrupt that the country was rising up against him. The Allies had few compunctions about the regimes with which they were allied, including the Greek dictatorship, which expressed its open admiration for Hitler and Mussolini; Britain's main ambition in the war in the Eastern Mediterranean was to put the Greek king back on his throne.

The Allies also had an utterly cynical approach to self-determination. In August 1941, British Prime Minister Winston Churchill and US President Roosevelt signed the Atlantic Charter, in which they pledged to respect 'the right of all peoples to choose the form of government under which they will live.' Later, Stalin also declared 'full adhesion of the Soviet Union to the principles of the Atlantic Charter.' But Churchill was adamant that the Charter did not apply to India; and, at the Yalta conference in 1945, he insisted that it exclude the entire British empire. Russia was equally opposed to self-determination. What was called the 'Soviet Union' was not a voluntary federation of republics, but an internal empire dominated by Russia. Russia's annexation of Poland and the Baltic states in 1939 showed what Stalin thought of national self-determination and, by war's end, Russia's sphere of influence had extended much further across the European continent. In standing up to Japanese imperialist aggression, Britain and the US were happy to overlook its atrocities in China so long as the rising Asian power did not threaten British possessions.

Nor was it an anti-fascist war. Senior figures in the British and Australian ruling establishments expressed sympathy for Hitler and Mussolini during the 1930s. Roosevelt wrote that he was 'deeply impressed by what [Mussolini] has accomplished and by his evidenced honest purpose of restoring Italy and seeking to prevent general European trouble.'[19] Britain and France had had every opportunity to fight fascism in Spain in 1936; instead, they held back and allowed Franco to impose a dictatorship, while Stalin's Russia destroyed the anti-fascist fight from the inside. Following the German invasion, many in the French ruling class were happy to serve under the collaborationist Vichy regime.

The war was not, therefore, one to save democracy or smash fascism. Rather, it arose from increasing tensions between the imperialist powers, old and new, after the Great Depression. The collapse of world trade in the early 1930s drove the ruling classes to build protectionist blocs to defend their weakened economies. Inevitably, economic competition burst into open warfare to grab markets and territory from rival states. Britain and France sought to defend their positions by closing off trade in their blocs. This put pressure on Japan and Germany, who could only get access to markets and raw materials by challenging the existing imperialist balance of power. This explains Japan's invasion of China and Germany's seizure of Sudetenland. Eventually, there had to be an armed clash between the imperialists.

Britain and France, victors of World War I but economically weaker than before, sought desperately to cling to their empires. They were thus able to pass themselves off as 'reasonable' countries seeking to avoid war. Germany and Japan struggled against the stranglehold of the more established imperialists. The US and Russia, for their part, angled to take advantage of conflicts to build their own empires. The US only agreed to enter the war on Britain's side in late 1941 after it was agreed that the British empire would be dismantled after the war. The US considered Russia as much a threat to its interests as

Germany. Vice President Harry Truman declared in June 1941, when war broke out between Germany and Russia:

> If we see that Germany is winning, we ought to help Russia, and if Russia is winning, we ought to help Germany, and in that way let them kill as many as possible.[20]

The US was happy to allow Germany to seize territory, but when it became obvious that a German conquest of Europe would eventually lead to a German advance into Africa, Asia and Latin America and, ultimately, to an attack on the US itself, the US prepared to fight.

In the Pacific theatre, only when Japan began to encroach on Western possessions in Shanghai and then Indochina did the US and other Western powers grow alarmed. Roosevelt's problem was that there was little domestic appetite for another war. The president had to invent a pretext, something that would galvanise the population behind the war effort. Simply attacking Japan without any obvious provocation was not going to win popular support. Goading Japan into attacking the US was the solution. In July 1941, the US, which supplied 80 percent of Japan's oil needs, imposed an oil blockade, adding to a string of sanctions it had introduced since 1938. To rise as an imperialist power, Japan needed access to oil; with US supplies cut off, that meant annexing the oil-rich Dutch East Indies. But that would involve an attack on the Philippines, a US colony in all but name, which lay between the two countries. To succeed in this venture, Japan must firstly destroy US naval power. In December 1941, Japan attacked Pearl Harbour, home to America's Pacific fleet. With the fleet lying in ruins, Roosevelt clearly had his *casus belli*, and the US joined the Pacific War with the backing of the immense majority of the US public.

This is the context for Australia's involvement in the Pacific War. Australia was no innocent party, a helpless and peaceful victim of Japanese aggression. As a white dominion in the Asia-Pacific, Australia supported European colonialism, particularly British colonialism, seeing in it the best guarantee of its own security. It was itself a rising imperialist power in the Pacific. At the time of the outbreak of war, Australia effectively controlled and exploited New Guinea, Nauru and Fiji. Like the US, Australia was deeply concerned about the Japanese threat to the existing imperial structures of domination in the Asia-Pacific, but the Curtin government could hardly use defence of French colonialism in Indochina or Dutch colonialism in the East Indies as the basis for Australia's involvement in the war. The threat of Japanese invasion of

Australia, however, was quite different. This was a cynical propaganda campaign. The Curtin government continued to invoke that threat for the next 18 months, despite receiving intelligence by May 1942 that the Japanese high command had rejected any plan to invade Australia, and even after Japanese reversals at the battles of Midway and the Coral Sea in May–June 1942 had halted any further Japanese naval advance in the Pacific.[21] Australia's Pacific War was as much an imperialist venture as Japan's.

The CPA promotes the war effort

None of this mattered to the CPA. Under orders from Moscow, it aggressively encouraged the war effort, arguing that 'In the prosecution of a just war…it is obvious that *the working class must become the leading force.*'[22] Communists threw their energies into the home front: sending comfort parcels to the armed forces; selling war bonds; serving in rural fire brigades; and mobilising labour for fruit canning. The CPA supported Curtin's introduction of conscription for service outside Australia, denouncing opposition to it from within some quarters of the ALP. In the factories and mines, on the waterfront and in the merchant marine, the CPA did its best to increase productivity – whatever the cost to workers. CPA union leaders enthusiastically joined industry commissions set up by the Curtin government to boost output. The Miners' Federation, for example, accepted cancellation of holidays, suspension of compulsory retirement and introduction of extra shifts in certain mines. The miners' leaders spoke so often of the need to avoid strikes that historian of the union Robin Gollan argues: 'By 1945 the leadership was regarded by many miners as a bureaucracy which was failing to protect the interests of miners.'[23] The shop committees built by the CPA in the 1930s to advance workers' struggle now subverted it.

The Curtin government rewarded the party for its support, easing the Menzies government's strictures. After the CPA signed an undertaking with Attorney-General Bert Evatt, promising to 'do its utmost to promote harmony in industry, to minimise absenteeism, stoppages, strikes or other hold-ups,'[24] Curtin lifted the ban on the party altogether in December 1942. The CPA continued to talk of internationalism but became a super-nationalist party, flying the Australian and British flags alongside the Russian at its rallies and opening its congresses with 'Advance Australia Fair.'

The party did not successfully quash all industrial militancy. When the invasion scare of 1942 passed, strikes quickly recovered. At Austral Bronze in Sydney in 1943, management tried to introduce a speed-up scheme, and the workers struck. Communist FIA officials led strikebreakers onto the job. The engineers' union refused to work with the scabs, and the strikebreaking move collapsed.

Militant coal miners openly defied Miners' Federation and government attempts to stop strikes. In May 1942, the coal owners, the Miners' Federation and the Curtin government drafted the Canberra Code, giving the Federation legal sanction to expel striking members. Those strikers who persisted could be drafted into military service. Curtin stated that stoppages amounted to treason, prompting police prosecutions and fines. Nothing worked, however; the number of strikes in the coal mines rose every year throughout the war. Miners' Federation officials admitted that they could never convince some of the militants that the war was anything other than a bosses' war.[25]

The CPA's patriotic fervour extended to the armed forces, where 1,500 party members enlisted. The CPA did its best to enhance military effectiveness. The *Communist Review* stated in January 1942:

> Above all, our work in the armed forces is positive work which must be concerned with getting rid of antiquated methods of training, incompetency, inefficiency, and undemocratic methods on the part of sections of the commanding staff. Our object is to play our part in transforming our soldiers, airmen and sailors into first class fighting forces capable of dealing devastating blows against Nazi Germany and its allies.[26]

The party started to raise its profile by surreptitiously circulating leaflets in army camps. These demanded improvements in conditions, greater accountability of officers and the establishment of committees to organise sporting and cultural activities and to discuss grievances. Members distributed Communist literature, ran study circles and set up some unit newspapers. On the Atherton Tablelands in North Queensland, the CPA was even able to hold an interdivisional conference of 60 delegates. In the 9th AIF division in Palestine, the CPA recruited several hundred members and raised funds to send home to the party. In Papua New Guinea, CPA members in the armed forces used their experience in conducting illegal work to issue leaflets, coordinate protests about conditions, recruit to the party, sell *Tribune*, run classes on political economy and raise funds. When the war ended, the CPA played a leading role in organising protests by soldiers demanding to be sent home; the army command was using the available shipping to transport equipment back to Australia.

Much of this work was illegal, breaching army protocols. It was certainly far more aggressive than anything the CPUSA would sanction: the US party regarded strikes to win better conditions on base as 'traitorous.' Some of this work had a progressive edge; for example, the CPA fought for equal pay for women and took a stand against racist treatment of Aboriginal, Torres Strait Islander and African American personnel. The party's work in the military netted it 2,500 new members.

The officers mostly turned a blind eye to this activity, because it was in the service of the war. 'Lifting morale' meant imbuing the soldiers, not with militant class consciousness and hatred towards the officer class, but with readiness to fight Japanese, Italian and German workers in uniform. The party recruited by emphasising its support for the war and the wartime exploits of the Russian army. There was nothing left wing in admiring the Russian war effort. The mainstream media, including the notoriously anti-communist *Sunday Telegraph* and *Sydney Morning Herald*, glorified Stalin's Russia. The Curtin government ordered that the red flag be flown from the Sydney Town Hall and other public buildings in 1941 in honour of its new ally. General Blamey publicly praised the Russian war machine. The CPA was able to hold public forums featuring the Sydney Lord Mayor, a major-general, the Anglican Canon of Sydney, the president of the Rural Bank and the private secretary to Attorney-General Bert Evatt – all calling for support for Russia and the war effort. In February 1942, the CPA invited the NSW Returned Servicemen's League president, Colonel Arthur Hyman, the minister for aircraft production, Senator Don Cameron, and the managing director of military supplier Amalgamated Wireless, Sir Ernest Fisk, to speak at a Congress of National Unity and Allied Victory. Communist author Frank Hardy noted that in these years 'being a communist was as easy as a piece of cake,'[27] because it did not involve standing against your own ruling class.

The CPA fought racism in the armed forces, but it turned a blind eye to national chauvinism when it suited Russian foreign policy, especially around the supposed collective war guilt of the population of the Axis powers from whom Stalin was demanding reparations. In 1944, the CPA's *Guardian* ran the headline: 'Romanians Must Pay for Crimes,' as though Romanian workers were responsible for the war crimes of their rulers. The CPA generally did not go along with the Curtin government's blatant yellow peril racism, but it did support the atomic bombing of Hiroshima and Nagasaki and ran a racist caricature of the Japanese leaders being blown up, with the heading 'Jappy Ending.'

During the war, the CPA dropped its support for national liberation struggles – something which had distinguished it – because they diverted

Allied troops from the fight against the Axis powers. CPA leaders had to explain to the leaders of the Indonesian Communist Party, who were based in Australia following the Japanese invasion of their homeland, why they should support Dutch colonialism in their country. Only when the war was close to victory did the CPA shift back to supporting independence struggles in the Asia-Pacific.

Class struggle on the home front

In 1944, class struggle on the home front began to pick up speed. With many more workers in jobs than at the outset of the war, working class households enjoyed higher incomes, but these came with long hours of overtime and tiring shift work. The Curtin government's wartime regulations froze the real value of the Basic Wage, while the margin for skilled and semi-skilled workers fell in real terms.[28] Income tax, levied on workers for the first time in 1943, cut take-home pay. Working conditions in hastily built factories producing for the war effort were onerous and dangerous. Housing standards declined because money was diverted to war production. Availability of most consumer goods was drastically curtailed by rationing of food and clothing. Black markets favoured the rich in the general search for illegal supplies of controlled commodities, ranging from housing to beer. Faced with these challenges, workers fought for their rights, and strikes increased rapidly. One journalist summarised the situation:

> New South Wales, during the 20 months ending August 31 [1944], had 1,432 industrial disputes [depriving] the neutral citizen of meat, bread, laundry, newspapers, tyres, theatrical entertainment, hospital attention, buses and trams, coke for stoves, potatoes, restaurants, hot baths, country and inter-state travel and other amenities.[29]

The October 1944 Sydney newspaper strike for a 40-hour week and four weeks' leave was a key battle. It was sparked by low-paid women workers brought into the industry during the war and was a decisive victory that paved the way for a 40-hour week for all workers.

Women workers were active elsewhere as well. The government's Women's Employment Bureau had established female wages at 90 percent of the male rate in war-related industries – a significant increase on the previous rate – but bosses found every opportunity to avoid paying the higher rate. Well aware of the labour shortage and their important contribution to the war effort, women workers refused to be fobbed off and walked out on strike. This willingness to have a go was not restricted to women in the strategically important metal industries. In Perth, female textile workers struck in the summer and spring of 1943 over bad conditions and low pay. Nurses employed at Perth's Claremont Hospital, working extremely long hours and subjected to intrusive regulation of their private lives, walked out. Their strike was only for six hours, but its significance in an industry where staff were expected to bear any hardship made it exceptional.

The CPA only maintained support among industrial workers in the later stages of the war because it was prepared to bend to the mood of workers. This distinguished it from the CPUSA, which promoted a rigid anti-strike line throughout the war. Australian CPA union officials did, however, move firmly when they faced a direct political challenge – for example, by the hated Trotskyists, routinely described as 'fascist rats' and 'criminals.' The most striking example of Stalinist thuggery occurred in 1945 on Sydney's Balmain docks in the iron workers' union (FIA).

The CPA, under Ernie Thornton, had won the national leadership of the FIA in 1938. Within four years, it succeeded in winning control over every FIA branch except one. Thornton aimed to transform the union into a top-down monolith run by the national leadership, just like the CPA itself. The one branch not under CPA control was Balmain, the biggest. The Balmain branch was a running sore for the CPA. In its ranks was a smattering of Trotskyists, led by Nick Origlass and Laurie Short, and a number of anti-Stalinist independents. With operations on the Balmain waterfront running at full capacity, workers were in a strong position to make gains via short, snap actions and, in 1943, a five-month overtime ban. The CPA was furious at what it saw as the branch's sabotage of the war effort. An attempt to push the branch leadership out in the 1943 elections failed, with the incumbents defeating a CPA ticket by two to one. The CPA's second try, later that year, was successful: the Stalinists made a clean sweep of the branch executive in a rigged election. The following year saw constant skirmishes between the members, who used direct action to resolve their grievances, and the executive, which was determined to stamp it out. Early in 1945, the Thornton leadership sacked the job delegates, including Origlass and his comrades, and imposed CPA loyalists in their place. Members reacted with fury. Three thousand walked off the job in an unauthorised strike lasting six weeks. This strike not only won Origlass's reinstatement but created a new, independent branch of the FIA, led by Trotskyists and other militants, which lasted for some time after the war.

Balmain was a rare setback. The CPA reached the pinnacle of its size and influence towards the end of the war. Membership had risen from 4,000 in 1940 to 15,000 by 1942 and climbed to 23,000 in January 1945. Relative to population, the CPA was the largest Communist party in the English-speaking world. The party had significant sway within the union bureaucracy: Communists held controlling positions in unions with a membership of 275,000 and had some influence in unions with a membership of 480,000 – 40 percent of all unionists.

The CPA also made electoral inroads for the first time, taking advantage of workers' hopes that the end of the war would see real social change and capitalising on the widespread sympathy for Russia. In 1944, the party made a big push in NSW council elections, running 70 candidates, mostly in working class industrial areas; 16 were elected. The northern coalfields remained a CPA stronghold. In Kearsley, just outside Cessnock, the party won five of the eight seats at the 1944 council elections, the first time Communists had won a majority in municipal government anywhere in the English-speaking world. In neighbouring Lake Macquarie, the CPA won three seats on the council; in Cessnock itself, they won two seats out of nine. The party's other stronghold was North Queensland. In the 1944 state election, the CPA's Fred Paterson won the state seat of Bowen on the back of strong support from sugar workers and mine workers.

The CPA built support beyond blue collar workers. In the early years of the war, when the party was illegal and opposed the war effort, about 70 percent of CPA recruits were factory workers. The lifting of the ban on the party prompted an influx of middle class professionals, attracted by the CPA's apparent anti-fascist credentials and sympathy for Russia and no longer scared away by its outlaw status. The party recruited journalists, teachers, scientists and engineers, university students and intellectuals on the basis of what Ralph Gibson called 'an advanced liberal-democratic rather than a revolutionary outlook.'[30]

Conclusion

The decade reviewed in this chapter demonstrates how the CPA leadership switched direction on Moscow's orders. Dropping the worst of its social fascist line gave the CPA some room to move in the early years; it made ground in the unions on the basis of solid work by rank and file militants. The adoption of Popular Front politics, however, saw the party become class collaborationist, advocating alliances with the ALP and even sections of the UAP. Soon after the Stalin–Hitler pact, the CPA switched course again, leading strikes and rediscovering the crimes of the British empire. Just 18 months later, the

Stalin–Hitler alliance broke down; the CPA was back to saluting the Union Jack alongside the Russian flag.

The CPA's support for World War II was a rejection of the whole socialist, internationalist tradition argued for by Lenin during the previous imperialist war. In World War I, socialists had fought conscription; in World War II, the CPA proudly promoted it. After World War I, anti-war sentiment was widespread – not just within the left but across broader swathes of the working class; the CPA's promotion of the second great imperialist war as a 'people's war,' a 'just war' or 'the good war' allowed the ruling class to undermine opposition to imperialism. The Australian ruling class was able to evoke the supposedly heroic status of World War II to justify future military interventions.

The CPA jettisoned the very principles that created it and so sacrificed its raison d'être. Given the existence of the ALP, why was another, much smaller, nationalist, pro-capitalist party necessary in the labour movement? Dissolution of the party still lay far in the future, but the CPA had taken its first steps down that road.

FURTHER READING

A. Davidson, *History of the Communist Party of Australia*, Stanford, Hoover Institution Press, 1969.

R. Gollan, *Revolutionaries and Reformists: Communism and the Australian Labour Movement 1920–1950*, Sydney, Allen and Unwin, 1975.

H. Greenland, *Red Hot: The Life and Times of Nick Origlass*, Sydney, Wellington Lane Press, 1998.

S. Macintyre, *Reds: The Communist Party of Australia from origins to illegality*, Sydney, Allen and Unwin, 1998.

T. O'Lincoln, *Into the Mainstream*, Melbourne, Red Rag Publications, 2009 [1985].

T. O'Lincoln, *Australia's Pacific War: Challenging a National Myth*, Melbourne, Interventions, 2011.

A. Smith, 'World War II: The Good War', *International Socialist Review*, no. 10, 2000.

14.

ANTI-FASCIST RESISTANCE IN ITALY AND GREECE

Chapter 13 explored the nature of World War II: it was not an anti-fascist war for democracy but a struggle for power between the dominant imperialists and their challengers. At its most general, the war was between the Allied and Axis camps, but within the Allies, a three-way jockeying for power emerged as the US, Britain and Russia argued over spheres of influence. When it became clear that Germany was losing the war, the Allied powers held a series of meetings to divide the spoils. In November 1943, Churchill, Stalin and Roosevelt met in Tehran and agreed on a plan to draw new borders for Europe. In May 1944, the British and Russian governments agreed that Western Europe was to fall into the British and US camp, Eastern and Central Europe into the Russian. In October 1944, Churchill and Stalin met in the Kremlin to draft the notorious 'percentages agreement.' With the stroke of a pen and without any acknowledgement of the wishes of the people, the two imperialists allocated Romania and Bulgaria to the Russians, Greece to the British and Yugoslavia and Hungary to be split 50-50. The division of territories in Europe was confirmed by the three big powers at the Yalta conference in the Crimea in February 1945.

While the Allied leaders were drawing lines on maps, those living under Nazi occupation were fighting for their liberation. In some regions, these struggles took on insurrectionary proportions. Workers were the bedrock of these revolts. They bore the heaviest burden of the war, suffering the sharpest decline in living standards and the heaviest repression. And they despised those ruling classes who collaborated with the Nazi occupation or did nothing to fight it. Allied leaders feared a repeat of the experience during and after World War I, when popular rebellions toppled kings and emperors. The Allies had to collaborate with the Resistance movements for military purposes, but they were wary of them; their desire for a new world order might hinder the imperialists' plans for their countries.

Communist parties played an important role in some of the biggest Resistance movements: building partisan squads, organising unions and leading strikes to fight the occupation. In Italy, workers under Communist leadership mounted the first strikes under Nazi occupation in the whole of Europe. Partisan squads in Italy tied up six German divisions. Backed by partisans, workers went on to free much of the north before the arrival of Allied forces. In Greece, Communist-led armed partisans dominated large swathes of the country. In Athens and the big cities, the organised workers' movement led great strikes which made it hard for the occupation forces and their puppet government to maintain control. In Yugoslavia, Tito's fighters destroyed the German occupation. Because of their leading role, the Communist parties exploded in size, from a few thousand at the beginning of the war to hundreds of thousands, if not millions, by the end. What the Communists did mattered. They held the balance of power.

The Communist parties had no intention of leading revolutions. They led mass Resistance movements whose ranks were inspired by a desire to rid their countries of the old political order that had brought them fascism, hunger, unemployment, war and occupation. This appetite for radical reform, if not revolution, penetrated far into the ranks of the Communist parties and required some acknowledgement by their leaders. But the leaders were also thoroughgoing Stalinists who had embraced the Popular Front in the 1930s. Their objective in occupied Europe was to purge the fascist dictators and monarchs and establish 'people's democracies' run by coalition governments. Communists would divide ministerial portfolios with representatives of the 'progressive capitalists' and the petit bourgeoisie, along with a smattering of university professors, religious leaders and other capitalist worthies.

The Stalinist leaders in the Resistance movements oriented to sections of the Russian ruling class as well as their own. What were Russia's goals as it advanced towards Berlin? One was to destroy local opposition in those countries that now fell within its sphere of influence. When the Russian army marched into Poland in 1944, Stalin ordered his troops to halt outside the capital to allow the Nazis to crush the Warsaw Uprising – at the cost of 150,000 lives. Russian troops entering Germany early in 1945 squelched Communist-led workers' committees that had taken over factories and local government. Chapter 17 will examine more such cases. Russia's second goal was to ensure that the Communist parties dominating the Resistance movements in the countries allocated to the British and US sphere of influence did not threaten the postwar carve-up. Because Stalin wanted Roosevelt and Churchill to confirm Russian control over the East, Stalin had to deliver them the West. That was his message for Communist parties in the relevant countries.

The local Communist leaders in occupied Europe saw themselves as a part of the international Communist movement. This was a movement which had been so seriously Stalinised that most Communist leaders regarded advancing what they saw as communism and defending the national interest of Russia as identical. While the best of the local leaders were not mere pawns of Moscow, they were not for workers taking power. Tito, for example, defied Moscow but still set up a Stalinist regime in Yugoslavia. Popular Front politics and loyalty to Stalin combined to ensure that Western Communist parties did not strive to take power when the Nazis were driven out. They turned their backs on the hopes of millions of workers, peasants and Resistance partisans for a new social and political order.

Two countries where the popular struggle was very advanced, Italy and Greece, demonstrate the Stalinists' counter-revolutionary practice.

ITALY

Italian workers suffered a catastrophic defeat in the 1920s with Mussolini's rise to power. Consequently, it was much harder to organise there in the early years of the war than in the rest of occupied Europe. Resistance only became possible when Italian troops suffered defeats in North Africa in early 1943. The industrial proletariat of Northern Italy were the first to move.[1]

The massive expansion of the armaments industry that had occurred in the key industrial centres of the north – Genoa, Turin and Milan – in the early 1940s increased the power and confidence of workers. They shook off the legacy of defeat in the 1920s. Confidence fused with immense bitterness over 60-hour working weeks, astronomical prices for black market food, wartime profiteering by the wealthy and the lack of air-raid shelters for the thousands who died in Allied bombing raids.

In March 1943, 200,000 workers struck in the north. Communists emerged from the underground to agitate and publicise the strikers' demands. Turin's giant FIAT Mirafiori factory, opened by Mussolini in 1939 with great fanfare as a symbol of fascist progress, was the centre of the struggle. Rank and file leaders, mostly radical socialists, suffered harsh repression, but the regime was forced to grant economic concessions. The Turin strike indicated that workers were beginning to overcome their fear and that the fascist order was starting to crumble, losing its ability to control an increasingly restive population. The parties of the left, the Communists (PCI), the Socialists (PSI) and the Action Party (Pd'A), signed a pact agreeing to cooperate in the overthrow of fascism. Big Italian capitalists could see the writing on the wall and began talks with the Allies.

In July 1943, the Allies invaded Sicily. In an attempt to preserve as much as possible of the political order, King Emmanuel, who had installed Mussolini as prime minister in 1922, organised a coup against the dictator and installed in his place Field Marshal Pietro Badoglio. Badoglio had been a loyal servant of Mussolini, chief of the armed forces between 1925 and 1940 and was responsible for war crimes during Italy's wars of conquest in Africa. He quickly showed his colours as head of state. When civilians came out onto the streets to celebrate Mussolini's downfall, Badoglio ordered the military to fire on them, killing dozens. Neither his past record nor his actions in government caused the Allies any qualms; they set up secret negotiations with him for an armistice. They saw in him and King Emmanuel useful guardians of order, bulwarks against revolution. Winston Churchill welcomed the bloody repression of the anti-fascist demonstrations, arguing that the alternative was 'rampant Bolshevism.'

Hearing of Badoglio's negotiations with the Allies, Germany poured soldiers into the country to replace Italian military units. By 3 September, when the Italian government signed an armistice with the Allies, German troops occupied much of the country. The Nazis appointed Mussolini to head a puppet government. Rather than organise the Italian army to fight the Germans, Badoglio and the royal family fled Rome and set up court in the south of the country, leaving the unprepared Italian army to be slaughtered by the German military or captured and transported to work in slave labour camps for German war industries. Many former soldiers and civilians seized what guns they could from the disintegrating Italian army and headed into the mountains to join the burgeoning partisan bands. By the end of 1943, there were 9,000 partisans under arms.

With the Nazis occupying the bulk of the country, and the traditional elite having fled or offered themselves as collaborators, tentative steps to cohere the burgeoning Resistance came to fruition in the form of a national liberation committee (CLN). The CLN included representatives of every anti-fascist party opposed to the German occupation and its puppet government, ranging from the Communists to the traditional party of the bosses, the Liberals. It was led by Ivanoe Bonomi, from a small social democratic party. The CLN constituted itself as a government in waiting and sought to organise the partisan forces springing up all around the country.

The first major victory for the anti-fascist struggle came in Naples at the end of September 1943. The German occupation had driven residents into extreme poverty. Allied bombing compounded their misery. The middle class had fled the bombing, leaving the workers in the most wretched circumstances. Fearing an imminent Allied attack, the German commander ordered the destruction of the city. He also ordered the immediate transportation of every man of working age to work in factories in Northern Italy and Germany and threatened severe punishment to any who resisted. The population erupted in a spontaneous insurrection. Hundreds died in the fighting, but they drove the Germans out after four days. When the Allied armies marched into the city, they found the people in control.

By winter, Italy was divided into two. Germany occupied the North, supported by local Italian fascists; Britain and the US gradually won ground in the South. Each side had its own puppet leader, Mussolini and Badoglio respectively. In the North, the German occupation forces sought to squeeze the population dry. Italian workers and peasants resisting attempts to conscript them to work in Germany were massacred.

Despite the repression, the Resistance fought. In the countryside, partisans blew up bridges, ripped up railways, attacked ammunition dumps, sabotaged power lines and communications and ambushed German soldiers, seizing their weapons. In the cities, partisans organised armed action groups to attack the occupation forces and their fascist collaborators. Women increasingly found their way into the fray, taking part in military actions and carrying out support activities for other fighters. Some took charge of partisan squads. The working class, especially the strikers, were central to crippling the German occupation. In the Emilia Romagna region and its capital Bologna, the three largest categories of recruits to the Resistance were industrial workers (32%), agricultural workers (32%) and artisans (11%). The Communists constituted the largest group of Resistance fighters. Their Garibaldi Brigades made up at least half the total forces under arms, even more in the early period. The Pd'A's Justice and Freedom Brigades accounted for about 20 percent.

The Allied commanders were extremely wary of the Resistance. Their main priority was to defeat German occupation and to eliminate the most prominent fascist leaders in the towns that fell under their control. They were prepared to leave the existing state authorities, including the police, in control in every other respect, provided that they transferred their loyalty to the Allies. Churchill feared that Italy would parallel the situation unfolding in neighbouring Yugoslavia and Greece, where Communist partisans were rapidly establishing control. At best, he treated the Resistance as an auxiliary in defeating the Germans; at worst, he viewed them as an enemy. When the partisans in the North drove out the Germans in a number of places and formed partisan republics in 1944, the Allies disowned them. Lacking military support, the partisan republics fell to Nazi attack. In the South, British commanders struck deals with the landlords and Mafia – who only recently had been loyal to Mussolini – thus ensuring continued mass starvation, unemployment and the new curse of hyperinflation. Peasants began to occupy the land and to protest against grain seizures by the authorities.

The workers' movement and the left

The PCI was the biggest party on the left, the driving force in the Resistance. It had suffered enormous repression under fascism and fought to survive as an underground organisation. At the outset of the war, it had only 6,000 members. But its experience of underground work during peacetime was enough to give the PCI a head start when mass resistance developed. Party cadres certainly did not lack bravery: thousands suffered imprisonment or death in combat fighting the occupation. The PCI impressed and attracted many militants through their courage. The PCI could also draw on the tremendous goodwill that existed towards Stalin and the Russian army, currently forcing the Wehrmacht back on the eastern front. As the Resistance advanced, the PCI began to recruit tens of thousands of members. By February 1945, membership stood at 90,000 and kept growing.

In the early years of the war, the PCI was not a typical monolithic Stalinist party. Fascist rule had cut the workers' movement off from the political debates absorbing the communist movement in the 1930s. The leadership, based until 1940 in Paris and then in Moscow, was headed by Stalin's acolyte Palmiro Togliatti who had fled Italy in 1926 to escape fascist repression. Togliatti rose to high office in the Comintern, where he carried out Stalin's dirty work. In 1937 he was sent to Spain, where he oversaw the torture and assassination of anarchists and supporters of the POUM. However, he was incapable of imposing the Popular Front line on Italian-based PCI activists from afar. The party therefore retained a substantial left wing: many members were sympathetic to Bordiga, who had defended Trotsky against Stalin and been expelled by Togliatti in 1930. Numerous other local, independent communist groups also emerged outside the PCI. Some had considerable support and their own fighting groups, rivalling those of the Communists. In Rome, the dissident communist group Bandiera Rossa was equal in size to the PCI and challenged its accommodation to the Allies. Restricted to Rome, however, it could not match the PCI as a national force, particularly in the northern cities which were the crucible of the Resistance.

The isolation of the PCI from the debates in the Comintern also had a negative side. Key issues at stake – united front versus popular front, socialism in one country, Trotsky versus Stalin – had not been fully clarified. No clear cadre organisation had emerged that could unify and politically educate the plethora of left communist groups to form a party that challenged the PCI for hegemony over the working class. This lack of political clarity rendered the independent communists unable to combat the concerted attacks mounted on them by the Stalinists. Many of their members ended up joining the PCI.

The Pd'A and PSI were the two main alternatives to the PCI. The Pd'A was founded in 1942 out of an earlier anti-fascist and anti-Stalinist organisation, Justice and Freedom. The second biggest party on the left, it had tens of thousands of members at the end of the war, 20,000 under arms in the mountains and 11,000 in the cities. It was a very heterogeneous party: one wing was reformist, the other revolutionary. The latter rejected Russia as a model for socialism; towards the end of the war, it stood well to the left of the PCI. The Pd'A attracted many anti-fascist middle class professionals to its ranks, but it lacked a stable working class base.

The PSI was too small and weak to make a decisive difference in the 1920s. Like the Pd'A, it was highly factionalised and divided between revolutionary and reformist wings, lacked a strong base in the industrial working class and had built no serious underground organisation during the 1930s. Moreover, while the PSI was highly critical of the Badoglio government, it was almost as pro-Russian as the PCI itself, and some of its leaders envisaged fusion with the PCI. It was politically disarmed by Stalin's betrayal of the movement.

The PCI's domination of the Resistance had a disastrous effect on the course of the struggle late in the war and afterwards. At a time when the ruling class had been discredited by its support for fascism, and state institutions were fracturing under the stress of military occupation, the PCI played the decisive role in propping up an unpopular monarchist government and preserving Italian capitalism.

The Communists lurch to the right

In March 1944, Stalin dropped a bombshell on the Italian Resistance. In line with his agreement with Roosevelt and Churchill to assign Italy to the Western sphere of influence, Stalin announced Russia's official recognition of the Badoglio government and its figurehead leader, King Emmanuel. Togliatti was sent home to enforce the new line. This rightward turn, the Salerno Turn, transformed the PCI's role in the Resistance. In late 1943, the party had argued that 'The struggle of peasants and workers for their immediate demands is sacrosanct' and, along with the Pd'A and the PSI, denounced Badoglio and the king. Now it promoted a classic Popular Front of the type Togliatti had helped to enforce in Spain. Socialism was to be put off indefinitely. In place of struggle against the old elite, the party now championed national unity with the bosses, the monarchy, ex-fascists and anyone not immediately identified with the Nazis. The PCI leadership also sought to eliminate party traditions of saluting with clenched fists, brandishing the red flag and singing revolutionary songs, replacing them with rhetoric about 'progressive democracy.' In return for giving the monarchy and fascist general a certificate of anti-fascist credibility, seven PCI members, including Togliatti, were admitted to Badoglio's revamped cabinet.

The Salerno Turn was the result of Stalin's decision to recognise Badoglio and the king but it was quite in keeping with the PCI's counter-revolutionary character. PCI leaders returning from exile were Stalinist bureaucrats who fundamentally distrusted workers' self-activity. They opposed any working class action not controlled by them and tried to turn the unions they founded into appendages of the party.

Because the PCI was the dominant force in the Resistance, it was easily able to persuade the CLN and its local offshoots to support Badoglio and the monarchy. The disorganised and divided PSI, some of whose members initially condemned the PCI's turn, were no match for the hardened PCI bureaucrats in manoeuvring within the Resistance. The Pd'A was incapable of resisting it because it had failed to build a mass following among the working class and peasantry. Other oppositional revolutionary organisations which attained some size in Turin and Rome were too small or weak to challenge the PCI.

The PCI's main orientation now was not to the parties of the left but to the Christian Democrats (DC). This was a new bourgeois party which, unlike the traditional capitalist parties, sought to build a mass base on a confessional and populist basis. The DC promised various groups what they wanted: for the middle class, security for its property and respect for the family; for workers and peasants, modest reforms; for the capitalists, the best means to stabilise Italian capitalism; and for the Catholic hierarchy, a vehicle to influence politics in the postwar world and to marginalise the Communists, reducing their competition with the church for hearts and minds. The Christian Democrats played a very minor role in the fighting, but Vatican support enabled them to grow rapidly towards the end of the war.

The PCI now clung onto this party in coalition, assuring its supporters that the DC was a trustworthy partner.

Two developments at the end of 1944 crushed hopes for genuine liberation by the end of the year. In November, Allied Commander Field Marshal Montgomery Alexander announced that the Allies would suspend their military campaign in the North for the duration of the winter. He instructed the Resistance forces to go to ground. The effect – deliberate or not – was to weaken the Resistance and embolden Mussolini's National Guard, who with German support killed thousands of partisans and deported tens of thousands of young men to labour camps. In December, the leaders of the CLN met Allied commanders in the capital and signed the Protocols of Rome, signifying their surrender as an independent force. In return for financial support, CLN leaders agreed to submit to an Italian general appointed by the Allies. They further agreed that, on the defeat of the Germans, they would place themselves under the command of Allied generals and would disband and surrender their weapons when ordered to do so.

Many rank and file PCI militants, particularly in the underground ranks of the party in the North, were sceptical about Togliatti's Salerno Turn and shared the enthusiasm of many in the Resistance for revolutionary change. But they were prepared to give the leadership the benefit of the doubt. They had tremendous faith in Stalin and the Russians and believed that the Russian army was going to smash through the German forces in northern Italy to liberate the country. They reassured themselves that Togliatti was only playing a tactical game to trick the bourgeoisie into lowering its defences. The PCI leadership encouraged this misunderstanding, a strategy that became known as *doppiezza*, duplicity. While dropping hints that it was planning to launch an insurrection at some point in the future, and tolerating rank and file members and even some leaders who espoused a revolutionary line, the PCI leadership steered the party steadily towards class collaboration and integration into the old state apparatus which was being rapidly rebuilt by the Allies. The tremendous struggles, sacrifices and heroism of the working class were sacrificed to build a postwar order that fell far short of their hopes and dreams.

Liberation of the North

Workers were not waiting passively while negotiations were going on between the Allies and CLN leaders to decide their fate. In March 1944, more than a million workers came out on strike, starting in Milan and spreading to Bologna, Florence and Venice. They raised openly political demands:

immediate peace and an end to war production for Germany. The *New York Times* reported: 'In terms of mass demonstrations, in occupied Europe, nothing can come close to the revolt of Italian workers.'[2] In August, the Resistance liberated Florence after a battle lasting three weeks, with thousands of civilians spontaneously joining partisan groups in the streets to drive the Nazis out. In September, widespread sabotage, strikes and go-slows in Turin crippled supplies of military goods. When bosses at FIAT demanded Sunday working hours to make good the shortfall, workers struck across the city, forcing management to retreat.

The peasants and landless labourers in the South were active too. The region was now under Allied control, but the peasants and rural workers understood that real liberation lay in their hands. In the autumn of 1944, an enormous protest movement gathered strength in the villages, inspired by the decision of the PCI Minister of Agriculture to grant peasants a greater share of their produce, protection from eviction and the right to take over all uncultivated land, on the proviso that they organise themselves into cooperatives. This was the only progressive reform enacted by any of the Communist representatives in government. At the same time, the PCI leader of the newly reconstituted union federation tried to force on the landlords a better deal for rural wage labourers. Three years of rural struggle for peasant and rural worker rights ensued. This far exceeded in size anything that had come before and reached down to the lowest, most oppressed villagers. Against bloody opposition from landlords, the Mafia and local politicians in their pay, big crowds of armed peasants took the fight to the landlords in their grand mansions and won a fairer share.

Industrialists in the north played both sides. Preparing for German defeat, FIAT managing director Vittorio Valletta paid hundreds of millions of lire in cash and aid to the Resistance, even while producing tanks and V2 rocket parts for Germany. FIAT bosses tried to head off violent intervention by German forces by settling strikes while also giving the Nazis lists of anti-fascist militants.

The great uprising came in April 1945. The Resistance had survived the terrible winter months and now stood 200,000 strong.[3] They issued a call for a national insurrection as the Allies approached the big cities of the north:

> Partisan formations will attack and eliminate the Nazi-fascist headquarters and effect the liberation of cities, towns and villages. We will proclaim a general strike…the culmination of the people's long campaign for freedom and the expression of their unshakable determination.[4]

In Bologna and Milan, the Germans were driven out before the arrival of the Allies and workers seized the factories. Turin was a much tougher fight. The Germans had planned to seize industrial machinery and deport thousands of industrial workers to Germany. A mass strike brought the city to a halt. Armed workers took on the Nazis and, rejecting all attempts by the German commander to negotiate safe passage for his troops, forced the commander and his army to surrender. In Genoa, 3,000 poorly armed citizens took on 15,000 well-armed Germans. Nine thousand Germans, followed by another 6,000, surrendered unconditionally to the far smaller force of armed urban partisans. In every big city, when the Allies arrived, the workers were armed, transport and electricity were functioning, and a democratic council was in control.

The people in the north of Italy freed themselves, not relying on the Americans and British. They were denied the chance to take power because the PCI had already repudiated such a step, and there was no other force strong enough in the working class to pose an alternative leadership. The potential that existed for social and economic transformation was never realised. The partisans were ordered to hand in their arms to the Allies. Those who hid their weapons, in the hope that the order might come for insurrection at some point, were to be sorely disappointed.

Meet the new boss

Ex-partisans returning to their hometowns after Liberation found that little had changed. The country was now run by a Popular Front-style government with representatives from the PCI, PSI and DC, but the same company bosses who had collaborated with the Nazis were still in charge of the factories. Very few state functionaries lost their jobs. Those who had made fortunes out of the war kept their money. The most significant change was the abolition of the monarchy by a referendum in 1946.

The PCI supported this continuity. By far the largest party, with nearly two million members by 1946, it had no intention of using its power to carry out thoroughgoing changes to Mussolini's state apparatus. As Justice Minister, Togliatti passed an amnesty which allowed many fascists responsible for torture, rape and murder to escape unpunished. Togliatti kept on judges who had served the fascists and these unsurprisingly dismissed most cases brought against fascists in the post-war years.

The PCI also strove to make peace with the Vatican which had supported Mussolini for two decades. In 1947, citing 'respect for the family,' the PCI voted to enshrine Roman Catholicism as the state religion in the new constitution, handing the church a veto over divorce and control over education in state schools. Even as DC prime minister Alcide de Gasperi squeezed PCI and PSI representation in the Cabinet, the Communists loyally served his government.

The big industrialists who had feared expropriation of their factories soon realised that the PCI had no intention of coming after them. Togliatti described national economic planning as utopian, called for an anti-inflationary policy to protect small savers and urged unions to be concerned more with increasing production than with wages. No effort was made to nationalise industry. Communist union leaders agreed to national wage agreements that included safeguards against inflation but banned local strikes over wages. Power in the unions was quickly centralised. Bosses took full advantage of the situation; mass sackings followed, with militants especially targeted. In February 1947, Togliatti complained:

> In the last years, no political strike has taken place in Italy… This is a country where the unions have signed a wage truce… This is the striking and absurd feature of the present economic situation: the working class and the unions are giving the best example and taking the necessary steps to preserve production, order and social peace to enable reconstruction to take place. On the other side, a bunch of political and economic speculators are taking advantage of the situation.[5]

Togliatti only complained. He did nothing to resolve the inequities.

After Liberation, the PCI envisaged that it would govern the country as part of a coalition with other anti-fascist parties for a prolonged period. Over time, its leaders believed, as the country's largest party it would gradually come to dominate the government. However, the tide was running in the opposite direction. In 1945, the DC could not simply push aside the Communists. But with the PCI demobilising the popular forces that had given it strength, the DC grew more powerful. In May 1947, in an environment of growing Cold War tensions, with the United States intervening to try to force the Communists out, the DC president expelled the PCI and the PSI from the government. Rather than fight this purge by mobilising the party's enormous base in the industrial working class, Togliatti let it pass. Passivity cost the party dearly. With the PCI demonstrating its impotence, the middle class rallied behind the DC. The conservatives won a decisive victory over a combined PCI–Socialist ticket at the April 1948 national elections.

Three months later, on 14 July 1948, the endgame played out. An assassination attempt on Togliatti by a far right student in Rome prompted a working class explosion. With Togliatti lying critically injured, workers across the north spontaneously walked out on strike, bringing industry, offices and transport to a halt. Those who had hidden their weapons in preparation for an insurrection brought them out. In the industrial triangle of Genoa, Milan and Turin, strikers set up barricades, disarmed soldiers and police, took over factories and held bosses, including FIAT's president, hostage. The PCI leadership, fearing escalation to a broader confrontation with the state, slammed on the brakes overnight. In Genoa, they urged workers to take down the barricades and let the police and armed forces move freely. In Milan, they instructed workers to end their demonstrations and return to work. In the absence of any alternative political lead, the workers were forced to accept the PCI's instructions to return to work after three days. Any loyal Communists who had believed that the leadership was waiting for the right moment to launch an insurrection had a bitter awakening in those July days. What the mainstream newspapers called 'normality' now returned. Christian Democracy rode high. In the following years, the Cold War climate intensified; thousands of former PCI partisans were arrested and jailed.

Was a revolution possible?

The outcome of the massive struggle in Italy during the war years was miserable. Was there an alternative? The best chance for a revolutionary outcome came in the last year of the war. The old order had been shaken to its core by military defeat and invasion. The rural poor, suffering acute hardship, were demanding an end to their centuries-old oppression. Urban workers demanded urgent solutions to their poverty, abysmal housing conditions and lack of rights at work. Paul Ginsborg argues: 'For them, the fight against the Nazis and the struggle for a new dignity as human beings, both at home and in the factories, went hand in hand.'[6] And tens of thousands had joined the Resistance, wanting not just to liberate the country but to transform it.

Certainly, as Ginsborg argues, any bid for power in Italy in 1944–45 would have faced immense problems. Fascist terror and German reprisals intimidated many from joining in the fight. The Resistance was weak in the South, and once the Allies had established control they represented a formidable obstacle to any attempt to link up struggles by southern peasants with the workers' uprising in the northern cities. Had the Resistance rejected the Allied commanders' demand to submit, the Allies would have done their utmost to crush any uprising in the north. There was also the fact that, although factory CLNs were established in hundreds of workplaces in the north, there were no soviets or workers' councils capable of bringing together workers on a city-wide basis, with delegates elected from workplaces and subject to recall. Dual power was absent.

But such apparently insuperable obstacles might have been overcome. The traditional hostility of the peasants in the south to communism could be overcome, as the popularity of the PCI's land reform legislation demonstrated. Peasants flocked to the PCI. What of the hostility of the Allies? It is not a given that British and US soldiers would have fired on those they were liberating. The international dimension is also relevant. The Allied command had already lost control of Tito's partisans in Yugoslavia and was struggling to crush a rising in Athens (see below). Had the British been compelled to fight the Italian Resistance as well in the latter half of 1944, the outcome is uncertain.

The truth is that we can never know whether a revolution was possible in Italy at this time, because there was no attempt to lead one. The PCI was determined to obstruct any revolutionary struggle for power, and it had the strength to prevent one. There was no equivalent of the Bolshevik Party in Italy. The PCI failed, however, even to achieve significant reforms of the existing state. It wasted its strong bargaining position in 1944 and reined in its supporters in the name of national unity when every other social force – the king, Badoglio and his successors, the Allies, the Vatican, the southern landowners and the northern capitalists – was fighting to assert its agenda. The PCI's Popular Front strategy and support for the Russian state tempered its demands for radical change, ensuring that few reforms took place at the end of the war. Some modest anti-fascist purges of the state apparatus, the introduction of a democratic constitution and an end to the monarchy were the limit. Most of the fascists remained at their posts or were shuffled around. The capitalists faced few repercussions for their longstanding support for the fascists, and the DC emerged as the strongest parliamentary party and went on to rule Italy for decades. When we look at why the Italian working class and peasantry failed to make a real breakthrough, having suffered and resisted so much during the war, we must sheet home responsibility to the PCI.

GREECE

The Resistance to Nazi occupation in Greece was even stronger than in Italy.[7] With the Germans evacuating in October 1944 to reinforce the home front and the British military yet to arrive in significant numbers, the

Communist-dominated Resistance held the future of the country in the palm of its hand. It suffered a crushing defeat. Like the Italian, the Greek Resistance was sacrificed on the altar of big power politics – Britain's determination to regain its hold on the country and Russia's willingness to let it do so. But the Greek Communists (KKE) were complicit in their fate. Committed to the Popular Front strategy and to Stalin, the KKE surrendered its advantage and lost to those who were prepared to fight for power.

In Italy, the PCI wasted a great opportunity to enact far-reaching social and economic reforms. In Greece, the outcome of the KKE's strategy was far more severe – thousands of party members lay dead and tens of thousands were forced into exile. While the Allies could tolerate Communists in the Italian government that took office after the war, this was not an option for Britain in Greece: the Communists had to be destroyed. Britain had much at stake in Greece. British shareholders held controlling interests in many of the country's big industries, but more important was Greece's position in the Eastern Mediterranean. Without controlling Greece, Britain risked losing access to the Suez Canal and India. Greece was also a gateway to the oil fields of Persia, which were rapidly becoming a critical imperialist asset. Churchill was determined to hold on to Greece and that meant restoring the British puppet king, George II, and crushing the Communists. Greece is the only case of the European conflict where the British used their military to smash the Resistance and mobilised Nazi collaborators to join them in this fight. Stalin, who had cynically handed over Greece to Britain earlier, did nothing to prevent the British offensive, even as thousands of his supporters were killed.

Invasion and occupation

In 1936, the fascist General Ioannis Metaxas, an admirer of Hitler, seized power in league with King George II. He crushed an emerging liberal democracy and unleashed a reign of terror on the left, arresting and jailing thousands. Tens of thousands of leftists – far more than the membership of the Communist Party – were forced to sign declarations recanting loyalty to the party. Fewer than 1,000 Communists refused to repent; they were sent to rot in prisons on remote Aegean islands. Only 200 Communists remained free.

When war was declared in September 1939, Metaxas initially sought to strike a balance between Germany and Britain. But when Italy invaded Greece in September 1940, Metaxas threw his lot in with the Allies. Popular resistance to Mussolini's army soon drove the Italians back, deep into Albania. Embarrassed by the failure of its junior partner, Germany sent in its much more formidable army in April 1941. Within three weeks, the Greek government surrendered. The Axis powers divided up the country. Germany controlled the big cities – Athens and its port Piraeus and the northern hub of Salonika, the centres of political and economic power – while Italy and Bulgaria controlled the rest of the country. The Greek ruling class split into two camps. Metaxas had died in January 1941. Emmanouil Tsouderos now led the government, which fled Athens with the king. Under British protection, they went first to Crete, then to London. They finally set up a government in exile in Cairo in 1943. The other camp collaborated with the occupation forces and set up a quisling government in Athens.

The German occupation was a catastrophe for the civilian population. During the winter of 1942, 250,000 people starved to death because of food requisition, pillaging and looting by the occupying armies. Thousands of men were conscripted to work in Germany and its ally Bulgaria. In March 1943, virtually the entire 50,000-strong Jewish community of Salonika was deported to Auschwitz. Only a few survived. The German puppet government of Ioannis Rallis established 'security battalions' – fascist hoodlums – which committed terrible atrocities, including widespread rape, theft and murder of anyone suspected of leftist activities.

Birth of the Resistance

Resistance emerged within months of the German occupation. The KKE played a pivotal role. It was led by George Siantos, but the supporters of his predecessor, Nikos Zachariadis, who had been deported by the Germans to Dachau, retained control over the Central Committee. Zachariadis was a classic Stalinist apparatchik. He had spent most of the 1920s in Russia, receiving a thorough Stalinist indoctrination at the Lenin School in Moscow. In 1931, Stalin sent him back to Greece to purge the KKE of oppositionists, which included an influential Trotskyist current as well as other anti-Stalinist communists. Zachariadis imposed a dictatorial regime on the party, driving out oppositionists and demanding unthinking loyalty from those who remained. In 1934, having eliminated internal opposition, Zachariadis dumped the ultra leftism of the Third Period, which had prevented the party from making any inroads into the working class, and took up the Comintern's Popular Front line. The task of Communists, the KKE leadership argued, was to encourage the formation of a government led by the 'progressive bourgeoisie' to foster capitalist development in Greece. The consequences of this became clear in the first half of 1936. Following a general election in which neither of the two major capitalist parties, the Liberal Party and the People's Party, won a majority, the KKE, with 15 seats in the chamber, put all its efforts into trying to cobble together a parliamentary deal with the Liberals rather than leading workers, who were out on strike in huge numbers, into a challenge to the policies of both of the capitalist parties. The defeat of the strike paved the way for Metaxas's seizure of power, and the KKE leadership quickly joined thousands of other leftists in the dictator's jails.

All wings of the ruling class were discredited by their decision to collaborate with the Nazi occupation or to flee into exile. The KKE moved in to fill the vacuum, setting up the EAM (National Liberation Front) in September 1941 to organise the resistance to occupation. In line with its Popular Front strategy, the KKE invited all 'anti-fascist forces,' regardless of any previous collaboration with Metaxas, to join EAM. Unsurprisingly, the bourgeois parties feared the KKE more than they did the Germans, and none took up this invitation. The EAM remained in the hands of the KKE and two other, smaller left parties. As the only visible force, EAM was soon swamped by an influx of recruits. KKE members quickly became a minority in the Resistance, but the party's disciplined, centralised organisation and experience working underground meant that its political line prevailed. In February 1942, EAM established a labour section, the EEAM; in April, it set up ELAS, the Greek Popular Liberation Army.

EAM, and in particular EEAM, quickly won a following in Athens. During the terrible winter famine of 1942, EAM mobilised food supplies to the capital, saving thousands of lives. In March, 3,000 students defied a ban and celebrated Greek Independence Day. In April, civil servants struck for better pay and food rations, forcing the government to make concessions. ELAS stepped up its attacks, derailing trains and blowing up buildings. The situation escalated early the following year, with repeated mass actions of resistance. On 24 February 1943, a big crowd demonstrated against attempts to conscript men to serve in German munitions factories. German and Italian troops fired into the crowd, killing or wounding 100 as the crowd broke through the lines of soldiers. Parts of Athens became no-go zones for the occupation forces as Greeks fought back, while in the provinces, German and Italian troops did not dare leave their barracks. On 4 March 1943, major strikes broke out in the press, civil service and Bank of Athens. The following day, a huge crowd marched in central Athens in support of the strikers. Forced into a corner by the violent opposition, the German command suspended its attempt to conscript labour – the first such victory in occupied Europe. On 25 June, the EEAM called another general strike, and 100,000 marched in Athens in defiance of occupation forces.

The Resistance also established liberated zones in rural areas. Greece's mountain ranges made it suitable territory for guerrilla warfare. The partisans built a powerful base among the peasantry and increasingly took control of mountain villages from Italian troops. In late March 1943, a popular uprising in a small town in western Macedonia drove out the Italian forces. It was the first liberated town in Europe. The victory sparked a further rush of recruits to ELAS. In the spring of 1943, ELAS had 5,000 men and women under arms; five months later, the figure was close to 40,000.

Where they took control in the rural areas, ELAS introduced a range of democratic reforms, including self-government and the election of councillors and judges in mass assemblies. Monty Woodhouse, a British agent operating alongside ELAS, but not a sympathiser, wrote in his memoirs:

> The initiative of EAM/ELAS justified their predominance, though not their tyranny. Having acquired control of almost the whole country, except the principal communications used by the Germans, they had given it things that it had never known before. Communications in the mountains, by wireless, courier, and telephone, have never been so good before or since... The benefits of civilisation and culture trickled into the mountains for the first time. Schools, local government, law-courts and public utilities, which the war had ended worked again... All the virtues and vices of such an experiment could be seen; for when the people whom no one has ever helped started helping themselves, their methods are vigorous and not always nice. The words 'liberation' and 'popular democracy' filled the air with their peculiar connotations.[8]

Women took up arms as well. They began to enjoy new freedoms under the Resistance. In villages run by EAM, women were entitled to vote in local elections, challenging traditional norms. EAM called these village councils *laokratia*, or 'people power.' This was also meant to refer to a future 'state of the people,' a democratic government. The term *laokratia* would serve a usefully ambiguous purpose for the KKE leadership, evoking the idea of social liberation while being quite consistent with parliamentary democracy.

The KKE supported the Allied war effort and looked to Britain to help it fight the German occupation. Initially, the British reciprocated, recognising ELAS as the most effective resistance force. They supplied weapons to ELAS, and British special forces and ELAS guerrillas undertook joint actions to blow up bridges and railway lines. From the middle of 1943, however, with the war swinging the Allies' way and Churchill increasingly anxious about ELAS's growing power, the British switched tack. They threw their weight behind a rival organisation, EDES (the Greek Republican Liberation League). The leader of EDES, Napoleon Zervas, who had turned down a power-sharing offer by EAM, offered his services as a British puppet. EDES had a fraction of the political support garnered by EAM and ELAS, but it received the lion's share of British supplies from this point on, generating bloody clashes between the two wings of the Resistance, with ELAS generally gaining the upper hand.

EAM chokes the Resistance

The Greek Resistance, like the Italian, was characterised by internal tensions. EAM/ELAS and, through these, the KKE, won tremendous support for their role in leading the Resistance. They maintained a left face as the voice of national liberation and republicanism. While the monarchist government was content to sit out the war in Cairo, the ranks of the KKE were filled with those who wanted to fight not only against the Nazi occupation but for a future free of fascism and monarchy. Russia was also a strong point of attraction for many Greek anti-fascists. Communist-led partisans in Yugoslavia, immediately to the north, were driving out the German occupation: why not Greece? Support for EAM was naturally strongest among workers and peasants, but many army officers, university professors and church clergy, including bishops, backed EAM as the embodiment of Greek national pride. In response to these layers, the KKE often sought to muffle their mass base's demands for political transformation.

In March 1944, EAM held a clandestine general election to elect a provisional government. It took place in the liberated areas and in occupied cities under the noses of the German army. More than one million cast their votes, out of a population of seven million – a stunning exercise of mass defiance. The KKE won the lion's share of the vote. The Communists took only a minority of positions in the new cabinet, but the others – religious leaders, professors, capitalists and others not tainted by collaboration with the Axis powers – were generally believed to be KKE sympathisers, if not secret members, and it was the KKE that set the new government's agenda.

The EAM's decision to set up a provisional government in the mountains worried the British and Cairo governments. Germany was clearly losing the war. If it withdrew from Greece abruptly, the provisional government would be in place with a popular mandate to take power. In the event, Churchill had two big advantages: Stalin's determination to deliver on his side of the bargain with the British; and the EAM's commitment to bourgeois democracy as the supposed 'first stage' of the Greek revolution, but really its terminus.

The first clash occurred on 31 March 1944 when Greek troops stationed in Egypt mutinied and declared their loyalty to EAM's provisional government. They had served under British command in campaigns in North Africa but were now keen to return to their homeland to join the Resistance. Anti-monarchist officers and soldiers, led by the Military Anti-Fascist Organisation, took over command of several military units in Cairo. In the port of Alexandria, popular committees of sailors and sympathetic officers took charge of the ships, throwing monarchist officers overboard.

The Cairo government was helpless, but the British stepped in to save it. Churchill ordered the British Army, backed by loyalist sailors and officers, to round up the mutineers. Fifty were killed or wounded and thousands sent to prison camps in the desert. Throughout the mutiny and subsequent repression, Stalin and the EAM stood aside, not saying one word to encourage the mutineers or to condemn the British. Later, at the party congress held in September 1945, the KKE denounced the Egyptian uprising as a British plot to destroy democracy and even initiated an investigation against the party cadres who had led it.

Churchill was alarmed by the mutiny in Egypt and by the fact that the Russian army was poised to descend on the Balkans. He moved on two fronts. Firstly, in a precursor of the percentages agreement (above), he confirmed with Stalin Russian support for British control over Greece, in return for which Britain would recognise Russian control over Romania. Secondly, he approved negotiations by the Cairo government with the Resistance about forming a government of national unity. George Papandreou, a liberal anti-monarchist but reliably anti-communist and loyal to Britain, was appointed prime minister. The first attempt to construct such a government at an all-party conference in Lebanon in May fell apart within days because an internal revolt among KKE partisans in the mountains, disgusted at the shoddy deal its representatives had accepted, forced EAM to repudiate it. As a condition of EAM involvement, they demanded much more power in the government, along with Papandreou's resignation. That was rejected by the British, creating a stalemate.

The stalemate was broken in August at another all-party conference held in the Italian town of Caserta. The EAM leadership backed down and agreed to join a national unity government led by Papandreou. EAM also agreed that:

> All guerrilla forces operating in Greece place themselves under the orders of the Greek Government of National Unity, [which in turn]

places these forces under the orders of [Britain's] General Scobie who has been nominated by the Supreme Allied Commander as General Officer Commanding Forces in Greece.[9]

Two factors explain why the KKE capitulated to Papandreou and the British at Caserta: Russian pressure and its own limitations. In July 1944, with the Russian army active in the Balkans, Stalin was able to parachute eight military attachés into the ELAS HQ in the mountains. These advisers did their best to convert ELAS, a relatively egalitarian guerrilla force, into a more formal army structure. They stripped it of the popular revolutionary elements of the Resistance and introduced a regular military hierarchy, including ranks, saluting and official decorations, just as Stalin's functionaries had done in Spain in 1936–37. They were not always successful; many of the partisans in the mountains did not jump to every order from the leadership in Athens, still less to Moscow's. However, Moscow now had much more sway over ELAS, and Stalin was determined to ensure ELAS did not overstep the role he had allocated to it. The KKE was to fight for representation in an all-party Popular Front government, not to rule in its own right. Stalin was pushing at an open door, of course. His view was consistent with that of the KKE leadership in Athens whose Popular Front politics committed the party to forming a government with capitalist representatives. The Caserta Agreement was to doom the Greek Communists to a bloody defeat.

The Dekemvriana

British fears that the German occupation might collapse 'prematurely', that is, before an alternative to the KKE was put in place, were soon realised. In the autumn of 1944, Germany lost ground on every front. On 12 October, it withdrew its troops from Greece, fearing that they would be cut off by Russian forces advancing through the Balkans. The withdrawal of the Wehrmacht and the resulting power vacuum caught the British unprepared. They now had to move quickly to establish forces in a country where they had none. The British promptly shipped the Papandreou government to Athens, accompanied by a small British expeditionary corps. Reluctantly, Churchill agreed to leave the king in Cairo pending a plebiscite to decide his fate.

On any assessment of the balance of forces, EAM/ELAS were dominant at the time of the German withdrawal. ELAS forces numbered 60,000; the KKE claimed a membership of 350,000 in a population of just seven million; and EAM had 1.5 million members, with strong support in rural areas and the big cities. ELAS fighters heading down from the mountains towards Athens were greeted as liberators. Any time in the weeks that followed the German withdrawal, EAM could have taken power. In Athens, workers were champing at the bit and, in some cases, taking matters into their own hands. On 4 November, workers in the capital demonstrated in huge numbers against British plans to impose the old order. Many partisans also believed that they were going to march into Athens to claim power. But the KKE leadership ensured that none of this would happen. They halted the ELAS fighters and kept them outside the capital. They supported measures by the Papandreou government that cut wages, provoking a storm of criticism within the party and EEAM, EAM's labour wing.

The British and Papandreou had no such compunctions about advancing their cause. While they had formally agreed in the Caserta Agreement to punish those who had collaborated with the German occupation, they instead resurrected the fascist security battalions and inducted them into a new National Guard to wage war on EAM. The British also began to pour soldiers into the country.

In the first week of December, matters in Athens came to a head. On 1 December, General Scobie ordered ELAS to disband but allowed other military forces, including the fascists, to continue to operate unchecked. Disarmament would have been suicidal for ELAS because it would ensure its annihilation at the hands of the fascists and the destruction of EAM. EAM refused to agree to Scobie's orders, and its representatives resigned from Papandreou's Cabinet. Even now, EAM urged its supporters to avoid a confrontation with 'our British allies.'

On 3 December, EAM organised a massive demonstration of 200,000 Athenians (in a city of 600,000) to protest against General Scobie's disarmament order. This was meant as a show of strength, to improve EAM's bargaining leverage. EAM may have had no intention of fighting the British, but police fired on the crowd, killing 28 and seriously wounding another 150. Scobie declared martial law. Thus began the Dekemvriana (December events).

EAM called a general strike. The effect was total: all shops, factories, ministries and public and private installations in Athens were paralysed. ELAS seized 21 of the 28 police stations in the city. On 5 December, hundreds of thousands turned out for the funeral of the 28 martyrs. They appealed to British soldiers: 'Let us choose our own government.' EAM told General Scobie that, in view of the massacre, it would not be surrendering its arms. By 12 December, EAM had taken control of most of Athens. The British kept control of only a few blocks in the city centre. But ELAS did not deploy the tens of thousands of fighters stationed outside Athens to the capital. Rather, the KKE's time was taken up with purging its political opponents on the left. Taking advantage of its control over the city, the KKE leadership directed the party's paramilitary security force, OPLA, to kill hundreds of anarchists, Trotskyists and KKE dissidents.

General Scobie and Churchill had to move quickly to retrieve the situation, which boded ill for British interests in Greece. Churchill ordered thousands of British soldiers then engaged in the Italian campaign to ship to Athens to fight the Greek Resistance. With the arrival of fresh forces and heavy weapons, including tanks, the British turned their experience of crushing colonial revolts to good use. Churchill instructed Scobie to act as if he were 'in a conquered city, confronted by local rebellion.' The British used heavy artillery to pound working class districts, while the Royal Air Force strafed apartment blocks. The British were backed by the National Guard and openly fascist gangs under the command of Colonel Grivas. It took 37 days of bitter fighting, with 50,000 Greek dead and 2,000 British casualties, before the British succeeded in crushing the resistance. Careful to observe his agreement with Churchill, Stalin abandoned the Greek Communists to their fate.

A ceasefire in mid-January was followed in mid-February by the Varkiza agreement. ELAS undertook to disarm, to withdraw 160 kilometres outside Athens and to evacuate Salonika, one of its other strongholds. In return, the British promised an amnesty for 'political' crimes and a plebiscite on the monarchy, to be followed by democratic elections.

ELAS's surrender, as anticipated, saw the fascists conduct a reign of terror against their opponents. Thousands of former ELAS members were arrested and tortured. Many were executed, their bodies left in public squares as a warning to others. Thousands of former partisans fled to Albania and Yugoslavia, now in the hands of the Communists. By contrast, most fascists escaped punishment. Those who had collaborated with the Nazi occupation were now lauded as national heroes by the middle class and the wealthy; those who had fought it were condemned as criminals and terrorists.

In March 1946, a farcical election took place in an environment of systemic fascist harassment of any left or liberal representatives. The KKE boycotted it as an undemocratic travesty, and the right swept the board. British, French and US observers declared the election 'on the whole' free and fair, and Stalin welcomed the new government. Six months later, a plebiscite held in only slightly less illegitimate circumstances voted in favour of the monarchy. At the end of September, King George II returned to the throne.

The terror unleashed against EAM in the cities drove thousands to the mountains. The Communists resumed the guerrilla war, although without the support of their former EAM partners. But there was no orientation to mass struggle, either in the villages or cities. Zachariadis was back in Greece, ordering ELAS – now renamed the Democratic Army – to abandon guerrilla tactics and fight as a regular army. In such a contest, the war would be won by whichever side had the most weapons and the best trained soldiers; there was no doubt who would prevail. The Democratic Army, equipped with weapons and rear bases in Yugoslavia, did score some early successes against the disorganised and badly led national army. But the decision by US President Truman, in the first act of the Cold War, to supply the Greek Government with much superior weapons and military advisers quickly saw the momentum shift. By the summer of 1949, the Democratic Army was in retreat across the country. On 16 October 1949, the Civil War formally ended with the crushing defeat of the Communists. The war had cost 158,000 Greek lives, mostly from the left, the workers and the peasants. The fascists, by contrast, all found plum jobs in government and the army and remained in high office for many years afterwards.

THE LESSONS OF ITALY AND GREECE

Italian and Greek experiences confirm that World War II was not a fight for democracy. Britain and the US put their own interests first. They were happy to co-operate and even arm fascist forces in Greece and to leave many fascists in place in Italy. Stalin was content to let them do so.

The second great imperialist war shares much in common with the first, but there are some important differences. World War I ended in revolutionary overthrow of rulers across Europe and the advent of the first workers' state; World War II did not. Workers and peasants in Italy, Greece and elsewhere showed their willingness to fight to change the world. There was mass resistance. There were political and social crises. But whether there was a genuinely revolutionary situation, comparable to the end of World War I, we cannot know. The best sections of the working class were led by class collaborationist Stalinists, so the potential was never tested. The Stalinists were much more successful than the reformists had been in holding back workers' struggle after World War I. They helped to build mass resistance movements in occupied Europe, but the credibility they earned from this was used to channel these movements into a dead end. Blinded by Stalinism, they sacrificed the interests of the partisan movement to meet Russia's needs, believing them to be the same thing. Their domination of the more radical elements of the workers' movement enabled the Stalinist parties to prevent the emergence of mass revolutionary parties. Trotsky called Stalin 'the gravedigger of the revolution.' Italy and Greece demonstrated that this applied outside Russia too, everywhere that Communist parties were able to build a mass following.

FURTHER READING

ITALY

T. Behan, *The Italian Resistance: Fascists, Guerrillas and the Allies*, London, Pluto Press, 2009.

P. Ginsborg, *A History of Contemporary Italy*, London, Penguin Books, 1990.

D. Gluckstein, *A People's History of the Second World War*, London, Pluto Press, 2012.

GREECE

D. Eudes, *The Kapetanios: Partisans and Civil War in Greece, 1943 –1949*, New York, Monthly Review Press, 1972.

D. Gluckstein, *A People's History of the Second World War*, London, Pluto Press, 2012.

B. Potter, *Greek Tragedy*, Solidarity pamphlet no. 29, London, 1968.

E. Vulliamy and H. Smith, 'British perfidy in Greece: a story worth remembering', *Open Democracy*, 1 December 2014.

STALINISM AND ANTI-STALINISM AFTER WORLD WAR II

15.

POST-WAR UPSURGE IN AUSTRALIA AND THE COMMUNIST CHALLENGE

After World War II, hopes were high among civilians and returned soldiers alike for a new world order in peacetime. There could be no return to the horrors of the Great Depression and its aftermath – the tens of millions thrown onto the scrapheap, the triumph of fascism and the butchery of war. These hopes were highest in those countries that had been occupied by the Axis powers (Chapter 14), but they were also widespread in the victorious Allied powers. In Britain, workers turned on Churchill's Conservatives at the 1945 general election and delivered Labour a big majority for the first time. In the US, strikes swept the country. But Australian workers stand out for their militancy at this time. They fought for several years for shorter working hours, higher wages, improved annual leave and more control over work. Mostly, they won. Union membership soared.[1]

The situation presented the CPA with big opportunities to win an audience among worker militants. However, the CPA did little to seize the moment; it gave a lead in some important strikes but did not launch a broader offensive. This changed in 1948 when, at Moscow's behest, the party jagged left. In this later period, the CPA began to believe it could replace the Labor Party's dominance in the working class by leading aggressive political strikes. This project was not realistic, even in the immediate postwar years. By 1948, however, in a Cold War environment and with a more confident right, victories were harder to win. The CPA's ambition to overtake the ALP led it to overreach itself at a time when it was isolated in the labour movement. Its misorientation contributed to the defeat of a major battle in the coal mines which set back the workers' movement and helped consolidate the rightward shift in Australian society.

The balance of forces in 1945

Historian Tom Sheridan gives a sense of working class attitudes at the end of the war:

> All members of the work force retained vivid, and usually bitter, memories of the depression years. This meant not only that the victims of that economic disaster were determined that it should never happen again, but also that the attitude of organised labour was coloured by a desire for something akin to revenge, for a squaring of those industrial and social accounts left suspended with the outbreak of war. This time, it was felt, the bosses, the financiers, or however 'they' might be described, were not going to get away with it.[2]

The two main union demands were a 40-hour week and a rise in the Basic Wage. Coal miners had already won 40 hours in 1940 and in 1944, printers at Sydney newspapers struck and won shorter hours. Unions now pushed for a 40-hour week for all and an end to wartime wage restraint.

Bosses in private industry were in no position to withstand workers' demands. With low unemployment and shortages of skilled labour, workers' bargaining power was strong. Employers' identification with the unjust pre-war political and economic order only discredited them. With a few important exceptions, they were on the defensive, both industrially and politically.

Labor governments and the industrial tribunals were the main impediment to workers' victories in the immediate postwar years. Prime Minister Ben Chifley committed to continuing wartime austerity, ignoring Labor conference resolutions to meet workers' demands on pay and working hours and shunting union claims off to tribunals. The tribunals proved tortuously slow. Workers turned to strike action on a massive scale.

Mainstream union leaders were useless. The ACTU's Albert Monk and Percy Clarey, backed by the Victorian Trades Hall Council's Vic Stout and the NSW Labor Council's Jim Kenny, were keener to defend the Chifley government and its state Labor counterparts than to fight for workers' interests. Most union officials wanted nothing more than a quiet life; others were ideologically opposed to direct action. They preferred lobbying the ALP and making submissions to the industrial tribunals as a way of obtaining modest gains. But workers would not let them rest easy. Strikes broke out both in the traditional militant hotspots and also among usually quiescent groups, including waiters, bakers and postal and pastoral workers.

Nor were Communist union leaders leading the charge, although media coverage sought to blame them. The CPA was certainly a force in the labour movement. It reached the high-water mark of its influence in the unions in the immediate postwar years. It was well represented on the floor of ACTU Congresses and on its executive; it led five trades and labour councils, including the Queensland Trades and Labour Council. On one estimate, it counted 50 full-time and 250 part-time union officials in its ranks. The party had grown during the war and, while some recruits melted away fairly quickly in the last months of the war, it still had 16,000 members in the winter of 1945, a sizeable party by Australian standards. Membership fell further by 1947, to 12,000, but with the party's fair-weather friends quitting, the CPA became a harder and more serious organisation, both in terms of its ability to intervene in industrial disputes and its commitment to Stalinism.

The Russian leaders, however, made no effort to encourage the CPA to use this influence in the unions to aggressively champion strikes. The CPA was hardly a priority for Stalin in 1945, given the other demands on the Russian leader's time. More generally, though, Stalin at this time was attempting to maintain a working relationship with the British and US leaders to ensure that the agreed-upon division of wartime spoils went ahead smoothly. Russia had demonstrated its credentials during the war when it dissolved the Comintern in 1943 and formally renounced its call for revolution in the West. Collaboration between the wartime allies was still obvious at the Yalta conference in February 1945. Although relations between the Big 3 began to sour at the Potsdam conference in July, as the big imperialist powers fought over spheres of influence in Germany, Russia at this stage was not seeking to bring on a wider fight with its former wartime allies, as its intervention in Italy and Greece demonstrated (Chapter 14).

If the Russians were not pushing for a left turn in the Western Communist parties, they also wanted to prevent them from veering too far to the right and losing their identity as independent organisations. The risk was clearest in the US party where general secretary Earl Browder had taken Popular Front politics to their logical conclusion and dissolved the party, renaming it the 'Communist Political Association.' It was to act as a pressure group on the Democratic Party. The CPUSA also backed extending the wartime ban on strikes. In Britain, the CPGB argued that the wartime Conservative–Labour coalition should be returned to office at the July 1945 general election – when workers were preparing to sweep Labour to power in its own right. Forced by Labour's smashing victory to modify its approach, the CPGB became virtually uncritical supporters of the Attlee Government.

This tendency by the US and British Communists to orient too closely to their 'own' ruling class rather than to Moscow was not helpful to Stalin. These parties, even if relatively small, could still serve as one more weapon in Russia's diplomatic armoury. Stalin launched a campaign through a proxy, PCF leader Jacques Duclos, to fight this tendency, which resulted in Browder's removal as general secretary in February 1946.

Such international factors helped to shape the thinking of the CPA leaders in 1945: neither to aggressively attack the Australian ruling class, nor to drift to the right. An attempt by FIA leader Ernie Thornton to liquidate the Australian party, on the lines of Browderism, was roundly rejected. Local factors came into play as well. The CPA had grown strongly during the war when it backed the Curtin government. From the perspective of CPA leaders, there did not seem to be any great advantage to be gained from breaking with this approach. 'Constructive criticism' of the Chifley government was emphasised, and the CPA continued to support the return of Labor at elections. When in March 1946, Victorian party secretary Jack Blake tried to steer the party to a more critical approach to the ALP, stating in the draft of a resolution to the state conference that 'Workers will gain from Labor governments, only what they unite, organise, and fight for,' he was condemned by the rest of the national leadership for his 'left sectarianism' and the offending sentence was struck out. The CPA's industrial approach was also marked by moderation. Party members were urged to oppose any attempt to use strikes to break Labor's wartime wages controls and labour regulations. The postwar strike wave was not, therefore, the result of any adventurism on the part of the CPA, despite media assertions.

The final element in the postwar alignment of forces was the Industrial Groups, set up in 1945 by the NSW ALP in a bid to challenge CPA control over important unions. Initially united only in their hostility to Stalinist control, they were fairly politically mixed. Members ranged from the Catholic Right of the party to Nick Origlass's Trotskyist group inside the ALP. At the first conference of the NSW Industrial Groups in March 1947, a Trotskyist motion calling for the nationalisation of industry under workers' control was carried; another, to disband the armed forces and replace them with a workers' militia, was defeated by only one vote. These, however, were fluke results. The right now had the wind in its sails. As the Cold War began, the well-resourced Catholic Church-backed political group, 'The Movement,' headed by B. A. Santamaria, soon came to dominate the Industrial Groups. They became a stronghold of the right in the labour movement for the next decade.

Strike wave, 1945–48

As war came to a close, many Australian workers believed that a new Depression might not be far away and that wartime full employment would soon give way to lengthy dole queues. They knew that they had to act immediately to take advantage of their strong bargaining power before it was snatched away again. The Chifley Labor government, however, was determined to frustrate these aspirations. Industrial confrontation was inevitable. That Labor was in office federally and in most states gave the postwar strikes an additional political edge.

STEEL STRIKE

The steel industry experienced the first big blow-up. Broken Hill Proprietary (BHP) was determined to prevent the Communist-run FIA from having any say over how its steel mills were run. BHP management, long recognised as one of the most bloody-minded in the country, had maintained absolute control over the steelworks for many years by using lockouts, shutdowns, scabs, company unions, blacklists, victimisations and union deregistration proceedings. With the balance of power swinging towards the unions, BHP now faced resistance. In September 1945, management at BHP's Port Kembla plant sacked an FIA delegate. Before long, 6,000 Port Kembla workers were on strike. Four weeks later, they were joined by 7,000 workers at BHP's Newcastle plant. The company's seafarers and coal miners in the Hunter region then struck in support of the steelworkers.

The steel strike took place at a time when demand for the 40-hour week was hotting up. The ACTU had feebly pushed the issue through arbitration and – unsurprisingly – made no headway. Workers now turned to industrial muscle. In July 1945, 3,000 commercial printers struck for the 40-hour week. They were still out in September, when workers at Sydney's Bunnerong power station downed tools. In October, coal miners and transport workers prepared to strike in support of the power workers. The Bunnerong stoppage caused widespread power shortages and brought many industries in Sydney to a halt. With workers pressing ahead, the NSW Labor Council tried to run to the head of the movement by announcing a one-day statewide stoppage. The Chifley government invoked wartime national security regulations to end the power strike, while promising the Labor Council that it would amend the law to allow the Arbitration Court to introduce the 40-hour week for workers on federal awards. The Labor Council scrapped its plans for a statewide strike, and the power workers returned to work. With combined action for the 40-hour week delayed for many months, the commercial printers stayed out another month. They eventually voted to return to work in November to allow the Arbitration Court to hear their claim.

With the industrial temperature rising in NSW in the spring of 1945 there was strong union sympathy for the BHP workers. The strike was solid, and pressure built among more militant unions to broaden the dispute. Attempts by BHP to play the Newcastle workers off against the Port Kembla workers, and by the Labor Council to isolate the FIA, were rebuffed. The closely knit steel communities rallied around the strikers, with substantial local donations and large turnouts at public meetings and processions. Local traders offered their services free to strikers. Mining communities close to the steel plants also offered support, as did seafarers and building workers.

By November, even with the Bunnerong power workers back at work, action by coal miners made blackouts and industrial shutdowns a common occurrence. The right wing Labor Council leaders, anxious to bring the strike to an end, argued that it was a Communist plot to undermine the Chifley government. The Liberal Opposition weighed in, warning of 'revolution, anarchy and bloodshed.'[3] Eventually, as the dispute stretched into December, the Chifley government patched up a deal with BHP, who agreed to recognise union delegates and to re-employ workers sacked during the strike. But the steelworkers still refused to go back, staying out another three weeks until BHP agreed to negotiate with their chosen officials and to reinstate the delegate whose sacking had triggered the strike. By sticking to their guns, the steel workers had succeeded in inflicting a rare defeat on one of the country's biggest and most arrogant employers.

QUEENSLAND MEAT STRIKE

Weeks after NSW steelworkers returned to work, thousands of Queensland meat workers came out. Unfortunately, the employers came out on top in this case. Like the BHP bosses, meat industry bosses wanted to assert their right to hire and fire. They were up against workers with a reputation for militancy, members of the Amalgamated Meat Industry Employees Union (AMIEU). The union was run by the CPA, but workers in the big export meat works in Central and North Queensland often chafed at the restrictions placed on them by Brisbane union leaders. The bosses were supported by the Queensland Industrial Court, the Hanlon state Labor government and the AWU – which had a long record of working with the ALP government to smash militant unions.

The sacking of union activists at two small Brisbane meat works triggered the strike. It quickly escalated and became statewide on 29 March. The Industrial Court deregistered the union and ordered the workers to return to work. Bacon factory workers quickly folded, leaving workers at the big export meat works to carry on.

Appeals for support from other unions met with mixed success. Only the wharfies initially struck in support. Attempts by the ARU to pull members out were barred by the Industrial Court. A solidarity strike by coal miners in June, quickly restricting power supplies and transport services, gave fresh life to the strike. The Hanlon Government declared a state of emergency, while the media slammed the strike as a Communist plot. After more than three months on strike, a stormy mass meeting of AMIEU members voted to return to work on the basis of existing awards and preservation of pre-strike work practices.

The bosses drove home their advantage. They sacked union activists, eliminated seniority provisions and limited on the job representation by the union. Only in the militant Northern district, centred on Townsville, were workers able to hold onto their conditions. The Hanlon Government passed punitive amendments to industrial laws: toughening anti-strike laws, widening union deregistration provisions and giving the bosses greater leeway to sack union activists.

Meanwhile, federal Arbitration Court hearings on the 40-hour week had dragged on, month after month. When workers demanded action to put pressure on the court, CPA union leaders backed the ACTU in instructing them not to strike while the case was being heard, for fear of jeopardising the Chifley government's chances at the September federal election.

VICTORIAN TRANSPORT STRIKE

After the September election, which Labor won handsomely, unions began to move again. In October 1946, Victorian rail and tram workers struck for increased leave and penalty rates and improved rosters. This was the first Victorian rail strike since 1903 and the first ever combined rail and tram strike. As picketers prevented petrol wagons from making deliveries, petrol supplies quickly began to dry up. Strikers threatened to overturn the few private buses still running. Rail workers in Albury, NSW, prevented movement of goods to and from Sydney. Tram workers picketed bus services laid on to circumvent the strike. The Victorian government was forced to introduce electricity rationing in Melbourne because of the effects of the railway stoppage and a solidarity strike by Wonthaggi coal miners. The media and conservative opposition slammed the strike as 'the beginnings of the Communist new order' and 'an organised attempt at anarchy.'[4] After nine days, the transport workers were victorious. Historian of the CPA Alastair Davidson described the outcome as delivering: 'bigger gains to the workers than any other single strike in Victorian history.'[5]

VICTORIAN METAL TRADES LOCKOUT AND STRIKE

The transport strike was soon overshadowed by the biggest setpiece battle of the postwar era: the metal trades margins campaign. The wage premium for skilled workers above the labourers' wage, known as 'the margin,' had been stagnant for years. To restore the margin, the Amalgamated Engineering Union (AEU) submitted a claim for a 20 shilling wage increase for skilled metal workers. On 14 October 1946, the AEU in Melbourne imposed an overtime ban. The next day, 6,500 AEU members in Sydney stopped work for 24 hours. On 22 October, the combined metal trades unions in Victoria decided to join the overtime ban. This was accompanied by a campaign of mass resignations from foundries, a powerful weapon at a time of acute skill shortages. By the end of the week, 1,600 AEU members had withdrawn from 98 metal shops. The bosses retaliated, locking out 20,000 workers on 14 November. Far from being intimidated, AEU members voted not to return to work until they were granted the full 20 shilling wage increase. The AEU also pulled out 1,500 maintenance workers whom the employers had retained in the locked-out shops to service machinery.

The metal trades were not alone in fighting for their rights. On 17 October, coal miners at 13 NSW pits ceased work, and Sydney wharfies struck for a week. On 21 October, the South Australian railways stopped for 24 hours. On 6 December, gas workers embarked on a national strike characterised by unprecedented rank and file militancy, including sit-ins. The gas strike rolled on through the summer, eventually depriving Melbourne of all gas supplies. On 11 December, 20,000 wharfies stopped work for 24 hours. The Arbitration Court's decision in December to raise the Basic Wage by just 7 percent, far short of the ACTU's claim of 21 percent, heightened the union movement's understanding that the court, the Chifley government and the bosses were all doing their best to frustrate workers' demands.

The Victorian metal industry bosses who believed that locking out the tradespeople could bring them to heel were mistaken. With order books still healthy and shortages of skilled workers chronic, the bosses were in no position to hold out. Over summer, the lockout crumbled. On 20 January 1947, the Victorian Chamber of Manufacturers called it off. But the metal workers vowed to stay out. Within the AEU, rank and file members escalated pressure on their leaders to maximise the effectiveness of the strike by calling out more workers. The AEU executive's hope of confining the stoppage to select groups of workers was dashed; they were forced to call out another 7,000 members.

On 22 March, with all 49 Melbourne branches unanimously refusing to accept a mediocre Arbitration Court wage offer, the AEU executive pulled out 3,000 members in power and transport industries. These were joined by tradespeople in the railways, gas and tramways. On 24 March, 7,000 AEU members voted at a mass meeting to extend the strike to the Yallourn power complex in the Latrobe Valley. Pressure from the AEU Melbourne district committee saw the federal executive permit apprentices in the Newport power station to join the strike. By 14 April, with power supplies rapidly dwindling, all suburban trains had ceased running, country train services ran at only half capacity, and electricity supplies were rationed. On 15 April, gas supplies were severely restricted and tram services heavily cut. On 28 April, AEU members on the country railways stopped work, and all remaining staff and apprentice members were withdrawn from metropolitan power stations and the railways in Melbourne.

Conservative forces were outraged at the prospect of a power shutdown in Melbourne. The Liberal Party prophesied: 'complete chaos and bloodshed will be seen in the streets of Melbourne next week.'[6] The metal workers were unbowed. Strikes extended to larger groups of workers, forcing the bosses to agree to lift wages substantially for the skilled trades. On 7 May, AEU members agreed to return to work. Six months later, the Arbitration Court handed down its decision for the Metal Trades Award, lifting wages for the skilled trades by 16 shillings (a 15% increase) and granting the lesser grades increases of 11 to 13 shillings. Sheridan calls this: 'easily the biggest victory ever achieved by the AEU, a union well used to industrial success.'[7]

The AEU victory was testimony to the determination of the rank and file. They stayed solidly behind the strike, repeatedly confirming their support at successive mass meetings of thousands. They won despite opposition from the bosses and the Arbitration Court, state and federal Labor governments, leaders of other unions and even some within the AEU.

The metal trades breakthrough had far-reaching effects. The margins for hundreds of thousands of skilled and semi-skilled workers in varying occupations rose in line with the metal trades. The AEU had demonstrated its preparedness to fight for its rights, and the message was not lost on the authorities. Just one month after the metal workers had scored their historic victory, the NSW Government legislated a 40-hour week for workers on state awards; soon afterwards, the Queensland Government announced that it would do the same. This forced the hand of the Arbitration Court. After dragging its feet for 16 months, it finally introduced the 40-hour week in all federal awards, to take effect in January 1948. These were remarkable breakthroughs, described by Sheridan as 'the biggest ever won by the Australian working class.'[8]

VICTORIAN TRAMWAYS STRIKE AND ESSENTIAL SERVICES LEGISLATION

In January 1948, Victoria's Communist-led tram workers were on strike again, this time over the tramway board's refusal to introduce five-day rosters. The new Liberal–Country government of Thomas Hollway referred the strike to arbitration. The Arbitration Court ordered the workers back to work. A mass meeting of 2,500 tram workers refused to comply and in response, the state government announced draconian essential services legislation. The government's bill would make legal strikes almost impossible in a wide range of industries, including transport, fuel, light, power, water and sewerage. The government accompanied the bill with a barrage of anti-communist propaganda.

The response by Communist-led unions was immediate. Seafarers struck, wharfies and Newport power workers announced that they would follow suit, and building unions arranged stop-work meetings. Faced with this blitz of industrial action, the Arbitration Court retreated, handing down a decision that gave tram workers virtually everything they demanded. The government, however, rushed its essential services legislation into parliament. While the two chambers debated the bill, Trades Hall also convened an emergency meeting. Militant leaders demanded a statewide general strike, but the Trades Hall leadership tried to defuse the anger. The government offered the Trades Hall leaders a slight concession – that it would not proclaim the legislation without first consulting them – and this gave the Trades Hall leaders the opportunity to claim a great victory. Communist union leaders swallowed the line and, without consulting members, announced that they would call off the strikes.

Hollway had only backed off temporarily; the government proclaimed the *Essential Services Act 1948* in October. The Communist-led unions in public transport, the building industry and the Wonthaggi mines held a one-day protest strike on 16 November, and a mass meeting of 10,000 unionists demanded that the Act be repealed. One week later, the government used its new powers to issue summonses against 10 rail and tram workers for breaching the legislation. Militant unions immediately struck. The Seamen's Union blockaded the state, gas supplies soon ran short, cuts to rail operations loomed and a planned strike by coal miners threatened electricity supplies. Transport and building unions organised further stoppages. Faced with the almost complete breakdown of services, the Hollway government dropped the proceedings against the 10 workers.

The *Essential Services Act* still remained on the books, but the government was wary of using it. It attempted to invoke the legislation during the 1949 coal strike but backed off when the AEU and the Federated Engine Drivers and Firemen's Association (FEDFA) threatened to strike in support of the miners. In 1950, the government had the opportunity to use the law during two lengthy public transport strikes but stayed its hand. Industrial resistance had rendered the Act a dead letter.

QUEENSLAND RAIL STRIKE

State Liberal governments were not alone in reacting fiercely to militant unionists in 1948. In Queensland, the Hanlon Labor government took extraordinary measures to try to beat a strike on the state's railways. AEU members in the railway workshops had been denied the full flow-on of the margins increase in the Metal Trades Award, granted in 1947. Other governments had passed on the full increase, but the Queensland premier attempted to have much of the increase absorbed into existing rates. On 3 February 1948, AEU members in the Ipswich railway workshops, one of the largest workplaces in the state, struck for the full rate. The government retaliated by standing down the remaining 14,000 rail workers and locomotive drivers without pay, shutting down the state's railway network. Far from intimidating the strikers, the standdowns steeled AEU members' resolve and embittered the rest of the workforce. The AEU pulled its maintenance members off the Brisbane trams, bringing the city's tramways to a halt.

Recognising that the standdowns of rail workers had backfired, Hanlon reversed course and urged the Industrial Court to order them to return to work. The TLC disputes committee, dominated by ALP members, called upon the stood-down rail workers to join the strike instead. It added increases to margins and weekend penalty rates for all rail workers to the demands. On 27 February, Hanlon announced a state of emergency, describing the strike as 'a challenge now to democratically constituted government which has all the elements of civil war.'⁹ Picketing was banned; strikers were threatened with dismissal. The Chifley government came to Hanlon's aid, providing money to help organise scab road haulage operations and delaying social security payments to families of stood-down workers.

Repression only enlarged the numbers involved in the dispute. Under the leadership of the AEU's Ted Rowe and Joe Cranwell, who had led the metal trades dispute in Victoria the previous year, mass pickets of thousands gathered outside workshops at Ipswich and other centres, making a mockery of the anti-picketing laws. Mass meetings of rail workers rejected the Industrial Court's return to work order and joined the strike. The TLC now declared all work in railway workshops and depots banned. Ipswich miners refused to supply coal to the railways, and interstate unions weighed in with support. Seafarers and wharfies stopped work to block fuel supplies for the government's scab road haulage operation.

On 9 March, the Queensland government tightened the legal screws further, passing the *Industrial Law Amendment Act 1948*. This targeted any industrial solidarity action or any action that took place 'designed to prolong the strike' and even banned the media from carrying stories sympathetic to the strike. Hefty fines and up to six months' imprisonment were provided for anyone breaching the Act. Within three days, the government laid charges against three leading Communists involved in the strike. A few days later, relishing their new powers, police bashed a procession of unionists protesting against the new legislation – including Australia's only Communist MP, Fred Paterson, who was observing the march from the footpath. The attack on Paterson aroused a fierce response: 6,000 attended a mass protest rally and 1,600 wharfies marched in defiance of the Act.

The ACTU executive formally supported the strike and opposed the new emergency powers, but the majority of union leaders were horrified by what they saw as another Communist attack on a Labor government. Queensland rail workers did, however, win support from NSW ARU secretary Jack Ferguson. His union banned all freight movement to Queensland and persuaded the Grouper-dominated NSW land transport group of unions to do the same. The interstate rail blockade was critical in forcing Hanlon to negotiate.

As the weeks wore on, strike-weariness became apparent. The locomotive drivers decided not to support further work bans. Coal miners lifted their industrial action. In regional ARU branches, where members had been starved of hard news and exposed only to government and media lies, resolve weakened. Both sides moved towards a settlement. On 1 April, the government lifted its wage offer, offered weekend penalty rates for the first time and agreed not to victimise strikers. On 2 April, mass meetings of railway workers agreed to return to work.

After the strike, amid a storm of union protest, five Communist unionists were jailed for refusing to pay fines incurred under the *Industrial Law Amendment Act*. Not wishing to face another round of strikes, an anonymous donor, quite possibly the Queensland Government itself, paid the fines of the first three. Soon after, the other two were freed. The government repealed the Act and announced that it would neither proceed with outstanding prosecutions nor collect outstanding fines. By standing firm, supported by the all-important solidarity from NSW rail workers, Queensland rail workers had won most of their demands.

The CPA changes course

Communist-led unions were in the forefront of the postwar strikes, but the CPA tended not to distinguish itself as a particularly radical force. It criticised the Chifley government for blocking the immediate implementation of the 40-hour week and for its determination to hold down wages. But it continued to call for a united front with the ALP.

In the unions, Communist officials tended to *adapt to* rather than *lead* the militancy of workers; in some cases, they did not even go that far. In 1945–46, CPA officials backed ACTU efforts to prevent a national strike over the 40-hour demand, frustrating rank and file CPA members. As the campaign for shorter hours reached its peak in 1947, party leaders noted that even right wing officials 'sometimes made much more militant speeches than our own.'[10] In the Miners' Federation, CPA officials took a dim view of strikes that were not authorised by district officers. In 1947, CPA industrial strategist and editor of the Federation's *Common Cause*, Edgar Ross, condemned what he called a 'blind strike psychology' among NSW South Coast miners.[11]

The degree of militancy shown by Communist officials varied with the circumstances. The AEU's margins campaign of 1946–47 had been led by the CPA's Ted Rowe and Labor's Joe Cranwell. Both adhered to a militant line, including pressuring more conservative members of the leadership to maintain support for the strike. By contrast, the FIA's Thornton took a less aggressive stance during the dispute. The different situations of their two unions explains the varying stances: the AEU was wealthy and paid strike pay for the duration of the dispute, and it was comparatively easy for skilled engineers to find other work during the stoppage; the FIA was a poor union whose members lacked the easily saleable skills of engineers, making its industrial militancy correspondingly fragile.

Things began to shift in late 1947 when rising tensions with the US and Britain prompted Moscow to signal a political switch to its followers. The Cominform, set up by Stalin to dictate the ideological positions of the Communist governments of Eastern Europe and the West's two big Communist parties, the PCI and PCF, declared that the world was divided into two camps: the 'imperialist and anti-democratic camp' led by Washington, and an 'anti-imperialist and democratic camp' led by the Soviet Union. Communists in the West were now to adopt a more aggressive posture towards their ruling classes. The CPA had already begun pragmatically moving in this direction under the impact of the class struggle in Australia, so adopting the new line at its Fifteenth Congress in May 1948 did not represent an abrupt change. Party leaders told congress delegates that capitalism was approaching a deep crisis, war clouds were looming, and ALP governments would go on the offensive against workers. This presented an opportunity for the CPA to challenge Labor's domination of the working class. The party was already in a good position, Thornton claimed:

> Our mass support is very great... Our prestige is high, we are winning trades union elections, we are on top in the trade union movement ... We are a tremendous public force, greater than in most countries.[12]

Bright prospects lay ahead, the leadership declared. While the CPA had gone into the Depression as a marginal force with only a few hundred members, it would enter the new world depression as a powerful organisation, capable of making major breakthroughs.

The Queensland rail strike, which had concluded in the month before the Fifteenth Congress, provided much of the justification for the new policy. Hanlon's strikebreaking tactics were held up as proof of the bankruptcy of Laborism, and the success of the strike proved the potential of militant policies:

> The strike wave is not only beginning to embrace new sections of the working class and drawing them into active political life but is also resulting in exposing the role of the capitalist state, the Labor Party and reformist leaders and is opening the way to the passing of the masses over to the side of the Communist Party.[13]

Early in 1949, the CPA turned its hostility to Labor up a notch. The 'united front' with the ALP was unceremoniously buried, setting the scene for confrontation. The 1948 predictions of an economic bust were reiterated: 'There is no way out for the capitalist order…signs of an approaching crisis are becoming clearer from day to day.'[14] It was true, the leadership admitted, that the CPA had not grown over the previous 12 months, but workers' illusions in postwar 'so-called prosperity' would soon be shattered,[15] driving them into the CPA's arms.

It must be emphasised that, despite the CPA's shift to the left in 1948–49 and its condemnation of the ALP, it remained solidly committed to reformism. Its answer to rising US militarism and the coming economic collapse was not revolution or even 'anti-capitalism.' It advocated nationalisation of the big monopolies and the formation of a People's Front involving workers, middle class professionals, farmers and progressive capitalists. The party had not abandoned the Popular Front, only the ALP would not now be part of it, and the CPA would strive to fill its shoes.

The CPA's 'left turn' versus reality

The CPA's left turn seriously misoriented the party in its interventions in the class struggle in the late 1940s. Australia was entering a quarter century of unparalleled growth, not a new depression. Working class support for Labor was not being eliminated. Even if the CPA could win elections in some unions, it was routinely crushed by the ALP in state and federal elections. The CPA could hardly ignore its failure to beat Labor at the polls, so it turned to 'political strikes' as the vehicle to challenge Labor. Dixon explained at the Fifteenth Party Congress:

> There are strikes led by reformists and by some Communist trade union officials which are conducted as purely economic strikes, and this is most unsatisfactory. We must aim in strike struggles…to draw the masses…to the side of the Communist Party.[16]

There is nothing exceptional about socialists declaring their aim to win over workers from reformists in the course of struggle; indeed, it is incumbent on them to do so. The problem was that the CPA understood this as prioritising the party's needs above all else, which had disastrous consequences during the 1949 coal strike.

The CPA's left turn overlooked Australia's shift to the right in the late 1940s. A ruling class offensive against the left was gaining momentum, drawing behind it layers of the middle class and more backward sections of workers. The formation of the Liberal Party in 1944, under Robert Menzies's leadership, was one milestone. The new party rapidly gained tens of thousands of middle class recruits – wheat and dairy farmers, shopkeepers, small employers, accountants, doctors and lawyers. Menzies described them as 'the backbone of the nation,' and they in turn drew behind them such groups as clerks in private business.[17]

The Liberals mobilised the middle class as shock troops to defend the capitalists. Opposition to communism and strikes was the rallying cry. The first test came in August 1944, when the Labor government held a referendum to extend federal government economic powers to better coordinate the war effort. Conservative forces decried it as a step towards communism and mobilised to defeat it heavily in the popular vote.

In 1947, a much bigger battle blew up over the Chifley government's legislation to nationalise the banks. The banks immediately fought back, challenging the legislation in the High Court and running a big public campaign. They mobilised thousands of bank clerks to leaflet the suburbs, organised large public meetings and sent letters to bank customers. The Liberals seized on the issue, setting up a fighting fund from donations from big capitalists and condemning the proposal as 'a plan to destroy private enterprise and to create a Socialist State.'[18] Insurance companies joined the fray, fearing that they would be next. The Chifley government defended its legislation with far less confidence. In August 1948, the High Court declared the Act invalid.

The right wing mobilisation had an impact on the working class, with some workers enthusiastically joining the anti-communist campaign. For others, lasting social and economic trends blunted the class antagonism of the immediate postwar years. Big wins over shorter hours, higher pay and annual leave saw the edge begin to come off the class struggle. Jobs were plentiful, overtime easy to get and unemployment low; fears of a return to depression conditions abated. Living standards rose alongside a postwar baby boom, making home ownership a realistic option for young working class families. Property developers built suburban housing developments to meet the demand, and workers moved out of the inner city, fragmenting the working class communities that had been one of Labor's main bastions of support. The result was that some workers who had voted Labor in 1946 swung behind the Liberals at the 1949 election.

The ALP was not merely a victim of this right wing push. Its leaders were no laggards in 'fighting communism.' After the NSW ALP set up the Industrial Groups to fight the CPA in union elections, the Queensland, Victorian and SA branches soon followed. By 1948, the Groupers were beginning to register victories against Communist union leaders. Grouper influence in the Victorian and NSW ALP branch executives began to grow. In March 1949, Attorney-General Bert Evatt prosecuted CPA secretary Lance Sharkey for sedition. Sharkey had foolishly told the Sydney *Daily Telegraph*: 'If in the pursuit of aggressors, the soviet troops come to Australia, the Australian working class would welcome them.'[19] The following month, FIA assistant secretary and prominent Communist Jack McPhillips was jailed for a year for contempt of court for an innocuous statement that the Arbitration Court was subject to industrial pressure. Finally, during the 1949 coal strike, Chifley would not hesitate to fight the CPA and the Miners' Federation 'boots and all.'

The political tide was turning against the CPA and the left at the start of 1949. The party's prognosis of the opportunities that lay ahead was quite unrealistic. This, taken together with the party's Stalinist practices in the unions, all but guaranteed that the CPA would mishandle the looming coal strike.

The 1949 coal strike

Several factors favoured the coal miners as they prepared for an industrial campaign. Coal was the country's main fuel source, and stocks remained low throughout the postwar years. Strikes would quickly cause industrial shutdowns. The industry was virtually 100 percent unionised; the Miners' Federation organised 80 percent of workers, with the rest shared between the AEU, FEDFA and three small craft unions. The union was organised on a district basis. In NSW, accounting for three-quarters of the membership, there were three districts: Northern (66% of NSW production), Western (17%) and Southern (Illawarra; 16%). The union was relatively democratic. Pit head committees frequently struck without consulting the district executives or central council (national executive).

Mining communities in the established NSW and Victorian fields were tightly knit, with a strong sense of solidarity forged through a history of big strikes and lockouts. They shared a fierce hatred of mine owners for their neglect of basic safety, amenities and housing. Labor's failure to deliver on promises after the war and the CPA's diligent work over many years delivered the Communist Party a strong position in the union. The CPA held two of the top three national positions and, with its allies, majorities on the NSW Western and Southern district executives. Moderates controlled the bigger Northern district executive, but the CPA and its supporters held a majority on the larger board of management to which the executive was accountable.

The miners faced opposition on several fronts. Mine owners wanted an end to wartime controls that prevented them hiring and firing at will and changing working conditions. The miners' most intransigent opponents, however, were the Joint Coal Board, the Coal Industry Tribunal and the Chifley government. The Joint Coal Board was set up by the government in 1946 to boost production at the lowest possible cost; the welfare of mine workers was an afterthought. The Coal Industry Tribunal, also created by the Chifley government, aimed to reduce the industry's very high rate of strikes. It had jurisdiction over all industrial matters, including powers to impose fines and to sentence individuals to imprisonment for refusing to obey its directions. Its president, Justice Frank Gallagher, saw his main role as bringing militant mine workers to heel.

The Chifley government was determined to prevent the miners from using their industrial leverage to make gains. Gains won in the mines became the benchmark for workers in other industries, undermining Chifley's attempt to put a lid on wages. Chifley was also motivated by a desire to take on the CPA, which had made no secret of its desire to overtake the ALP. Accusations from conservative forces that the government was unwilling to 'take on the Commies' also made Chifley more determined to bring on and decisively win a confrontation with the CPA, proving his anti-communist credentials in time for the election later that year. Cabinet, the NSW Labor Government, the NSW Labor Council, the ACTU and the AWU all backed Chifley enthusiastically.

The combined mining unions council, on which the Federation was the main mover, believed that it must act quickly – because it anticipated an economic depression and was pressured by members threatening to take matters into their own hands. On 22 April 1949, the council served a log of claims containing four main demands: long service leave, a 35-hour week, a 30 shilling weekly wage increase and improvements to pit and town amenities. The mining unions immediately launched a campaign to build support on and off the coalfields, including big meetings and supporters' rallies in Sydney.

The owners rejected the 35-hour week claim, made their offer of long service leave conditional on changes unacceptable to the miners, proposed incentive payments instead of a wage increase and demanded the elimination of the compulsory retirement age of 60. In June, after weeks of stalling by the bosses and the Tribunal, the leaders of even the conservative craft unions had lost patience. By order of Justice Gallagher, they had deferred stop-work meetings while negotiations were under way, but this had only encouraged the mine owners and Coal Board to become more intransigent. All the unions now recognised that industrial pressure was needed. On 16 June, mass meetings voted nine to one in favour of a strike beginning on 27 June.

The Chifley government did its best from the outset to isolate the miners. It denounced the planned strike as a Communist plot that it would forcefully resist. Charles Anderson, the NSW Labor Council president, echoed Chifley's words: 'I ask the decent elements within the Miners' Federation to prevent their organisation being smashed by a few working-class traitors who are called Communists.'[20] In a largely successful attempt to turn public opinion against the miners, NSW authorities began to impose power restrictions even before the strike started, causing 130,000 stand downs and power cuts to households and transport services.

Negotiations continued. The mining unions withdrew two of their core demands – provision of pit and town amenities and the 30 shilling increase – in an attempt to extract concessions, but to no avail. The matter was no longer an industrial battle but a political contest. A senior Coal Board official told Edgar Ross, on the eve of the strike: 'Chif is determined to "pull you on".'[21]

On 27 June, receiving no concessions from the owners, 23,000 miners walked off the job. The Chifley government immediately swung into action. It passed legislation that froze the funds of the Miners' Federation and their supporting unions and prohibited individuals and unions from giving strikers and their families financial support. The Arbitration Court sentenced eight union leaders who had refused to reveal the whereabouts of union funds to jail terms of six to 12 months. Police raided CPA headquarters in Sydney.

Some ALP branches recorded protests, as did the Communist-led unions. The Seamen's Union, for example, stopped work for 24 hours. But supporters of the miners had difficulty getting their argument heard. The mining unions were prevented from presenting their case in the media – which, from start to finish, ran a hysterical campaign denouncing the strike. Labor politicians toured the coalfields condemning the strike. Chifley told an audience in Lithgow:

> This strike has been engineered by communists to destroy the arbitration system and wreck Labor governments. If it is their intention to wage a callous war on the community, then it will be a case of boots and all. I will never bend my knee to this unwarranted display of brute force.[22]

The miners resisted the government's attacks. The imprisonment of their leaders only welded them together. On 10 July, mass meetings overwhelmingly voted to continue the strike. Between 20 and 22 July, unofficial mass meetings in the key NSW Northern district voted to continue the strike. The Western, Southern and Victorian districts also remained solid.

In the last days of July, however, the strike front began to fray, and then to crack, in the face of opposition inside and outside the labour movement.

The ARU's Jack Ferguson played a particularly important role in breaking the strike. Ferguson had backed the Queensland rail workers in 1948, helping to ensure their victory; but he now campaigned hard against the miners. Ferguson faced opposition within the NSW ARU from shop committees that the CPA had helped organise. On 12 June, 5,000 rail workers marched in Sydney, demanding better pay and conditions, ending at the CPA platform in the Domain. Speakers attacking Ferguson were loudly applauded. Ferguson saw the coal strike as an opportunity to hit back at his Communist opponents. On 12 July, the ARU leader attended a meeting with representatives of the federal and NSW cabinets, the NSW Labor Council and ALP officials. They formulated a plan of attack that included ARU members shifting existing coal stocks 'at grass' to power stations. This alleviated pressure on industry in Sydney.

The AWU also offered its services to the Chifley government. Regarded by the bosses as more pliant than the Miners' Federation, the AWU had begun to make inroads in the mining industry, particularly in the open cut mines in the Northern district and in Queensland. Three weeks into the strike, Chifley suggested that the AWU scab on the Federation. He had no intention of going ahead with this, knowing the industrial mayhem that would result from two unions aggressively competing for members, but the threat that the AWU might take over struck fear into miners' hearts. They understood the AWU's willingness to do deals with bosses at workers' expense.

Coal shortages led to massive layoffs in mid-winter. They combined with the ferocious campaign by the ALP, ACTU and NSW Labor Council to reduce public support for the miners. Faced with a much tougher situation than they had expected, with no breakthrough in sight, the miners' morale began to waver.

Small mining communities on the fringe of the struggle, such as Collie in Western Australia, returned to work, as did miners in open cut Queensland mines under threat from the AWU. By the end of July, trouble was also brewing in the NSW Northern district. There were rumblings of dissatisfaction at a new open cut mine in Muswellbrook, where workers lacked the union traditions of the older underground mines. The Miners' Federation and its militant supporters on the combined mining unions council could have waged a campaign urging members to stay strong, engaging those who were not involved in strike support work and sending delegations to other unions and work sites to drum up support. That would have involved having the argument at mass meetings. Instead, the Federation leadership simply stonewalled the demand for mass meetings, opening up a split in the ranks of the mining unions.

Chifley's announcement that he would send troops into the mines piled on the pressure. On 1 August, 2,500 armed troops, backed by hundreds of police, were sent into three open cut fields. On 5 August, another 2,000 more troops started work at eight underground mines. These strikebreaking measures were fully backed by the NSW Labor Council. The ARU agreed to transport the coal dug by the soldiers to power stations, without which the whole operation would have failed. The amount of coal the soldiers extracted was insufficient to get industry moving again, but the government's willingness to take this step, with the support of the Labor Council, was a powerful blow to the miners' morale. It heightened their sense of isolation. It sent a clear signal that this was no ordinary industrial dispute against the employers; this was a political fight, and the ALP would use every arm of the state to crush them.

On 31 July, members of the Muswellbrook lodge called on the Northern district executive to organise mass meetings to vote on a back to work plan. If the district executive refused, lodge members threatened, they would call on other lodges to split from the Federation. On 1 August, a large public meeting in Cessnock echoed the demand for mass meetings, something now backed by AEU delegates in the northern collieries as well as smaller craft unions. The CPA still tried to hold back the growing call. In an unprecedented step, the party used its majority on the Northern district board of management to overrule a vote of lodge delegates to convene mass meetings. The CPA-dominated Southern district executive attempted to offset pressure from the Northern district to end the strike by convening meetings in Bulli and Wollongong which they hoped would strongly back staying out. Instead, the motion to continue the strike was only narrowly carried at Wollongong and was overwhelmingly defeated at Bulli.

The Federation leadership now had no alternative but to call mass meetings on 9 and 10 August. They recommended to members that they remain out for another week, hoping to find a face-saving formula to resolve the strike in the meantime. Members had had enough, however. They voted three to one to return to work. Every district but Victoria voted to end the strike. The defeated miners returned to work on 15 August. Jailed union leaders were released on 24 August, but the fines remained. Soon after the end of the strike, Justice Gallagher reopened hearings on the union's claims, ruling in favour of long service leave for miners but denying them the 35-hour week.

The defeat of the coal strike was a big win for the right in the labour movement. Chifley believed, correctly, that fighting the Communists would be popular: three-quarters of the electorate approved of his fund freezing legislation. Those in the ALP who opposed the government's handling of the strike were expelled and oppositional branches purged. At the September 1949 ACTU Congress, the CPA and its supporters were pushed back by a resurgent right whose delegates held a two to one majority on the floor. The biggest winners of the miners' defeat were the right in broader society. At the December federal election, the Liberals capitalised on the growing anti-communist mood. The disenchantment among ALP members at the use of troops to break a strike ensured that many of them had little appetite to campaign for the party. The outcome was that the Liberals were narrowly returned to power. In following years, they attempted to capitalise on the anti-communist atmosphere encouraged by Chifley.

The role of the CPA in the coal strike

Historians commonly argue that the CPA's 'adventurism,' its attempt to promote itself at the expense of the ALP to advance its political ambitions, largely triggered the 1949 coal strike. Edgar Ross had said as much when he spoke in early 1949 of 'an impending struggle in the coalfields' to be 'conducted under our political inspiration.'[23] However, while the CPA certainly played a leading role in the Miners' Federation, coal miners were not mere dupes of the party.

Fundamentally, miners struck in 1949 because they saw it as their best opportunity to succeed in their demands before a new economic depression took hold. Further, the Coal Industry Tribunal, the Joint Coal Board, the mine owners and federal and state governments had all shown that they would not concede the miners' claims without pressure. The miners' demands were not particularly radical – New Zealand miners already worked a 35-hour week, and long service leave was widespread in the public sector. Communist union leaders did not drag an unwilling membership into a confrontation; they were themselves dragged. Nearly five months before the strike, delegates to the annual meeting of the Federation's central council explained: 'The rank and file are waiting for a clear lead on major claims and will certainly follow when it is given...now is the time for a showdown' and 'If we do not do something... quickly, then the rank and file will take matters into their own hands.'[24] Miners had a militant history. Whether Labor or Communist, they were all united on the justice of their fight.

While the CPA was not responsible for the strike, its defeat had an impact on the party. Initially, the CPA declared it 'a great victory.' Labor had exposed its own anti-working class politics and created the possibility for 'further offensives' by the CPA.[25] In 1951, the party changed course, arguing that the strike had been a mistake. The party's enthusiasm for a confrontation was now attributed to its mistaken 'left sectarian' approach to the ALP. The leadership made Jack Blake and Jack Henry scapegoats for a policy that had been agreed by the whole leadership. The CPA concluded that it had to repudiate the left turn of the late 1940s and again pursue a 'united front' approach to the ALP. This argument bears some interrogation.

The CPA based its left turn on two premises: that a depression was looming which would radicalise workers and make them more predisposed to favour the CPA; and that Labor was going on the attack against workers. Workers would only make gains in these circumstances by waging militant struggles. The CPA therefore decided to challenge the ALP on the industrial front.

The CPA's assessment of the situation in the late 1940s was flawed, but it was hardly alone in predicting that a depression was on its way; plenty of mainstream economists made the same prediction. And the notion that the Chifley government was shifting to the right was accurate. It had set its face against workers' demands, maintained wage restraint for as long as possible and refused to legislate a 40-hour week. The Queensland Labor government had imposed draconian measures during the 1948 rail strike. Chifley was no respecter of human rights – as the coal strike would demonstrate. What, then, was 'left sectarian' about attacking Labor's record in office, in saying that it did the bosses' bidding, and that workers would have to fight Labor governments? Mass strikes undoubtedly ended wage restraint and brought the 40-hour week.

The CPA argued retrospectively that it should never have abandoned its wartime and postwar 'united front' approach to the ALP. But how could the CPA have created a 'united front' with Queensland Labor in 1948 or Chifley in 1949, when Labor's leaders did their best to smash strikes?

The CPA's conclusion in 1951 that the problem in 1949 was 'left sectarianism' was really an attack on militancy. The party was now shifting to the right. As part of its rightward orientation in the 1950s, the CPA abandoned criticism of Labor and ran 'unity tickets' of CPA and ALP officials or agreed to a sharing of spoils in union elections. This may have allowed some CPA union leaders to hold onto their positions and, in a few cases, to win back those lost to Groupers. But holding union office alone, without any recovery in rank and file militancy, did nothing to rebuild the fighting strength of the unions.

The CPA's bureaucratic approach to trade unionism was well established by the late 1940s. The party had been very successful in winning union positions in the 1930s and 1940s; but the focus on gaining full-time positions came to substitute for rank and file-driven activism. Rank and file workers had to fit into the plans made, supposedly, on their behalf. During World War II, this involved quashing strikes. In the late 1940s, it involved promoting strikes but directing them from on high. Rank and file power was nowhere prioritised.

A few examples suffice to show the CPA's top-down approach in the unions. On the jailing of the FIA's McPhillips in April 1949, Communist Miners' Federation leaders simply announced a general 24-hour stoppage in defence of McPhillips, without consulting fellow officials, delegates or the membership. A storm of protest erupted; the leadership was riding roughshod over members and flouting the union's democratic traditions. The strike went ahead, but lodges in all districts, particularly the Northern district, refused to obey the directive and continued working.

The CPA Miners' Federation officials' refusal to call mass meetings late in the coal strike fitted this general pattern of manipulation. By denying members a voice, the CPA union leaders only gave the right a weapon. The 'back to work' elements in the union could, rightly, claim that the Communist leaders were manipulators who trampled on the democratic right of members. The CPA certainly felt the backlash after the strike ended. In elections in the Northern district later in 1949, the Groupers threw their weight behind the moderates, who won big majorities on both the executive and board of management. The CPA subsequently lost its majority on the Federation central council, for the first time since 1934.

The same tendency to bureaucratic pronouncements was obvious in the FIA. The FIA lacked the democratic traditions of the AEU and Miners' Federation. The Communists did little to change this when they took over in 1937 (see Chapter 13 for its treatment of the Balmain branch late in the war). When McPhillips was jailed, FIA leaders convinced branch meetings in Sydney and Newcastle, stacked with CPA members, to call an immediate protest strike. Balmain militant Nick Origlass had had repeated run-ins with the FIA leaders; he nonetheless understood the need for action to protest the jailing but wanted to ensure members were given a say on the matter. He urged the union leadership to call special branch meetings to ascertain members' feelings and to give the leadership the opportunity to convince members of the action. His call fell on deaf ears, but the membership had their say. At a mass meeting in Newcastle the following day, thousands of rank and file members drove the FIA leaders off the stage and marched back to work. A few days later, 6,000 iron workers at the Leichhardt Oval in Sydney did the same. If the CPA leadership wanted a strike, many FIA members instinctively thought this a good reason not to have one, regardless of the merits of the case.

The same kind of contempt for FIA members was at play in union elections. In December 1949, Thornton and McPhillips beat the opposition ticket, led by Laurie Short – Origlass's former Balmain collaborator, but now moving sharply to the right – by 1,700 votes. Short appealed in the courts, alleging that 4,000 ballot papers had been forged, and the Industrial Registrar granted Short's application in June 1950. At the subsequent election for FIA national secretary, Short again lost. Again, Short appealed. Finally, in November 1951, the Industrial Court's Justice Dunphy concluded that there had been 'forgery, fraud and irregularities on a grand scale' in the 1949 FIA election. Short was declared elected national secretary. In March 1952, in court-supervised elections, the Grouper ticket drove the Communists out of office by a two to one majority. After 15 years, the CPA had lost control of the FIA and gained a shocking reputation for manipulative practices, something which Short, who went on to run the union for three decades, regularly reminded members of at every union election.

Conclusion

The postwar years saw one of Australia's biggest strike waves, winning some of the biggest breakthroughs in pay and conditions. ALP governments, in office federally and in most states, did little to help workers. The Chifley government did not stamp out all strikes, but, with the help of the industrial courts, it succeeded in slowing down the fight for shorter hours and higher wages. Many union leaders saw strikes as a threat to their comfortable existence, and they also lent their weight to the government's efforts.

In 1948–49, the pendulum was swinging away from militancy. The impact of the Cold War and some lessening in the urgency of working class struggle contributed. When the CPA jagged left and advocated confrontation with the ALP, the conditions were not favourable. The CPA's bureaucratic approach reduced its capacity to bring workers with it; resorting to top-down edicts further alienated workers. The defeat of the coal strike marked the point at which the right began to dominate national politics, pushing the left onto the defensive for the best part of two decades. Only a fresh wave of worker and student militancy in the late 1960s swung politics back towards the left, in circumstances where an anti-Stalinist left had the space to grow. Revolutionary socialist politics would revive in Australia for the first time since the 1920s.

FURTHER READING

D. Blackmur, 'The meat industry strike, 1946' and 'The railway strike, 1948', both in D.J. Murphy (ed.), *The Big Strikes: Queensland 1889–1965*, St Lucia,

University of Queensland Press, 1983.

K. Buckley and T. Wheelwright, *False Paradise: Australian Capitalism Revisited, 1915-1955*, Melbourne, Oxford University Press, 1998.

P. Deery (ed.), *Labour in Conflict: The 1949 coal strike*, Sydney, Hale and Iremonger, 1978.

H. Greenland, *Red Hot: The Life and Times of Nick Origlass*, Sydney, Wellington Lane Press, 1998.

T. O'Lincoln, *Into the Mainstream: The Decline of Australian Communism*, Melbourne, Red Rag Publications, 2009 [1985].

T. Sheridan, *Division of Labour: Industrial Relations in the Chifley Years, 1945-49*, Melbourne, Oxford University Press, 1989.

16.

THE COMMUNISTS COME TO POWER IN CHINA

Chiang Kai-shek's crushing of the Chinese Revolution in 1927 (Chapter 7) did nothing to solve the crisis of the Chinese nation.[1] It neither unified the country nor provided it with stable leadership. The GMD government in Nanjing was an unstable formation that never succeeded in imposing its rule on the country. It had little authority outside the cities and the areas the Nationalist Army occupied. Rival warlords controlled much of the Chinese landmass, and the GMD, while proclaiming its hostility to warlords, was partly made up of warlord interests. In the cities, criminal gangs held sway over whole industries and districts. Again, the GMD were in cahoots with these gangs, with Chiang himself closely connected to Shanghai's largest, the Green Gang. Imperialist governments vied both with each other and with the GMD for spheres of influence. Continuous instability was the outcome of the shifting alliances between the various actors.

The lack of any unified political authority prevented any deep-seated transformation of the country. In the ten years of Republican China (1927–37), the GMD undertook some modest economic development. It built power plants, extended the post office system, overhauled the national budget and drew up ambitious plans to build new railways, check river flooding and encourage mining and agriculture. In the first years of Chiang's rule, the economy grew. But many of Chiang's plans came to nothing. Constant warfare and the need to buy off the country's warlords saw the army swallow half the national budget. Despite tax reform, the government was chronically short of money, and interest payments on public debt took one-third of public revenues. Coal mining, iron foundries and banking developed in the modern sector, but traditional handicrafts and small enterprises predominated elsewhere. Foreign businesses continued to enjoy preferential treatment. Expatriates enjoyed the finest things of life in their walled-off concessions.

Eighty percent of the population lived in the rural areas. The defeat of the rural uprisings of 1926–27 left many peasants and landless labourers in squalor and misery. Local government officials in the villages worked hand in glove with magistrates, gentry and landlords, widening the gap between rich and poor. Regular famines and floods killed millions and sent rural refugees pouring into the cities. The Great Depression drove down prices for silk, cotton, soybeans and tobacco, bringing poverty and death to millions of peasants who had concentrated on cash crops for export.

The GMD introduced a labour code providing for the eight-hour day, paid holidays, paid maternity leave and the elimination of child labour, but it was not enforced. Masses of children as young as nine were employed in workshops. Industrial safety standards were non-existent. Workers suffered wage cuts, rising inflation and high unemployment as millions of rural refugees competed for jobs in the cities. The new health and education facilities were grossly inadequate for the demands upon them, even in the big cities. Destitution among the working class was rife and prostitution and begging widespread. The only 'unions' in existence were yellow unions run by gangsters; these acted as labour contractors, strike breakers, traders in child labour and dealers in opium. Worker militants were assaulted with impunity. Meanwhile, government officials lived in luxury, pocketing bribes and sending their children to top private schools.

Growing intellectual opposition to Chiang's corrupt rule was met by censorship and repression. The only answer Chiang had to offer disenchanted middle class supporters was the New Life movement, which espoused fascist ideology. Whampoa military academy graduates who had served as Chiang's anti-communist shock troops in 1927 formed a paramilitary apparatus known as the Blueshirts, openly modelled on Mussolini's Blackshirts, to attack GMD opponents.

Chiang's failure to develop a modern economy or to cohere a unified nation state made the country easy prey for Japanese imperialism. Japan had already established footholds in mainland China in the 1910s and 1920s. In the 1930s, the appetite of Japanese capitalism for markets, territory and raw materials drove Japan to seize Manchuria and then to attempt to grab the whole of China. Japanese invasion transformed politics in China, exposing the weaknesses of GMD rule and providing the Communists with the opportunity to rebuild their forces after years of devastating defeats. In the 1940s, the CCP began to challenge for power. After a three-year civil war, the

Communists drove out the GMD and established the 'People's Republic of China.' How the CCP triumphed, and what kind of state it established tell us much about China today.

The transformation of the CCP

Following its defeat by Chiang and the warlords in 1927, the CCP was reduced to a small rump in the cities. The Comintern's adoption of the adventurist Third Period line in 1928 compounded the party's urban isolation. At a time when the working class was trying to steady itself after a string of massacres, the CCP Central Committee in Shanghai sought to turn every strike into an offensive against the state. This invited massive police repression. Workers fled the party in fear of their lives. An internal circular of November 1928 admitted that:

> Unfortunately, our union organisations have been reduced to a minimum, our party units in the cities have been pulverised and isolated. Nowhere in China can we find one solid industrial cell.[2]

Urban workers, who had in 1926 constituted two-thirds of the party's membership, now made up less than 2 percent of party membership.[3]

In 1930, the Third Period line led to fresh disasters. The Comintern had written to the CCP Central Committee:

> It is now possible and necessary to prepare the masses for the revolution that will overthrow the political power based on the alliance between the landlord class and the bourgeoisie and establish the dictatorship of the workers and peasants in the Soviet form.[4]

In June, the CCP Central Committee, now under the leadership of Li Lisan, determined that: 'The situation for direct revolution is already in existence on a national basis and is very likely to be turned into a nationwide victory of the revolution.'[5] Revolution in China would be the trigger for world revolution. Guided by this unrealistic perspective, the CCP's Red Army mounted a widespread offensive over the summer months to capture key cities. The result was a debacle: the Communists were wiped out. Only by refusing an order to march on Nanchang were Mao and his military commander Zhu De able to escape obliteration. The Comintern scapegoated Li Lisan for the failure and, in early 1931, imposed Stalin's faithful servants Wang Ming and Bo Gu as party leaders to enforce Moscow rule.

Only a shell in the cities and militarily smashed elsewhere, the CCP now retained a hold only in Mao's mountain fastness in Jiangxi province. Abandoning the cities had enormous consequences for the Chinese Communists. The CCP's partisan bands had originally been established as the armed wing of a rising mass movement of workers and peasants. With the mass movement destroyed, the CCP's guerrilla forces in the countryside took on a life of their own and became the centre of the party's strategy. The working class was relegated to an ancillary. The CCP's power now depended on partisan guns rather than the strong arm of the worker in the factory or the peasant in the field. Nigel Harris explains the connections between the Comintern's Third Period strategy and the shift in the party:

> Rural guerrilla warfare imposed its own constraints. It was not a form of struggle open to a settled working class. To participate, a worker was obliged to become a professional soldier. For guerrilla warfare, secrecy and surprise were essential, not open debate. The mode of struggle determined the type of contender. The party in the cities could advance Third Period slogans only at the cost of its survival. The partisans alone could advance those slogans with impunity where they possessed military power, but the slogans did not secure their power, only their arms did that. Thus, Third Period politics in China made necessary the partisans and so identified a different social stratum to propagate them, those who were socially rootless, members of the intelligentsia, workers who had abandoned their place of work and rural vagrants.[6]

How did the CCP square the circle, claiming loyalty to working class revolution while building a party in which the working class was irrelevant? By the expedient of proclaiming the *party itself* to be the proletariat. Class struggle was no longer the fight by the oppressed masses but by the party as the embodiment of the proletariat.

In November 1931, Mao convened the misleadingly named First All China Soviet Congress in Jiangxi. Misleading because the CCP's geographic reach was extremely limited at this time and because soviets on the lines of Russia in 1917 existed nowhere in the country. Regardless, the congress declared the formation of the 'Chinese Soviet Republic' in Jiangxi, complete with a constitution, a labour law and a land law. The constitution declared the party's goal of overthrowing imperialism and the GMD. This Soviet Republic, the constitution boasted, was a 'state based on the democratic dictatorship of the workers and peasants.' All power would 'belong to the workers, peasants, and Red Army soldiers and the entire toiling population.'[7] Militarists, bureaucrats, landlords, gentry, village bosses and monks, described as exploiting and counter-revolutionary elements, lost any political rights. All big private landowners, including landlords, village bosses, gentry and militarists were to have their land confiscated without compensation. Land would be distributed among the poor and middle peasants, while 'hired farm hands, coolies and toiling labourers' were entitled to equal rights to land allotments.

The CCP also created numerous 'mass organisations' in Jiangxi. The party paid particular attention to winning support among women by taking steps to lift their social status, banning arranged marriages and the buying and selling of women. Marriage and divorce were to be by consent. The territory controlled by what the party called the 'Jiangxi Soviet' steadily expanded on the basis of limited, but real, practical reforms.

In practice, the CCP attack on the rich farmers was not nearly as thoroughgoing as party statements suggested. The partisans were too weak to collectivise land ownership and were dependent on rich farmers, who fed them, paid the taxes needed to buy the guns and uniforms and supplied sons and daughters to join their ranks. Similarly, the CCP might declare equality for women, but it deferred to the rural gentry hostile to such a notion. The result was that Mao and his followers proclaimed radical transformation in the areas under Communist control but refrained from implementing it.

The CCP's militaristic turn towards partisan warfare in the early 1930s transformed its internal regime. Bloody purges of factional rivals replaced open debate. At least 12,000 people were killed in purges instigated by Mao and other leaders in Jiangxi in 1931-32.

The 'Jiangxi Soviet' came under constant attack by Chiang's armies. The Communists initially got the better of the Nationalists, but, by the latter half of 1934, the CCP's 'liberated areas' were under threat of annihilation. The Communists were forced to flee, and the 'Jiangxi Soviet' collapsed. In October, between 80,000 and 90,000 Red Army partisans left their bases and headed inland with their supporters and family members. Fighting off pursuing GMD forces and warlord armies, the Red Army suffered terrible casualties in the remote countryside as they marched west and then north towards remote Shaanxi province. Hunger and thirst, extreme weather and inhospitable terrain also took their toll over the course of the 8,000 kilometre, year-long march. When they joined the Communists who had established bases in northern Shaanxi, their numbers were down to just 10,000.

The Long March was significant for the survival of the Red Army. It also enabled Mao to advance his position within the party and the Red Army. During a three-day conference in January 1935, Mao attacked the policies that had led to the fall of the 'Jiangxi Soviet,' laying the blame on others for the disaster. His distinctive strategy was to recognise that the party's strength was in guerrilla fighting, not in a conventional military force fighting fixed field battles against the GMD. His views laid the basis for the CCP to become a purely nationalist party. He won the support of Zhou Enlai and Zhu De, now emerging as the party's leading military tactician, and decisively sidelined Stalin's man, Wang Ming.

The 'Second United Front'

In December 1936, Mao and the Red Army moved their headquarters in Shaanxi province to the small town of Yan'an. From its Yan'an base, the CCP grew dramatically in the following years on the basis of its support for national resistance and land redistribution.

In September 1931, Japan had invaded Manchuria, establishing a puppet government led by the last Manchu emperor, Puyi. The GMD government, far more interested in fighting the CCP, did little to halt the Japanese invasion; in May 1933, Chiang signed the Tanggu truce, formally recognising the Japanese occupation. Popular resentment over the GMD's capitulation grew rapidly. The CCP sought to put itself at the head of this mood, contrasting its willingness to fight with the GMD's abject surrender. It condemned the Chiang government as 'a government of national betrayal and national disgrace' and urged its overthrow as a condition of successfully prosecuting the 'national revolutionary war against the Japanese and other imperialists.'[8] On 1 August 1935, the CCP issued an 'Appeal to Fellow Countrymen to Resist Japan and for National Salvation,' calling on all classes and armies in China to form a political and military alliance against Japan. The appeal aroused widespread support. In December 1935, students in Beijing rose up, demanding that the GMD government fight. Students on campuses across eastern China followed. Fired by patriotism, thousands of young people fled the cities in the east to join the Red Army in Shaanxi.

The CCP's appeal did not explicitly invite Chiang Kai-shek to join the alliance to fight Japan. Chiang's forces had killed thousands of CCP members, and the party called the GMD leader 'the butcher of Shanghai.' Still, the GMD's armies constituted the biggest fighting force in the country. In August 1936, the CCP finally sent an Open Letter to the GMD calling for a 'strong revolutionary, united front' with the Red Army and other nationalist forces.

Chiang was by no means convinced of the need for a pact. He saw an opportunity to wipe out the CCP once and for all. However, the mood for national unity to fight Japan was growing within the army. When Chiang ordered two of his generals to attack the Red Army in Shaanxi, they refused and instead kidnapped Chiang and held him prisoner in his residence in Xi'an. They demanded that Chiang mobilise the army to fight the Japanese. Aware that refusal might spark off a wholesale revolt against him, Chiang reluctantly agreed to join forces with the Communists. The CCP leadership, whose first response to news of Chiang's kidnapping was to urge his captors to execute him, now dropped any criticism of the GMD leader, hailing him as 'the leader of the nation's anti-Japanese unity,' in whom 'the party has placed unquestioning confidence.'[9] Anyone who challenged the united front was 'an enemy of the Chinese people' and 'an agent of Japanese imperialism.'

In the first months of 1937, GMD and CCP leaders drafted a 'Second United Front.'[10] (The first was 1924–27.) The new united front saw the CCP abandon any class-war rhetoric in the name of national unity against the Japanese invader. The CCP embraced Sun Yat-sen's 'Three Principles of the People' – 'nationalism, democracy and welfare.' It ended forcible confiscation of land; agrarian transformation now went only as far as the landlords who supported the GMD would accept. The party called off the 'sovietisation' movement and agreed to rename 'soviet' governments as local authorities of the GMD. The Red Army would join the Nationalist army as the Eighth Route Army and New Fourth Army.

Although the CCP's pact with the GMD was driven by local considerations, it coincided with Stalin's aspirations for China. Alarmed by the prospect of further Japanese encroachment on Russia's eastern borders, Stalin signed a pact with the GMD against Japan in 1935. Good relations between the local Communists and the GMD therefore suited Stalin's needs.

The CCP's pact with Chiang differed in important respects from the Popular Front strategy introduced elsewhere by the Comintern. It shared the language of 'national unity' but did not subordinate the CCP to its bourgeois partners. Mao had no intention of placing the CCP's heads in the noose Chiang had prepared for them. The CCP refused to hand over command of its army to GMD officers; nor would it accept GMD control over its 'soviet' governments. The 'united front' strategy therefore strengthened the CCP, rather than weakening it, although its project still had as little to do with communism as the

Comintern's Popular Front. The CCP's basic program was the same as it had been in 1927 – to fight for a bourgeois democratic regime – but now the Red Army would fight for it in parallel with, not as part of, the GMD armies. The degree of separation and subordination would depend on circumstances.

Mao spelled out the CCP's strategy in his 1939 document, 'The Chinese Revolution and the Chinese Communist Party.'[11] The first goal was to defeat Japanese occupation and overthrow Chinese 'feudalism' by means of a 'national and democratic revolution.' This initial stage was 'not against capitalism and capitalist private property' but the establishment of a 'New Democracy,' under which China would be ruled by 'a joint dictatorship of several anti-imperialist classes.' The proletariat and the CCP would lead China under a New Democracy, but 'the republic will neither confiscate capitalist private property in general nor forbid the development of such capitalist production.' Over time, state-run industry would overwhelm capitalist industry; China, under CCP leadership, would transition peacefully into the next stage, socialism.

As with all such Stalinist 'two-stage' revolutionary schemas, the Chinese version was opposed to genuine working class power. The forces the CCP charged with carrying out the first stage – the party leaders, made up of urban intellectuals leveraging themselves to power on the backs of the peasants – ensured that the 'second stage' was never going to happen. The CCP leaders had no interest in allowing it.

Eager to build its support in the 'liberated zones' it controlled, the CCP sought to balance the interests of the rural classes. For the poorer and middle peasants, the party cut rent, taxes and interest on loans. For the landlords, the party stopped poor peasants from seizing their land. For the moneylenders, the party forced peasants to pay their repayment arrears. The landlords obviously resented the lower rents forced on them by the CCP, but some of them profited from the industries the Red Army established in the Communist-controlled areas. The peasants resented having to repay loans to moneylenders, but the party was less brutal in enforcing repayment than the old masters of the villages. The party also imposed hierarchical relations within the Red Army and appeased the local gentry in the villages it controlled by winding back the measures it had introduced in Jiangxi encouraging sexual equality.[12]

The CCP broadened its appeal among the peasantry by coupling land reform with political reform. District and regional councils, elected by all villagers, became the chief organs of government. The councils represented some measure of democracy and accountability in the villages, where hitherto the landlord's word had been law; but the CCP took an instrumentalist approach to them. The councils included representation from all classes and could determine minor matters with some degree of freedom, but they were never to stray from the party line or to encourage 'extreme' measures such as attacks on landlords and rich peasants.

The party's bureaucratic conception of democracy was reproduced in its own ranks. The CCP boasted of egalitarianism in its Yan'an headquarters, but an elite soon became evident. The leaders were hardly living a life of luxury. The territory was inhospitable, living conditions were extremely sparse, and those working at the Yan'an base were forced to live in caves after Japanese attacks flattened the town. Still, the higher ranked in the party had access to better food and clothing, and many showed little concern for the welfare of the people. It was in Yan'an that the authoritarian nature of inner-party life in the CCP was finally consolidated. In early 1942, Mao began a purge of the party, dubbed the 'Rectification Campaign,' ostensibly to combat bureaucratism, dogmatism and sectarianism within the party, but actually to destroy his chief leadership rival, Wang Ming. Mao's initiative, however, soon began to take on a life of its own. Writers, intellectuals and artists began to criticise the CCP. Some, such as Ding Ling, charged with developing women's organisations in Yan'an, criticised the hypocrisy of the party over sexual equality, because the private lives of leaders diverged widely from the party's official support for women's liberation. Writer Wang Shiwei condemned the party's hierarchical structures and the privileges of those at the top.

Mao and his allies soon abandoned their campaign against Wang Ming and turned their fire on their critics. They launched the 'thought reform' movement, involving 'criticism and self-criticism' exercises. These were nothing less than brainwashing techniques demanding repeatedly rewritten confessions of 'errors' by victims. Those who refused to recant their 'errors' were publicly humiliated and beaten and, in many cases, imprisoned and tortured by Mao's Moscow-trained security chief Kang Sheng. Wang Shiwei was put to death. Such techniques were routinely used thereafter by Mao and other party leaders to smother internal criticisms, creating an internal culture of stifling conformism and driving thousands of members to suicide or mental breakdown.

The fight against Japanese occupation

In July 1937, the Imperial Japanese Army stepped up its invasion, aiming to seize the whole country. It captured Beijing and the neighbouring port city of Tianjin. In August, it opened a second front, attacking and seizing Shanghai in the south. In September, Japanese planes began to bomb the

Nationalist capital, Nanjing. In December, the Imperial army captured Nanjing and carried out a barbaric massacre, killing up to 300,000. Chiang and his entourage had fled Nanjing long before the Japanese arrival and set up a new capital in Wuhan.

The Nanjing massacre galvanised the Chinese resistance. Chiang's forces briefly held up the Japanese advance in Shandong in the spring of 1938 and bogged down the Japanese over the summer by bursting the dykes of the Yellow River, flooding vast tracts of the country at the cost of hundreds of thousands of civilian lives. The Japanese army resumed its offensive in September. It took Wuhan after a bloody battle, forcing Chiang to move his capital again, this time far west to Chongqing. Wang Jingwei, the former leader of the 'left GMD' who had turned on the CCP in 1927, was installed as head of Japan's puppet government in Nanjing.

The country was now divided between the Japanese Imperial Army, which controlled the towns and railway lines in the eastern and most populous half of the country, the GMD forces, who held on in the south west, and the CCP, which occupied areas of the north west. Despite his formal alliance with the CCP, which obliged the two parties to observe a truce, Chiang understood that independent Communist military forces were a threat to his power and the two sides clashed regularly. After the most significant battle in 1941, the truce between them was formally suspended, and the GMD diverted many of its troops to blockading the CCP.

The Communists avoided setpiece battles with the Japanese army and used guerrilla tactics instead, engaging where the enemy was weak, then retreating. Guerrilla warfare depended on popular backing – people to feed and hide partisans after hit and run operations and to provide enthusiastic fighters capable of local initiative, using local knowledge. But peasants did not automatically back the Communists. They were not naturally Chinese nationalists like student and middle class recruits to the CCP. Many initially withheld judgement about the Japanese occupation, because it seemed that nothing could be worse than the GMD. Two things changed their minds: the brutality of the Japanese occupation and the CCP's land reform measures. The rural elites had fled to the cities, and only the Communists could organise the defence of the villages. The land reform measures lightened many peasants' crushing financial burden.

The CCP emerged as a major force during the war against Japanese occupation, growing from 40,000 in 1937 to 490,000 in 1940 and 1.2 million by 1945. The leadership continued to hail overwhelmingly from the 'respectable' classes, particularly among students from the families of small farmers, merchants and even aristocratic officials.¹³ The CCP's armies grew too, from 50,000 in 1937 to one million by 1945 (along with another two million peasants in local guerrilla bands). By the end of the war, advances by the Eighth Route Army and the New Fourth Army saw the Communists control territory with a combined population of 125 million, one-quarter of the national total. Their guerrilla bands operated over much larger areas.

The GMD armies were obviously incapable of reining in the landlords, who were the social base of their officer class, but they were also half-hearted in attacking the Japanese. By the end of 1940, the GMD and the Japanese had reached a stalemate. Not even US entry into the war on China's side after the Japanese attack on Pearl Harbour in December 1941, which significantly changed the balance of forces in Asia, was enough to stir GMD generals to fight. Appointed by US President Roosevelt as Supreme Commander of the Allied forces in China, Chiang welcomed the US money and the huge quantities of weapons that followed. He gloried in the boost to his prestige when he was invited to the Cairo conference in November 1943 alongside Roosevelt and Winston Churchill. But Chiang's chief of staff, US General Joseph Stilwell, soon came to realise that Chiang had no intention of using US money and weapons to fight the Japanese. Chiang was prepared to leave that job to the US and to keep US weapons for use against the Communists in the civil war that would follow Japan's defeat.

In the spring of 1944, Japan broke the stalemate. It seized large tracts of Chinese territory, including strategic railway lines linking Korea with Vietnam. GMD military losses in the war now totalled more than 1.3 million, and civilian loss of life was even greater.

The rotten structures of Chiang's regime were clearly demonstrated by its inability to defend the country against Japanese aggression, even with substantial US aid and an army of nearly four million. The economic collapse and inflation that was running out of control also reflected on the government. Thieving generals were making fortunes from lucrative war contracts and US aid, rather than fighting Japan. Charlie Hore notes that it revealed:

> the inability of the old ruling classes to solve any of China's fundamental problems – imperialism, warlordism and the land question. The Guomindang represented classes which had lost any confidence in their own future.¹⁴

The political and military bankruptcy of the GMD government allowed Mao to discredit it as failing at one of the most elementary tasks of any capitalist government – national self-defence. Mao also used Nationalist failure to promote the CCP as the rightful rulers of the land. The CCP and its armies garnered nationalist support from every social class as a new force, less corrupt and more disciplined. This formed the basis of its claim to leadership of the country after the war.

Civil war and CCP victory

Japan was driven out of China in 1945 not by Chiang's Nationalist Army, nor by the Communists, but by the combined impact of US saturation bombing of its cities and Russia's invasion of Manchuria in early August.

With Japan defeated, the battle for supremacy between the Nationalists and Communists now started again in earnest. The US and Russia initially favoured a coalition government. A few days before Japan's formal surrender, US ambassador to China, Patrick Hurley, accompanied Mao and Zhou from Yan'an to Chongqing for negotiations with Chiang over a united government to run the country. US President Truman wanted to limit Russia's influence in East Asia, but knew that there was no appetite at home for the deployment of US ground forces to China. Truman was also well aware of the ramshackle state of the GMD regime and that Mao's Red Army was highly motivated and poised to advance. Mao had also done his best to convince the US that the CCP were simply reformers who wanted to modernise their country and were no threat to US interests. A coalition government served Truman's interests in reining in the CCP while giving the US time to rearm the Nationalists. On Russia's side, Stalin recognised the GMD as the country's legitimate government, signing a Treaty of Friendship with Chiang in August, but wanted to keep his options open. Stalin was also wary that aggressive action by the CCP against the GMD might provoke the US to intervene to rescue Chiang, forcing Russia to take sides, something he was keen to avoid. The Russian leader therefore urged Mao to join the negotiations overseen by the US ambassador.

Neither Chiang nor Mao, however, had any intention of sharing power. They played along with the coalition negotiations, signed truces, agreed to merge their armies and even sat together in a Political Consultative Conference to prepare for a coalition government; in practice, both sides were preparing for war. In June 1946, full-scale hostilities began.

The civil war was not a repeat of the guerrilla war of the 1930s but a series of setpiece battles between the CCP's renamed People's Liberation Army (PLA) and Chiang's Nationalist armies. The latter initially had a huge advantage over the Communists, in no small part due to the US airlifting half a million

Nationalist soldiers, along with heavy artillery, from Chongqing to the regions evacuated by departing Japanese troops. So keen was the US to ensure that Chiang's armies took control that it ordered the defeated Japanese to remain in place to hold off the PLA until the Nationalists were able to assume power. Such assistance helped the GMD secure a string of victories in the first 12 months, which seemed to herald a quick victory over Mao's forces. The PLA, however, seized substantial quantities of Japanese war materiel from Manchuria when Russia withdrew its forces in 1946 and used these with great effect.

Civil wars are decided by politics as much as by military power. The PLA foot soldiers were mostly former peasants who believed that they were fighting for a China free of oppression and foreign domination. The GMD armies were made up of half-starved, unwilling conscripts, kept in line only by terror and led by corrupt and cowardly officers with no confidence in their ability to win. The GMD forces were incapable of holding on in the longer term. From the summer of 1947, whole divisions simply surrendered to the PLA, handing over their US-supplied weapons. Hundreds of thousands of Nationalist soldiers switched sides. Others deserted to rejoin their families in their home villages. The number of GMD troops under Chiang's command fell from four million at the end of the war to an extremely demoralised and disloyal group of 2.2 million in mid-1948. Meanwhile, the PLA had grown to 5.5 million men and women under arms.[15]

Chiang's support in the cities was also slipping away. The economy was in freefall despite massive US economic aid. Shortages of basic goods and runaway inflation made everyday life unbearable for all but a tiny minority of war profiteers. The gap between rich and poor widened to an unprecedented extent. For the poor, everyday life was a struggle to survive. The middle classes, who had formed the base for the Nationalists during the 1930s, were ruined by inflation. Some switched their allegiances to the Communists in the hope that their victory might restore stability and security. Their student sons and daughters organised waves of protest against the GMD. Chiang cracked down hard, killing and wounding many, driving the student movement to support the CCP. With Chiang's supporters abandoning him, the PLA met little resistance from the local populace when they entered the cities.

In mid-1948, the Communists advanced on three fronts: the north east, the Beijing–Tianjin area and east-central China. In November, the PLA seized Shenyang, the biggest city in Manchuria, completing the conquest of what under Japanese rule had become China's industrial heartland. Tianjin and Beijing fell soon after, and a third offensive culminated in the capture of Chiang's capital Nanjing in April 1949 and Shanghai in May. By now, even the GMD's most loyal supporters and army officers realised that the war was lost. Tens of thousands fled mainland China, accompanied by foreign businesspeople and missionaries. On 1 October, with much of the country in PLA hands, Mao presided over a large rally in Tiananmen Square at which he declared the establishment of a new regime: the People's Republic of China. There was no mention of socialism. Two weeks later, Guangzhou fell to the PLA, with the Nationalist army simply abandoning the city without a shot being fired. Chiang and his retinue flew to Taiwan and established a US-backed government, claiming sovereignty over the mainland.

China under Communist rule

For several decades, socialists from a variety of different political traditions described China as socialist or as advancing towards socialism. Even today, some socialists believe this to be true. They dismiss as Western media lies or exaggerations accounts of massive exploitation of Chinese workers at the hands of local and foreign capitalists; the destruction of the natural environment; the oppression of national minorities; the authoritarian character of the CCP regime; and its alliances with other repugnant regimes. Where they admit the substance of these criticisms, they argue that such practices are justified by imperialist attempts to destroy the supposed socialist motherland.

More common today than open adulation of the CCP is the argument that China was socialist (or some variant of 'workers' state') until the 1990s but has since 'turned capitalist.' Supposedly, the advent of foreign investment and multinationals and the privatisation of state enterprises – a process of 'opening up' that culminated in China's joining the World Trade Organisation in 2001 – changed the country from socialist to capitalist. This is to mistake form for content. If we adhere to Marx's conception of socialism as working class rule, the 'People's Republic of China' was never socialist. The changes that have taken place since the 1980s, undoubtedly significant, do not alter the fundamental fact that workers do not rule in China and never have.

Mao claimed the state that came into existence in 1949 was a 'new democratic state...under the leadership of the working class (through the Communist Party).'[16] In fact, the CCP had no organic relationship to the working class in 1949. For a start, it had virtually no working class members. Of its membership of 4.5 million, 72 percent were poor and middle-poor peasants; 25 percent were rich peasants and members of the urban middle class; and merely 2 percent were workers. While only a minority, rich peasants and landlords held substantial influence in the party. The party was still overwhelmingly a rural party with few forces in the cities. The CCP had just 3,300 members in Beijing, in a population of 1.7 million. Yet, Mao made this distinctly non-proletarian party stand in for the working class. This is not Marxism. This is idealism, whereby what the party says it stands for determines its character, not what it is.

A party's orientation to the working class is also obvious from its practice. The Communists had no intention of leading workers to power. During the war against Japan, the CCP opposed strikes in GMD-run areas and undertook no independent organisation of workers. During the civil war workers in Shanghai repeatedly struck, but the CCP made no attempt to link their strikes to the struggles of either the peasants or the city's students. In 1949, when the PLA began to overrun Nationalist-held cities, workers took this as a signal to fight for their rights. But the CCP had neither the intention nor the capacity to foster an uprising among the workers of the cities. The central committee complained that 'the struggle between capital and labour was such as to result in a state of anarchy.' As the PLA marched into the cities, party cadres were instructed to avoid 'the mistake of applying in the cities the measures used in rural areas for struggling against landlords and rich peasants.'[17] The priority was to ensure that businesses in the cities were able to run at a profit, 'giving consideration to both public and private interests and benefiting both labour and capital.' Workers and capitalists were to be encouraged to 'organise joint committees for the management of production and to do everything possible to reduce costs, increase output and stimulate sales.'[18] The CCP discouraged even simple demands, such as higher wages and food relief. The party would decide what reforms were to be implemented once it gained power.

When the PLA marched into Shanghai in May, the Communist soldiers were greeted with a mixture of curiosity and enthusiasm by a population that had grown sick of the misery, chaos and corruption of GMD rule. But there was no expectation that the people themselves might take power. It was a straight switch of master, with PLA commander Chen Yi assuming the post of mayor. Owner of the *Shanghai Evening Post* Randall Gould observed:

> The changeover was like nothing that had been imagined. We had feared days of lawless disorder. Nothing of the sort occurred. One day the Nationalists, the next day the Communists, while our erstwhile defenders rode down the Yangtze River and over to Formosa. It was as simple as that.[19]

It was the same in Beijing earlier in the year following the Nationalist surrender; *Time* magazine reported the scene as 20,000 uniformed PLA troops marched in accompanied by brass bands:

> Picked Nationalist soldiers grimly guarded the Reds' line of march. Beneath pictures of Communist boss Mao Tse-tung... sound trucks blared: 'Long live the liberation'. Crowds watched the Reds in silence.[20]

The new masters of the cities drove out the old from their positions of power, but in other respects tried to maintain the status quo. In Shanghai, Mayor Chen kept the GMD police in their positions and held meetings with senior business leaders to reassure them of Communist support. Encouraged by the PLA's stance, some foreign businesspeople decided to remain in Shanghai in the hope that new opportunities might open up under CCP rule. The US Consul-General noted the response of the US Chamber of Commerce which met on the day after the PLA's arrival:

> The rejoicing couldn't have been greater if the city had been liberated by American forces. American and British businessmen were convinced – I can't think why – that they would do better under the Communists.[21]

US business executives in Shanghai were to be disappointed, but this was due initially to action by the workers themselves, not the CCP. In the second half of 1949, the number of strikes in the city soared to 3,324, dwarfing the previous record of 280 disputes in 1946. The CCP leaders did their best to put a lid on the outbreak. Former party leader Li Lisan, now deputy chair of the new All China Labour Federation, told workers that 'the redistribution of factory installations would spell ruin for the workers' and that the time 'had not yet arrived' for the 'complete abolition of capitalist exploitation.'[22]

Mao's hostility to workers' self-activity had a clear material basis. The CCP leaders did not want to have to deal with urban workers fighting for their rights and establishing workers' councils, as they had in the 1920s. Genuine soviets did not fit into Mao's 'New Democracy,' where the bourgeoisie could flourish. It would be the party that would rule.

The CCP's constant invocation of the peasantry did not extend to giving them any say over a liberated China. During the war against Japan, the Communists instituted land reform measures in the areas they captured, expropriating land held by 'traitors' (defectors to the Japanese) but protecting that held by 'progressive gentry.' This continued until 1947, when the CCP's land program briefly jagged to the left and revived the old Jiangxi program of land confiscation. Under the new law, CCP cadres were to be charged with taking the land, but its distribution was to be in the hands of committees of poor peasants and landless labourers. This new measure was a genuinely revolutionary step, but there were insufficient party cadres to take on the task, so confiscation of land was slow. In Hebei province, the poor peasants would not wait. They took land without waiting for permission, demanding complete equality and the right to supervise the CCP. They then marched to the towns to seize the properties of the rural rich. The party leadership very quickly swung hard to the right in response to this spontaneous movement from below. Mao condemned such 'left excesses' and instructed the poor peasants to protect the industrial and commercial holdings of landlords and rich peasants.[23] Land redistribution, Mao argued, could wait until after the end of the Civil War and should on no account be left to 'the spontaneous activity of the masses.' In the interim, policy returned only to rent and interest reduction. Peasant insurrection – indeed, any popular movement from below – was not to contribute to the defeat of the GMD.

Prior to the Russian Revolution, lively and passionate debates characterised the Bolshevik Party, fuelled by the close relationship between the party and the advanced sections of the working class. The CCP could not have been more different. Mao's 1942–44 Rectification Campaign, with its suppression of dissent and imposition of thought reform, laid the basis for the creation of a leadership cult. 'Mao Zedong Thought,' a flexible ideology that could contain multiple contradictory ideas to suit Mao's needs at any time, was invented, along with the slogan 'Long Live Chairman Mao!' The CCP's Seventh Congress in the spring of 1945 confirmed this trend, rewriting the party's history, laying the blame for its errors on Mao's adversaries and absolving him and the Comintern of any responsibility. By August 1945, every major position in the party lay in Mao's power, and his writings held the status of sacred texts. What need was there for democracy in a Communist party which had no orientation to working class democracy and emancipation?

Other than Mao himself, whose social interests did the CCP represent? Here, Trotsky's theory of permanent revolution discussed in Chapters 1 and 7 has relevance. The 1949 Chinese Revolution demonstrated a real problem with Trotsky's theory. Trotsky's argument was that the bourgeoisie in a late-developing country is cowardly and incapable of carrying through the basic national tasks of unification and modernisation. The failure of the Chinese bourgeoisie's main political representatives, the GMD, to unite and defend the country confirms that argument. Trotsky also pronounced on the revolutionary incapacity of the peasantry. Again, the Chinese Revolution confirmed this historical fact. Peasants seized land, where they were not beaten back by the GMD or CCP, but they did nothing to form themselves into a government or to cohere themselves into a new ruling class. They were unable to solve the big questions confronting China as a backward country in a world system of capitalist states. Those peasant sons and daughters who joined the Communist guerrillas were declassed as peasants and converted into full-time soldiers by that process, following the orders of whichever class commanded them.

In the situation where the bourgeoisie would not, and the peasantry could not, lead, Trotsky maintained that the working class could step in to lead a revolutionary struggle and liberate the late-developing nations. Such a struggle, Trotsky argued, would inevitably pass over into a struggle for socialism. A state in the hands of the workers could then legislate for land to the peasantry, directly solving the rural question that lay at the heart of Chinese politics for centuries. The problem in China was that the working class did not play a leading role after its historic defeat in 1927. The road to a socialist resolution to China's crises was, therefore, closed off.

But history does not stop. In the age of imperialism, China could not languish as it did for several centuries before the Opium Wars. Either the nation would be swallowed up by more advanced capitalist states, such as Japan or the US, or another class would have to emerge from within China that could break the fetters holding back the nation's productive forces. The circuit-breaker came in the form of the middle class intelligentsia from the cities. These intellectuals constituted the leadership of the CCP in the 1930s and 1940s. They were frustrated by the backward state of the Chinese economy, desperate to break foreign control of the country and keen to impose themselves as leaders of a new nation. They built an army based on the peasantry to smash the GMD and then hoisted themselves into power, creating a new regime based on a Communist party state apparatus which incorporated significant elements of the old. The permanent revolution that Trotsky envisaged became *deflected* thereby – and, British Marxist Tony Cliff points out, in a purely nationalist direction.[24] The 'two-stage' revolution was simply window dressing for this project. Many in the CCP may have genuinely believed that they were fighting for emancipation of the workers and peasants; but that was not the party leadership's project.

The Chinese Revolution demonstrated the role urban intellectuals could play in other countries dominated by an old, corrupt ruling class or a weakened colonial power. In countries such as Cuba, Vietnam, Algeria and Egypt in the 1940s and 1950s, middle class social layers felt most keenly the effects of imperialist domination. By virtue of their relative wealth and access to education and international travel, they enjoyed a superior status to the mass of the population. This same access to the scientific and technical world of the imperialist countries also made them acutely aware of how far their nation lagged behind Europe and North America. Imperialist domination deprived them of any hope of leading their countries, something that would have been their birthright elsewhere. As an intermediate layer, standing between the propertied capitalists and the propertyless working class, the middle classes were also the natural representatives of the 'national interest' and the most imbued with the idea of 'national culture.' Their nationalism was at once a rejection of Western imperialism and a desire to emulate its economic development.

The political weight of these intellectual layers depended on the preparedness of the working class to fulfil the destiny that Trotsky had attributed to it. The characteristic of the nationalist revolutions of the 1950s and 1960s, led by these intellectual layers in military uniform or guerrilla battle dress, was the working class's failure to pose a proletarian solution to imperialist domination. That was the product of Stalinism, which destroyed the working class revolutionary alternative in the colonial world or prevented it from ever emerging.

What of China since 1949? The Communist victory achieved the old desire of Chinese nationalism for a strong and independent country that could begin the process of independent economic development. But the state, not the old bourgeoisie, was in control: the CCP came to power as a force in its own right, standing above all the classes of the old society. Yet, the CCP was not free to act as it wished. A competitive and hostile world economy dictated the need for a strong national economy, so industrialisation was the priority. The main source of funds to drive industry had to come from the workers and peasants – as it had in Stalinist Russia in the 1930s. The CCP forced up production targets in industry year after year during the 1950s. Piecework became widespread. Initially, the CCP protected private capitalist interests, but the government changed course in 1953 and nationalised swathes of private industry. Three years later, the CCP introduced collectivisation of land in rural cooperatives. Slowly but surely, China began to adopt the state capitalist model of economic management. This had nothing to do with any transition to socialism. State ownership was necessary to enable the new ruling class to step up the pace of industrialisation in a competitive imperialist world where China lagged.

The changes in the Chinese economy since the early 1990s, far from 'turning China capitalist,' represent the bureaucracy's attempt to insert China into international circuits of capital accumulation; to capture new markets for state-run businesses; to attract foreign investment and, with it, foreign managerial know-how and advanced technologies; and to rationalise areas of industry where productivity in China lagged behind international norms, releasing labour and capital to other sectors. No counter-revolution was involved. This economic shift was undertaken in the first instance by party leader Deng Xiaoping, a member of the CCP since 1923, with the backing of the large majority of his colleagues who understood the need for the change of strategy.

One outcome of the economic changes in recent decades has been a shift in the ownership of industry. A bigger share is now in the hands of local and overseas private capitalists. But this has not involved 'abandonment of socialism' and the embrace of capitalism, as some on the left argue. The 'new economy' is very much a product and a beneficiary of the old. Brand new cities such as Shenzhen, sites of extensive private domestic and foreign investment, depend on state infrastructure developed over decades. Chinese private businesses that flourish on the basis of international connections depend on loans from China's state-owned banks. While many state-owned enterprises (SOEs) collapsed in the 1990s because of reduced state subsidies, others have flourished. *Forbes* lists 75 Chinese SOEs in its top 500 global companies.[25] Whether in the hands of the private sector or of the state, the purpose of Chinese enterprises remains the same: capital accumulation, not the satisfaction of the needs of workers and peasants. Nor do the business owners constitute a separate class in China itching to overthrow the CCP. They are very closely integrated into the party, and the party leadership has repeatedly demonstrated its ability to bring them to heel when required.

China's foreign policy has undergone no qualitative change since 'opening up' was introduced in 1992. Realpolitik, not any conception of socialist internationalism, has always ruled, despite China's claims in the 1960s to be a defiant anti-imperialist and principled supporter of national liberation struggles. Following the rupture of relations with Russia in 1960 and US President Nixon's visit to China in 1971, the guiding principle of Chinese foreign policy for several decades was to undermine Russia. This often involved backing up some of the most reactionary Western-backed despotic regimes, ranging from Pakistan's General Zia, Zaire's President Mobutu and the Shah of Iran, to Cambodia's Khmer Rouge and Ethiopia's Emperor Haile Selassie. China had been a warm supporter of Chile's reformist Allende government, but then became the first 'communist' country to support coup leader General Pinochet when he seized power in 1973. Today, China lines up with Syrian dictator Bashar al-Assad, the reactionary Iranian regime, the racist Sri Lankan Government and the Philippines' authoritarian leader Rodrigo Duterte.

Until the 1990s, the CCP's focus was on economic development. China's transformation from a peripheral, developing economy to the world's second largest imperialist power is now underpinning a more aggressive international role. China's nuclear capability, which it has possessed since 1964, further illustrates its distance from anything progressive. Nuclear bombs do not distinguish between the capitalists and the workers of the cities on which they are dropped.

The Chinese government continues to practice neo-colonialism closer to home. It colonised Tibet in 1950 and continues to oppress the region today by encouraging mass migration of Han Chinese. The government does the same in Xinjiang, suppressing local cultural autonomy and detaining hundreds of thousands of Uyghurs.

In 1949, a massive peasant army led by Communists smashed forever the old ruling classes, broke the power of Western imperialism and laid the basis for a new social order. But this was in no sense a socialist revolution. Working class power in China remains to be won.

FURTHER READING

T. Cliff, *Deflected Permanent Revolution*, London, Socialist Workers Party, 1986 [1963].

J. Fenby, *The Penguin History of Modern China*, London, Penguin Books, 2013.

D. Gluckstein, 'China: revolution and war', in D. Gluckstein (ed.), *Fighting on all Fronts: Popular Resistance in the Second World War*, London, Bookmarks, 2015.

N. Harris, *The Mandate of Heaven: Marx and Mao in Modern China*, Chicago, Haymarket Books, 2015 [1978].

C. Hore, *The Road to Tiananmen Square*, London, Bookmarks, 1991.

17.

ANTI-STALINIST REVOLTS IN EASTERN EUROPE

The imperialist carve-up of Europe late in World War II dashed the hopes of the people of Greece and Italy for socialism.[1] It also denied the people of Eastern Europe[2] any choice over the regimes that took power after the war in their countries. Within a few years, anti-Stalinist revolts began to break out. These revolts demonstrated that the regimes that ruled Eastern Europe in the postwar decades were not socialist in any way; workers were not in charge. As workers struck and took to the streets of Berlin, Poznan and Budapest, they began to revive the real socialist tradition of workers' power that their Stalinist rulers had done their best to bury. In every case they were beaten, but their willingness to fight for their rights, even in the most repressive circumstances, revealed the tenacity of the working class and its thirst for justice.

Russia takes over Eastern Europe

In the years following Hitler's defeat, Russian armies occupied Eastern Europe and installed loyal governments, but not to spread socialism. Russia wanted a defensive barrier against the West and was not deterred by general hostility and scepticism about communism. In Poland, Stalin allowed the Nazis to crush the 1944 Warsaw Uprising. In Germany, anti-fascist committees flourished after the Nazis' defeat, but the Stalinists crushed them. In Germany's wartime allies – Bulgaria, Hungary and Romania – military defeat was followed by revolutionary upheaval, most pronounced in Bulgaria, where soldiers' councils were formed. The Communist parties[3] of these countries derailed the upsurge; in Hungary, the initial joy that greeted the arrival of Russian soldiers turned to horror at the looting and rapes that followed.[4] In Yugoslavia, where Marshal Tito's Communist party had a mass base, workers took over their factories and established workers' councils, but Communist opposition brought these to an end.

Like the Western imperialists, the Russian occupying forces used extreme nationalism and anti-German racism to cement their rule. In Czechoslovakia and Poland, the Russian occupation and its local allies deported millions of Germans and Hungarians and confiscated their property. The German population in Czechoslovakia had been a Communist party stronghold before the war. Many had died in Nazi concentration camps. Yet, supposedly socialist regimes drove these workers out of the country.

Initially, Russia instructed the Communist parties to enter broad coalition governments with a range of explicitly pro-capitalist parties. In Bulgaria, the Communists entered a government headed by General Kimon Georgiev, who had briefly ruled the country in 1934 following a military coup that abolished parliamentary rule and banned trade unions. In Romania, the Communists joined the government of General Nicolae Rădescu and dissolved their armed militia as a condition of membership. Elsewhere, Communists formed blocs with social democratic parties which were in some cases well to the left of the Communists. But whatever the composition of these coalitions, Russia ensured that Communists were given control over the police, internal security and military portfolios. The Communists used these ministries to build up their power in state apparatuses that were in many respects carryovers from the past, both in personnel and structure. They certainly did not use them to build up workers' power. Mátyás Rákosi, Communist Party general secretary and deputy prime minister in Hungary in 1946, banned strikes, stating that they were 'a luxury only the American economy could afford.'[5]

While most Eastern European Communist parties had been weak in 1945, with few followers, this changed with Russian occupation. The parties began to grow rapidly. Although they did recruit some worker members, they also enrolled former fascist supporters, middle class careerists and opportunists seeking a well-paid job in the state apparatus; others joined for more idealistic reasons, seeing bureaucratic state capitalism as a way to lift their predominantly rural and poverty-stricken countries out of backwardness. Party leaders, with the exception of Tito, distinguished themselves by their subservience to their masters in Moscow.

The situation in Europe changed dramatically in 1947 with the advent of the Cold War. Keen to build Western Europe as an anti-communist bloc, the US poured financial aid into Europe, on condition that recipient governments expel their Communist coalition partners. In the East, Russia purged the coalition governments, creating what they called 'people's democracies' – governments run by Communist parties, sometimes in alliance with peasant parties.

These people's democracies were far from socialist. Rákosi defined them as 'the dictatorship of the proletariat without the soviet form' – workers' power without the organs of workers' power.[6] Most workers had no faith in the old prewar social order, so they acquiesced (partly out of fear) to the Stalinist takeover. The old bourgeois forces were discredited by their fascist pasts. The opposition of the social democratic parties to the new regimes was broken by a combination of cooption and repression. In Russian-occupied Germany, the old SPD had been re-established in 1945 and quickly won working class support; the Stalinists forcibly took them over. There was resistance, above all in Poland, where the Socialist Party was strong and had moved to the left during the war. Here, rank and file worker members of the Socialist Party offered concerted resistance to the Stalinist takeover.

There was nothing progressive about the Russian takeover. Russia was in no sense what Stalinists called a 'helpful big brother.' It was an imperialist power and dominated, much as Britain had with its colonies. The first phase was looting – 'reparations' – in which gold reserves and massive amounts of equipment, including entire factories, were seized and sent back to Russia. This was particularly true for Germany and its former Axis allies, but also for Czechoslovakia and Poland. Looting in Poland was accompanied by direct annexation of the country's territory. Another form of imperialist exploitation by Russian occupation forces was the setting up of mixed companies; they provided only a small amount of capital but took a disproportionate share of the profits. Finally, the Russians imposed exploitative trading relationships. Eastern Europe was forced to supply raw materials and other commodities to Russia at well below world market prices, often below cost price, and to buy Russian goods at inflated prices. The Eastern Bloc was certainly not characterised by fraternal relationships between socialist governments led by Russia, as the Stalinists trumpeted.

As might have been expected, Western Communist parties welcomed the Communist advances in the East as a triumph for socialism. With the Chinese Communist Party also vying for power, the 'socialist' world appeared to be going from strength to strength. Capitalism was surely doomed. Not only hardline Stalinists saw the new regimes in Eastern Europe as socialist; many supporters of the Western labour and social democratic parties also viewed them positively. Once the new governments nationalised heavy industry, social democrats believed that they were on the way to building socialism.

Nationalisation of industry in the Stalinist states provoked a debate in the Fourth International (FI), founded by Trotsky in 1938 to advance the struggle for genuine socialism. The FI argued that – despite the degeneration of the 1917 Revolution under Stalin – Russia remained a workers' state that must be defended against Western capitalism. They called Russia a 'degenerated workers' state.' They admitted that Stalinism was thoroughly counter-revolutionary. Under no circumstances could Stalinism overthrow capitalism. That, after all, was the rationale for the existence of the FI, to build genuinely revolutionary parties.

The FI's argument that Russia was any kind of workers' state after World War II was clearly wrong. Workers had absolutely no control over the Russian state, and the regime is much better understood as state capitalist. Nonetheless, the FI position did not break with the central tenet of Marxism – that only the working class could overthrow capitalism. There had, after all, been a genuine workers' revolution in Russia.

But what should the FI make of the new regimes in Eastern Europe, imposed by Russian occupation? Initially, the FI argued that the regimes in Eastern Europe remained capitalist. But once the Stalinist governments in Eastern Europe started to nationalise heavy industry, and once they had driven out their former coalition partners, the regimes ruling Eastern Europe and Russia began to look exactly the same. Logically, one should call them *all* workers' states or *all* capitalist.

The FI could not simply look to Trotsky's writings for answers. Trotsky had believed that Stalinist Russia would collapse during World War II and never considered a situation where Stalinism would conquer half of Europe. The FI majority decided that, because Russia was a workers' state, albeit degenerated, then the Eastern European states must also be workers' states, albeit 'deformed workers' states' not born out of revolutions. This conclusion represented a break with Marxism. It meant that workers' states, no matter how qualified by the label 'deformed,' could be brought into existence by Russian tanks. In that case, what need was there for the FI?

The main argument the FI majority used to justify this stance paralleled that of the Stalinists – and every right winger in the West: Eastern Europe was socialist/communist/a workers' state because industry was in state hands. But, as Engels had pointed out decades previously:

> The modern state, no matter what its form, is essentially a capitalist machine – the state of the capitalists, the ideal personification of the total national capital. The more it proceeds to the taking over of productive forces, the more does it actually become the national capitalist, the more citizens does it exploit.

> The workers remain wage-workers – proletarians. The capitalist relation is not done away with. It is, rather, brought to a head.[7]

That state ownership does not in itself constitute socialism or even a workers' state should have been clear to the FI. A lot of industry in Eastern Europe had been state owned before World War II, in countries with extreme right wing governments strongly tinged by fascism. The war only increased state control. With many countries devastated by war, it was only the state that was in a position to get industry running again afterwards. Had the Russians not occupied Eastern European nations, their economies would still have been predominantly state run in the late 1940s. The trend to state ownership was also apparent in Britain and France where eminently capitalist governments nationalised basic industries in the postwar years because private capitalists were incapable of making the kind of investments needed to re-equip them. Socialism requires the creation of a workers' state, and that may or may not immediately proceed to nationalisation. The Russian Bolsheviks, for example, only reluctantly engaged in widespread nationalisation of industry more than six months after the October 1917 Revolution. It is workers' control that is the fundamental property of socialism, and the regimes in Eastern Europe were far from being under workers' control.

If the majority of the FI opted to describe the Stalinist regimes as workers' states, British Marxist Tony Cliff drew the opposite conclusion. Cliff argued that Russia was state capitalist, as were the Eastern European regimes that mirrored it. Only by drawing this conclusion were Marxists able to hold to the basic tenet that socialism is about workers' control, not whether industry is in government hands. Any other conclusion opens the door to the idea that some other agency, not the working class, is capable of creating workers' states. Once that is accepted, everything that generations of Marxists had argued for must be abandoned. Holding firm to the idea that socialism is the act of the working class and that the Eastern European states were in no sense progressive – let alone socialist – enabled Cliff's supporters to make sense of the political crises that blew up in Eastern Europe within a few years of the Communists taking power.

Splits in the Stalinist apparatus – rumblings below

For the first few years of their existence, the Stalinist governments in Eastern Europe enjoyed some working class support. Workers in many countries experienced a rise in their living standards. Some won privileged jobs in the new state bureaucracy. The nationalisation of industry seemed to fit with traditional working class demands, and much of the repression seemed to be aimed at the discredited old order. In Hungary, the Communist Minister of Agriculture carried out widespread land reform, breaking up big estates and giving land to the peasants.

Two developments changed this. One was turmoil at the top. In June 1948, Stalin tried to bring Yugoslav leader Tito to heel. Tito, the only leader who had come to power without Russian assistance and who therefore enjoyed unusual autonomy, broke with Moscow. Stalin responded by launching a purge of Communist parties throughout Eastern Europe, targeting potential Tito supporters. The purge was far reaching and bloody: the biggest series of trials and executions since the 1936 Moscow show trials. Among those executed were the general secretaries of the Bulgarian and Czech Communist parties. The general secretary of the Polish Communist Party and the Romanian foreign secretary were arrested. The purge was most violent in Hungary. Rákosi and his security police, the AVH – officered in many cases by former fascists and operating out of the very dungeons used by the fascists – began a three-year reign of terror. They tortured and executed thousands of supposed 'Titoist-Trotskyite spies,' 'capitalist restorationists' and 'supporters of Admiral Horthy' (the wartime dictator). Rákosi's victims included Foreign Minister and long-time party loyalist, László Rajk, executed as a traitor, and Interior Minister János Kádár, imprisoned and held in solitary confinement for three years. Not only leaders were purged. All open opposition, working class, peasant, middle class and former ruling class alike, was suppressed. All told, half a million Hungarians, in a population of less than 10 million, were jailed during Rákosi's reign of terror.

The other indication that the initial phase of relatively stable Stalinist rule was over was the decision to ramp up the exploitation of workers. Cold War competition forced the Stalinist governments to build heavy industry in countries that were quite poor and agrarian in character, compared with Western Europe. The five-year plans introduced by these governments diverted resources from consumer goods, intensified the pace of work, extended shift work, imposed piece rates and reduced living standards. Initially, workers did not openly resist; but absenteeism rose, and the quality of work deteriorated. The five-year plans also targeted the peasantry, who were forced into state collective farms or compelled to sell produce to the state at fixed prices.

The suffering of the masses in Eastern Europe contrasted with the fortunes of the privileged. Top party bureaucrats and state functionaries enjoyed high salaries and numerous perks, including private holiday homes and imported luxury cars. Even party members lower down the chain of command enjoyed better food, clothes and housing. People seethed in anger over the injustice. A pressure cooker atmosphere developed.

Stalin's death in March 1953 led to a chain of events that threatened to bring down the whole postwar Communist order. In Russia, Stalin's death brought to a head tensions in the ruling apparatus. Contending groups fought for power. Stalin's minister of the interior, Lavrentiy Beria, responsible for savage repression of his master's opponents, was condemned and executed. Many thousands of party functionaries in Russia lost their jobs; new leader Nikita Khrushchev prepared to sweep away thousands more.

In July 1953, 18,000 coal miners, many of them political prisoners, went on strike at the Vorkuta labour camp in Siberia. This camp held 60,000 slave labourers. After a 10-day stand-off, the camp commander ordered the shooting of the striking miners; dozens were slain. Vorkuta sent a clear signal to Moscow of discontent among the populace.

The power struggle at the top in Russia was partly a battle to succeed Stalin. But rising social tensions demonstrated that the Russian party needed to broaden its base in the population. Gradually, political prisoners were released, and other strictures of the Stalinist regime loosened.

Stalin's death had even more far-reaching effects outside Russia, because the Eastern European regimes had weaker roots in society. De-Stalinisation campaigns brought down thousands of party officials and state functionaries. Political repression was relaxed, and Russia began to ease its financial demands on its satellites. The combination of instability within the apparatus of the regimes and growing resentment from below created an opening for workers.

The first outburst came in East Germany. In June 1953, a strike by East Berlin construction workers against increased productivity norms led to a generalised uprising against the hardline Stalinist regime of Walter Ulbricht. Resentment over cuts to living standards had been growing throughout the spring, as government investment was diverted to heavy industry. Russia stepped in to advise a change of course: it forced Ulbricht to backtrack on some measures but not to scrap the hated productivity norms. The government's retreat disoriented party cadres, but the wider population viewed it as a sign of weakness. A few small demonstrations and petitions on 14 and 15 June quickly escalated to a strike the following day; 300 workers at two Berlin construction sites demanded the restoration of the old work norms. They then began to raise political slogans expressing their discontent with the government and called a general strike and mass demonstration for the 17th. Alarmed by the growing threat, Ulbricht scrapped the higher productivity norms, but this was no longer enough to quell workers' demands for change. They demanded lower work norms, price cuts, free elections and amnesty for those arrested.

On the following morning, massive crowds began to form up in columns from different areas of Berlin to march to the city centre. They called out 'Down with the government!' and 'Butter, not arms!' They attacked party posters and statues of Communist leaders. By 11am, elements of the crowd had begun to move on police headquarters. At that point, Russian tanks opened fire. Fighting quickly broke out and continued into the night. The Russian army and East German police brutally repressed demonstrators, arresting hundreds and executing dozens, including several Russian soldiers who refused to shoot on the crowds.

Outraged by the massacre, tens of thousands of East Germans demonstrated in every town and city. More than 200,000 workers from 330 factories struck. Protesters assaulted party functionaries, freed political prisoners from jails and looted party shops that sold scarce consumer goods to party loyalists. They demanded the dissolution of the government, free elections and an end to the privileges enjoyed by party functionaries. Some called for the reinstitution of the SPD. They demanded the government address bread shortages, unsafe workplace facilities and excessive night work. The Russian army and East German police violently attacked these demonstrations, killing dozens. It took several days to put down the revolt.

The East German rising, the first in the Eastern Bloc, was a tremendous shock to the Ulbricht government and to Moscow. In an attempt to rebuild Ulbricht's credibility, Russia sent substantial aid to the country and cancelled reparations. The workers may have been driven off the streets, but they did achieve something. Never again would the East German government try an economic shock program of the same scale.

The monolith cracks

The impact of Stalin's death and the rumblings from below weakened the Stalinist monolith. It cracked in 1956. Khrushchev, who had been gradually purging Stalin's acolytes, stepped up his attacks in February. At the 20th Congress of the Russian Communist Party, Khrushchev gave a six-hour speech in which he unmasked the late dictator as a mass murderer responsible for the imprisonment, torture and execution of vast numbers of Russians over a prolonged period. He condemned the obscene Stalin cult that had dominated Russian life. Khrushchev was careful, however, not to disown the entire Stalinist apparatus.[8] How could he, as a product of this same system?

By cleverly sheeting home terror to the psychological neuroses of one man, he exempted his audience of thousands of party apparatchiks, making it clear that they would not be prosecuted.

Khrushchev's denunciation of Stalin threw Communist parties around the world into chaos. The leader who had been held up as a godlike figure was now being trodden into the dirt. In Eastern Europe, this inevitably cast doubt on the legitimacy of the Stalinist governments. Debate could not be confined only to privileged bureaucrats and disenchanted party officials.

Poland saw the first outbreak of popular protest. Dissident intellectuals were increasingly dissatisfied with Russian control, mismanagement of the economy, repression of free speech and the constant rewriting of history to suit the party's interests. Their illegal publications now reached a wider audience, when authorities were not confident to carry out mass arrests. Polish workers were experiencing the same kind of conditions that had driven their colleagues in East Berlin to rise up three years earlier. Metal workers in Poznan's largest factory drew up a petition demanding overtime pay and a relaxation of work quotas. A delegation of workers took it to the capital, Warsaw. Receiving no satisfaction, the Poznan workers struck on 27 June. They marched to the city centre and were quickly joined by tens of thousands of other workers. They sang the 'Internationale' and held banners reading 'We demand bread.' Soon the demonstration, now 100,000 strong, turned into a riot. Sections of the crowd seized an arms depot. They attacked the local Communist Party office and a string of government buildings, including police stations, a prison camp and the military school, grabbing more weapons.

The city's authorities feared a repeat of the East Berlin experience. Concerned that local units would not be reliable, they called on military units outside Poznan for help. Ten thousand troops and the internal security corps arrived in a procession of 400 tanks, armoured cars and field guns. Party leader Edward Ochab condemned the protests as the work of Western agents and declared on the local radio station: 'Any provocateur or lunatic who raises his hand against the people's government may be sure that this hand will be chopped off.' Resistance, armed and unarmed, continued heroically for several days, but the troops finally took control of the city by 30 June.

The Poznan workers' revolt caused renewed debate inside the Polish Communist Party. To assuage popular anger, the government announced wage rises. In the autumn, 'reform Stalinist' Władysław Gomułka, who had been jailed as a 'Titoite' and was opposed by Khrushchev, was installed. This divided the movement, allowing Gomułka to send in the riot police to drive off the streets those demanding complete democratisation of the regime.

Breakout in Hungary

It was in Hungary that divisions in the Communist regime and mass discontent came together to produce the biggest explosion of popular unrest. The Hungarian Communist Party, like others, was split after Stalin's death, between those who wanted to maintain a hard line and those open to a more liberal approach. In July 1953, Moscow pushed the butcher Rákosi to one side and appointed Imre Nagy, a reform-minded Stalinist, as general secretary. One of Nagy's first acts was to release Kádár from jail. Nagy, however, proved incapable of consolidating his hold on the party. A change in the balance of power in Moscow in 1955 turned the tables. Nagy was ousted in favour of Rákosi and expelled from the party. Months later, Khrushchev's secret speech changed the political landscape once again. Rákosi was again the wrong man for the job. Moscow replaced him with another figure from the old guard, Ernő Gerő. Gerő was a veteran Communist who had won Stalin's approval after his work, alongside Togliatti, crushing the CNT and POUM in Barcelona in 1937.

Divisions at the top of the Hungarian party created space for middle class artists, writers, technicians and other intellectual layers to meet to discuss their grievances. The focus was the Petofi circle, founded by Young Communists in 1955 to promote Nagy and his program of gradual reform. In the turmoil of 1956, the Petofi circle became the lightning rod for much broader social tensions. The circle's public debates drew audiences of hundreds, then thousands, predominantly from the middle classes. The Petofi circle reflected a growing public mood of discontent. Even secret police sent to spy on the participants ultimately declared themselves in sympathy with their ideas.

The first show of mass defiance came on 6 October with a 200,000 strong rally to ceremonially re-bury Rajk, the Communist minister executed by Rákosi. Rajk had been a Stalinist and loyal to Moscow; but, by virtue of his execution by the hated Rákosi in 1949, he was now reborn in popular consciousness as an oppositionist. Next, student groups organised a march for 23 October, in solidarity with the rebels in Poznan. The organisers of the 20,000 strong march had no intention of launching an insurrection. Their demands were a hodgepodge: the evacuation of Russian forces from their bases in Hungary; the formation of a new government under Nagy; elections by secret ballot open to all parties; an end to speed-ups in the factories; the introduction of a minimum living wage; the right to strike; press freedom; and the restoration of traditional national regalia, including the old coat of arms.

Although the crowd that gathered on the 23rd was initially peaceful, its mood changed when Gerő broadcast a speech attacking them as a 'trouble-making mob' intent on 'national subversion.' One section of the crowd marched off to tear down a huge statue of Stalin. The other marched on the radio station to demand the right to broadcast their views to the nation. When AVH security police opened fire on those assembled outside the radio station, killing 16 and wounding dozens of others, the die was cast. Within the space of hours, the protest had become an armed insurrection, and a general strike took effect from midnight.

Groups of protesters, particularly young workers, immediately began to arm themselves, seizing weapons from military depots. They attacked security police, set police cars ablaze and vandalised symbols of the Stalinist regime. Soldiers sent to relieve the security police instead sided with the crowd, while the police could not be induced to fight. Only the AVH now remained 'reliable,' and they were incapable of holding back the crowds. Fearful that the protest in Budapest, coming so soon after Poznan, would spark uprisings elsewhere, the Russians deployed 1,100 tanks and 30,000 troops overnight to crush the rising. They were quickly confronted by protesters wielding their newly acquired weapons. The Hungarian workers' revolution had begun.

The first days of street fighting were chaotic, fired by spontaneous fury. The Hungarian word for revolution is *forraldom*, the boiling over of the masses. This is just what occurred. Protesters turned on anything and anyone associated with the old regime. They smashed statues and monuments associated with Stalinist rule, invaded Communist party offices and killed suspected police spies. Youths as young as 13 or 14 threw Molotov cocktails at the lumbering Russian tanks – easy targets in crowded streets. While students and intellectuals dominated in the first couple of days, soon the majority of the armed fighters were factory workers and apprentices from the industrial districts. One report, based on a subsequent survey of thousands of refugees, described them:

> They were amongst the poorest of Hungarians – the ones communism was supposed to have helped the most but did not. On the whole, they were the young people who had the worst jobs, the worst education and the least hope. They wanted an end to communism...not reforms to a system they despised. They had less to lose by rebelling so spectacularly than any other group.[9]

Some of the most determined fighters were the city's football supporters, ingrained with a deep hatred of the authorities. One student said: 'It is touching that it was the hooligans of Ferencvaros [a famous football team] who created ethics out of nothing during the revolution.'[10]

After years of repression, cultural expression blossomed in the atmosphere of revolution. Taking the place of half a dozen dull party publications, 25 lively daily newspapers emerged and built a circulation of millions within a few days. The revolutionary youth, the different sections of workers, peasants, police and army all had their papers, publishing exposés of the privileged lives of Communist leaders. New political parties emerged, including a social democratic party which grew quickly. Solidarity flourished: donations for the families of those killed in the fighting piled up in open suitcases left unguarded on street corners. Doctors and nurses staffed makeshift emergency hospitals to treat those injured by the Russian army. Strikes erupted in working class districts. Workers in the regional industrial centres soon followed, with 30,000 coal miners calling for free elections.

The Hungarian state virtually fell apart. Many police and soldiers handed over their weapons to the insurgents, as did some Russian soldiers. Some army officers who had fought in the clandestine anti-fascist resistance during the war went over to the revolutionaries, while others simply stood back. Not one army unit, not even the military cadets, handpicked sons of loyal party members, could be persuaded to help the Russians crush the revolt. As the state lost authority, the 800,000 strong Communist Party disintegrated.

Workers' power

After several days of street fighting in Budapest, organised workers began to put their stamp on events. Workers' councils mushroomed, starting in the capital, home to half the country's industrial workers. They established the first council on 23 October and soon set up others across the working class districts of the city. On 31 October, a parliament of workers' councils for Budapest was attended by delegates from 24 factories. The delegates declared:

> The supreme controlling body of the factory is the workers' council democratically elected by the workers… The director is employed by the factory. The director and highest employees are to be elected by the workers' council… The director is responsible to the workers' council in every matter which concerns the factory.[11]

The councils also demanded a range of democratic measures – above all, the withdrawal of Russian troops.

The workers' councils movement spread across the industrial regions and took control of every aspect of life, including organisation of food supplies and maintenance of public order. In Borsod county – home to heavy industries, including a cement and brickworks, a textile mill, and iron, steel and rolling stock production – committees joined up to form workers' councils. Miskolc, one of the county's biggest towns, went furthest. After workers beat off an attack by the security forces, government authority collapsed. The town's workers' council and the newly formed student parliament soon imposed their authority. Workers' councils across Borsod then forged a county-wide workers' council. A similar process happened in town after town. Government authorities attempted to hold onto power by force, shooting workers in the streets, but the workers fought back and overwhelmed them.

Budapest and the industrial cities saw the most action, but the rural areas also stirred on hearing news of the urban revolt. Village committees were elected. Understanding that they faced a common enemy, villagers loaded carts with food to take to towns to help those fighting back.

The emergence of the workers' councils posed the question of who ruled Hungary. Government structures were crumbling. Moscow had installed Nagy in place of Gerő on the first night of the revolution, in the hope that he would derail it. Nagy's orientation was to try to reform the Communist system in order to save it. Initially, Nagy set his face firmly against the revolution, condemning rebels fighting Russian tanks as 'counter-revolutionaries.' Under pressure from the revolution, Nagy had to switch tack and passed a string of reforms that loosened the grip of the Stalinist bureaucracy. But the reforms were always too little, too late for the steadily radicalising revolutionaries. His instructions to clear the streets were simply ignored. The Communist Party was in chaos, the security police had been abolished, and neither police nor army would lift a finger in support of the Russian army.

The workers' councils were now running Hungary. Although many workers had participated in the uprising without clear demands, or only hoping to see Nagy returned to office, the revolution gave them the confidence to demand more. The brutal attacks by Russian troops solidified their determination. Calls began to emerge for a Central Workers' Council. The general strike continued, workers refusing to return to work until Russian troops had evacuated.

British Communist journalist Peter Fryer, sent by the party's *Daily Worker* to tell readers about the supposed 'counter-revolution' under way in Hungary, found quite the opposite:

> In their spontaneous origin, in their composition, in their sense of responsibility, in their efficient organisation of food supplies and of civil order, in the restraint they exercised over the wilder

elements among the youth, in the wisdom with which so many of them handled the problem of Soviet troops, and, not least, in their striking resemblance at so many points to the soviets or councils of workers', peasants' and soldiers' deputies which sprang up in Russia in the 1905 revolution and again in February 1917, these committees, a network of which now extended over the whole of Hungary, were remarkably uniform. They were at once organs of insurrection – the coming together of delegates elected by factories and universities, mine and Army units – and organs of popular self-government, which the armed people trusted. As such they enjoyed tremendous authority, and it is no exaggeration to say that until the Soviet attack of November 4 the real power in the country lay in their hands.

Of course, as in every real revolution 'from below,' there was 'too much' talking, arguing, bickering, coming and going, froth, excitement, agitation, ferment. That is one side of the picture. The other side is the emergence to leading positions of ordinary men, women and youths whom the AVH dominion had kept submerged. The revolution thrust them forward, aroused their civic pride and latent genius for organisation, set them to work to build democracy out of the ruins of bureaucracy.[12]

The *Daily Worker* refused to publish Fryer's reports. The editor's response was typical of the Communist Parties who asserted that the Hungarian revolt was a counter-revolution by fascist elements, backed by Western imperialism.

Stalinist opponents of the Hungarian Revolution argued that the rebels were all right wing and intent on reinstituting rule by landlords, big business and the Catholic Church. Of course, ideological confusion existed among the mass of Hungarian workers. Right wing elements, clerical tendencies and even open fascists hovered around, hoping to see the overthrow of the regime. The fact that the traditional language of socialism had been usurped by the Stalinist dictatorship enhanced the confusion. Many rebels believed that they were fighting communism, which was to be expected when there was no organised party promoting socialism as the politics of workers' power. But it is nonsense to believe that workers who had taken control of their workplaces, set up workers' councils and were virtually running every aspect of political life only aimed to set up a regime run by private capitalists. Politically, they were very mixed. Many leaders of the workers' councils were young, with no political experience; others were old social democrats and union militants; still others, former Communists with memories of the 1919 Hungarian Revolution. But all agreed on the core demands:

> WITHDRAWAL OF RUSSIAN TROOPS
> WORKERS' CONTROL OF THE FACTORIES
> NO RETURN TO STALINISM
> NO RETURN OF THE PREWAR FACTORY OWNERS.

Although the movement was fairly unformed politically, the important thing was that the masses were involved and groping towards a solution.

Russian withdrawal

After several days of fighting in Budapest, and with the general strike holding across the country, the Russians realised that they could not crush the resistance with the forces at their disposal. They had lost 500 men, and their troops were exhausted and hungry. They had suffered a tremendous blow, their biggest setback in Eastern Europe to date. Russian emissaries negotiated a ceasefire with Nagy. It took effect on 29 October. Celebrations in the streets of Budapest were muted; anger and bitterness were not. Big crowds showered the departing troops with jeers and abuse and attacked Communist Party headquarters, wreaking vengeance on those who had persecuted them for years.

Following the departure of Russian troops from the capital, Nagy tried to assert his authority. He freed 8,000 political prisoners and announced the abolition of the one-party system and the formation of a multi-party Cabinet, with Kádár appointed Minister of State. He urged workers to end their strikes, which, he said, were injuring the revolution. He sought to integrate the rebel forces into a new National Guard as a way of controlling them.

Most in the workers' councils were willing to give Nagy time to implement his reforms. The councils in the two main workers' districts of Budapest agreed to call off their strike and advised that work would resume on Monday 5 November. There was opposition, however, particularly among those with arms. They had just brought a mighty army to heel and wanted to see their demands met in full. These rebels, whose voice was not fully represented in the workers' councils, saw the ceasefire as the start of negotiations. Arms and the general strike had won them much, and they were their best hope for winning more. They refused to hand over their weapons. They demanded that Russian troops be evacuated, not just from Budapest, but from Hungary, and that the country declare its neutrality.

The leadership in Moscow was split on the next step. Hardline Stalinists argued that the withdrawal of Russian troops had severely weakened Moscow's authority, and the revolution should be crushed. Others still hoped that Nagy could bring the revolution under control. As the days went on, the hardliners got the upper hand. The calculation was simple: Russia could not let the revolution succeed for fear of the consequences. The signs of revolutionary 'contagion' in other countries were unmistakable. On 30 October, huge demonstrations in support of the Hungarian rising took place in Poland; 300,000 gathered in Warsaw. In Romania, where authorities had already stepped up security to reinforce control over train stations, airports, broadcasting stations and university campuses, students held big protest marches. A KGB report from Czechoslovakia described student demonstrations in Bratislava and other provincial cities and 'a growing hostility and mistrust of the Soviet Union.' The Czech Government informed Moscow that the revolution in Hungary was having 'a deleterious psychological effect' and 'creating a hostile anti-socialist mood' among Czech troops sent to reinforce the border with Hungary: 'If we don't embark on a decisive move, things in Czechoslovakia will collapse.' Reports coming into the politbureau from Russian intelligence services and other Warsaw Pact governments all suggested that the Russian position was precarious. Inside the USSR itself, the de-Stalinisation campaign had sparked disturbances in Georgia earlier in the year: riots in Tbilisi were suppressed by tanks and martial law, and there were fears of worse to come. Students and faculty at several campuses in Russia, including the prestigious Moscow State University, protested against the first military intervention in Budapest, and the KGB cracked down hard.[13] Khrushchev decided to act. Hungary must be taught a lesson as a warning to others.

Fresh invasion and worker resistance

On Thursday 1 November, reports came flooding into Nagy's office of Russian troops sweeping across the border. Nagy dithered. Having been a loyal Communist for so long, he blindly believed Russian denials that the troops had aggressive intentions. His chief concern was that the revolutionaries not give Russia 'a pretext to break off negotiations.' Unwilling to lead popular resistance, he refused to tell the people the news of Russia's military mobilisation. Instead, Nagy called for outside assistance, announcing Hungary's exit from the Warsaw Pact and calling on the four Great Powers – the US, Britain, France and Russia – to guarantee Hungary's neutrality. Nagy had no illusions that the US would send military aid but hoped that it would at least use the UN to impose pressure on Russia – a vain hope.

In the early hours of Sunday 4 November, Russian forces attacked Budapest, this time with overwhelming force. Furious fighting ensued as between 10,000 and 15,000 workers rose up to fight Russia's 150,000 troops, 2,500 tanks and squadrons of fighter jets. Nagy took sanctuary in the Yugoslav embassy and ordered the National Guard not to resist the Russian invasion. It fell on workers to fight back. It was the workers' districts of Budapest that suffered the worst damage from Russian shelling, and it was workers, many of them teenagers, who died or were injured in their thousands. And it was workers who held out the longest. While most of the city fell to Russian arms within two days, rebel groups in the working class district of 'Red' Csepel, whose population of 70,000 was besieged for five days, hung on until 11 November. Their bravery, however, proved no match for Russian firepower. In the first Russian intervention, the armed forces had been instructed to take control of the city but not to level it; this time, restraint was cast aside. Fryer wrote:

> I have just come out of Budapest, where for six days I have watched Hungary's new-born freedom tragically destroyed by Soviet troops... Vast areas of the city – the working class areas above all – are virtually in ruins. For four days and nights Budapest was under continuous bombardment. I saw a once lovely city battered, bludgeoned, smashed and bled into submission.[14]

The stately villas of the fashionable middle class districts were, by contrast, hardly touched.

Communist Party leaders from Eastern Europe and China – worried that they would be next if workers in Hungary were able to challenge Communist rule – backed the invasion, some begging to be allowed to send their armies to join the Russians.

On 7 November, the Russians flew in their replacement for Nagy. It was Kádár, who had left Budapest for Moscow several days previously and now re-entered the country as Russia's man. On 22 November, Nagy and his entourage were kidnapped by Russian soldiers and flown to Romania where they were thrown in jail.

Russian tanks had won control of the streets and imposed Kádár as prime minister, but they could not control the factories. Workers' councils launched a general strike and brought industrial production to a halt for a full month.

They retained total control of the key workplaces into December. A journalist writing for the British *Observer* reported the situation in mid-November:

> A fantastic aspect of the situation is that although the general strike is in being…the workers are nevertheless taking it upon themselves to keep essential services going, for the purposes which they themselves determine and support. Workers' councils in industrial districts have undertaken the distribution of essential goods and food to the population in order to keep them alive. The coal miners are making daily allocations of just sufficient coal to keep the power stations going and supply the hospitals in Budapest and other large towns. Railwaymen organise trains to go to approved destinations for approved purposes.[15]

On 14 November, a new Central Workers' Council of Greater Budapest, based in Csepel, met for the first time. Fifty delegates represented all the major factories of Budapest; others came from the provincial centres of Miskolc and Gyor. This became the organising centre of the resistance. Before long, the council decided on a basic platform and leadership. Its democratic nature became obvious when delegates from Csepel tried to undermine the strike but were thrown out by workers from the district and replaced by representatives supporting the strike.

Debates raged on the Central Workers' Council. Should they negotiate with Kádár and call off the strikes? What concessions could the councils make in negotiations, and what were their bottom lines? The mood swung back and forth between concessions and outright opposition. Events had unfolded so rapidly that many workers were uncertain about the way forward. Years of deceitful rhetoric of 'Marxism' spouted by the Stalinists had taken their toll. Many workers were disoriented, caught between their spontaneous revolutionary actions and the old habits of the past. Unfortunately, with no revolutionary party, it was difficult for the more militant factory delegates, many of them from industrial regions outside Budapest, to hold the line against those keen to compromise.

In negotiations with representatives from the Central Workers' Council and in a series of announcements to the public, Kádár used both carrot and stick to beat back opposition. The government offered a series of concessions to workers, peasants and to the Catholic Church, which had been suppressed by his predecessors. The most hated Stalinist leaders – Rákosi and Gerő – were prevented from returning from exile in Moscow, and Kádár indicated that he would not reintroduce the repression associated with their rule. Kádár stated his willingness to afford the workers' councils government recognition as legitimate bodies.

But workers' councils would be tolerated only so long as they were willing to restrict themselves to handling minor workplace grievances and to disown any political ambitions. Any attempt to organise politically would invite harsh repression. And so, when the Central Workers' Council invited workers' councils from around the country to meet in Budapest on 21 November, delegates found the venue surrounded by Russian tanks. Fearing, incorrectly, that delegates had been arrested *en masse*, Budapest workers resumed their strike on the 22nd and 23rd, pulling out big numbers. The government now began to denounce the workers' councils as 'counter-revolutionary.' Kádár attempted to ban the Central Council's regular bulletin, although this only increased its popularity. Ominously, the regime used former AVH officers to begin rebuilding the secret police. By a combination of such concessions, chicanery and brute force, Kádár was gradually able to wear down the opposition.

Resistance continued for several weeks. On 4 December, 30,000 women defied martial law, staging a silent demonstration in Budapest against the invasion. On 8 December, in response to the arrest of the coal miners' leaders and the shooting of 39 demonstrating miners, the Central Workers' Council called another 48-hour general strike, the most widely observed yet. The government responded by declaring the councils illegal; it instituted a state of emergency and rounded up 200 workers' council leaders. When strikes and demonstrations in solidarity with arrestees were called, workers were shot down on the streets. Opposition was increasingly forced underground. On 5 January 1957, the government announced the death penalty for those 'inciting strikes.' On 8 January, workers in Budapest demonstrating their support for the Central Workers' Council were met by Russian tanks. The revolt was finally crushed by the end of January, at a cost of 2,500 lives.

The Kádár government now launched a dragnet to catch anyone suspected of playing a leading role in the uprising. Some were hanged within days of their arrest. In April, Nagy was brought back from Romania and imprisoned in Budapest. In June 1958, Kádár had him executed. By the end of 1959, 22,000 had been jailed and more than 300 executed. Most of those targeted were young workers and those involved in the workers' councils. Two hundred thousand fled into exile.

The Western powers shed only a few crocodile tears for the martyrs. In line with the postwar division of spheres of influence, NATO accepted that Russia had a free hand in Hungary. The NATO allies had plenty on their plates at this time. Egyptian President Gamal Nasser had nationalised the Suez Canal in June, so Britain and France, in partnership with Israel, invaded Egypt in late October to seize the waterway. France was also pouring troops into Algeria to try to defeat the independence movement. Neither Britain nor France had any interest in encouraging an oppressed people to resist foreign invasion. The US made it clear that it had no intention of intervening. The Eisenhower administration had boasted for years about 'liberating the captive peoples of Eastern Europe,' with CIA radio station Radio Free Europe urging the revolutionaries to fight the Russians. But when the Hungarian revolutionaries appealed for help, the US let them be crushed: images of Russian tanks rolling through Budapest were good propaganda material to undermine Russian prestige.

The Hungarian Revolution and Stalinism

The Hungarian Revolution shattered the myth that Russia and Eastern Europe – the so-called socialist bloc – were societies in which workers held power. This dealt a blow to many Western Communist Parties. Khrushchev's speech had already caused significant confusion and doubt in the minds of Communist cadres: how could their parties have followed Stalin unquestioningly for so long? Russia's brutal invasion of Hungary, backed by most Communist leaders, brought the crisis to a head. In France, some militants of the CGT union federation, dominated by the Communists, refused to distribute leaflets supporting the Russian action. This opposition made itself felt on the CGT executive, where the PCF was unable to get a motion carried supporting Moscow's invasion. In Italy, the PSI opposed the Russian intervention. The executive of the CGIL union federation, in which the PSI and PCI worked alongside each other, carried a motion deploring the intervention of Russian troops.

Opposition in the ranks of the Communist parties caused mass resignations. In France, membership dropped from 360,000 to 290,000; in Italy, from two million to 1.8 million; and in Britain from 33,000 to 25,000. In the US, the *Daily Worker* initially denounced the first Russian intervention, but Stalinist orthodoxy was reinforced after several months. By 1957, membership of the CPUSA stood at 10,000, well down from its peak of 75,000 in 1947. The impact on the left varied. In the US, the combination of the Cold War atmosphere and the postwar prosperity persuaded most ex-Communists to drop out of politics or drift to the right. In Britain, however, the trend was partly counteracted by the Suez Crisis. Mass protests took place against Britain's attack on Egypt, and many drew the conclusion that both sides, West and East, were equally bad. The Australian experience with the fallout from Hungary was somewhere between the US and British cases, with the CPA losing members and prestige but without suffering collapse.

From the late 1950s onwards, Stalinism on the Russian model suffered a long historical decline in the West. The revolts against Stalinism in East Germany, Poland and Hungary in the 1950s were the harbingers of others. Each uprising and the bloody repression that greeted it drove another nail in the Stalinist coffin. Khrushchev's revelations of (some of) Stalin's crimes had also permanently tarnished Russia's image. The emergence of a number of rival 'socialist' countries further weakened the attractive power of Russia as the homeland of socialism. Stalin's split with Tito in 1948 was followed in 1960 by a much more serious split between Russia and China.

Russia also became less involved in the affairs of the Western Communist Parties once it acquired the atomic bomb in 1949. Russia's nuclear capability meant that the Western parties, which had been a valuable bargaining chip in Moscow's relations with the Western powers, were no longer a significant factor in the Russian bureaucracy's foreign policy. The threat of mutually assured destruction, not Communist support for class struggle in the West, could now stay America's hand, By the time of the 1962 Cuban missile crisis, in which the US and Russia came within hours of firing nuclear missiles at each other, the Western parties were largely irrelevant to Khrushchev. They were therefore allowed greater freedom to forge their own path somewhat independently of the Kremlin.

Finally, Stalinism had been the product of defeat and despair. The Russian myth had been at its strongest in the 1930s, when Western workers saw Stalin as the only alternative to mass unemployment and fascism. The postwar period was one of economic expansion and full employment, strengthening workers' bargaining position with the bosses. Workers who had much more confidence in their own strength felt less desire for a distant paradise.

These factors left the Stalinist parties with two choices. A minority longed to retreat into sectarian sentimentality, nostalgia for the days when Stalin was in charge. The majority pursued an alternative option. They gradually transformed their organisations into social democratic parties or, in the Italian and Spanish cases, 'Eurocommunist' parties, which combined social democracy with a residual core of hard Stalinism. Eventually, even the Eurocommunist parties evolved into straightforward social democratic parties. Most dissolved altogether after the collapse of the Soviet Union in 1991.

Today, Stalinism still exists as state ideology in China, little more than nationalism and veneration of the strong state. It also has a following in mass parties in India. In a few smaller countries, it continues to provide a supposedly

Marxist veneer to a set of politics that are thoroughly anti-working class. In the Western left, although the Communist parties have virtually all vanished, their legacy lives on in 'campism.' This is the belief that the world is divided into an imperialist bloc, dominated by the United States, and a progressive, anti-imperialist bloc, populated by whoever is opposed at any point in time to the US – Putin's Russia, Assad's Syria or Xi Jinping's China. Stalinism also persists in popular front politics, in the idea that the working class should look for allies in supposedly 'progressive' sections of the bourgeoisie. Open worship of Stalin may be a fringe activity in the Western left, but some of the key tenets of Stalinism are still accepted as good coin by leftists.

Rebirth of revolutionary Marxism

The Hungarian Revolution heralded an early step towards the destruction of Stalinism in Eastern Europe. It also created the potential for the rebirth of revolutionary Marxism. Hungary demonstrated that, in even the most oppressive circumstances, workers are able to rise up and create organs of mass democracy – workers' councils, just like the soviets of 1917 in Russia – which can begin to take over every aspect of life. The Hungarian Revolution vindicated Trotsky's basic contention, discussed at the beginning of this book: revolutions are, first and foremost, 'the forcible entrance of the masses into the realm of rulership over their own destiny.' In the 1960s, with working class and student radicalism gathering momentum around the world, anti-Stalinists were able to win an audience for their argument that Marxism is the self-emancipation of the working class or it is nothing.

We are now many decades from the struggles that feature in this book. Much has changed, but much remains the same. The media and the education system never tire of telling us that revolutions are obsolete, but multiple intersecting crises ravage the lives of working class and oppressed people in rich and poor countries alike, generating rebellions. Revolts of every kind will continue while capitalist barbarism rules the world. The chief question is: what will become of them? Will they be sent down a blind alley by reformists or other forces opposed to fundamental change, or will they build into a broad revolutionary challenge to capitalism?

Many episodes discussed in this book show that a precondition for a successful outcome to future struggles for workers' power is the existence of revolutionary parties built ahead of time. Rosa Luxemburg found, to her cost, that trying to set a revolutionary party in motion when millions of workers are on the move is too late.

What do the experiences detailed in this book tell us are the necessary characteristics of such a party? Firstly, clarity on the major political questions: a commitment to working class struggle and self-emancipation. The system of world capitalism we face today cannot be overturned by any means short of mass insurrection, a thoroughgoing revolution on an international scale that systematically dismantles the huge apparatus of capitalist rule and replaces it with new institutions of workers' power and popular control. Building this entails opposing reformism and other political ideologies that appear to promise change but capitulate to the capitalist system. It involves opposing nationalism and imperialism, especially important for socialists in an imperialist country like Australia. Self-emancipation also involves supporting the struggles of the oppressed, because divisions in the working class only weaken our ability to fight for liberation.

Secondly, theoretical understanding must be combined with practice. Revolutionary parties are combat organisations. We wage political fights, not only against the capitalist class but against rival currents within the workers' and student movements, in a bid to win hegemony, or leadership. The revolutionary party needs an active and engaged membership, with the mass of members fighting to build class struggle politics in the trade unions, among students and in social movements. Marxism is not a holy scripture handed down on tablets, like Moses's Ten Commandments; it is a living science. Like all sciences, it must be tested and re-tested in practice, revised where it is found to be deficient and consolidated where it is not. An active membership is also a prerequisite for internal democracy. Leaders are held to account by members involved in the day to day work of the party – an approach entirely absent from the Stalinist monoliths that came to dominate the Comintern from the late 1920s.

Thirdly, the experience of Russia's Bolsheviks demonstrates the importance of building and renewing cadres, experienced members who understand what they are doing, take their tasks seriously and have the capacity to pull others around them and build the influence of the party. Class struggle does not move in a smooth, linear fashion but through rapid and sharp changes, both advances and retreats. Party cadres need the capacity to form their own judgement and make snap decisions. Developing such cadres requires intensive and continuous involvement and a commitment to studying the lessons of class struggle over generations. It means taking account of the experiences of struggle, the successes and the failures, discussed in this book. To guide the practice of the present, a revolutionary party must learn the lessons of history.

Building such revolutionary parties is not straightforward. There will be many twists and turns along the way. But the histories of struggle recounted here demonstrate clearly that there is no alternative to the hard work involved. Nothing short of constructing revolutionary socialist parties offers humanity a way forward from its crises. We hope that this book convinces you, the reader, to join us in this task.

FURTHER READING

I. Birchall, *Workers against the Monolith: The Communist Parties since 1943*, London, Pluto Press, 1974.

S. Bloodworth, 'Lenin and a theory of revolution for the West', *Marxist Left Review*, no. 8, 2014.

P. Fryer, *Hungarian Tragedy*, Melbourne, Red Flag Publications, 2020.

C. Harman, *Class Struggles in Eastern Europe*, London, Pluto Press, 1983.

M. Haynes, 'Hungary: workers' councils against Russian tanks', *International Socialism*, no. 112, 2006.

C. Oakley, 'What kind of organisation do socialists need?', *Marxist Left Review*, no. 5, 2013.

B. Lomax, 'The workers' councils of Greater Budapest', in R. Miliband and J. Saville (eds.), *The Socialist Register 1976*, London, Merlin Press, 1976.

V. Sebestyen, *Twelve Days: The Story of the Hungarian Revolution*, London, Vintage, 2007.

ACRONYMS AND ABBREVIATIONS

ACTU	Australian Council of Trade Unions
AEU	Amalgamated Engineering Union (Australia)
AFL	American Federation of Labor
ALP	Australian Labor Party
AMIEU	Amalgamated Meat Industry Employees Union (Australia)
ARTUC	Anglo-Russian Trade Union Council
ARU	Australian Railways Union
AVH	State Protection Authority (Államvédelmi Hatóság) (Hungary)
AWU	Australian Workers' Union
BOC	Workers and Peasants Bloc (Bloque Obrero y Campesino) (Spain)
CCP	Communist Party of China
CEDA	Spanish Confederation of Autonomous Right Wing Groups (Confederación Española de Derechas Autónomas) (Spain)
CGL/ CGIL	General Federation of Labour (Confederazione Generale del Lavoro) (before 1927)
	Italian General Federation of Labour (Confederazione Generale Italiana del Lavoro) (after 1944) (Italy)
CGT	General Confederation of Labour (Confédération Générale du Travail) (France)
CGT-U	General Confederation of Labour – Unitary (Confédération Générale du Travail – Unitaire) (France)
CIO	Committee for Industrial Organizations (later, Congress of Industrial Organizations) (US)
CLN	National Liberation Committee (Comitato di Liberazione

	Nazionale) (Italy)
CLNAI	National Liberation Committee of Northern Italy (Comitato di Liberazione Nazionale Alta Italia)
CNT	National Confederation of Labour (Confederación Nacional del Trabajo) (Spain)
CPA	Communist Party of Australia
CPGB	Communist Party of Great Britain
CPUSA	Communist Party of the United States of America
DC	Christian Democrats (Democrazia Cristiana) (Italy)
EAM	National Liberation Front (Ethnikó Apeleftherotikó Métopo) (Greece)
ECCI	Executive Committee of the Communist International
ELAS	Greek Popular Liberation Army (Ellinikós Laïkós Apeleftherotikós Stratós)
FAI	Iberian Anarchist Federation (Federación Anarquista Ibérica) (Spain)
FEDFA	Federated Engine Drivers and Firemen's Association (Australia)
FI	Fourth International
FIA	Federated Ironworkers' Association (Australia)
GM	General Motors (United States)
GMD	Nationalist People's Party (Guomindang) (China)
IWW	Industrial Workers of the World (Australia/US)
KAPD	Communist Workers' Party of Germany (Kommunistische Arbeiter Partei Deutschlands)
KKE	Communist Party of Greece (Kommounistikó Kómma Elládas)
KMT	See GMD (Kuomintang) (China)
KPD	Communist Party of Germany (Kommunistische Partei Deutschlands)
MMM	Militant Minority Movement (Also, MM: Minority Movement) (Australia)
NAACP	National Association for the Advancement of Colored Peoples (US)
NATO	North Atlantic Treaty Organization
NEP	New Economic Policy (Russia)
NUR	National Union of Railwaymen (Britain)
OMS	Organisation for the Maintenance of Supplies (Britain)
PCE	Spanish Communist Party (Partido Comunista de España)

PCI	Italian Communist Party (Partito Comunista Italiano)
Pd'A	Action Party (Partito d'Azione) (Italy)
PLA	People's Liberation Army (China)
POUM	Workers Party of Marxist Unification (Partido Obrero de Unificación Marxista) (Spain)
PSI	Italian Socialist Party (Partito Socialista Italiano)
PSOE	Socialist Workers' Party of Spain (Partido Socialista Obrero Español)
PSUC	United Socialist Party of Catalonia (Partido Socialista Unificado de Catalunya)
RSDLP	Russian Social Democratic and Labour Party
RSS	Revolutionary Shop Stewards (Germany)
SFIO	French Socialist Party (Parti Socialiste, Section Française de L'Internationale Ouvrière)
SPD	Social Democratic Party of Germany (Sozialdemokratische Partei Deutschlands)
TLC	Trades and Labour/Labor Council (Australia)
TUC	Trades Union Congress (Britain)
UAP	United Australia Party
UAW	United Auto Workers (United States)
UGT	General Union of Workers (Unión General de Trabajadores) (Spain)
UMW	United Mine Workers (United States)
USI	Italian Syndicalist Union (Unione Syndicale Italiana)
USPD	Independent Social Democratic Party of Germany (Unabhängige Sozialdemokratische Partei Deutschlands)
UWM	Unemployed Workers' Movement (Australia)
VKPD	United Communist Party of Germany (Vereinigte Kommunistische Partei Deutschlands)
WWF	Waterside Workers' Federation (Australia)

ENDNOTES

Note: Where a second date is shown in square brackets, it is the original date of production of the work. Detailed sources for classic works of Marx, Lenin, Trotsky etc are not provided. Many are available on the Marxists Internet Archive www.marxists.org. Some URLs for less well known works are included.

INTRODUCTION

1. L. Trotsky, *The History of the Russian Revolution*, London, Pluto Press, 1977 [1933], p. 17. Emphasis added.

1. REFORMIST BETRAYAL, REVOLUTIONARY HOPE

1. Main sources used: S. Bloodworth, *How Workers Took Power: The 1917 Russian Revolution*, Melbourne, Socialist Alternative, 2008; S. Bloodworth, 'Lenin vs "Leninism"', *Marxist Left Review*, no. 5, 2013; P. Broué, *The German Revolution 1917-1923*, Chicago, Haymarket Books, 2006 [1971]; H. Grossman, 'The Internationals: The Second International (1889-1914)', in R. Kuhn (ed.), *Henryk Grossman Works, volume 2*, Leiden, Brill, 2 020 [1932]; D. Hallas, *The Comintern*, Chicago, Haymarket Books, 2008 [1985]; M. Haynes, *Russia: Class and Power 1917-2000*, London, Bookmarks, 2002; R. Hostetter, 'The SPD and the general strike as an anti-war weapon, 1905-1914', *The Historian*, 13, 1, 1950; J. Molyneux, *Marxism and the Party*, London, Pluto Press, 1978; C. Oakley, *The Socialist Movement: Our History*, Melbourne, Socialist Alternative, 2007 [2006]; C. Post, 'Leninism?', www.rs21.org.uk/2015/03/08/leninism-2/, 8 March 2015; C. Schorske, *German Social Democracy, 1905-1917: The Development of the Great Schism*, Cambridge, Harvard University Press, 1983 [1955].
2. E.H. Carr, *The Bolshevik Revolution*, volume 3, Harmondsworth, Penguin Books, 1983 [1953], pp. 135-36.
3. *Manifesto* of the First Congress of the Communist International, March 1919.
4. V.I. Lenin, 'The position and tasks of the Socialist International', *Sotsial-Democrat*, no. 33, 1 November 1914.
5. S. Berger and S. Braun, 'Socialism', in M. Jefferies (ed.), *The Ashgate Research Companion to Imperial Germany*, London, Routledge, 2020, p. 184.
6. Cited in M. Salvador, *Karl Kautsky and the Socialist Revolution, 1880-1938*, London, New Left Books, 1979, p. 162.
7. K. Kautsky, *The Road to Power*, 1909.
8. The British and Australian social democratic parties, which never expressed any revolutionary aspirations, were the exception, not the rule, in the Second International.
9. Cited in S. and B. Webb, *History of Trade Unionism*, 2nd edn., London, Longmans, 1920, pp. 466-70.
10. S. and B. Webb, *Industrial Democracy*, London, 1897, pp. 12 and 59. This trend was welcomed by the Webbs, who abhorred strikes.

11. Cited in S. and B. Webb, *History of Trade Unionism*, p. 594.
12. Grossman, 'The Internationals', p. 371.
13. Schorske, *German Social Democracy*, p. 48.
14. Hostetter, 'The SPD and the general strike', p. 39.
15. Hostetter, 'The SPD and the general strike', p. 27.
16. Hostetter, 'The SPD and the general strike', pp. 27-28.
17. Cited in Schorske, *German Social Democracy*, p. 290.
18. 'Opportunism' is the word Lenin and other revolutionaries frequently used for reformism. V.I. Lenin, 'The position and tasks of the Socialist International'.
19. For more on Kautsky, see D. Roso, 'Kautsky: the abyss beyond parliament', *Marxist Left Review*, no.14, 2017.
20. Cited in T. Cliff, *Rosa Luxemburg*, London, Bookmarks, 1986, p. 44.
21. V.I. Lenin, 'The War and Russian Social Democracy', 28 September 1914. The Bolsheviks were not entirely solid; the Paris Bolshevik group split, and some of its members volunteered to serve in the French army. I. Birchall, 'The Comintern's encounter with syndicalism', *Marxist Left Review*, no. 20, 2020; I. Birchall, 'Rereading Rosmer', *International Socialist Review*, no. 97, 2015.
22. S.A. Smith, *Red Petrograd*, Cambridge, Cambridge University Press, 1983, pp. 109-10.
23. V.I. Lenin, *One Step Forward, Two Steps Back*, 1904.
24. Bloodworth, 'Lenin vs "Leninism"', p. 24.
25. Bloodworth, 'Lenin vs "Leninism"', p. 25.
26. St Petersburg was renamed Petrograd in 1914 and Leningrad in 1924.
27. Cited in Bloodworth, 'Lenin vs "Leninism"', p. 40.
28. V.I. Lenin, 'The position and tasks of the Socialist International'.
29. V.I. Lenin, 'The position and tasks of the Socialist International'.
30. V.I. Lenin, 'Imperialism and the split in socialism', 1916.
31. L. Trotsky, *The History of the Russian Revolution*, London, Pluto Press, 1979 [1930], pp. 216-17.
32. Figures from Haynes, *Russia: Class and Power*, p. 22.
33. V.I. Lenin, 'Letters from Afar: First Letter: The First Stage of the First Revolution', 7 March 1917.
34. L. Trotsky, *The Permanent Revolution*, 1931.
35. V.I. Lenin, 'Lecture on the 1905 Revolution', 22 January 1917.
36. Cited in Haynes, *Russia: Class and Power*, p. 33.

2. THE CREATION OF MASS REVOLUTIONARY PARTIES

1. Main sources used: C. Bambery, 'Hegemony and revolutionary strategy', *International Socialism*, no. 114, 2007; P. Broué, *The German Revolution 1917-1923*, Chicago, Haymarket Books, 2006 [1971]; D. Gluckstein, 'Remember, remember the 9th of November', *International Socialism*, no. 160, 2018; D. Hallas, *The Comintern*, Chicago, Haymarket Books, 2008 [1985]; C. Harman, *The Lost Revolution: Germany 1918 to 1923*, London, Bookmarks, 1982; R. Hoffrogge, *Working Class Politics in the German Revolution: Richard Müller, the Revolutionary Shop Stewards and the Origins of the Council Movement*, Chicago, Haymarket Press, 2015; J. Rose, 'Luxemburg, Muller and the Berlin workers' and soldiers' councils', *International Socialism*, no. 147, Summer 2015; L. Tavan, 'Gramsci, Bordiga and the factory occupations' and 'Revolutionary Italy: rise and fall of the factory occupations', *Red Flag*, 28 July and 21 August 2020.
2. The Second International was formally reconstituted only in 1923.
3. Cited in C. Coutinho, *Gramsci's Political Thought*, Chicago, Haymarket Books, 2013, p. 6.
4. Cited in A. Rosmer, *Lenin's Moscow*, London, Pluto Press, 1971, p. 22.
5. Rosmer, *Lenin's Moscow*, p. 21.
6. Cited in Broué, *The German Revolution*, p. 130.
7. Cited in Broué, *The German Revolution*, p. 142.
8. Cited in Broué, *The German Revolution*, p. 144.
9. Cited in Harman, *The Lost Revolution*, p. 9.
10. Cited in Broué, *The German Revolution*, p. 149.
11. P. Frölich, *Rosa Luxemburg*, Chicago, Haymarket Books, 2010, p. 262.
12. Broué, *The German Revolution*, p. 174.
13. Cited in Gluckstein, 'Remember, remember the 9th of November', p. 158.
14. Cited in Broué, *The German Revolution*, p. 175.
15. R. Luxemburg, 'The National Assembly', 20 November 1918.
16. Luxemburg, 'The National Assembly'.
17. Cited in Broué, *The German Revolution*, p. 184.
18. Hoffrogge, *Working-Class Politics in the German Revolution*, p. 95.

19. Cited in Broué, *The German Revolution*, p. 197.
20. Proceedings of the Second Congress of the Comintern, sixth session, 29 July 1920, www.marxists.org/history/international/comintern/2nd-congress/ch06.htm.
21. Proceedings of the Second Congress of the Comintern, sixth session.
22. T. Kemp, *Stalinism in France*, London, New Park Publications, 1984, p. 66.
23. The party was named the Communist Party of Italy (PCd'I), only later changing its name to the Italian Communist Party (PCI), but we will use the later name, by which it is better known.
24. J. Braunthal, *History of the International: 1914–43*, Volume 2, London, Thompson Nelson, 1967.
25. F. Claudin, *The Communist Movement: From Comintern to Cominform*, Harmondsworth, Peregrine Books, 1975, p. 108.
26. P. Broué, '1921: The March Action', 1964, www.marxists.org/history/etol/writers/Broué/works/1964/summer/march-action.htm.
27. Proceedings of the Second Congress of the Comintern, sixth session.
28. Proceedings of the Second Congress of the Comintern, sixth session.

3. THE FIGHT AGAINST ULTRA LEFTISM

1. Main sources used: M. Armstrong, 'Socialist trade union strategy in the Bolshevik era', *Marxist Left Review*, no. 6, 2013; P. Broué, *The German Revolution 1917–1923*, Chicago, Haymarket Books, 2006 [1971]; T. Cliff and D. Gluckstein, *Marxism and Trade Union Struggle: The General Strike of 1926*, London, Bookmarks, 1986; R. Darlington, *Syndicalism and the Transition to Communism*, Aldershot, Ashgate, 2008; D. Hallas, *The Comintern*, Haymarket Books, 2008 [1985]; C. Harman, *The Lost Revolution: Germany 1918 to 1923*, London, Bookmarks, 1982; V.I. Lenin, *'Left-Wing' Communism – An Infantile Disorder*, 1920.
2. T. Behan, *The Resistible Rise of Benito Mussolini*, London, Bookmarks, 2003, pp. 92–93.
3. Lenin, *'Left-Wing' Communism*.
4. The KPD had both a Central Committee and a 'Zentrale', a subset of the Central Committee comprising the core leadership. In this chapter, we will use 'Central Committee' to refer to both.
5. Cited in Harman, *The Lost Revolution*, p. 84.
6. Harman, *The Lost Revolution*, p. 88.
7. 'Proclamation by the KPD Zentrale opposing the General Strike' in B. Fowkes (ed.), *The German Left and the Weimar Republic: A Selection of Documents*, Chicago, Haymarket Books, 2015, pp. 114–15.
8. Harman, *The Lost Revolution*, p. 190.
9. Cited in Broué, *The German Revolution*, p. 453.
10. Narodnism refers to a populist current dominant in the Russian radical circles in the 1880s and 1890s.
11. Lenin, *'Left-Wing' Communism*.
12. Lenin, *'Left-Wing' Communism*.
13. *The Communist International in Lenin's Time, Vol. 1, Workers of the World and Oppressed Peoples, Unite! Proceedings and Documents of the Second Congress, 1920*, New York, Pathfinder Press, 1991, p. 434.
14. Lenin, *'Left-Wing' Communism*.
15. Lenin, *'Left-Wing' Communism*.
16. Lenin, *'Left-Wing' Communism*.
17. Lenin, *'Left-Wing' Communism*.
18. Lenin, *'Left-Wing' Communism*.
19. Lenin, *'Left-Wing' Communism*.
20. Lenin, *'Left-Wing' Communism*.
21. Lenin, *'Left-Wing' Communism*.
22. L. Trotsky, 'Speech on Comrade Zinoviev's report on the role of the party', in *The First Five Years of the Communist International*, volume 1, London, New Park Publications, 1973, p. 126.
23. I. Birchall, 'The Comintern's encounter with syndicalism', *Marxist Left Review*, no. 20, 2020.
24. All quotes from 'From the Third International to the Trade Unions of all Countries', 8 August 1920, *Theses, Resolutions and Manifestos of the First Four Congresses of the Third International*, London, Ink Links, 1983, p. 176.
25. Cited in Birchall, 'The Comintern's encounter with syndicalism'.
26. G. Zinoviev, 'Call for the Third World Congress', in J. Riddell, *To the Masses: Proceedings of the Third Congress of the Communist International, 1921*, Chicago, Haymarket Books, 2015, p. 62. The Amsterdam International actually survived until 1945, eight years after the Profintern was formally wound up in 1937.

27. V.I. Lenin, *Imperialism, the Highest Stage of Capitalism*; G. Zinoviev, 'The Social Roots of Opportunism', 1916.
28. V.I. Lenin, 'The collapse of the Second International', 1915, www.marxists.org/archive/lenin/works/1915/csi/iii.htm.
29. Cited in Cliff and Gluckstein, *Marxism and Trade Union Struggle*, p. 39.
30. V.I. Lenin, 'Preface', *Imperialism: the Highest Stage of Capitalism*, 1917.
31. For much fuller critiques, see C. Post, 'Exploring Working-Class Consciousness: A Critique of the Theory of the "Labour-Aristocracy"', *Historical Materialism*, vol. 18, no. 4, 2010; T. Bramble, 'Is there a labour aristocracy in Australia?', *Marxist Left Review*, no. 4, 2012.
32. K. Marx, 'Preface: A Contribution to the Critique of Political Economy', 1859.
33. Cited in Cliff and Gluckstein, *Marxism and Trade Union Struggle*, p. 64.
34. Cited in Cliff and Gluckstein, *Marxism and Trade Union Struggle*, p. 53.

4. GERMANY: AN OPPORTUNITY LOST

1. Main sources used: P. Broué, *The German Revolution 1917–1923*, Chicago, Haymarket Books, 2006; C. Harman, *The Lost Revolution: Germany 1918 to 1923*, Bookmarks, 1982; J. Riddell, 'The origins of the united front policy', *International Socialism*, no. 130, 2011; J. Riddell (ed.), *To the Masses: Proceedings of the Third Congress of the Communist International, 1921,* Chicago, Haymarket Books, 2015; D. Roso, 'Review: A Jewish Communist in Weimar', *Marxist Left Review*, no. 20, 2020.
2. Harman, *The Lost Revolution*, p. 221.
3. R. Levine-Meyer, *Inside German Communism*, London, Pluto Press, 1977, p. 56.
4. L. Trotsky, *Lessons of October*, 1924.
5. Most accounts of the Open Letter's origins attribute authorship to Levi and Radek; for example, J. Riddell, 'Editorial introduction', in *To the Masses*, p. 35. Larson, however, suggests that Levi had no hand in it and that it was solely the work of KPD members in the Stuttgart branch of the metal workers' union in consultation with Jakob Welcher and Heinrich Brandler; S. Larson, 'Activate the Party: Reassessing the Origins of the United Front Policy in German Revolution 1920-21', *Taking on the Right*, Proceedings of the 15th Annual Historical Materialism Conference, 8–11 November 2017, SOAS University of London.
6. Cited in Larson, 'Activate the Party'.
7. Riddell (ed.), *To the Masses*, p. 21.
8. Cited in Riddell, 'Editorial Introduction', *To the Masses*, p. 18.
9. 'Theses on the March Action. Adopted by the KPZ Zentrale on 7 April 1921', in B. Fowkes, *The German Left and the Weimar Republic: A Selection of Documents*, Chicago, Haymarket Books, 2015, pp. 91–92.
10. P. Levi, 'Our Path: Against Putschism', in D. Fernbach (ed.), *In the Steps of Rosa Luxemburg: Selected Writings of Paul Levi*, Chicago, Haymarket Books, 2011, p. 148.
11. L. Trotsky, 'Report on World Economic Crisis', in Riddell (ed.), *To the Masses*, p. 133.
12. Letter from Lenin to Zinoviev, 10 June 1921, in Riddell (ed.), *To the Masses*, pp. 1,098–1,099.
13. Broué, *The German Revolution*, p. 539.
14. Riddell (ed.), *To the Masses*, p. 578.
15. From this point on, we will revert to the name KPD in place of the VKPD, because the latter dropped out of use soon after the merger.
16. L. Trotsky, 'On the United Front', 1922.
17. B. Fowkes, *Communism in Germany under the Weimar Republic*, Springer, 1984, p. 92.
18. Harman, *The Lost Revolution*, pp. 246–47.
19. Harman, *The Lost Revolution*, p. 247.
20. Harman, *The Lost Revolution*, p. 248.
21. Harman, *The Lost Revolution*, p. 260.
22. Harman, *The Lost Revolution*, p. 261.
23. Broué, *The German Revolution*, p. 764.
24. Trotsky, *Lessons of October*.
25. Cited in Roso, 'A Jewish Communist in Weimar'.
26. The following section draws heavily from a Marxism 2010 conference talk in Melbourne by Corey Oakley: 'Was setting up the Comintern a mistake?', unpublished.
27. P. Levi, 'Our Path: Against Putschism', p. 163.

5. COUNTER-REVOLUTION IN RUSSIA

1. Main sources used: T. Cliff, *Trotsky: Fighting the Rising Stalinist Bureaucracy 1923-1927*, London, Bookmarks, 1991; J. Geier, 'Zinovievism and the degeneration of world Communism', *International Socialist Review*, no. 93, 2014; M. Haynes, *Russia: Class and Power 1917-2000*, London, Bookmarks, 2002; J. Molyneux, *Leon Trotsky's Theory of Revolution*, Brighton, Harvester Press, 1981; J. Rees, 'In defence of October', *International Socialism*, no. 52, 1991.
2. K. Marx, *The German Ideology*, 1845.
3. Haynes, *Russia: Class and Power*, p. 50.
4. V.I. Lenin, 'The New Economic Policy and The Tasks Of The Political Education Departments', 17 October 1921.
5. All figures in this paragraph are from Haynes, *Russia: Class and Power*, pp. 71, 50, 53.
6. V.I. Lenin, 'Conditions for Admitting New Members to the Party', 26 March 1922.
7. V.I. Lenin, 'Report on the Substitution of a Tax In Kind for the Surplus Grain Appropriation System', speech given to the Tenth Party Congress, 15 March 1921.
8. L. Trotsky, *The Revolution Betrayed*, Chapter 5, 1936.
9. Petrograd was renamed Leningrad after Lenin's death. It reverted to its Tsarist name St Petersburg in 1991.
10. Trotsky, *The New Course*, London, New Park Publications, 1972 [1923], p. 64.
11. Quotes in this paragraph from 'Resolution of the Fifth Comintern Congress on the Russian Question', July 1924, in J. Degras (ed.), *The Communist International 1919-1943 Documents, Volume II 1923-1928*, 1959, pp. 140-42.
12. Zinoviev Speech: 'Discussion on E.C. Report and World Situation', Fifth Congress of the Communist International, in *Abridged Report of Meetings held at Moscow June 17th to July 8, 1924*, London, Communist Party of Great Britain, pp. 129-30.
13. 'Theses on Tactics adopted by the Fifth Comintern Congress', July 1924, in: Degras, *The Communist International, volume II*, p. 142.
14. J. Stalin, 'Speech to industrial managers, February 1931', academic.shu.edu/russianhistory/index.php/Stalin_on_Rapid_Industrialization.
15. M. Reiman, *The Birth of Stalinism. The USSR on the Eve of the 'Second Revolution'*, London, I.B. Taurus, 1987, pp. 110-111.
16. Haynes, *Russia: Class and Power*, p. 9.
17. J. Harris, 'Introduction', in *The Great Fear: Stalin's Terror of the 1930s*, Oxford University Press, 2016 (online).
18. J. Arch Getty, G. Rittersporn and V. Zemskov, 'Victims of the Soviet penal system in the pre-war years: a first approach on the basis of archival evidence', in P. Waldron (ed.), *The Soviet Union*, London, Routledge, 2007.
19. R.G. Suny, 'Stalin and his Stalinism: Power and Authority in the Soviet Union, 1930-53', in I. Kershaw and M. Lewin (eds.), *Stalinism and Nazism: Dictatorships in Comparison*, Cambridge, Cambridge University Press, 1997, p. 19.
20. This section draws heavily from Molyneux, *Leon Trotsky's Theory of Revolution*, pp. 110-12.
21. A. Joffe, 'Letter to Leon Trotsky', 16 November 1927, www.marxists.org/archive/joffe/1927/letter.htm.

6. THE BRITISH GENERAL STRIKE

1. Main sources used: T. Cliff and D. Gluckstein, *Marxism and Trade Union Struggle: The General Strike of 1926*, London, Bookmarks, 1986; C. Farman, *The General Strike, May 1926*, St Albans, Panther Books, 1974; D. Hallas, 'The Communist Party and the General Strike', *International Socialism* (first series), no. 88, 1976; C. Harman, 'The General Strike', *International Socialism* (first series), no. 48, June-July 1971.
2. Cited in Cliff and Gluckstein, *Marxism and Trade Union Struggle*, p. 84.
3. Cited in Harman, 'The General Strike'.
4. See M. Armstrong, 'Socialist trade union strategy in the Bolshevik era', *Marxist Left Review*, no. 6, 2013.
5. Cited in Harman, 'The General Strike'.
6. Cited in Farman, *The General Strike*, p. 42.
7. Cited in Harman, 'The General Strike'.
8. Cited in Hallas, 'The Communist Party and the General Strike'.
9. Cited in Hallas, 'The Communist Party and the General Strike'.
10. Cited in Harman, 'The General Strike'.

11. 'Trotsky on the problems of the British labour movement', *International Socialism* (first series), no. 48, June–July 1971.
12. Farman, *The General Strike*, pp. 86, 90, 93.
13. Cited in R. Page Arnot, *The General Strike May 1926*, London, EP Publishing, 1975 [1926], p. 153.
14. Cited in Farman, *The General Strike*, p. 192.
15. Cited in Farman, *The General Strike*, p. 192.
16. Cited in Cliff and Gluckstein, *Marxism and Trade Union Struggle*, p. 203.
17. Cited in Farman, *The General Strike*, p. 145.
18. Cited in Cliff and Gluckstein, *Marxism and Trade Union Struggle*, p. 201.
19. Cited in Farman, *The General Strike*, p. 204.
20. The two representatives of the Miners' Federation were both absent from this meeting.
21. Cited in Farman, *The General Strike*, p. 287.
22. Cited in Cliff and Gluckstein, *Marxism and Trade Union Struggle*, p. 246.
23. L. Trotsky, 'Where is Britain Going?', 1925.
24. L. Trotsky, 'The fundamental principal errors of syndicalism', 1930.
25. B. Penrose, 'Herbert Moxon, a victim of the "Bolshevisation" of the Communist Party', *Labour History*, no. 70, May 1996, p. 93.
26. Cited in Hallas, 'The Communist Party and the General Strike'.

7. THE CHINESE REVOLUTION

1. Main sources used: M. Armstrong, *From Little Things, Big Things Grow: Strategies for Building Revolutionary Socialist Organisations*, Melbourne, Socialist Alternative, 2007; G. Benton, 'Introduction' in G. Benton (ed.), *Prophets Unarmed: Chinese Trotskyists in Revolution, War, Jail and the Return from Limbo*, Chicago, Haymarket Books, 2015; D. Bing, 'Sneevliet and the early years of the CCP', *China Quarterly*, vol. 48, 1971; N. Harris, *The Mandate of Heaven: Marx and Mao in Modern China*, Chicago, Haymarket Books, 2015 [1978]; C. Hore, *The Road to Tiananmen Square*, London, Bookmarks, 1991; H. Isaacs, *The Tragedy of the Chinese Revolution*, 2nd edn., Stanford, 1961 [1938]; J.P. Roberts, *China: From Permanent Revolution to Counter-Revolution*, London, Wellred Books, 2015; A. Shawki, 'China: From Mao to Deng', *International Socialist Review*, no. 1, 1997; S.A. Smith, *A Road is Made: Communism in Shanghai, 1920-1927*, London, Routledge, 2000; N. J. Spence, *The Search for Modern China*, 3rd edn., New York, W.W. Norton, 2013.
2. V.I. Lenin, 'Draft Theses on the National and Colonial Question', Second Congress of the Communist International, 1920.
3. Cited in C. Mackerras, *China in Transformation, 1900-1949*, London, Longman, 1999, p. 95. A tael was equivalent to about one imperial ounce (28g).
4. Alternatively, 'Kuomintang.'
5. Guangzhou was commonly called Canton in sources at this time.
6. Hanyu pinyin will be used in this book when referring to the names of Chinese provinces, institutions or people, except, as in the cases of Hong Kong, Peking University, Chiang Kai-shek, Sun Yat-sen and Wang Ching-wei, when they are better known under other names.
7. The party was at this stage called the Communist Party of China (CPC) but we refer to it throughout this book by the name by which it is more commonly known today, the Chinese Communist Party (CCP). As elsewhere, the change in name in the late 1930s signified a nationalist turn.
8. J. Riddell (ed.), *Workers of the World and Oppressed Peoples, Unite! Proceedings and Documents of the Second Congress, 1920, Volume One*, New York, Pathfinder Press, p. 272.
9. V.I. Lenin, 'Address to the Second All-Russia Congress of Communist Organisations of the Peoples of the East', 22 November 1919.
10. J. Riddell (ed.), *Workers of the World and Oppressed Peoples, Unite!* p. 281.
11. J. Riddell (ed.), *Workers of the World and Oppressed Peoples, Unite!* p. 295.
12. V. I. Lenin, The Right of Nations to Self-Determination, 1914.
13. V. I. Lenin, 'On the National Pride of the Great Russians'.
14. V.I. Lenin, *Collected Works*, volume 31, pp. 241.
15. V.I. Lenin, *Collected Works*, volume 31, pp. 241-42.
16. Cited in F. Claudin, *The Communist Movement: From Comintern to Cominform*, Harmondsworth, Peregrine, 1975, p. 261.
17. J. Degras (ed.), *The Communist International, 1919 to 1943, Documents, Volume 1, 1919-1922*, 1955, p. 144.

18. 'Manifesto of the 2nd Congress of the CCP', in C. Brandt, B.I. Schwartz and J.K. Fairbank, *A Documentary History of Chinese Communism*, London, Allen and Unwin, 1952, p. 65.
19. 'Manifesto of the 3rd Congress of the CCP', in Brandt et al., *A Documentary History of Chinese Communism*, pp. 71-72.
20. Isaacs, *The Tragedy of the Chinese Revolution*, p. 49.
21. Isaacs, *The Tragedy of the Chinese Revolution*, p. 71.
22. Isaacs, *The Tragedy of the Chinese Revolution*, p. 72.
23. L. Shaffer, 'Modern Chinese labor history, 1895-1949', *International Labor and Working Class History*, no. 20, 1981.
24. Cited in Harris, *The Mandate of Heaven*, p. 10.
25. L. Trotsky, 'Stalin and the Chinese Revolution', *The Militant*, vol. IV, no. 37, 26 December 1931.
26. Cited in Isaacs, *The Tragedy of the Chinese Revolution*, p. 87.
27. Cited in Harris, *The Mandate of Heaven*, pp. 11-12.
28. Isaacs, *The Tragedy of the Chinese Revolution*, p. 116.
29. Isaacs, *The Tragedy of the Chinese Revolution*, p. 132.
30. Isaacs, *The Tragedy of the Chinese Revolution*, p. 136.
31. Isaacs, *The Tragedy of the Chinese Revolution*, p. 137.
32. Isaacs, *The Tragedy of the Chinese Revolution*, p. 137.
33. Cited in Smith, *A Road is Made*, p. 198.
34. 'Extracts from the resolution of the Eighth ECCI Plenum on the Chinese question', in J. Degras (ed.), *The Communist International, 1919-1943, Documents Volume II, 1923-1928*, 1959, p. 389.
35. Isaacs, *The Tragedy of the Chinese Revolution*, p. 207.
36. Isaacs, *The Tragedy of the Chinese Revolution*, p. 211.
37. Hu Sheng (ed.), *A Concise History of the Communist Party of China*, Beijing, Foreign Languages Press, 1994, p. 108.
38. Cited in Hu, *A Concise History of the Communist Party of China*, p. 114.
39. L. Trotsky, 'Stalin and the Chinese Revolution', *The Militant*, vol. IV, no. 37, 26 December 1931, p. 4.
40. Shaffer, 'Modern Chinese labor history', p. 33.
41. Hu, *A Concise History of the Communist Party of China*, p. 105.
42. Hu, *A Concise History of the Communist Party of China*, p. 106.
43. Cited in Smith, *A Road is Made*, pp. 198-99.
44. See Chapter 3 of L. Trotsky, *The Third International after Lenin*: 'Summary and perspectives of the Chinese Revolution: its lessons for the countries of the Orient and for the whole of the Comintern'.
45. L. Trotsky, *My Life: An Attempt at an Autobiography*, 1930.

8. 'SOCIAL FASCISM': THE PATH TO NAZI VICTORY IN GERMANY

1. 'Extract from the Theses of the Sixth Comintern Congress on the International Situation and the Tasks of the Communist International', in J. Degras, *The Communist International 1919-1943, Documents, Volume II*, 1959, p. 456.
2. L. Haro, 'Entering a theoretical void: the theory of social fascism and Stalinism in the German Communist Party', *Critique*, vol. 39, no. 4, 2011, p. 565.
3. J. Stalin, 'On the International Situation', *International Press Correspondence*, vol. 4, no. 72, 1924, p. 792.
4. 'Extracts from the Theses of the Tenth ECCI Plenum on the International Situation and the Tasks of the Communist International', in J. Degras (ed.), *The Communist International 1919-1943, Documents, Volume III, 1929-1943*, 1965, p. 44.
5. Main sources used on Germany: T. Cliff, *Trotsky: The Darker the Night, the Brighter the Star*, London, Bookmarks, 1993; D. Gluckstein, *The Nazis, Capitalism and the Working Class*, London, Bookmarks, 1999; Haro, 'Entering a theoretical void'; Trotsky's numerous works on fascism, cited in the Chapter 8 end notes.
6. L. Trotsky, 'What is national socialism?', 1933.
7. R.F. Hamilton, *Who Voted for Hitler?*, Princeton, Princeton University Press, 1982, p. 304.
8. L. Trotsky, 'What next? Vital questions for the German proletariat', 1932.
9. L. Trotsky, 'Germany, the key to the international situation', 1931.
10. L. Trotsky, 'What Next?'
11. L. Trotsky, 'For a workers' united front against fascism', 1931.
12. Cited in R. Schwarzwald, 'Introduction', in D. Guérin, *The Brown Plague: Travels in Late Weimar and Early Nazi Germany*, Durham NC, Duke University Press, 1984, pp. 18-19.

13. Trotsky, 'Germany, the key to the international situation'.
14. Trotsky, 'For a workers' united front'.
15. Trotsky, 'For a workers' united front'.
16. Trotsky, 'For a workers' united front'.
17. Trotsky, 'For a workers' united front'. Albert Grzesinski was Minister of the Interior in the Prussian government between 1926 and 1930, notorious for ordering the Berlin police to attack Communist May Day rallies in 1929, resulting in 25 deaths.
18. Trotsky, 'Germany, the key to the international situation'.
19. Trotsky, 'What Next?'
20. Cited in I. Deutscher, *The Prophet Outcast: Trotsky, 1929-1940*, Oxford University Press, 1987, p. 143.
21. Cited in: R. F. Hamilton, *Who Voted for Hitler?*, p. 306.
22. *Communist International*, Volume 11, no. 8, 1 May 1933.
23. Cited in L. Trotsky, 'Fascism and democratic slogans', 1933.

9. COMMUNISM IN AUSTRALIA DURING THE GREAT DEPRESSION

1. Main sources used on Australia: M. Armstrong, 'Socialist trade union strategy in the Bolshevik era', *Marxist Left Review*, no. 6, 2013; J. D. Blake, 'The Australian Communist Party and the Comintern in the early 1930s', *Labour History*, no. 23, November 1972; R. Bozinovski, *The Communist Party of Australia and Proletarian Internationalism, 1928-1945*, PhD thesis, School of Social Sciences, Victoria University, 2008; T. Bramble and R. Kuhn, *Labor's Conflict: Big Business, Workers and the Politics of Class*, Melbourne, Cambridge University Press, 2010; R. Cooksey, *Lang and Socialism: A Study in the Great Depression*, Canberra, ANU Press, 1976; A. Davidson, *History of the Communist Party of Australia*, Stanford, Hoover Institution Press, 1969; C. Fox, *Fighting Back: The Politics of the Unemployed in Victoria in the Great Depression*, Carlton, Melbourne University Press, 1996; R. Gollan, *Revolutionaries and Reformists: Communism and the Australian labour movement 1920-1950*, Sydney, Allen and Unwin, 1975; D.W. Lovell and K. Windle, *Our Unswerving Loyalty: A document survey of relations between the Communist Party of Australia and Moscow, 1920-1940*, Canberra, ANU E Press, 2008; S. Macintyre, *Reds: The Communist Party of Australia from origins to illegality*, Sydney, Allen and Unwin, 1998; J. Moss, *Representatives of Discontent: History of the Communist Party in South Australia, 1921-1981*, Melbourne, Globe Press, 1983; B. Penrose, *The Communist Party and Trade Union Work in Queensland and the Third Period: 1928-1935*, PhD thesis, Department of History, University of Queensland, 1993; B. Penrose, 'Herbert Moxon, a victim of the "Bolshevisation" of the Communist Party', *Labour History*, no. 70, May 1996; N. Wheatley and D. Cottle, 'Sydney's anti-eviction movement: community or conspiracy?', in R. Markey (ed), *Labour and Community: Historical Essays*, University of Wollongong Press, 2001.
2. Executive Committee of the Communist International, 'To the United Communist Party of Australia', December 1922, in Lovell and Windle, *Our Unswerving Loyalty*, pp. 153-58. See also Armstrong, 'Socialist trade union strategy in the Bolshevik era' for more on Garden's role in the early CPA and its relationship to the ALP.
3. The following assessment of the Kavanagh leadership is based on P. Kelloway, '*Three major industrial disputes 1928--30: rank and file action and the Communist Party of Australia*, PhD thesis, University of Melbourne, 2020.
4. Different sources give quite disparate figures for CPA membership in the 1920s. The figure of 300 for the end of 1928 is from Macintyre, *Reds*, p. 150.
5. Political Secretariat ECCI, 'Open Letter to the CEC of the Communist Party of Australia', in Lovell and Windle, *Our Unswerving Loyalty*, pp. 283-287.
6. Praesidium CPA telegram, 30 December 1929, in Lovell and Windle, *Our Unswerving Loyalty*, p. 290.
7. Moore was also known as Harry Wicks. B. Curthoys, 'The Comintern, the CPA and the Impact of Harry Wicks', *The Australian Journal of Politics and History*, vol. 39, no. 1, 1993.
8. Kavanagh, who, unlike Sharkey, was a sincere and well-read Marxist, went on to join the tiny Trotskyist organisation, the Communist League of Australia, in 1940 in opposition to the CPA's Popular Front politics.
9. CPA conferences were relabelled 'Congresses' in 1931, in line with Comintern practice.
10. Penrose, 'Herbert Moxon', p102.
11. Macintyre, *Reds*, p. 175.
12. Cooksey, *Lang and Socialism*, p. 51.

13. M. Cathcart, *Defending the National Tuckshop: Australia's secret army intrigue of 1931*, Sydney, McPhee Gribble, 1988.
14. Penrose, 'Herbert Moxon', pp. 102–05.
15. Cited in Macintyre, *Reds*, p. 240.
16. T. O'Lincoln, 'The Militant Minority: organising rank and file workers in the thirties', 1986, sa.org.au/interventions/minority.htm.
17. Cited in Penrose, *The Communist party and trade union work*, p. 271.
18. Cited in Penrose, *The Communist party and trade union work*, p. 315.
19. Cited in Bozinovski, *The Communist Party of Australia*, p. 126.
20. Macintyre, *Reds*, p. 199.
21. Cooksey, *Lang and Socialism*, p. 28.
22. Cited by Comintern representative B. Freier in 'Memorandum of the Anglo-American Secretariat for the Political Commission', in Lovell and Windle, *Our Unswerving Loyalty*, p. 329.
23. *Workers' Weekly*, 21 July 1933.
24. Cited in H. Greenland, *Red Hot: The Life and Times of Nick Origlass*, Sydney, Wellington Lane Press, 1998, p. 60.

10. THE POPULAR FRONT IN FRANCE

1. Main sources used: S. Bloodworth, 'From revolutionary possibility to fascist defeat: The French Popular Front of 1936-38', *Marxist Left Review*, no. 19, 2020; F. Claudin, *The Communist Movement: From Comintern to Cominform*, Harmondsworth, Penguin Books, 1975; J. Danos and M. Gibelin, *June '36: Class Struggle and Popular Front in France*, London, Bookmarks, 1986 [1952]; T. Kemp, *Stalinism in France: Volume One*, London, New Park Publications, 1984; L. Trotsky, 'Once again: Whither France, parts 1-5' and 'The French Revolution has begun', 1936.
2. 'ECCI May Day Manifesto, April 1936', in J. Degras (ed.), *The Communist International, 1919-1943, Documents, Volume III 1929-1943*, 1965, p. 390.
3. 'Resolution of the Seventh Comintern Congress on the danger of a new world war', in Degras, *The Communist International, Volume III*, 1965, p. 375.
4. Cited in Claudin, *The Communist Movement*, pp. 173–74.
5. The PCF joined this demonstration because it also denounced the Radicals. Given its later alliance with this party, the PCF subsequently denied its presence on the day.
6. J. Wardhaugh, *In Pursuit of the People: Political Culture in France, 1934-39*, Basingstoke, Palgrave Macmillan, 2009, p. 48.
7. Claudin, *The Communist Movement*, p. 687.
8. Danos and Gibelin, *June '36*, p. 42.
9. Cited in Claudin, *The Communist Movement*, p. 201.
10. Claudin, *The Communist Movement*, p. 201.
11. Cited in Claudin, *The Communist Movement*, p. 201.
12. Cited in Claudin, *The Communist Movement*, p. 202.
13. Danos and Gibelin, *June '36*, p. 135.
14. Kemp, *Stalinism in France*, p. 132.
15. Kemp, *Stalinism in France*, p. 134.
16. The PCF claimed higher membership figures: 163,000 in May 1936, 246,000 in July and 380,000 in October, although these included significant padding. Kemp, *Stalinism in France*, p. 139.
17. For the Spanish Civil War, see Chapter 11.
18. ECCI, 'Manifesto on the 22nd anniversary of the Russian Revolution', 7 November 1939, http://ciml.250x.com/archive/comintern/english/ecci_1939_11_november_manifesto_22_years_october_revolution.html.
19. L. Trotsky, 'The French Revolution has begun!', 9 June 1936.
20. L. Trotsky, 'The decisive hour in France', *Socialist Appeal*, 24 December 1938.

11. THE SPANISH REVOLUTION: ANARCHISM PUT TO THE TEST

1. Main sources used: G. Bailey, 'Anarchists in the Spanish Civil War', *International Socialist Review*, no. 24, 2002; M. Bookchin, *The Third Revolution, Volume 4: Popular Movements in the Revolutionary Era*, London, Continuum, 2005; P. Broué, 'The "May Days" of 1937 in Barcelona', 1988; P. Broué and E. Témime, *The Revolution and the Civil War in Spain*, Cambridge, MIT Press, 1972; E. H. Carr, *The Comintern and the Spanish Civil War*, New York, Pantheon Books, 1984; A. Durgan, 'Trotsky and the POUM', *International Socialism*, no. 147, 2015; C. Ealham, 'Social history, (Neo-)revisionism and mapping the 1930s Spanish left', *Labor History*, vol.

58, no. 3, 2017; R. Fraser, *Blood of Spain*, New York, Pantheon Books, 1986; D. Hallas, *The Comintern*, Chicago, Haymarket Books, 2008 [1985]; C. Hore, *Spain 1936*, London, Bookmarks, 1986; F. Morrow, *Revolution and Counter Revolution in Spain*, New York, Pathfinder Press, 1974 [1938]; L. Trotsky, 'The class, the party and the leadership', 1940.
2. Trotsky was referring to the Russian context, but the parallel is clear.
3. Published estimates of the PCE's size in 1936 vary substantially.
4. Fraser, *Blood of Spain*, pp. 44–45.
5. Broué and Témime, *The Revolution and the Civil War*, p. 127.
6. Broué and Témime, *The Revolution and the Civil War*, p. 100.
7. Cited in Fraser, *Blood of Spain*, p. 137.
8. G. Orwell, *Homage to Catalonia*, London, Folio Society, 1970 [1938], p. 10.
9. R. Fraser, *Blood of Spain*, p. 286.
10. Broué and Témime, *The Revolution and the Civil War*, p. 127.
11. B. Bolloten, *The Spanish Civil War: Revolution and Counterrevolution*, Chapel Hill, NC, University of North Carolina Press, 1987, p. 81.
12. L. Trotsky, 'The Lessons of Spain: the last warning', 17 December 1937.
13. Broué and Témime, *The Revolution and the Civil War*, p. 130.
14. The following account comes from Fraser, *Blood of Spain*, pp. 111–12.
15. Bookchin, *The Third Revolution*, p. 188.
16. The following assessment is drawn from Broué and Témime, *The Revolution and the Civil War*, p. 189.
17. Broué and Témime, *The Revolution and the Civil War*, pp. 207–08
18. R.J. Alexander, *The Anarchists and the Spanish Civil War*, vol. 2, London, Janus Publishing, 1999, p. 876.
19. Broué and Témime, *The Revolution and the Civil War*, pp. 236, 238.
20. Morrow, *Revolution and Counter-Revolution in Spain*, p. 94.
21. Durgan, 'Trotsky and the POUM', p. 201.
22. Morrow, *Revolution and Counterrevolution in Spain*, p. 95.
23. Morrow, *Revolution and Counterrevolution in Spain*, p. 95.
24. Fraser, *Blood of Spain*, p. 255.
25. Cited in Broué and Témime, *The Revolution and the Civil War*, p. 231.
26. Broué and Témime, *The Revolution and the Civil War*, p. 235.
27. Fraser, *Blood of Spain*, p. 340.
28. Broué and Témime, *The Revolution and the Civil War*, p. 283.
29. Broué and Témime, *The Revolution and the Civil War*, p. 285.
30. Trotsky, 'The Lessons of Spain: The Last Warning'.
31. Trotsky, 'The Lessons of Spain: The Last Warning'.

12. SIT-DOWN FEVER! US WORKERS' STRUGGLE AND THE ROOSEVELT ADMINISTRATION

1. Main sources used: M. Davis, *Prisoners of the American Dream*, London, Verso, 1986; M. Goldfield, 'Worker insurgency, radical organization, and New Deal labor legislation', *American Political Science Review*, vol. 83, no. 4, 1989; M. Goldfield and C.R. Melcher, 'The myth of Section 7(a): worker militancy, progressive labor legislation and the coal miners', *Labor: Studies in Working-Class History of the Americas*, vol. 16, no. 4, 2019; D. Guérin, *100 Years of Labor in the USA*, London, Ink Links, 1979; D. Lucia, 'Bringing misery out of hiding: the unemployed movement of the 1930s', *International Socialist Review*, no. 71, 2010; D. Milton, *The Politics of US Labor: From the Great Depression to the New Deal*, New York, Monthly Review Press, 1982; M. Naison, 'The Great Rent strike war of 1932 in the Bronx', *International Socialist Review*, no. 81, 2012 [1986]; C. Post, 'The New Deal and the Popular Front: Models for contemporary socialists?', *International Socialist Review*, no. 108, 2018; A. Preis, *Labor's Giant Step: Twenty Years of the CIO*, New York, Pathfinder Press, 1972; S. Smith, *Subterranean Fire: A History of Working Class Radicalism in the United States*, Chicago, Haymarket Books, 2006.
2. 'Bernie Sanders defines his vision for democratic socialism in the United States', 12 June 2019, www.vox.com/2019/6/12/18663217/bernie-sanders-democratic-socialism-speech-transcript.
3. Preis, *Labor's Giant Step*, p. 41.
4. Davis, *Prisoners of the American Dream*, p. 55.
5. Cited in Preis, *Labor's Giant Step*, p. 12.
6. Preis, *Labor's Giant Step*, p. 17.
7. Milton, *The Politics of US Labor*, p. 50.
8. Goldfield, 'Worker insurgency', p. 1,273.

9. Davis, *Prisoners of the American Dream*, p. 54.
10. Smith, *Subterranean Fire*, p. 140.
11. Preis, *Labor's Giant Step*, p. 60.
12. Cited in Smith, *Subterranean Fire*, p. 141.
13. Guérin, *100 Years of Labor*, p. 112.
14. Personal communication, October 2020.
15. Smith, *Subterranean Fire*, p. 134.
16. Smith, *Subterranean Fire*, p. 144.
17. Preis, *Labor's Giant Step*, p. 69.
18. Smith, *Subterranean Fire*, p. 148.
19. Davis, *Prisoners of the American Dream*, p. 73.
20. Smith, *Subterranean Fire*, p. 134.

13. SALUTING THE FLAG: AUSTRALIAN COMMUNISTS DURING WORLD WAR II

1. Main sources used: R. Bozinovski, *The Comintern, The Communist Party of Australia and Illegality*, BA Honours thesis, School of Social Sciences, Victoria University, 2003; R. Bozinovski, *The Communist Party of Australia and Proletarian Internationalism, 1928-1945*, PhD thesis, School of Social Sciences, Victoria University, 2008; P. Cochrane, 'The Wonthaggi Coal Strike, 1934', *Labour History*, no. 27, November 1974; A. Davidson, *History of the Communist Party of Australia*, Stanford, Hoover Institution Press, 1969; R. Gollan, *Revolutionaries and Reformists: Communism and the Australian Labour Movement 1920-1950*, Sydney, Allen and Unwin, 1975; H. Greenland, *Red Hot: The Life and Times of Nick Origlass*, Sydney, Wellington Lane Press, 1998; S. Macintyre, *Reds: The Communist Party of Australia from origins to illegality*, Sydney, Allen and Unwin, 1998; D. Menghetti, 'The Weil's disease strike, 1935', in D.J. Murphy (ed.), *The Big Strikes: Queensland 1889-1965*, St Lucia, UQ Press, 1983; M. Mowbray, 'The red shire of Kearsley, 1944-1947: Communists in local government', *Labour History*, no. 51, November 1986, pp. 83-94; T. O'Lincoln, *Australia's Pacific War: Challenging a National Myth*, Melbourne, Interventions, 2011; T. O'Lincoln, *Into the Mainstream*, Melbourne, Red Rag, 2009 [1985]; G. Reekie, 'Industrial action by women workers in Western Australia during World War II', *Labour History*, no. 49, 1985; A. Smith, 'World War II: The Good War', *International Socialist Review*, no. 10, Winter 2000; B. Symons, 'All-out for the People's War: Communist soldiers in the Australian army in the Second World War', *Australian Historical Studies*, vol. 26, issue 105, 1995.
2. *Workers Voice*, 1 November 1935, cited in O'Lincoln, *Into the Mainstream*, p. 51.
3. Cited in Macintyre, *Reds*, p. 253.
4. Cited in O'Lincoln, *Into the Mainstream*, p. 45.
5. As late as February 1940, Menzies told the Australian High Commissioner in London that he envisaged 'a new alignment of nations in which not only Great Britain and France, but Germany and Italy combined to resist Bolshevism.' K. Buckley and T. Wheelwright, *False Paradise: Australian Capitalism Revisited, 1915-1955*, Sydney, Oxford University Press, 1998, p. 138.
6. R. Dixon, 'Towards a People's Front', *Communist Review*, September 1938.
7. L. Sharkey, 'Congress for the People's Front', *Communist Review*, January 1939.
8. Cited in Macintyre, *Reds*, p. 314.
9. L. Harry Gould, 'Ruling class, working class and the defence of Australia', *Communist Review*, January 1939.
10. Cited in Macintyre, *Reds*, p. 347.
11. Cited in Macintyre, *Reds*, p. 386.
12. Cited in Bozinovski, *The Comintern*, p. 40.
13. Cited in Gollan, *Revolutionaries and Reformists*, p. 80.
14. According to Davidson, membership grew from 4,000 in July 1940, when it was declared illegal, to 7,200 in May 1942. By October 1942, membership had jumped to 15,000. Davidson, *The Communist Party of Australia*, p. 82.
15. Cited in Symons, 'All-out for the People's War', p. 597.
16. Symons, 'All-out for the People's War', p. 598.
17. O'Lincoln, *Australia's Pacific War*, pp. 56-57.
18. O'Lincoln, *Australia's Pacific War*, pp. 56-57.
19. Cited in Smith, 'World War II'.
20. 'Harry S. Truman. Decisive President', *New York Times*, 27 December 1972, p. 46.
21. P. Stanley, *Invading Australia: Japan and the Battle for Australia, 1942*, Melbourne, Viking Penguin, 2008, p. 158; O'Lincoln, *Australia's Pacific War*, pp. 140-42.

22. Cited in Symons, 'All-out for the People's War', p. 598; emphasis in original.
23. Gollan, *Revolutionaries and Reformists*, p. 132.
24. B. Evatt, Hansard, 18 December 1942.
25. R. Cahill, 'Home front WW2: myths and realities', *The Queensland Journal of Labour History*, 19 September 2014, http://ro.uow.edu.au/cgi/viewcontent.cgi?article=2800&context=lhapapers.
26. Cited in Symons, 'All-out for the People's War', p. 599.
27. Cited in Symons, 'All-out for the People's War', p. 608.
28. The Basic Wage was the award wage set for unskilled labourers and was meant to be a 'living wage' for a man and his family. It was lifted in line with inflation on a regular basis by the Arbitration Court, maintaining its real value. The 'margin for skill' came on top of the Basic Wage and was paid to semi-skilled and skilled workers. Unlike the Basic Wage, the margin was not indexed in line with inflation by the Court.
29. Cited in O'Lincoln, *Australia's Pacific War*, p. 130.
30. Cited in Symons, 'All-out for the People's War', p. 609.

14. ANTI-FASCIST RESISTANCE IN ITALY AND GREECE

1. Main sources on the Italian Resistance: T. Behan, *The Italian Resistance: Fascists, Guerrillas and the Allies*, London, Pluto Press, 2009; I. Birchall, *Bailing out the System: Reformist Socialism in Western Europe, 1944-1985*, London, Bookmarks, 1986; D. Broder, 'Assessing Togliatti', *Jacobin*, 16 March 2017; P. Ginsborg, *A History of Contemporary Italy*, London, Penguin Books, 1990; D. Gluckstein, *A People's History of the Second World War*, London, Pluto Press, 2012.
2. Cited in Behan, *The Italian Resistance*, p. 84.
3. There are widely varying estimates of the strength of the Resistance: Ginsborg suggests 100,000, Behan 200,000-300,000.
4. Cited in Gluckstein, *A People's History*. p. 157.
5. Cited in D. Sassoon, 'The rise and fall of West European Communism, 1939-48', *Contemporary European History*, vol. 1, no. 2, p. 161.
6. Ginsborg, *A History of Contemporary Italy*, p. 52.
7. Main sources used on the Greek Resistance: R. Clogg, *A Concise History of Greece*, 3rd edn., Cambridge, CUP, 2013; D. Eudes, *The Kapetanios: Partisans and Civil War in Greece, 1943-1949*, New York, Monthly Review Press, 1972; D. Gluckstein, *A People's History of the Second World War*; B. Potter, *Greek Tragedy*, Solidarity pamphlet no. 29, London, 1968; H. Richter, 'The Greek Communist Party and the Communist International', *Jahrbuch für Historische Kommunismusforschung*, 2002; E. Vulliamy and H. Smith, 'British perfidy in Greece: a story worth remembering', *Open Democracy*, 1 December 2014.
8. Cited in Gluckstein, *A People's History, p.* 44.
9. Cited in Gluckstein, *A People's History*, p. 49.

15. POST-WAR UPSURGE IN AUSTRALIA AND THE COMMUNIST CHALLENGE

1. Main sources used: D. Blackmur, 'The meat industry strike, 1946' and 'The railway strike, 1948', both in D.J. Murphy (ed.), *The Big Strikes: Queensland 1889-1965*, St Lucia, University of Queensland Press, 1983; K. Buckley and T. Wheelwright, *False Paradise: Australian Capitalism Revisited, 1915-1955*, Melbourne, Oxford University Press, 1998; A. Davidson, *History of the Communist Party of Australia*, Stanford, Hoover Institution Press, 1969; P. Deery, 'Chifley, the army and the 1949 coal strike', *Labour History*, no. 68, May 1995; P. Deery, 'Communism, security and the Cold War', *Journal of Australian Studies*, nos. 54-55, 1997; P. Deery (ed.), *Labour in Conflict: The 1949 coal strike*, Sydney, Hale and Iremonger, 1978; R. Gollan, *Revolutionaries and Reformists: Communism and the Australian Labour Movement 1920-1950*, Sydney, Allen and Unwin, 1975; H. Greenland, *Red Hot: The Life and Times of Nick Origlass*, Sydney, Wellington Lane Press, 1998; D. Jordan, *Conflict in the Unions: The Communist Party of Australia, Politics and the Trade Union Movement, 1945-1960*, PhD thesis, Victoria University, 2011; T. O'Lincoln, *Into the Mainstream: The Decline of Australian Communism*, Melbourne, Red Rag Publications, 2009 [1986]; E. Ross, *Of Storm and Struggle: Pages from Labour History*, Sydney, New Age Publishers, 1982; T. Sheridan, *Division of Labour: Industrial Relations in the Chifley Years, 1945-49*, Melbourne, Oxford University Press, 1989.
2. T. Sheridan, 'Labour vs Labor', in J. Iremonger, J. Merritt and G. Osborne (eds.), *Strikes: Studies in Twentieth Century Australian Social History*, Sydney, Angus and Robertson, 1975, p. 177.
3. Cited in Sheridan, *Division of Labour*, p. 108.
4. Cited in Sheridan, *Division of Labour*, p. 189.

5. Davidson, *The Communist Party of Australia*, p. 131.
6. Cited in Sheridan, *Division of Labour*, p. 143.
7. Sheridan, *Division of Labour*, p. 147.
8. Sheridan, *Division of Labour*, p. 244.
9. Cited in Sheridan, *Division of Labour*, p. 217.
10. Cited in Sheridan, *Division of Labour*, p. 239.
11. Cited in Sheridan, *Division of Labour*, p. 237.
12. Cited in Sheridan, *Division of Labour*, p. 243.
13. Cited in Sheridan, *Division of Labour*, p. 245.
14. Cited in Sheridan, *Division of Labour*, p. 247.
15. Cited in Sheridan, *Division of Labour*, p. 247.
16. Deery, *Labour in Conflict*, p. 37.
17. R. Menzies, 'The forgotten people', Speech to Sydney radio station 2UE, 22 May 1942.
18. Cited in Buckley and Wheelwright, *False Paradise*, p. 199.
19. Cited in Deery, 'Communism, security and the Cold War', p. 170.
20. Cited in Sheridan, *Division of Labour*, p. 288.
21. Ross, *Of Storm and Struggle*, p. 104.
22. Cited in Deery, 'Communism, security and the Cold War', p. 162.
23. Cited in Deery, 'Communism, security and the Cold War', p. 165.
24. Cited in Sheridan, *Division of Labour*, p. 272.
25. Deery, *Labor in Conflict*, pp. 97–99.

16. THE COMMUNISTS COME TO POWER IN CHINA

1. Main sources used: J. Fenby, *The Penguin History of Modern China*, London, Penguin Books, 2013; D. Gluckstein, 'China: revolution and war', in D. Gluckstein (ed.), *Fighting On All Fronts: Popular Resistance in the Second World War*, London, Bookmarks, 2015; N. Harris, *The Mandate of Heaven: Marx and Mao in Modern China*, Chicago, Haymarket Books, 2015 [1978]; C. Hore, *The Road to Tiananmen Square*, London, Bookmarks, 1991; G. Hutchings, *China 1949: Year of Revolution*, London, Bloomsbury Academic, 2021; E. Liu, *Maoism and the Chinese Revolution: A Critical Introduction*, Oakland, PM Press, 2016; C. Mackerras, *China in Transformation, 1900–1949*, London, Longman, 1999; J.P. Roberts, *China: From Permanent Revolution to Counter-Revolution*, London, Wellred Books, 2015.
2. Cited in Hore, *The Road to Tiananmen Square*, p. 33.
3. H. Isaacs, *The Tragedy of the Chinese Revolution*, 2nd edn., Stanford, 1961 [1938], Chapter 18.
4. Hu Sheng (ed.), *A Concise History of the Communist Party of China*, Beijing, Foreign Languages Press, 1994, p. 148.
5. Hu, *A Concise History of the Communist Party of China*, p. 149.
6. Harris, *The Mandate of Heaven*, pp. 21–22.
7. Mackerras, *China in Transformation*, p. 58.
8. Harris, *The Mandate of Heaven*, p. 25.
9. Harris, *The Mandate of Heaven*, p. 26.
10. We use the CCP's terminology of a 'united front', although the conception of an alliance between the CCP and GMD was not in any sense a united front in the meaning used by the early Comintern.
11. Mao Zedong, 'The Chinese Revolution and the Chinese Communist Party', 1939, www.marxists.org/reference/archive/mao/selected-works/volume-2/mswv2_23.htm.
12. Gluckstein, 'China: revolution and war', pp. 278–79.
13. Harris, *The Mandate of Heaven*, p. 29.
14. Hore, *The Road to Tiananmen Square*, p 39.
15. Estimates of the size of the Communist armies in the 1940s vary widely. In this chapter, we use figures provided in G. Benton, *New Fourth Army: Communist Resistance along the Yangtze and the Huai, 1938–1941*, Oakland, University of California Press, 1999; and PLA sources.
16. Mao Zedong, 'On some important problems of the party's present policy', January 1948, www.marxists.org/reference/archive/mao/selected-works/volume-4/mswv4_26.htm.
17. Mao Zedong, "On the policy concerning industry and commerce', February 1948, www.marxists.org/reference/archive/mao/selected-works/volume-4/mswv4_31.htm.
18. Mao Zedong, "On the policy concerning industry and commerce'.
19. G. Hutchings, *China 1949: Year of Revolution*, p. 176.
20. G. Hutchings, *China 1949: Year of Revolution*, p. 87.
21. G. Hutchings, *China 1949: Year of Revolution*, p. 176.

22. G. Hutchings, *China 1949: Year of Revolution*, p. 220.
23. Mao Zedong, 'On some important problems of the party's present policy'.
24. T. Cliff, *Deflected Permanent Revolution*, London, Socialist Workers Party, 1986 [1963].
25. K.J. Lu, X. Lu, J. Zhang and Y. Zheng, 'State-owned enterprises in China: A review of 40 years of research and practice', *China Journal of Accounting Research*, vol. 13, 2020, p. 32.

17. ANTI-STALINIST REVOLTS IN EASTERN EUROPE

1. Main sources used: I. Birchall, *Workers against the Monolith: The Communist Parties since 1943*, London, Pluto Press, 1974; P. Fryer, *Hungarian Tragedy*, London, Dennis Dobson, 1956; C. Harman, *Class Struggles in Eastern Europe*, London, Pluto Press, 1983; M. Haynes, 'Hungary: workers' councils against Russian tanks', *International Socialism*, no. 112, 2006; B. Lomax, 'The workers' councils of Greater Budapest', in R. Miliband and J. Saville (eds.), *The Socialist Register 1976*, London, Merlin Press, 1976; V. Sebestyen, *Twelve Days: The Story of the Hungarian Revolution*, London, Vintage, 2007.
2. The descriptor 'Eastern Europe' will be used to include countries often described as 'Central European' (e.g. Czechoslovakia, Hungary and Poland) for purposes of simplicity.
3. Communist parties in Eastern Europe went by many different names; for the sake of simplicity, they will all be referred to as Communist parties.
4. Sebestyen, *Twelve Days*, pp. 10-12. The Russian army was not unique in this respect, of course. US, French and Australian troops all earned notoriety for their crimes against the people in the defeated Axis powers.
5. Cited in Sebestyen, *Twelve Days*, p. 26. Readers will recall Rákosi from Chapter 4 when he was the Comintern's agent at the Italian Socialist Party's 1920 Livorno Congress.
6. Birchall, *Workers against the Monolith*, p. 46.
7. F. Engels, *Socialism: Utopian and Scientific*, 1880.
8. Nor did he disown the horrors associated with Stalin's first Five Year Plan. In Khrushchev's rewriting of history, Stalin's crimes only began in 1934 with the murder of Kirov, which was the pretext for the Moscow Trials.
9. Cited in Sebestyen, *Twelve Days*, p.195.
10. Cited in Haynes, 'Hungary: workers' councils against Russian tanks'.
11. Cited in Haynes, 'Hungary: workers' councils against Russian tanks'.
12. Fryer, *Hungarian Tragedy*, pp. 50-51.
13. All quotes in this paragraph from Sebestyen, *Twelve Days*, pp. 217-18.
14. Fryer, *Hungarian Tragedy*, p. 83.
15. Cited in Haynes, 'Hungary: workers' councils against Russian tanks'.

ALSO BY INTERVENTIONS

Lenin's Interventionist Marxism

By Tom Freeman
Edited and introduced by Sandra Bloodworth

This book is an edited version of Tom Freeman's PhD thesis "Lenin's conception of the party: organisational expression of an interventionist Marxism". Freeman makes a groundbreaking contribution to our knowledge of the early revolutionary movement in tsarist Russia and Lenin's theory and politics. Tom Freeman died in 2005 at the young age of 51.

"Tom Freeman's work stands as a valuable contribution to what can be considered the field of 'Lenin Studies' that has been blossoming over the past decade, taking its place with the varied, important contributions of Lars Lih, Antonio Negri, Alan Shandro, Tamas Krausz, August Nimtz and others. This clear and meticulous research reveals a continuity between Lenin's revolutionary organisation perspectives of the early 1900s with those advanced during the revolutionary mass upsurge of 1905 - and this in a way that can be useful for revolutionary activists of today and tomorrow. Freeman highlights the dynamic interplay of theory and practice, of Marxism and mass struggle, of intellectual activists and radicalising workers and mass insurgencies that shaped the past and are the hope of the future."

—Paul Le Blanc
Author of Lenin and the revolutionary party.

ALSO BY INTERVENTIONS

Into the Mainstream:
The Decline of Australian Communism

By Tom O'Lincoln

How are the mighty fallen. At the end of World War II, the Communist Party was a major force in Australian working class life. Yet by the 1980s it had diminished to a demoralised rump, and today it's only a memory. Did the party deserve this fate? its courage and hard work brought together thousands of working class fighters. It led them in important struggles. But then it inflicted on them the bitterest of disappointments.

Into the Mainstream traces the party's decline from an influential movement, plagued by its bureaucratic Stalinist politics, to a shrinking organisation trying desperately to re-invent itself as a radical force, but finally drifting into the political mainstream. The story is set against such historic events as the cold war, the Sino-Soviet split, and the social radicalisation of the late sixties. It offers lessons for revolutionary activists today.

―― ALSO BY INTERVENTIONS ――

Australia's Pacific War: Challenging a National Myth

By Tom O'Lincoln

War is such a nightmare it's hard to believe any war can retain a positive aura for decades. Yet the vast conflict in the Pacific is a shibboleth for Australian politics to this day. Politicians in particular use its appeal to legitimise modern wars. Tom O'Lincoln's book questions every aspect of this syndrome. He argues that the Pacific War was an imperialist one on both sides, that the west cannot claim the moral high ground, and that wartime Australia was riven with class and other social conflicts. His aim is to challenge an Australian national myth.

"This thought-provoking book challenges us to re-consider what we assumed we knew about the Pacific war."

—Dr Peter Stanley
National Museum of Australia

www.ingramcontent.com/pod-product-compliance
Lightning Source LLC
Chambersburg PA
CBHW070246010526
44107CB00056B/2361